FIX-IT
and
FORGET-IT®
5-ingredient
favorites

Cover and interior illustrations by Cheryl Benner
Cover design by Cliff Snyder
Interior design by Dawn J. Ranck

FIX-IT AND FORGET-IT 5-INGREDIENT FAVORITES
Copyright © 2007 by Good Books, Intercourse, PA 17534

FIX-IT
and
FORGET-IT®
5-ingredient
favorites

Comforting *Slow-Cooker* Recipes

By *The New York Times*
bestselling author
Phyllis Pellman Good

Good Books®

Table of Contents

About
Fix-It and Forget-It 5-Ingredient Favorites

Too little time to cook?

Worried about your skills in the kitchen?

Fix-It and Forget-It 5-Ingredient Favorites can be your steady kitchen companion. **This packed-full collection has more than 700 recipes, each with 5 or fewer ingredients.**

And each recipe's instructions spell out every step so you won't get stranded along the way. This book makes cooking manageable.

Think of *Fix-it and Forget-It 5-Ingredient Favorites* as your inspiration and encourager. All of its recipes come from home cooks. These are their favorite dishes, loved by families and households across the country. So get out your slow cooker—or cookers—and choose from these flexible, forgiving, and absolutely scrumptious recipes.

What qualifies as a 5-ingredient recipe?

1. Any recipe with 5—or fewer—ingredients.
2. Water does *not* count.
3. Salt and pepper count as *one* ingredient.
4. Ingredients listed as *optional* do *not* count.
5. Non-stick cooking spray does *not* count.
6. The "base" over which the recipe is to be served (for example, crackers or chips, rice, pasta, or potatoes) does *not* count.

A word about slow cookers

These great little appliances can vary considerably in their heat intensity and speed of cooking. Older models often require more cooking time than newer ones. That's why we give a range of cooking times for many of the recipes. Experiment by using the shorter cooking time first. Then make a note right on the recipe page itself about what you discovered works best for your cooker. Personalize this cookbook!

Variables to keep in mind

Ideally, you should fill your slow cooker about 2/3 full. You may need to increase the cooking time if you've exceeded that amount, or reduce it if you've put in less than that.

- The fuller your slow cooker, the longer it will take its contents to cook.
- The more densely packed the cooker's contents are, the longer they will take to cook.
- The larger the chunks of meat or vegetables, the longer they will take to cook.

If you put ingredients into the cooker straight out of the refrigerator, you may need to add 20-30 minutes to the cooking time.

If you put frozen meat into the cooker, you should add 4-6 hours of cooking time on Low, or 2 hours on High.

If you're using a slow cooker at an altitude over 3,500 feet, you will need to cook its contents somewhat longer than the recipe states. Allow time to experiment, and then write what worked next to the recipe.

If you want to check that the meat in your slow cooker is fully cooked, use a food thermometer:

- Beef should reach an internal temperature of 170° F;
- Pork should reach an internal temperature of 180° F;
- Poultry should reach an internal temperature of 190° F.

Don't miss the Quickie Go-Alongs at the back of the book

If you want to round out a meal that has a slow-cooker main dish, turn to the "Quickie Go-Alongs" chapter beginning on page 253. Most of these recipes have more than 5 ingredients, but I added them because they meet two important tests: 1. They're quick to prepare; 2. They are irresistibly delicious. Don't miss them.

The pass-it-on tradition

Good cooks love to share their recipes. They don't possess them; they pass them on. This collection is rich because of all the home cooks who generously offered their favorite recipes, so that all of us could fix satisfyingly delicious food at home. Thank you to each of you who has shared your gems. This book holds your precious food traditions, and we are all grateful.

So relax and let this collection of 5-ingredient recipes be your friendly kitchen companion. Mark your favorites—but don't hesitate to keep trying new ones.

Fix-It and Forget-It 5-Ingredient Favorites makes it possible for you to sit at the dinner table *together*, with your family and friends, around absolutely tasty food, no matter how wild and crazy your day.

—Phyllis Pellman Good

Soups, Stews, and Chilis

Bean and Bacon Soup

Jeanette Oberholtzer
Manheim, PA

Makes 6 servings

Prep Time: 25 minutes
Cooking Time: 11-13 1/2 hours
Ideal slow cooker size: 4-qt.

1 1/4 cups dried bean soup mix, *or* any combination of mixed dried beans
5 cups water
1 onion, chopped
3 cups water
4 slices fried bacon (precooked bacon works well), crumbled
1 envelope taco seasoning
2 14-oz. cans diced tomatoes, undrained

1. Place dried beans in large stockpot. Cover with 5 cups water. Cover pot and bring to a boil. Cook 2 minutes over high heat.

2. Remove pot from heat and allow to stand, covered, for 1 hour. Return pot to stovetop and cook covered for 2 1/2-3 hours, or until beans are tender. Drain.

3. Combine cooked beans, onion, 3 cups water, bacon, and taco seasoning in slow cooker. Mix well.

4. Cook on Low 8-10 hours.

5. Add tomatoes. Stir well. Cook another 30 minutes.

Tip: If you like a thickened soup, mash some of the beans before adding the tomatoes.

Black Bean Soup

Dorothy VanDeest, Memphis, TN

Makes 8 servings

*Prep Time: 10 minutes
to precook beans
Cooking Time: 6½-8½ hours
Ideal slow cooker size: 4-qt.*

1 lb. dried black beans
9 cups water
3 cups water
¼ lb. bacon, fried crisp
and crumbled, *or* ½ lb.
smoked ham, chopped
2 medium-sized onions,
chopped
1 tsp. garlic salt
¼ tsp. coarsely ground
pepper

1. Place dried beans in
large stockpot. Cover with 9
cups water. Cover pot and
bring to a boil.
2. Boil 10 minutes. Reduce
heat and simmer, covered, for
1½ hours, or until beans are
tender. Discard cooking water.
3. Combine cooked beans, 3
cups water, bacon, onions, garlic salt, and pepper in slow
cooker, stirring well.
4. Cover and cook on High
4-6 hours.

Tip: To serve beans as a side
dish, add a 4-oz. can of
chopped green chilies, 1 tsp.
powdered cumin, and ¼ tsp.
dried oregano to 5-6 cups of
fully cooked beans. Simmer for
25 minutes to blend flavors.
— **Bonita Ensenberger**
Albuquerque, NM

Holiday Soup

Ruth Retter
Manheim, PA

Makes 12-16 servings

*Prep Time: 10 minutes to
precook the beans
Cooking Time: 6½-9 hours
Ideal slow cooker size: 4-qt.*

1 lb. holiday soup mix of
dried beans, *or* your
choice of 1 lb. of mixed
dried beans
9 cups water
6 cups water
1 large onion, chopped
14-oz. can stewed *or* whole
tomatoes
juice of one lemon
2 ham hocks

1. Place dried beans in
large stockpot and cover with
9 cups of water. Cover and
bring to a boil on your stovetop. Continue boiling for 10
minutes.
2. Remove beans from
heat, keeping covered. Allow
to stand for 1 hour.
3. Return covered pot of
beans to stove and bring to a
boil. Then turn to simmer
and continue cooking, covered, for 2½-3 hours, or until
beans are soft. Drain.
4. Place drained beans in
slow cooker. Add 6 cups
water, chopped onion, tomatoes, lemon juice, and 2 ham
hocks. Mix together well.
5. Cover and cook on High
3 hours, or on Low 5 hours.
6. Remove ham from bone.
Cut meat into small pieces
and stir into soup before serving.

Variations:
*1. Add 1 tsp. chili powder to
Step 4.*
— **Ruth Ann Hoover**
New Holland, PA

*2. Add 1 cup carrots, 1 bay
leaf, and salt and pepper to
taste, to Step 4.*
— **Deb Herr**
Mountaintop, PA

Beans with Tomatoes and Ham

Kristin Tice
Shipshewana, IN

Makes 10 servings

Prep Time:
10-20 minutes
Cooking Time: 7¹/2-9¹/2 hours
Ideal slow cooker size:
5- to 6-qt.

3 cups dried beans
(northern, navy, black,
or pinto, *or* a
combination of any of
them)
12 cups water
4 cups fresh tomatoes,
chopped, *or* 28-oz. can
stewed *or* diced
tomatoes
¹/2 cup chopped onion
1 tsp. salt
4 cups water
2 cups ham

1. Place beans and 12 cups water in a large stockpot. Cover and bring to a boil.
2. Uncover and boil for 2 minutes.
3. Cover, remove from heat, and set aside for 1 hour. Drain beans.
4. Place beans in slow cooker. Add tomatoes, onion, salt, and 4 cups water.
5. Cover and cook on High 6-8 hours, or until beans are tender.
6. After beans are tender, stir in ham and cook an additional 30 minutes on Low.

Old-Fashioned Bean Soup

Shirley Sears
Sarasota, FL

Makes 8-10 servings

Prep Time: 10 minutes
Cooking Time: 13-20 hours
Ideal slow cooker size:
4- to 5-qt.

1 lb. dried navy beans,
soaked overnight
16 cups water, *divided*
1 lb. meaty ham bones, *or*
ham pieces
1 tsp. salt
¹/2 tsp. pepper
¹/2 cup chopped celery
leaves
1 medium onion, chopped
1 bay leaf, *optional*

1. Place dried beans and 8 cups water in a large stockpot. Cover and allow to soak for 8 hours or overnight. Drain.
2. Place soaked beans and 8 cups fresh water in your slow cooker.
3. Add all remaining ingredients.
4. Cover and cook on Low 10-12 hours, or on High 5-6 hours, or until the meat is falling off the bone and the beans are tender but not mushy.

Sauerkraut-Sausage Bean Soup

Bonnie Goering
Bridgewater, VA

Makes 8-10 servings

Prep Time: 10 minutes
Cooking Time: 2-3 hours
Ideal slow cooker size:
3- to 4-qt.

3 15-oz. cans white beans,
undrained
16-oz. can sauerkraut,
drained and rinsed
1 lb. link sausage, sliced
¹/4 cup brown sugar
¹/2 cup ketchup

1. Combine all ingredients in slow cooker.
2. Cover. Cook on High 2-3 hours.
3. Serve with cornbread, applesauce, or coleslaw.

Note: You may add tomato juice or water if you prefer a thinner soup.

A Tip —

Adding salt to dry beans before they are cooked soft will prevent them from getting soft.

Split Pea Soup with Ham

Elena Yoder
Carlsbad, NM

Makes 8 servings

Prep Time: 15 minutes
Cooking Time: 4 hours
Ideal slow cooker size: 4-qt.

2½ qts. water
1 ham hock *or* pieces of
    cut-up ham
2½ cups split peas, dried
1 medium onion, chopped
3 medium carrots, cut in
    small pieces
salt and pepper to taste

1. Bring water to a boil in a saucepan on your stovetop.
2. Place all other ingredients into slow cooker. Add water and stir together well.
3. Cover and cook on High for 4 hours, or until vegetables are tender.
4. If you've cooked a ham hock, remove it from the soup and de-bone the meat. Stir cut-up chunks of meat back into the soup before serving.

Italian Bean Soup

Eylene Egan
Babylon, NY

Makes 8 servings

Prep Time: 10 minutes
Cooking Time: 8-10 hours
Ideal slow cooker size: 4-qt.

1 lb. dried baby lima
    beans
9 cups water
2 8-oz. cans tomato sauce
3-4 cloves garlic, minced
6 cups water
salt and pepper to taste

1. Place dried beans in large stockpot. Cover with 9 cups water. Cover pot and bring to a boil.
2. Boil for 10 minutes. Remove from heat and allow beans to stand for 1 hour, covered.
3. Return to stovetop, keep covered, and bring to a boil. Reduce heat to a simmer, and continue cooking for 2½-3 hours, or until beans are tender. Drain.
4. Place drained, cooked beans in slow cooker. Add remaining ingredients and stir together well.
5. Cover and cook on High 1 hour, and then cook on Low 4-5 hours.

Mountain Bike Soup

Jonathan Gehman
Harrisonburg, VA

Makes 4 servings

Prep Time: 10 minutes
Cooking Time: 2-6 hours
Ideal slow cooker size:
    2- or 3-qt.

12-oz. can chicken broth
12-oz. can V-8 juice,
    regular *or* spicy
⅓ cup uncooked barley,
    rice, *or* broken spaghetti
    noodles
⅓ cup chopped pepperoni,
    ham, *or* bacon
15-oz. can cut green beans
    with liquid

1. Dump it all in. Put on the lid. Turn it on Low.
2. Go for a long ride on your bike, from 2-6 hours.

Tip: *This soup seems to accept whatever vegetables you throw in: a little corn, okra, diced potatoes, shredded zucchini, whatever . . . I often add more liquid before serving if it seems to be getting more like stew and less like soup.*

Smoked Sausage Stew

Carol Sherwood
Batavia, NY

Makes 4-5 servings

Prep Time:
35-40 minutes
Cooking Time: 4-5 hours
Ideal slow cooker size: 5-qt.

4-5 potatoes, peeled and cubed
2 15-oz. cans green beans
1 lb. smoked sausage, sliced
1 onion, chopped
2 Tbsp. butter

1. Layer potatoes, green beans, sausage, and onion in slow cooker in the order they are listed.
2. Dot top with butter.
3. Cook on Low 4-5 hours, or until potatoes are tender but not mushy.

Toscano Soup

Sheila Soldner
Lititz, PA

Makes 4-6 servings

Prep Time: 20-25 minutes
Cooking Time: 6-8 hours
Ideal slow cooker size: 4-qt.

2 medium-sized russet potatoes
1 lb. spicy Italian sausage
5½ cups chicken stock, *or* low-sodium chicken broth
2 cups chopped kale
½ tsp. crushed red pepper flakes, *optional*
½ cup cream, *or* evaporated milk

1. Cut potatoes into ½" cubes. Place in slow cooker.
2. Grill, broil, or brown sausage in a non-stick skillet. When cool enough to handle, cut into ½" thick slices.
3. Add sliced sausage to slow cooker. Stir in all remaining ingredients, except cream.
4. Cover and cook on Low 6-8 hours.
5. Fifteen to 20 minutes before serving, add cream or evaporated milk and cook until soup is heated through.

Tip: If you don't want the soup to be too spicy, use ½ lb. sweet sausage and ½ lb. spicy sausage.

Hearty Lentil and Sausage Stew

Cindy Krestynick
Glen Lyon, PA

Makes 6 servings

Prep Time: 5-10 minutes
Cooking Time: 4-6 hours
Ideal slow cooker size: 6-qt.

2 cups dry lentils, picked over and rinsed
14½-oz. can diced tomatoes
8 cups canned chicken broth, *or* water
1 Tbsp. salt
½-1 lb. pork *or* beef sausage, cut into 2" pieces

1. Place lentils, tomatoes, chicken broth, and salt in slow cooker. Stir to combine. Place sausage pieces on top.
2. Cover and cook on Low 4-6 hours, or until lentils are tender but not dry or mushy.

Sauerkraut Soup

Norma Grieser
Clarksville, MI

Makes 4 servings

Prep Time: 10 minutes
Cooking Time: 4-6 hours
Ideal slow cooker size:
3- to 4-qt.

2 14.5-oz. cans stewed
tomatoes
2 cups sauerkraut
1 cup diced potatoes
1 lb. fresh *or* smoked
sausage, sliced

Optional ingredients:
1 medium-sized onion,
chopped
1/3 cup brown sugar

1. Combine all ingredients
in slow cooker.
2. Cover and cook on Low
4-6 hours, or until the flavors
have blended and the soup is
thoroughly heated.

Pork-Veggie Stew

Ruth E. Martin
Loysville, PA

Makes 8 servings

Prep Time: 15 minutes
Cooking Time: 6 hours
Ideal slow cooker size: 4-qt.

2 lbs. boneless pork loin,
cut into 1" cubes
8 medium potatoes, peeled
and cut into 2" pieces
6 large carrots, peeled and
cut into 2" pieces
1 cup ketchup
2 1/4 cups water, *divided*

1. Brown pork cubes in a
large non-stick skillet.
2. Lightly spray slow
cooker with non-stick cooking
spray.
3. Place all ingredients
except ketchup and 1/4 cup
water in slow cooker.
4. Cover and cook on High
5 hours. One hour before
serving, combine ketchup
with 1/4 cup water. Pour over
stew. Cook one more hour.

*Tip: To prevent potatoes from
turning black or discoloring,
toss in water with a small
amount of cream of tartar
(6 cups water to 1 tsp. cream of
tartar).*

Pork Potato Stew

Kristin Tice
Shipshewana, IN

Makes 4 servings

Prep Time: 20 minutes
Cooking Time: 4 hours
Ideal slow cooker size: 3-qt.

1 lb. ground pork
1/2 cup onion, chopped
1 sweet potato, cubed and
peeled, approximately
3 cups
2 beef bouillon cubes
1/2 tsp. dried rosemary
3 cups water

1. Place meat and onion in
non-stick skillet. Brown on
stovetop.
2. Place drained meat,
along with onion, into slow
cooker. Add remaining ingredients.
3. Cover and cook on Low
for 4 hours.

*Optional ingredient: Add a
bit of hot sauce to make the
soup spicy, or serve on the side
to accommodate those who
don't like hot food.*

A Tip —

Try to have vegetable and meat pieces all cut about the
same size and thickness. Pieces of uniform size tend to finish
cooking at the same time.
Mary Puskar, Forest Hill, MD

Chili-Taco Soup

Frances L. Kruba
Dundalk, MD

Makes 8 servings

Prep Time: 25-30 minutes
Cooking Time: 5-7 hours
Ideal slow cooker size:
 1- to 2-qt.

2 lbs. lean stew meat
2 15-oz. cans stewed
 tomatoes, Mexican *or*
 regular
1 envelope dry taco
 seasoning mix
2 15-oz. cans pinto beans
15-oz. can whole-kernel
 corn
3/4 cup water

1. Cut large pieces of stew meat in half and brown in large non-stick skillet.
2. Combine all ingredients in slow cooker.
3. Cover and cook on Low 5-7 hours.

Beef and Black-Eyed Pea Soup

Jeanette Oberholtzer
Manheim, PA

Makes 6 servings

Prep Time: 25 minutes
Cooking Time: 8-10 hours
Ideal slow cooker size: 6 qt.

16-oz. pkg. dried black-
 eyed peas
10-oz. can condensed bean
 and bacon soup
3-4 cups water
4 large carrots, peeled and
 sliced
3-lb. beef chuck roast, cut
 into 2" cubes
1/2 tsp. each salt and
 pepper

1. Rinse and drain the peas.
2. Combine all ingredients in slow cooker.
3. Cook on Low 8-10 hours, or until peas and beef are tender.

Variation: For added flavor, add chopped onion and minced garlic, or a 14.5-oz. can chopped tomatoes, to Step 2.

Busy Cook's Stew

Denise Nickel
Goessel, KS

Makes 4-6 servings

Prep Time: 30-40 minutes
Cooking Time: 6-8 hours
Ideal slow cooker size: 3-qt.

1 lb. boneless stew meat,
 cut up
10 3/4-oz. can cream of
 mushroom soup
2 cups water
3 potatoes, cubed
3 carrots, diced
1 onion, chopped

1. Brown meat in large non-stick skillet. Don't crowd the skillet so the meat browns on all sides. (If your skillet is 10 inches or smaller, brown the beef in 2 batches.)
2. Place meat in slow cooker. Add remaining ingredients in the order listed. Stir well after each addition.
3. Cover and cook on Low 6-8 hours, or until meat and vegetables are tender but not mushy. Stir occasionally.

Variation: If you wish, add salt and pepper to taste.

Beef Barley Soup

Stacie Skelly
Millersville, PA

Makes 8-10 servings

Prep Time: *15 minutes*
Cooking Time: *9 1/4-11 1/2 hours*
Ideal slow cooker size: *6-qt.*

3-4 lb. chuck roast
2 cups carrots, chopped
6 cups vegetable, *or*
   tomato, juice, *divided*
2 cups quick-cook barley
water, to desired
   consistency
salt and pepper to taste,
   optional

1. Place roast, carrots, and 4 cups juice in slow cooker.
2. Cover and cook on Low 8-10 hours.
3. Remove roast. Place on platter and cover with foil to keep warm.
4. Meanwhile, add barley to slow cooker. Stir well. Turn heat to High and cook 45 minutes to 1 hour, until barley is tender.
5. While barley is cooking, cut meat into bite-sized pieces.
6. When barley is tender, return chopped beef to slow cooker. Add 2 cups juice, water if you wish, and salt and pepper, if you want. Cook for 30 minutes on High, or until soup is heated through.

Easy Slow-Cooker Vegetable Soup

Beth Peachey
Belleville, PA

Makes 8-10 servings

Prep Time: *10 minutes*
Cooking Time: *6-8 hours*
Ideal slow cooker size: *3-qt.*

1 cup carrots, chopped *or*
   sliced
1 cup green beans, fresh,
   frozen, *or* canned
1 cup corn, fresh, frozen *or*
   canned, and drained
1 qt. canned tomatoes
1 cup cooked beef, cut in
   bite-size pieces

1. Combine all ingredients in slow cooker.
2. Cover and cook on Low 6-8 hours, or until vegetables are tender.

Beef Vegetable Soup

Margaret Moffitt
Bartlett, TN

Makes 12 servings

Prep Time: *15 minutes*
Cooking Time: *6-8 hours*
Ideal slow cooker size: *4-qt.*

1 lb. chunks of stewing
   beef
28-oz. cans stewed
   tomatoes, undrained
1 tomato can of water
16-oz. pkg. of your favorite
   frozen vegetable
half a 10-oz. pkg. frozen
   chopped onions
1 1/2 tsp. salt and 1/4-1/2 tsp.
   pepper
2 Tbsp. chopped fresh
   parsley, *optional*

1. Combine all ingredients in slow cooker.
2. Cover and cook on High 6-8 hours.

Tip: Double this recipe (using a 7- to 8-qt. slow cooker). Freeze any leftovers for a quick second meal.

Homemade Beef Soup

Eleanor Larson
Glen Lyon, PA

Makes 6-8 servings

Prep Time: 10 minutes
Cooking Time: 3 hours
Ideal slow cooker size: 12-qt., or 2 6-qt. cookers

2 lbs. beef cubes
2 onions, chopped *or* sliced
2 16-oz. bags frozen vegetables
6 potatoes, cubed
6 beef bouillon cubes
5 cups water

1. Heat slow cooker to High. Brown beef cubes and onions in slow cooker, stirring frequently.
2. Stir in frozen vegetables and potatoes. Stir in bouillon cubes and water.
3. Cover and cook on Low 3 hours, or until meat is tender and vegetables are cooked to your liking. (Cooking it longer makes it even more tasty!)

Tip: Add more flavor by stirring in salt and pepper to taste, and/or fresh parsley, basil, and thyme.

Ground Beef Bean Soup

Dale Peterson
Rapid City, SD

Makes 8 servings

Prep Time: 25 minutes
Cooking Time: 3-4 hours
Ideal slow cooker size: 6-qt.

2 lbs. ground beef
3 15-oz. cans pinto beans, drained
2 10¾-oz. cans tomato soup
10¾-oz. can cheddar cheese soup
salt and pepper to taste

1. Brown beef in large non-stick skillet. Drain.
2. Place browned beef in slow cooker. Add remaining ingredients and mix well.
3. Cover and cook on Low 3-4 hours, or until soup is hot and until flavors have blended.

Variation: Serve this as a topping over rice or baked potatoes.

— **Carol Eveleth**
Wellman, IA

Chili with Two Beans

Patricia Fleischer
Carlisle, PA

Makes 6-8 servings

Prep Time: 15 minutes
Cooking Time: 4½-5 hours
Ideal slow cooker size: 6-qt.

1 lb. ground beef
6-oz. can tomato paste
40½-oz. can kidney beans, undrained
2 15½-oz. cans pinto beans, undrained
2 Tbsp. chili powder

1. Brown beef in large non-stick skillet. Drain.
2. Combine all ingredients in slow cooker.
3. Cover and cook on Low 4½-5 hours.

Extra Easy Chili

Jennifer Gehman
Harrisburg, PA

Makes 4-6 servings

Prep Time: 10 minutes
Cooking Time: 4-8 hours
Ideal slow cooker size: 4-qt.

1 lb. ground beef *or* turkey, uncooked
1 envelope dry chili seasoning mix
16-oz. can chili beans in sauce
2 28-oz. cans crushed or diced tomatoes seasoned with garlic and onion

1. Crumble meat in bottom of slow cooker.
2. Add remaining ingredients. Stir.
3. Cover. Cook on High 4-6 hours or Low 6-8 hours. Stir halfway through cooking time.
4. Serve over white rice, topped with shredded cheddar cheese and chopped raw onions.

I decided to make this chili recipe one year for Christmas. Our family was hosting other family members—and we had had guests for about a week prior to Christmas. Needless to say, I was tired of cooking so this seemed easy enough. It was so nice to put the ingredients in the slow cooker and let it cook all day long. Not only did the chili warm us up on a cold day, but it was a welcomed change

from the traditional Christmas meal. It has been my tradition ever since!

Mexican Chili Mix and Fritos

Melanie Thrower
McPherson, KS

Makes 4-6 servings

Prep Time: 10-15 minutes
Cooking Time: 4 hours
Ideal slow cooker size: 2- to 3-qt.

1 lb. ground beef
14³/4-16-oz. can cream-style corn, drained
¹/2 cup chunky picante sauce
16-oz. can pinto *or* black beans, drained
half an envelope dry taco seasoning

1. Brown ground beef in a large non-stick skillet. Drain.
2. Mix beef, corn, picante sauce, beans, and taco seasoning in slow cooker.
3. Cover and cook on Low 4 hours.
4. Serve over corn chips with optional garnishes of shredded cheese, chopped olives, sour cream, and salsa.

Tip: *I like to substitute ground elk or venison for the beef in this recipe.*

Easy Spicy Chili

Becky Gehman
Bergton, VA

Makes 9-12 servings

Prep Time: 15 minutes
Cooking Time: 4-10 hours
Ideal slow cooker size: 4- to 5-qt.

2 lbs. lean ground beef
3 15¹/2-oz. cans red kidney beans, drained
2-3 14¹/2-oz. cans diced tomatoes, undrained
2 onions, chopped
1 green pepper, chopped, *optional*
2-3 Tbsp. chili powder

1. Brown ground beef in a large non-stick skillet. Drain.
2. Place beef in slow cooker. Add kidney beans, tomatoes, onion, and green pepper, if you wish, to the cooker. Fold together well.
3. Cover and cook on Low 8-10 hours or on High 4-6 hours.
4. Add chili powder 2 hours before the end of the cooking time.

Tips:
1. This can be successfully frozen and reheated later.
2. You may want to pass salt and pepper as you serve the chili.
3. You may add about 2 Tbsp. of flour along with the chili powder in Step 4 if you want to thicken the chili.

Versatile Slow-Cooker Chili

Margaret Moffitt
Bartlett, TN

Makes 6-8 servings

Prep Time: 25 minutes
Cooking Time: 6 hours
Ideal slow cooker size: 3-qt.

1 lb. ground beef, *or* turkey
2 15-oz. cans tomato sauce
2 15-oz. cans kidney beans *or* black beans, drained
1 envelope dry chili seasoning
15-oz. can of water, *or* more *or* less

1. Brown ground beef or turkey in a non-stick skillet. Drain.
2. Combine all ingredients in the slow cooker.
3. Cover and cook on Low 6 hours.

Tip: If you do not have time to brown your ground beef or turkey, just put it in your slow cooker without browning it. It will cook sufficiently during the 6 hours.

A Tip —

Keep hot dishwater in the sink so you can clean up the kitchen as you go and while the food is baking or cooking.

Flavorful Chili

Sharon Hannaby
Frederick, MD

Makes 10-12 servings

Prep Time: 15-20 minutes
Cooking Time: 6-8 hours
Ideal slow cooker size: 5- to 6-qt.

2 lbs. ground beef
52-oz. can kidney beans, rinsed and drained
2 28-oz. cans diced tomatoes with garlic, basil, and oregano
2-3 Tbsp. chili powder, *or* 2-3 tsp. Tabasco sauce, according to your preference for heat
10$\frac{1}{2}$-oz. can tomato soup

1. Brown beef in a large non-stick skillet, breaking up the chunks of meat. Drain.
2. Place in slow cooker. Mix in all other ingredients.
3. Cover and cook on Low 6-8 hours.

Tips:
1. Serve over baked potatoes or rice.
2. Serve with chopped scallions or onions, shredded cheese, and sour cream as toppings.

Chunky Chili

Eleanor Larson
Glen Lyon, PA

Makes 4-5 servings

Prep Time: 10 minutes
Cooking Time: 4-5 hours
Ideal slow cooker size: 3-qt.

1$\frac{1}{2}$ lbs. cubed beef stew meat, *or* venison
1 medium-sized onion, chopped
1 *or* 2 8-oz. cans tomato sauce, depending upon how thick *or* thin you prefer chili to be
1$\frac{1}{2}$-3 tsp. chili powder, depending upon your taste preference
16-oz. can kidney beans, drained

1. Place all ingredients in slow cooker. Mix well.
2. Cover and cook on High 4-5 hours, or until the meat is tender but not over-cooked.

Beef and Beans

Margaret H. Moffitt
Bartlet, TN

Makes 4-6 servings

Prep Time: 20-25 minutes
Cooking Time: 4-6 hours
Ideal slow cooker size: 3-qt.

1½ lbs. ground beef
15-oz. can tomato sauce
  with garlic and onion
2 15-oz. cans kidney beans,
  undrained
salt and pepper to taste

1. Brown beef in a non-stick skillet, just until the pink is gone. Drain.
2. Place beef in bottom of slow cooker.
3. Add tomato sauce, beans, and salt and pepper.
4. Cover and cook on Low 4-6 hours.

Variations:
1. For a juicier dish to serve over rice, use two cans of tomato sauce.
2. For more texture, substitute petite-cut tomatoes with garlic and onion in place of the tomato sauce.
— **Anita Wansley**
Meridian, MS

Green Chili Stew

Colleen Konetzni
Rio Rancho, NM

Makes 4 servings

Prep Time: 30 minutes
Cooking Time: 6-8 hours
Ideal slow cooker size: 4-qt.

1 lb. ground beef
6 potatoes, peeled and
  cubed
1 onion, sliced
salt and pepper to taste
3/4 cup chopped green
  chilies

Optional ingredients:
1 tsp. garlic powder
1 bouillon cube

1. Brown ground beef in non-stick skillet. Drain. Place in slow cooker.
2. Add remaining ingredients to slow cooker. Stir together thoroughly.
3. Cover and cook on Low 6-8 hours, or until the vegetables are tender.

Chili Pie

Andrea Cunningham
Arlington, KS

Makes 6 servings

Prep Time: 15 minutes
Cooking Time: 6-8 hours
Ideal slow cooker size:
  4- to 6-qt.

1 lb. ground beef
2 12-oz. cans chili beans,
  drained
4 large tomatoes, diced
salt and pepper to taste
1 Tbsp. chili powder,
  optional
small onion, chopped,
  optional
corn chips, *optional*
1½ cups shredded cheese
  of your choice, *optional*

1. Brown ground beef in a non-stick skillet. Drain.
2. Spray the interior of the cooker with non-stick cooking spray. Combine ground beef, chili beans, tomatoes, and any of the optional ingredients you want in the slow cooker.
3. Cover and cook on Low 6-8 hours.
4. Serve over corn chips and top with cheddar cheese if you wish.

A Tip —

Put your cooker meal together the night before you want to cook it. The following morning put the mixture in the slow cooker, cover, and cook.
Sara Wilson
Blairstown, MO

Taco Soup

Norma Grieser
Clarksville, MI

Makes 4-6 servings

Prep Time: 10-12 minutes
Cooking Time: 4-6 hours
Ideal slow cooker size: 3-qt.

1 lb. ground beef
1 qt. tomato juice
15-oz. can kidney beans
1 envelope dry taco
  seasoning
10½-oz. can tomato soup
medium-sized onion,
  chopped, *optional*

1. Brown beef in non-stick skillet. Drain. Place in slow cooker.
2. Add remaining ingredients to slow cooker and stir until well combined.
3. Cover and cook on Low 4-6 hours.

Tip: Serve with Doritos, sour cream, and shredded cheddar cheese as toppings, if you wish.

Variation: Instead of tomato juice and tomato soup, substitute 1 14½-oz. can stewed tomatoes and 1 8-oz. can tomato sauce.
— **Sharon Shank**
Bridgewater, VA

Taco Pizza-Sauce Soup

Mary E. Shrock
Sugarcreek, OH

Makes 8 servings

Prep Time: 30 minutes
Cooking Time: 30 minutes
Ideal slow cooker size: 4-qt.

2 lbs. ground beef
1 small onion, chopped
1 Tbsp. taco seasoning
16-oz. can refried beans, *or*
  chili beans
3 qts. pizza sauce
salt and pepper to taste,
  optional

1. Brown meat with onion in large non-stick skillet. Drain.
2. Place browned beef and onions in slow cooker. Add taco seasoning, and then beans. Stir in pizza sauce and additional seasonings, if you wish.
3. Simmer on High for 30 minutes. Turn to Low and keep warm until ready to serve.

Tips:
1. Serve with sour cream, shredded cheese, and tortilla chips.
2. If the soup is too thick, add water or more pizza sauce.

Veggie-Beef Soup

Char Hagner
Montague, MI

Makes 6 servings

Prep Time: 10 minutes
Cooking Time: 3-8 hours
Ideal slow cooker size:
  4- to 5-qt.

1 lb. ground beef
14½-oz. can beef broth
1½ cups water
10-oz. pkg. frozen mixed
  vegetables
14½-oz. can diced
  tomatoes
1 Tbsp. dried minced
  onion

1. Brown meat in a non-stick skillet. Drain.
2. Place all ingredients in slow cooker.
3. Cover and cook on Low 6-8 hours, or on High 3-4 hours.

Variation: Stir in 1 cup dry macaroni 1 hour before the end of the cooking time.

Ground Beef Vegetable Soup

Renee Baum
Chambersburg, PA
Janet Oberholtzer
Ephrata, PA

Makes 10 servings

Prep Time: 15 minutes
Cooking Time: 8-9 hours
Ideal slow cooker size: 5-qt.

1 lb. ground beef
46-oz. can tomato, *or* V-8, juice
16-oz. pkg. frozen mixed vegetables, thawed
2 cups frozen cubed hash browns, thawed
1 envelope dry onion soup mix

1. Brown beef in non-stick skillet on stovetop. Drain.
2. Place beef in slow cooker. Stir in remaining ingredients.
3. Cover and cook on Low 8-9 hours, or until vegetables are cooked through.

Variations:
1. Instead of hash browns, use 2 cups cubed cooked potatoes.
— Elsie Schlabach
Millersburg, OH

2. Instead of tomato or V-8 juice, use 2 beef bouillon cubes dissolved in 2 cups boiling water. And instead of dry onion soup mix, use salt and pepper to taste.
— Sharon Wantland
Menomonee Falls, WI

Tomato Pea Soup

Ruth Ann Penner, Hillsboro, KS

Makes 4 servings

Prep Time: 10-12 minutes
Cooking Time: 2 hours
Ideal slow cooker size: 3-qt.

1 lb. ground beef
1/4 cup dried onions
5- *or* 10-oz. can diced tomatoes, depending upon how much you like tomatoes
15-oz. can peas
1/2 tomato can of water
2 beef bouillon cubes

1. Brown beef in non-stick skillet. Drain.
2. Combine all ingredients in slow cooker.
3. Cover and cook on High for 2 hours, stirring occasionally.

Campfire Stew

Sharon Wantland
Menomonee Falls, WI

Makes 4 servings

Prep Time: 15 minutes
Cooking Time: 2-3 hours
Ideal slow cooker size: 2-qt.

1 lb. ground beef
1 medium onion, chopped
half a green pepper, chopped

salt and pepper to taste
2 cans vegetable soup, your favorite variety

1. Brown ground beef with onions and green pepper in a non-stick skillet, stirring until crumbly. Drain.
2. Combine all ingredients in slow cooker.
3. Cover and cook on Low 2-3 hours.

Quick Taco Chicken Soup

Karen Waggoner
Joplin, MO

Makes 4-6 servings

Prep Time: 5 minutes
Cooking Time: 1 hour
Ideal slow cooker size: 4-qt.

12-oz. can cooked chicken, undrained
14-oz. can chicken broth
16-oz. jar mild thick-and-chunky salsa
15-oz. can ranch-style beans
15-oz. can whole-kernel corn

1. Mix all ingredients in slow cooker.
2. Cover and cook on High 1 hour. Keep warm on Low until ready to serve.

Buffalo Chicken Wing Soup

Mary Lynn Miller
Reinholds, PA
Donna Neiter
Wausau, WI
Joette Droz
Kalona, IA

Makes 8 servings

Prep Time: 10 minutes
Cooking Time: 4-5 hours
Ideal slow cooker size: 3-qt.

6 cups milk
3 10³/4-oz. cans condensed cream of chicken soup, undiluted
3 cups (about 1 lb.) shredded *or* cubed cooked chicken
1 cup (8 ozs.) sour cream
1-8 Tbsp. hot pepper sauce, according to your preference *for heat!**

1. Combine milk and soups in slow cooker until smooth.
2. Stir in chicken.
3. Cover and cook on Low 3³/4-4³/4 hours.
4. Fifteen minutes before serving stir in sour cream and hot sauce.
5. Cover and continue cooking just until bubbly.

Start with a small amount of hot sauce, and then add more to suit your—and your diners' tastes!

Split Pea with Chicken Soup

Mary E. Wheatley
Mashpee, MA

Makes servings

Prep Time: 20 minutes
Cooking Time: 4-10 hours
Ideal slow cooker size: 5-qt.

16-oz. pkg. dried split peas
³/4 cup finely diced carrots
3 cups cubed raw potatoes
8 cups chicken broth
1 cup diced cooked chicken

1. Combine peas, carrots, potatoes, and chicken broth in slow cooker.
2. Cook on High 4-5 hours, or on Low 8-10 hours, or until all vegetables are tender. Stir after the soup begins to slowly boil.
3. Ten minutes before serving, stir in cooked chicken.

Chunky Chicken Vegetable Soup

Janice Muller
Derwood, MD

Makes 6 servings

Prep Time: 20 minutes
Cooking Time: 2-6 hours
Ideal slow cooker size: 3¹/2 to 4-qt.

2¹/2 cups water
8-oz. can tomato sauce
10-oz. pkg. frozen mixed vegetables, partially thawed
1¹/2 tsp. Italian seasoning
1 envelope dry chicken noodle soup mix
2 cups cut-up cooked chicken *or* turkey

1. Combine all ingredients in slow cooker.
2. Cook on Low 2-6 hours, depending upon how crunchy you like your vegetables.

Mary's Chicken and Rice Soup

Becky Frey, Lebanon, PA

Makes 8-10 servings

Prep Time: 10-20 minutes
Cooking Time: 3-4 hours
Ideal slow cooker size: 3½-qt.

4.4-oz. pkg. chicken-
flavored rice and sauce
2 cups diced, cooked
chicken
15-oz. can diced tomatoes
and green chilies
49½-oz. can chicken broth

1. Prepare rice and sauce according to package directions.
2. Place all ingredients in slow cooker. Stir until well mixed.
3. Cover and cook on Low 3-4 hours.

Tips:
1. Serve over corn chips and sprinkle with shredded cheese, if you wish.
2. If you can't find tomatoes with chilies, add a 4-oz. can of diced green chilies. Or add them anyway for extra heat.
3. You can add the rice and sauce without preparing them according to their package directions. Just stir them in uncooked, and simmer the soup an hour longer in the slow cooker, or until the rice is thoroughly cooked.

Chicken Noodle Soup

Jean Butzer
Batavia, NY

Makes 6-8 servings

Prep Time: 15 minutes
Cooking Time: 3½-8½ hours
Ideal slow cooker size: 4-qt.

2 10¾-oz. cans creamy
chicken mushroom soup
5 cups water
2 cups chopped cooked
chicken
10-oz. pkg. frozen mixed
vegetables
½-1 tsp. pepper
1½ cups dried egg noodles

1. Place soup in slow cooker. Blend in water. Stir in chicken, vegetables, and pepper.
2. Cover and cook on Low 6-8 hours, or on High 3-4 hours.
3. Turn to High if using Low setting. Stir in noodles.
4. Cover and cook another 20-30 minutes, or until noodles are just tender.

Tips:
1. You may substitute other flavors of cream soups.
2. You may use chicken broth in place of all, or part of, the water.

Chicken Rice Soup

Norma Grieser
Clarksville, MI

Makes 8 servings

Prep Time: 30 minutes
Cooking Time: 4-8 hours
Ideal slow cooker size:
4- to 6-qt.

4 cups chicken broth
4 cups cut-up chicken,
cooked
1⅓ cups cut-up celery
1⅓ cups diced carrots
1 qt. water
1 cup uncooked long-grain
rice

1. Put all ingredients in slow cooker.
2. Cover and cook on Low 4-8 hours, or until vegetables are cooked to your liking.

Tasty Chicken Soup

Rhonda Freed
Lowville, NY

Makes 12 servings

Prep Time: 10-15 minutes
Cooking Time: 6-7 hours
Ideal slow cooker size: 4-qt.

12 cups chicken broth
2 cups chicken, cooked
and cut into small
pieces

1 cup shredded carrots
3 whole cloves
small onion
16-oz. bag of dry noodles,
  cooked, *optional*

1. Place broth, chicken,
and carrots in slow cooker.
2. Peel onion. Using a
toothpick, poke 3 holes on
the cut ends. Carefully press
cloves into 3 of the holes
until only their round part
shows. Add to slow cooker.
3. Cover and cook on High
6-7 hours.
4. If you'd like a thicker
soup, add a bag of cooked
fine egg noodles before serving.

*Tip: You can make the broth
and cook the chicken in your
slow cooker, too. Just put 2-3
lbs. of cut-up chicken pieces
into the slow cooker. Add 12
cups water. Cook on High 4-5
hours, or until chicken is tender
and falling off the bone.*

*Remove the chicken with a
slotted spoon. Debone when
cooled enough to handle.*

*Measure 2 cups of chicken
meat and return to slow cooker.
Completely cool the remaining
chicken and freeze or refrigerate for future use.*

*Continue with the recipe
above to make the soup.*

Vegetable Chicken Soup

Annabelle Unternahrer
Shipshewana, IN

Makes 6 servings

Prep Time: 10 minutes
Cooking Time: 4-8 hours
Ideal slow cooker size: 5-qt.

2 14½-oz. cans chicken
  broth
1 Tbsp. dried, minced
  onion
16-oz. pkg. frozen mixed
  vegetables
2 cups pre-cooked chicken
  breast, cubed
2 10¾-oz. cans cream of
  chicken soup

1. Combine the broth,
minced onion, vegetables,
and chicken in slow cooker.
2. Cover and cook on Low
3-7 hours, depending upon
how crunchy you like your
vegetables.
3. Add chicken soup and
continue cooking 1 more
hour.
4. Stir and serve.

Tips:
*1. Don't allow mixture to
boil after adding the chicken
soup.*
*2. For a heartier meal, serve
over steamed rice, allowing
about ½ cup cooked rice for
each serving.*

Chinese Chicken Soup

Karen Waggoner
Joplin, MO

Makes 6 servings

Prep Time: 5 minutes
Cooking Time: 1-2 hours
Ideal slow cooker size: 4-qt.

3 14½-oz. cans chicken
  broth
16-oz. pkg. frozen stir-fry
  vegetable blend
2 cups cooked cubed
  chicken
1 tsp. minced fresh
  gingerroot
1 tsp. soy sauce

1. Mix all ingredients in
slow cooker.
2. Cover and cook on High
for 1-2 hours, depending
upon how crunchy or soft
you like your vegetables to
be.

Creamy Corn and Turkey Soup

Janessa Hochstedler
East Earl, PA

Makes 5-6 servings

Prep Time: 15 minutes
Cooking Time: 3-8 hours
Ideal slow cooker size: 3-qt.

2 cups shredded cooked
  turkey
1 cup milk
2 cups chicken broth
15-oz. can Mexican-style
  corn
4 ozs. (half an 8-oz. pkg.)
  cream cheese, cubed
1 red bell pepper,
  chopped, *optional*

1. Place all ingredients in
slow cooker.
2. Cover and cook on Low
7-8 hours, or on High 3
hours.

Easy Turkey Chili

Dee Snyder
Lindenwold, NJ

Makes 6 servings

Prep Time: 10-15 minutes
Cooking Time: 6-8 hours
Ideal slow cooker size: 5-qt.

2 1-lb. rolls of ground
  turkey (found in freezer
  case of grocery store),
  thawed
2 15½-oz. cans red kidney
  beans, drained
2 envelopes dry chili
  seasoning mix
24-oz. jar salsa

Optional ingredients:
1 large onion, chopped
1 large bell pepper,
  chopped

1. Place turkey in slow
cooker. Break it up with a
spoon into small chunks.
2. Add remaining ingredi-
ents to slow cooker. Stir
together until thoroughly
mixed.
3. Cover and cook on Low
for 6-8 hours.

Tips:
1. Do not add water.
*2. Top individual servings
with grated sharp cheese, if you
wish.*
*3. This versatile dish can be
served over baked potatoes,
spaghetti, noodles, rice, hot
dogs, or tortilla chips.*

Quick Clam and Corn Chowder

Carol L. Stroh
Akron, NY

Makes 4-6 servings

Prep Time: 5-10 minutes
Cooking Time: 3-4 hours
*Ideal slow cooker size:
1½- to 2-qt.*

2 10½-oz. cans cream of
  potato soup
1 pint frozen corn
6½-oz. can minced clams,
  drained
2 soup cans milk

1. Place all ingredients in
slow cooker. Stir to mix.
2. Cook on Low 3-4 hours,
or until hot.

Clam Chowder

Marilyn Mowry
Irving, TX

Makes 3 servings

Prep Time: 10 minutes
Cooking Time: 2-3 hours
*Ideal slow cooker size:
1-to 2-qt.*

15-oz. can New England-
  style clam chowder
1½ cups milk, *or* half-and-
  half
6½-oz. can minced clams,
  undrained

half a stick (1/4 cup) butter
1/4 cup cooking sherry

1. Mix all ingredients together in slow cooker.
2. Heat on Low for 2-3 hours, or until until good and hot.

Crabmeat Soup

Carol L. Stroh
Akron, NY

Makes 8 servings

Prep Time: 5-10 minutes
Cooking Time: 5-6 hours
Ideal slow cooker size: 3 1/2-qt.

2 10 3/4-oz. cans cream of tomato soup
2 10 1/2-oz. cans split pea soup
3 soup cans milk
1 cup heavy cream
1 *or* 2 6-oz. cans crabmeat, drained
1/4 cup sherry, *optional*

1. Pour soups into slow cooker. Add milk and stir to mix.
2. Cover and cook on Low for 4 hours, or until hot.
3. Stir in cream and crabmeat. Continue to cook on Low for 1 hour, or until heated through.

Shrimp Soup/Chowder

Joanne Good, Wheaton, IL

Makes 12 servings

Prep Time: 25 minutes
Cooking Time: 7-8 hours
Ideal slow cooker size: 4-qt.

1 medium onion, chopped
5 medium russet potatoes, peeled and cubed
1 1/2 cups diced, pre-cooked ham
4-6 cups water
salt and pepper to taste
2 lbs. shrimp, peeled, deveined, and cooked

Chowder option:
4 Tbsp. flour
1 cup heavy (whipping) cream

1. Place chopped onion in microwave-safe bowl and cook in microwave for 2 minutes on High.
2. Place onion, cubed potatoes, diced ham, and 4 cups water in slow cooker. (If you're making the Chowder option, whisk 4 Tbsp. flour into 4 cups water in bowl before adding to slow cooker.)
3. Cover and cook on Low for 7 hours, or until potatoes are softened. If soup base is thicker than you like, add up to 2 cups more water.
4. About 15-20 minutes before serving, turn heat to High and add shrimp. If making chowder, also add heavy cream. Cook until shrimp are hot, about 15 minutes.

Optional ingredients, to be added in Step 2:
1/2 tsp. thyme
1 bay leaf (remove before serving)

Oyster Stew

Linda Overholt, Abbeville, SC

Makes 4 servings

Prep Time: 15-20 minutes
Cooking Time: 2 hours
Ideal slow cooker size: 3 1/2- to 4-qt.

1 pt. oysters with liquor
half a stick (1/4 cup) butter
1 pt. milk
1 pt. half-and-half
salt and pepper to taste

1. In large non-stick skillet, heat oysters slowly in their own juice until edges begin to curl (do not boil).
2. Place oysters and their liquor in the slow cooker.
3. Add butter, milk, and half-and-half. Season with salt and pepper to taste.
4. Cook on Low for about 2 hours, or until heated through.

Variation: Use 1 qt. milk, instead of 1 pt. milk and 1 pt. half-and-half.
— **Sara Kinsinger**
Stuarts Draft, VA

Sunday Night Soup

Sara Harter Fredette,
Goshen, MA

Makes 4-6 servings

Prep Time: 10-15 minutes
Cooking Time: 4-5 hours
Ideal slow cooker size: 4-qt.

1.8-oz. pkg. dry Knorr
  Tomato Beef-flavored
  soup mix
4 cups water
2 cups diced potatoes
3 cups chopped vegetables
  (celery, carrots, peppers,
  onions), *or* 1-lb. pkg.
  frozen mixed vegetables
2 cups cooked chicken *or*
  cooked beef cubes, *or*
  browned ground beef,
  optional

1. In slow cooker, blend
powdered soup mix into
water. Add vegetables.
2. Cover and cook on High
1 hour, and then on Low 3
hours, or until vegetables are
tender.
3. One-half hour before
end of cooking time, stir in
meat, if you choose to
include it.

Emergency Soup

Elaine Sue Good
Tiskilwa, IL

Makes 8 servings

Prep Time: 10-15 minutes
Cooking Time: 6-12 hours
Ideal slow cooker size: 5-qt.

32-oz. pkg. frozen mixed
  vegetables
16-oz. pkg. cocktail
  wieners, *or* hot dogs cut
  into bite-size pieces
46-oz. can tomato juice
1 Tbsp. dried basil *or*
  parsley

1. Combine all ingredients
in slow cooker.
2. Cover and cook on Low
6-12 hours.

Tips:
*1. This is one of those emer-
gency recipes that I like to use
if I suddenly get called away for
the day at the last minute. I
know everyone will be hungry
when I get home.*
*2. You can use almost what-
ever is available in your pantry
and refrigerator in this recipe.*
*3. You can also adjust the
seasonings to your own preference.*

Cheesy Broccoli Soup

Dede Peterson
Rapid City, SD

Makes 4 servings

Prep Time: 15 minutes
Cooking Time: 5-6 hours
Ideal slow cooker size: 3-qt.

1 lb. frozen chopped
  broccoli, thawed
1 lb. Velveeta cheese,
  cubed
10¾-oz. can cream of
  celery soup
14½-oz. can chicken or
  vegetable broth
dash of pepper
dash of salt

1. Combine ingredients in
slow cooker.
2. Cover. Cook on Low 5-6
hours.

Broccoli Soup

Linda Overholt, Abbeville, SC

Makes 8 servings

Prep Time: 5-10 minutes
Cooking Time: 1-1½ hours
Ideal slow cooker size:
3½- to 4-qt.

1 lb. fresh broccoli,
  chopped
2 12-oz. cans evaporated
  milk
2 10½-oz. cans cheddar
  cheese soup
2 10½-oz. cans cream of
  potato soup
1-2 cups cubed Velveeta
  cheese, *optional*

1. Place chopped broccoli
in medium-sized saucepan.
Add ¼ cup water, cover, and
steam briefly. Remove from
heat while broccoli is still a
bit crunchy. Set aside.
2. Mix milk and soups
together in slow cooker.
3. Add broccoli and cook-
ing water and cover. Cook on
High for 1 hour, or on Low
for 1½ hours.
4. Twenty minutes before
serving, stir in cubed Velveeta
cheese, if you wish.

Variations:
*1. For a little more zest, stir
in ¼ tsp. black pepper in Step 3.*
*2. Substitute mushroom soup
for cheddar cheese soup.
Substitute shredded sharp cheddar cheese for Velveeta cheese.*
— **Jennifer Kuh**
  Bay Village, OH

Creamy Tomato Soup

Sara Kinsinger
Stuarts Draft, VA

Makes 6 servings

Prep Time: 20 minutes
Cooking Time: 1½ hours
Ideal slow cooker size: 4-qt.

26-oz. can condensed
  tomato soup, plus 6 ozs.
  water to equal 1 qt.
½ tsp. salt, *optional*
half a stick (4 Tbsp.) butter
8 Tbsp. flour
1 qt. milk (whole, *or*
  reduced-fat)

1. Put tomato soup, salt if
you wish, and butter in slow
cooker. Blend well.
2. Cover and cook on High
for 1 hour.
3. Meanwhile, place flour
and 1 cup milk in 2-qt.
microwave-safe container.
Whisk together until big
lumps disappear. Then whisk
in remaining milk until only
small lumps remain.
4. Place flour-milk mixture
in microwave and cook on
High for 3 minutes. Remove
and stir until smooth. Return
to microwave and cook on
High for another 3 minutes.
5. Add thickened milk
slowly to hot soup in slow
cooker.
6. Heat thoroughly for 10
to 15 minutes.

*Tip: Serve with freshly ground
pepper, dried chives, or your
choice of green herbs, and oyster crackers or croutons.*

Easy Potato Soup

Yvonne Kauffman Boettger
Harrisonburg, VA

Makes 8 servings

Prep Time: 10 minutes
Cooking Time: 5 hours
Ideal slow cooker size:
4- to 6-qt.

3 cups chicken broth
2-lb. bag frozen hash
  brown potatoes
1½ tsp. salt
¾ tsp. pepper
3 cups milk
3 cups shredded Monterey
  Jack, *or* cheddar, cheese

1. Place chicken broth,
potatoes, salt, and pepper in
slow cooker.
2. Cover and cook on High
4 hours, or until potatoes are
soft.
3. Leaving the broth and
potatoes in the slow cooker,
mash the potatoes lightly,
leaving some larger chunks.
4. Add milk and cheese.
Blend in thoroughly.
5. Cover and cook on High
until cheese melts and soup is
hot.

Potato Chowder

Susan Wenger
Lebanon, PA

Makes 12 servings

Prep Time: 15 minutes
Cooking Time: 8¹/2-10¹/2 hours
Ideal slow cooker size: 5-qt.

8 cups peeled, diced
  potatoes
3 14¹/2-oz. cans chicken
  broth
10³/4-oz. can cream of
  chicken soup
¹/4 tsp. pepper
8-oz. pkg. cream cheese,
  cubed

1. In slow cooker, combine
potatoes, chicken broth,
chicken soup, and pepper.
2. Cover and cook on Low
8-10 hours, or until potatoes
are tender.
3. Add cream cheese, stirring until well blended.
4. Heat until cheese melts
and soup is hot throughout.

Optional ingredients:
¹/3 **cup chopped onion**
¹/2 **lb. sliced bacon, cooked**
  and crumbled
snipped chives

1. Add chopped onion to
Step 1, if you wish.
2. Garnish individual servings of the soup with bacon
and chives, if you like.

Potato Soup with Possibilities

Janie Steele
Moore, OK

Makes 6 servings

Prep Time: 20-30 minutes
Cooking Time: 5-6 hours
Ideal slow cooker size:
  4- to 6-qt.

6-8 cups homemade
  chicken broth, *or* 2 14-
  oz. cans chicken broth,
  plus ¹/2 soup can water
1 large onion, chopped
3 celery stalks, chopped,
  including leaves, if you
  like
6 large white potatoes,
  peeled, chopped, cubed,
  or sliced
salt and pepper to taste

Optional ingredients:
shredded sharp cheddar
  cheese
2-3 cups chopped clams
10- *or* **16-oz. pkg. frozen**
  corn

1. Place all ingredients in
slow cooker.
2. Cover and cook on High
5 hours, or on Low 6 hours,
or until vegetables are soft
but not mushy.

Potato Soup with Ground Beef

Sharon Timpe
Jackson, WI

Makes 6-8 servings

Prep Time: 15-20 minutes
Cooking Time: 3¹/2-4 hours
Ideal slow cooker size: 4- to 5-qt.

1 lb. ground beef
4 cups potatoes, peeled
  and cut into ¹/2" cubes
1 small onion, chopped
3 8-oz. cans tomato sauce
2 tsp. salt
¹/2 tsp. pepper
4 cups water
¹/2 tsp. hot pepper sauce,
  optional

1. Brown the ground beef
in a non-stick skillet. Drain
well. Place meat in slow
cooker.
2. Add cubed potatoes,
chopped onion, and tomato
sauce.
3. Stir in salt, pepper,
water, and hot pepper sauce,
if you wish.
4. Cover and cook on High
until mixture starts to simmer, about 1 hour.
5. Turn to Low and con-
tinue cooking until potatoes
are tender, about 2¹/2-3 hours.

Tips:
  1. Garnish each bowl of
soup with chopped parsley.
  2. I like to use red potatoes,
because they stay more firm.

Curried Limas and Potato Soup

Barbara Gautcher
Harrisonburg, VA

Makes 6 servings

Prep Time: 15 minutes
Cooking Time: 4-10 hours
Ideal slow cooker size: 3-qt.

1½ cups dried large lima
   beans
4 cups water, *divided*
5-6 medium-sized potatoes,
   finely chopped
½ head cauliflower,
   optional
2 cups (16 ozs.) sour cream
2 Tbsp. curry
1-2 tsp. salt and pepper, to
   taste

For faster cooking:
1. In a medium saucepan,
bring dried limas to a boil in
2 cups water. Boil, uncovered, for 2 minutes. Cover,
turn off heat, and wait 2
hours.
2. Drain water. Place
beans in slow cooker.
3. Add 2 cups fresh water.
Cover and cook 2 hours on
High.
4. During the last hour of
cooking, add diced potatoes
and florets of cauliflower.
Cook longer if vegetables are
not as tender as you like after
1 hour.
5. Ten minutes before
serving, add sour cream,
curry, and salt and pepper to
taste.

For slower cooking:
1. Soak limas in 2 cups
water overnight. In the morning, drain water. Put limas in
slow cooker and follow directions above, beginning with
Step 3.

*Tip: Sprinkle grated cheese on
top of each serving. And/or,
serve with chopped fresh fennel
as a topping.*

Cheese Soup

Darlene G. Martin
Richfield, PA
Kaye Taylor
Florissant, MO
Esther Hartzler
Carlsbad, NM

Makes 4 servings

Prep Time: 15 minutes
Cooking Time: 2-6 hours
Ideal slow cooker size: 3-qt.

2 10¾-oz. cans cream soup
   (celery, mushroom, *or*
   chicken)
1 cup milk
1 lb. cheddar cheese,
   cubed
1 tsp. Worcestershire sauce
¼ tsp. paprika

1. Put all ingredients in
slow cooker.
2. Cover and cook on Low
4-6 hours, or on High 2
hours.

*Tip: Top each serving with
croutons.*

Vegetable Cheese Soup

Rosalie D. Miller
Mifflintown, PA

Makes 5 servings

Prep Time: 15-20 minutes
Cooking Time: 4-10 hours
Ideal slow cooker size: 3-qt.

2 cups cream-style corn
1 cup potatoes, peeled and
   chopped
1 cup carrots, peeled and
   chopped
2 14½-oz. cans vegetable,
   or chicken, broth
16-oz. jar processed cheese

Optional ingredients:
1 tsp. celery seed
½ tsp. black pepper
½ cup chopped onion

1. Combine all ingredients
except cheese in the slow
cooker.
2. Cover and cook on Low
8-10 hours, or on High 4-5
hours.
3. Thirty to 60 minutes
before serving, stir in the
cheese. Then cook on High
for 30-60 minutes to melt and
blend the cheese.
4. If you choose to use any
or all of the optional ingredients, add them in Step 1.

Super Cheese Soup

Kate Johnson
Rolfe, IA

Makes 6 servings

Prep Time: 15 minutes
Cooking Time: 4 hours
Ideal slow cooker size:
4- to 5-qt.

4 *or* 5 potatoes, diced
16-oz. pkg. frozen
    vegetables
2-3 tsp. chicken bouillon
    granules
2-3 cups water
3/4 lb. Velveeta cheese,
    cubed

1. Place potatoes, frozen
vegetables, chicken bouillon,
and water (use 1 tsp. bouillon
to 1 cup water) in large
saucepan on stovetop and
cook until tender.
2. Add Velveeta cheese and
mix well.
3. Place soup in slow
cooker and keep warm on
Low for up to 4 hours.

Tip:
Or, if you've made the soup
ahead of time and had it refrig-
erated, you may need to heat it
longer on Low. If you're nearby,
stir the soup after 2 hours in
order to move the colder soup
out of the center and along the
edges of the cooker.

Cheddar Cheese Chowder

Ruth Zendt
Mifflintown, PA

Makes 4 servings

Prep Time: 15 minutes
Cooking Time: 3 1/2-4 1/2 hours
Ideal slow cooker size:
3- to 4-qt.

10-oz. pkg. frozen mixed
    vegetables
10 3/4-oz. can cream of
    chicken soup
1 soup can milk
1 cup shredded cheddar
    cheese

1. In a saucepan, cook and
drain frozen vegetables
according to package directions. Combine vegetables,
soup, and milk in slow
cooker.
2. Cover and cook on Low
3-4 hours, or until vegetables
are done to your liking. Stir
occasionally if you're nearby.
3. Sprinkle individual servings with cheese.

Onion Soup with Cheese

Jean H. Robinson
Cinnaminson, NJ

Makes 10 servings

Prep Time: 25 minutes
Cooking Time: 4 hours
Ideal slow cooker size: 6-qt.

4 large sweet white onions,
    sliced very thin
1 stick (1/2 cup) butter
8-oz. loaf French bread,
    sliced very thin
2 48-oz. cans beef, chicken,
    or vegetable, broth
1 lb. Swiss cheese,
    shredded

1. Saute onion rings in butter in large non-stick skillet
or saucepan until soft and
golden, about 15 minutes.
2. Put one-third of the
onions in the bottom of the
slow cooker. Layer one-third
of the bread slices over top.
Repeat layering 2 more times.
3. Pour broth over all.
4. Cover and cook on High
4 hours.
5. Stir in cheese 10 min-
utes before serving.

Variation: Add 1 1/2 tsp.
Worcestershire sauce and 3 bay
leaves to Step 2, as the final
and top layer.
    — **Karen Waggoner**
    Joplin, MO

Onion Soup

Patricia Howard
Green Valley, AZ

Makes 6-7 servings

Prep Time: 15-20 minutes
Cooking Time: 6-8 hours
Ideal slow cooker size: 4-qt.

3 cups thinly sliced onions
half a stick (1/4 cup) butter
3 Tbsp. sugar
2 Tbsp. flour
1 qt. beef broth

1. Cook onions in butter in large non-stick skillet or saucepan. Cover and saute 15 minutes, stirring frequently. Then add sugar and flour, mixing well.
2. While onions are cooking, place broth in slow cooker on High. Add onion mixture to broth.
3. Cover and cook on Low 6-8 hours.

Tip: Serve topped with toasted bread and grated Parmesan cheese, if you like.

Butternut Squash Soup

Elaine Vigoda
Rochester, NY

Makes 4-6 servings

Prep Time: 5 minutes
Cooking Time: 4-8 hours
Ideal slow cooker size:
4- to 5-qt.

45-oz. can chicken broth
1 medium-sized butternut squash, peeled and cubed
1 small onion, chopped
1 tsp. ground ginger
1 tsp. garlic, minced, *optional*
1/4 tsp. nutmeg, *optional*

1. Place chicken broth and squash in slow cooker. Add remaining ingredients.
2. Cover and cook on High 4 hours, or on Low 6-8 hours, or until squash is tender.

A Tip —

Some new slow cookers cook hotter and faster than older models. So get to know your slow cooker.

We suggest a range of cooking times for many of the recipes since cookers vary. When you've found the right length of time for a recipe done in your cooker, note that in your cookbook.

Creamy Vegetable Soup

Lauren M. Eberhard
Seneca, IL

Makes 12-15 servings

Prep Time: 5 minutes
Cooking Time: 3-4 hours
Ideal slow cooker size: 7-qt., or 2 4-qt. cookers, soup divided equally between them

3 14-oz. cans chicken stock
3 15-oz. cans creamed corn
3 cups skim milk
48-oz. pkg. frozen mixed vegetables, *or* other vegetables of your choice
1 onion, chopped

1. Mix all ingredients in slow cooker.
2. Cover and cook on Low 3 hours.

Variations:
1. Add 2 potatoes, cubed, to Step 2.
2. Add seasonings of your choice—salt, pepper, fresh herbs—to Step 2.

Harry's Vegetable Soup

Betty B. Dennison
Grove City, PA

Makes 16 servings

Prep Time: *4-5 minutes*
Cooking Time: *2-4 hours*
Ideal slow cooker size: *4-qt.*

4 15¼-oz. cans mixed
  vegetables, drained
46-oz. can vegetable juice
4 cups beef broth
1 tsp. Mrs. Dash

1. Mix all ingredients in a greased slow cooker.
2. Cover and cook on Low 4 hours or on High 2 hours.

Tips:
  1. If you have a beef roast, you may want to add a pound of cut-up pieces in Step 1.
  2. Leftover vegetables may be used instead of canned vegetables.

Tomato Vegetable Soup (Clean-the-Fridge-Monday-Night Soup)

Elaine Sue Good
Tiskilwa, IL

Makes 8 servings

Prep Time: *10 minutes*
Cooking Time: *4-10 hours*
Ideal slow cooker size: *3½-qt.*

2 cloves garlic, pressed and
  chopped
8- *or* 16-oz. pkg. frozen
  peppers and onions
3 Tbsp. Italian seasoning
  mix, *or* basil, oregano,
  etc.
32-oz. pkg. frozen mixed
  vegetables, *or* leftover
  vegetables from your
  refrigerator, chopped
46-oz. can vegetable, *or*
  V-8 juice, *or* Bloody
  Mary mix, *or* beef broth

1. Place pressed garlic cloves into bottom of slow cooker. Add peppers and onions.
2. Sprinkle seasonings over top.
3. Add vegetables. Then pour juice over all ingredients.
4. Cover and cook on High 4 hours, or on Low 8-10 hours.

Tips:
  1. Being flexible is the key to this recipe. You can add whatever you have on hand.
  2. Add water if you like a thinner consistency.
  3. You may add leftover meat—and/or cooked pasta or rice or barley—to bowls when serving.
  4. Sometimes I add leftover or canned lentils or beans to each bowl before adding the soup.

This recipe came about when our family was given 3 cases of Bloody Mary mix!

Chicken & Turkey Main Dishes

Poached Chicken

Mary E. Wheatley
Mashpee, MA

Makes 6 servings

Prep Time: 15 minutes
Cooking Time: 7-8 hours
Ideal slow cooker size: 4½-qt.

1 whole broiler-fryer
 chicken, about 3 lbs.
1 celery rib, cut into
 chunks
1 carrot, sliced
1 medium-sized onion,
 sliced
1 cup chicken broth,
 seasoned, *or* water, *or*
 dry white wine

1. Wash chicken. Pat dry
with paper towels and place
in slow cooker.
2. Place celery, carrot, and
onion around chicken. Pour
broth over all.

3. Cover and cook on Low
7-8 hours, or until chicken is
tender.
4. Remove chicken from
pot and place on platter.
When cool enough to handle,
debone.
5. Strain broth into a container and chill.
6. Place chunks of meat in
fridge or feezer until ready to
use in salads or main dishes.

Herby Chicken

Joyce Bowman
Lady Lake, FL

Makes 4-6 servings

Prep Time: 10 minutes
Cooking Time: 5-7 hours
Ideal slow cooker size: 5-qt.

2½-3½-lb. whole roaster
 chicken
1 lemon, cut into wedges
1 bay leaf

2-4 sprigs fresh thyme,
 or ¾ tsp. dried thyme
salt and pepper to taste

1. Remove giblets from
chicken.
2. Put lemon wedges and
bay leaf in cavity.
3. Place whole chicken in
slow cooker.
4. Scatter sprigs of thyme
over the chicken. Sprinkle
with salt and pepper.
5. Cover and cook on Low
5-7 hours, or until chicken is
tender.
6. Serve hot with pasta or
rice, or debone and freeze for
your favorite casseroles or
salads.

Roast Chicken *or* Hen

Betty Drescher
Quakertown, PA

Makes 6 servings

Prep Time: 30 minutes
Cooking Time: 9-11 hours
Ideal slow cooker size:
  4- to 5-qt.

3-4-lb. roasting chicken, *or*
  hen
1½ tsp. salt
¼ tsp. pepper
1 tsp. parsley flakes,
  divided
1 Tbsp. butter
½-1 cup water

1. Thoroughly wash chicken and pat dry.
2. Sprinkle cavity with salt, pepper, and ½ tsp. parsley flakes. Place in slow cooker, breast side up.
3. Dot with butter or brush with melted butter.
4. Sprinkle with remaining parsley flakes. Add water around the chicken.
5. Cover and cook on High 1 hour. Turn to Low and cook 8-10 hours.

Tips:
  1. Sprinkle with basil or tarragon in Step 4, if you wish.
  2. To make it a more complete meal, put carrots, onions, and celery in the bottom of the slow cooker.

Easy Mushroom Chicken

Trish Dick
Ladysmith, WI
Janice Burkholder
Richfield, PA
Carol Shirk
Leola, PA
Carrie Darby
Wayland, IA
Sara Kinsinger
Stuarts Draft, VA
Clara Newswanger,
Gordonville, PA

Makes 4-6 servings

Prep Time: 5-10 minutes
Cooking Time: 3-8 hours
Ideal slow cooker size: 4-qt.

4-6 chicken legs and thighs
  (joined), skinned
salt and pepper to taste
½ cup chicken broth, *or*
  dry white wine
10¾-oz. can cream of
  mushroom *or* celery
  soup
4-oz. can sliced
  mushrooms, drained

1. Sprinkle salt and pepper on each piece of chicken. Place chicken in slow cooker.
2. In a small bowl, mix broth and soup together. Pour over chicken.
3. Spoon mushrooms over top.
4. Cover and cook on Low 6-8 hours, or on High 3-4 hours, or until chicken is tender but not dry.

Optional Ingredients:
1 clove garlic, minced,
  added in Step 2.
Scant ¼ tsp. rosemary
  leaves, fresh *or* dried,
  added in Step 2.
  — Carolyn Spohn
  Shawnee, KS

Yummy Slow-Cooker Chicken

Teresa Kennedy
Mt. Pleasant, IA

Makes 6 servings

Prep Time: 10-15 minutes
Cooking Time: 8 hours
Ideal slow cooker size: 4-qt.

3 lbs. uncooked chicken
  pieces
1 onion, cut up
7-oz. can mushroom
  pieces, drained
10¾-oz. can condensed
  cream soup, your choice
  of flavors
your choice of fresh herbs

Optional ingredients:
6 carrots, sliced *or* cut into
  chunks
rib of celery, sliced *or* cut
  into chunks

1. Place chicken in slow cooker.
2. Mix all remaining ingredients in a mixing bowl. Pour over chicken.
3. Cover and cook on Low 8 hours, or until chicken is tender.

4. Fifteen minutes before serving, toss in your choice of fresh herbs. Blend in well.

5. Serve over cooked rice, potatoes, or noodles.

Slow-Cooker Chicken and Gravy

Betty Moore
Plano, IL

Makes 6-8 servings

Prep Time: 5 minutes
Cooking Time: 6 hours
Ideal slow cooker size: 4-qt.

6-8 bone-in chicken breast halves
salt and pepper to taste
10³/4-oz. can cream of mushroom soup
1 Tbsp. flour
1/2 cup water
paprika to taste

1. Season chicken breasts with salt and pepper. Place in slow cooker.

2. Pour soup over chicken.

3. Cover and cook on Low 6 hours.

4. Remove chicken to a serving dish or platter. Cover to keep warm.

5. Turn slow cooker to High. In a small mixing bowl, blend flour into water until smooth. Stir into hot gravy in slow cooker.

6. Cook until thickened. Pour over chicken to serve.

7. Sprinkle with paprika just before serving.

Honey Baked Chicken

Mary Kennell, Roanoke, IL

Makes 4 servings

Prep Time: 15 minutes
Cooking Time: 3-6 hours
Ideal slow cooker size: 5-qt.

4 skinless, bone-in chicken breast halves
2 Tbsp. butter, melted
2 Tbsp. honey
2 tsp. prepared mustard
2 tsp. curry powder
salt and pepper, *optional*

1. Spray slow cooker with non-stick cooking spray and add chicken

2. Mix butter, honey, mustard, and curry powder together in a small bowl. Pour sauce over chicken.

3. Cover and cook on High 3 hours, or on Low 5-6 hours.

Variations:

1. Use chicken thighs instead of breasts. Drop the curry powder if you wish.
— **Cathy Boshart**
Lebanon, PA

2. Use a small fryer chicken, quartered, instead of breasts or thighs.
— **Frances Kruba**
Dundalk, MD

3. Instead of curry powder, use 1/2 tsp. paprika.
— **Jena Hammond**
Traverse City, MI

Honey Mustard Chicken

Jean Halloran
Green Bay, WI

Makes 8 servings

Prep Time: 15 minutes
Cooking Time: 3-7 hours
Ideal slow cooker size: 5-qt.

8 boneless, skinless chicken breast halves
1¹/2 cups honey mustard dressing
1/2 cup water

1. Spray the inside of your slow cooker with non-stick cooking spray.

2. Cut chicken into approximately 2″ pieces. Place in the slow cooker.

3. In a bowl, mix together the dressing and water. Pour over the chicken pieces.

4. Cover and cook on High 3-4 hours, or on Low 6-7 hours.

Tip: If you prefer a slightly milder flavor, add another 1/4 cup water to Step 3.

Chicken in Piquant Sauce

Beth Shank
Wellman, IA
Karen Waggoner
Joplin, MO
Carol Armstrong
Winston, OR
Lois Niebauer
Pedricktown, NJ
Jean Butzer
Batavia, NY
Veronica Sabo
Shelton, CT
Charlotte Shaffer
East Earl, PA

Makes 4-6 servings

Prep Time: 10-15 minutes
Cooking Time: 3-4 hours
Ideal slow cooker size:
3- to 4-qt.

**16-oz. jar Russian *or*
Creamy French, salad
dressing**
12-oz. jar apricot preserves
**1 envelope dry onion soup
mix**
**4-6 boneless, skinless
chicken breast halves**

1. In a bowl, mix together
the dressing, preserves, and
dry onion soup mix.
2. Place the chicken
breasts in your slow cooker.
3. Pour the sauce over top
of the chicken.
4. Cover and cook on High
3 hours, or on Low 4 hours,
or until chicken is tender but
not dry.

Variations:
*1. Serve over cooked brown
rice. Top individual servings
with broken cashews.*
— **Crystal Brunk**
Singers Glen, VA

*2. Substitute K.C.
Masterpiece BBQ Sauce with
Hickory Brown Sugar for the
salad dressing. Add 1 cup
pineapple chunks and/or 1 cup
mandarin oranges, with or
without juice, to Step 1.*
— **Jane Hershberger**
Newton, KS

*3. Drop the salad dressing
and use 2 12-oz. jars apricot
preserves. And substitute ham
or turkey for the chicken
breasts.*
— **Shirley Sears**
Sarasota, FL
— **Jennifer Eberly**
Harrisonburg, VA
— **Marcia S. Myer**
Manheim, PA

Chicken, Sweet Chicken

Anne Townsend
Albuquerque, NM

Makes 6-8 servings

Prep Time: 15 minutes
Cooking Time: 5-6 hours
Ideal slow cooker size: 3-qt.

**2 medium-sized raw sweet
potatoes, peeled and cut
into 1/4" thick slices**
**8 boneless, skinless
chicken thighs**
**8-oz. jar orange
marmalade**
1/4 cup water
1/4-1/2 tsp. salt
1/2 tsp. pepper

1. Place sweet potato slices
in slow cooker.
2. Rinse and dry chicken
pieces. Arrange on top of the
potatoes.
3. Spoon marmalade over
the chicken and potatoes.
4. Pour water over all.
Season with salt and pepper.
5. Cover and cook on High
1 hour, and then turn to Low
and cook 4-5 hours, or until
potatoes and chicken are both
tender.

Chicken ala Orange

Carlene Horne
Bedford, NH

Makes 8 servings

Prep Time: 7 minutes
Cooking Time: 4-6 hours
Ideal slow cooker size: 4-qt.

8 boneless, skinless chicken breast halves
1/2 cup chopped onion
12-oz. jar orange marmalade
1/2 cup Russian dressing
1 Tbsp. dried parsley, *or* to taste

1. Place chicken and onion in slow cooker.
2. Combine marmalade and dressing. Pour over chicken.
3. Sprinkle with parsley.
4. Cover. Cook on Low 4-6 hours.
5. Serve with rice.

Orange Glazed Chicken Breasts

Corinna Herr
Stevens, PA
Karen Ceneviva
New Haven, CT

Makes 6 servings

Prep Time: 15 minutes
Cooking Time: 4-9 hours
Ideal slow cooker size: 4-qt.

12 ozs. orange juice concentrate, undiluted and thawed
1/2 tsp. dried marjoram leaves
6 boneless, skinless chicken breast halves
salt and pepper to taste
1/4 cup water
2 Tbsp. cornstarch

1. Combine thawed orange juice and marjoram in shallow dish. Dip each breast in orange juice mixture.
2. Sprinkle each breast with salt and pepper; then place in slow cooker. Pour remaining orange sauce over breasts.
3. Cover and cook on Low 6 1/2-8 1/2 hours, or on High 3 1/2-4 1/2 hours, or until chicken is tender but not dry.
4. Half an hour before serving, remove chicken breasts from slow cooker and keep warm on a platter.
5. Mix water and cornstarch together in a small bowl until smooth. Turn slow cooker to High. Stir corn-starch water into liquid in slow cooker.
6. Place cover slightly ajar on slow cooker. Cook until sauce is thickened and bubbly, about 15-30 minutes. Serve sauce over chicken.

Picnic Chicken

Anne Townsend
Albuquerque, NM

Makes 4 servings

Prep Time: 5 minutes
Cooking Time: 6-7 hours
Ideal slow cooker size: 3-qt.

2 lbs., *or* 4 large, chicken thighs
1/4 cup dill pickle relish
1/4 cup Dijon mustard
1/4 cup mayonnaise
1/2 cup chicken broth

1. Rinse chicken well. Pat dry. Place in slow cooker with the skin side up.
2. In a mixing bowl, stir together the relish, mustard, and mayonnaise. When well blended, stir in chicken broth. Mix well.
3. Pour sauce over chicken.
4. Cover cooker and cook on Low 6-7 hours, or until chicken is tender but not dry or mushy.

Orange Garlic Chicken

Susan Kasting
Jenks, OK

Makes 6 servings

Prep Time: 15 minutes
Cooking Time: 2¹/2-6 hours
Ideal slow cooker size: 4-qt.

6 skinless, bone-in chicken
   breast halves
1¹/2 tsp. dry thyme
6 cloves garlic, minced
1 cup orange juice
   concentrate
2 Tbsp. balsamic vinegar

1. Rub thyme and garlic over chicken. (Reserve any leftover thyme and garlic.) Place chicken in slow cooker.
2. Mix orange juice concentrate and vinegar together in a small bowl. Stir in reserved thyme and garlic. Spoon over chicken.
3. Cover and cook on Low 5-6 hours, or on High 2¹/2-3 hours, or until chicken is tender but not dry.

Tip: Remove chicken from slow cooker and keep warm on a platter. Skim fat from sauce. Bring remaining sauce to boil in a saucepan to reduce. Serve sauce over chicken and cooked rice.

Oregano Chicken

Tina Goss
Duenweg, MO

Makes 6 servings

Prep Time: 5 minutes
Cooking Time: 4-6 hours
Ideal slow cooker size:
   4- to 5-qt.

3¹/2-4 lbs. chicken, cut-up
half a stick (¹/4 cup) butter,
   or margarine, melted
1 envelope dry Italian
   salad dressing mix
2 Tbsp. lemon juice
1-2 Tbsp. dried oregano

1. Place chicken in bottom of slow cooker. Mix butter, dressing mix, and lemon juice together and pour over top.
2. Cover and cook on High for 4-6 hours, or until chicken is tender but not dry.
3. Baste occasionally with sauce mixture and sprinkle with oregano 1 hour, or just before, serving.

Greek Chicken Pita Filling

Judi Manos
Wist Islip, NY
Jeanette Oberholtzer
Manheim, PA

Makes 4 servings

Prep Time: 10 minutes
Cooking Time: 6-8 hours
Ideal slow cooker size:
   2- to 3-qt.

1 onion, chopped
1 lb. boneless, skinless
   chicken thighs
1 tsp. lemon pepper
¹/2 tsp. dried oregano
¹/2 cup plain yogurt

1. Combine first 3 ingredients in slow cooker. Cover and cook on Low 6-8 hours, or until chicken is tender.
2. Just before serving, remove chicken and shred with two forks.
3. Add shredded chicken back into slow cooker and stir in oregano and yogurt.
4. Serve as a filling for pita bread.

A Tip —

Liquids don't boil down in a slow cooker. At the end of the cooking time, remove the cover, set dial on High and allow the liquid to evaporate, if the dish is soup-ier than you want.

John D. Allen
Rye, CO

Pacific Chicken

Colleen Konetzni
Rio Rancho, NM

Makes 6 servings

Prep Time: 10 minutes
Cooking Time: 7-8 hours
Ideal slow cooker size:
  3- to 4-qt.

6-8 skinless chicken thighs
1/2 cup soy sauce
2 Tbsp. brown sugar
2 Tbsp. grated fresh ginger
2 garlic cloves, minced

1. Wash and dry chicken. Place in slow cooker.
2. Combine remaining ingredients. Pour over chicken.
3. Cover. Cook on High 1 hour. Reduce heat to Low and cook 6-7 hours.
4. Serve over rice with a fresh salad.

Tangy Chicken Legs

Frances L. Kruba
Dundalk, MD

Makes 4-6 servings

Prep Time: 10-15 minutes
Cooking Time: 4-5 hours
Ideal slow cooker size:
  5- to 6-qt. (oblong is best)

8 chicken drumsticks
1/3 cup soy sauce
2/3 cup packed brown sugar
scant 1/8 tsp. ground ginger
1/4 cup water

1. Place chicken in slow cooker.
2. Combine remaining ingredients in a bowl and spoon over chicken.
3. Cover and cook on Low 4-5 hours, or until chicken is tender but not dry.

Simple Chicken

Norma Grieser
Clarksville, MI

Makes 8-10 servings

Prep Time: 10 minutes
Cooking Time: 4-8 hours
Ideal slow cooker size:
  5- to 6-qt.

1/2 cup water
4 lbs. boneless, skinless chicken breasts
garlic salt
1 3/4 cups (14 ozs.) barbecue sauce

1. Put water in bottom of slow cooker. Layer in chicken pieces, sprinkling each layer with garlic salt.
2. Pour barbecue sauce over all.
3. Cover and cook on Low 8 hours, or on High 4 hours, until chicken is tender but not dry or mushy.

Tips:
  1. You can add slices of onion to each layer if you wish.
  2. You can use legs and thighs in place of breasts, if you wish.

Tender Barbecued Chicken

Mary Lynn Miller
Reinholds, PA

Makes 4-6 servings

Prep Time: 10-15 minutes
Cooking Time: 8-10 hours
Ideal slow cooker size: 5-qt.

3-4-lb. broiler/fryer
  chicken, cut up
1 medium-sized onion,
  thinly sliced
1 medium-sized lemon,
  thinly sliced
18-oz. bottle barbecue
  sauce
3/4 cup cola

1. Place chicken in slow
cooker. Top with onion and
lemon slices.
2. Combine barbecue
sauce and cola. Pour over all.
3. Cover and cook on Low
8-10 hours, or until chicken is
tender but not dry.

Herby Barbecued Chicken

Lauren M. Eberhard
Seneca, IL

Makes 4-6 servings

Prep Time: 10 minutes
Cooking Time: 6-8 hours
Ideal slow cooker size:
  4- to 5-qt.

1 whole chicken, cut up, *or*
  8 of your favorite pieces
1 onion, sliced thin
1 bottle Sweet Baby Ray's
  Barbecue Sauce
1 tsp. dried oregano
1 tsp. dried basil

1. Place chicken in slow
cooker.
2. Mix onion slices, sauce,
oregano, and basil together in
a bowl. Pour over chicken,
covering as well as possible.
3. Cover and cook on Low
6-8 hours, or until chicken is
tender but not dry.

Come-Back-for-More Barbecued Chicken

Leesa DeMartyn
Enola, PA

Makes 6-8 servings

Prep Time: 10 minutes
Cooking Time: 6-8 hours
Ideal slow cooker size: 5-qt.

6-8 chicken breast halves
1 cup ketchup
1/3 cup Worcestershire
  sauce
1/2 cup brown sugar
1 tsp. chili powder
1/2 cup water

1. Place chicken in slow
cooker.
2. Whisk remaining ingre-
dients in a large bowl. Pour
sauce mixture over chicken.
3. Cover and cook on Low
for 6-8 hours, or until chicken
is tender but not overcooked.

Tip: If the sauce begins to dry
out as the dish cooks, stir in
another 1/2 cup water.

Quickie Barbecued Chicken

Carol Sherwood
Batavia, NY
Sharon Shank
Bridgewater, VA

Makes 4 servings

Prep Time: 20 minutes
Cooking Time: 3-7 hours
Ideal slow cooker size: 4-qt.

4 boneless, skinless
   chicken breast halves
3/4 cup chicken broth
1 cup barbecue sauce
1 medium-sized onion,
   sliced
salt to taste
pepper to taste

1. Place all ingredients in slow cooker. Stir gently.
2. Cook on High 3 hours, or on Low 6-7 hours, or until chicken is tender but not dry.
3. Serve the breast pieces whole, or cut up and stir through the sauce.

Chicken and Potatoes Barbecue

Betty B. Dennison
Grove City, PA

Makes 8 servings

Prep Time: 5-10 minutes
Cooking Time: 4-9 hours
Ideal slow cooker size:
   4- to 5-qt.

8 boneless, skinless chicken
   breast halves, *divided*
8 small or medium-sized
   potatoes, quartered,
   divided
1 cup honey barbecue sauce
16-oz. can jellied cranberry
   sauce

1. Spray slow cooker with non-stick cooking spray. Place 4 chicken breasts in slow cooker.
2. Top with 4 cut-up potatoes.
3. Mix barbecue sauce and cranberry sauce together in a bowl. Spoon half the sauce over the chicken and potatoes in the cooker.
4. Place remaining breasts in cooker, followed by the remaining potato chunks. Pour rest of sauce over all.
5. Cover and cook on Low 8-9 hours, or on High 4 hours, or until chicken and potatoes are tender but not dry.

Tip: You may peel the potatoes or leave the skins on. Red potatoes are especially appealing with their skins on.

Cranberry Chicken Barbecue

Gladys M. High
Ephrata, PA

Makes 6-8 servings

Prep Time: 10 minutes
Cooking Time: 4-8 hours
Ideal slow cooker size:
   4- to 5-qt.

4 lbs. chicken pieces,
   divided
1/2 tsp. salt
1/4 tsp. pepper
16-oz. can whole-berry
   cranberry sauce
1 cup barbecue sauce

Optional ingredients:
1/2 cup diced celery
1/2 cup diced onion

1. Place 1/3 of the chicken pieces in the slow cooker.
2. Combine all sauce ingredients in a mixing bowl. Spoon 1/3 of the sauce over the chicken in the cooker.
3. Repeat Steps 1 and 2 twice.
4. Cover and bake on High 4 hours, or on Low 6-8 hours, or until chicken is tender but not dry.

Cranberry Chicken

Janie Steele
Moore, OK
Sheila Soldner
Lititz, PA

Makes 6 servings

Prep Time: 10 minutes
Cooking Time: 6-8 hours
Ideal slow cooker size:
4- to 5-qt.

6 chicken breast halves, *divided*
8-oz. bottle Catalina *or* creamy French, salad dressing
1 envelope dry onion soup mix
16-oz. can whole cranberry sauce

1. Place 3 chicken breasts in slow cooker.
2. Mix other ingredients together in a mixing bowl. Pour half the sauce over chicken in the cooker.
3. Repeat Steps 1 and 2.
4. Cover and cook on Low 6-8 hours, or until chicken is tender but not dry.

A Tip —

Keep a supply of cream of mushroom soup in your pantry. It is a quick and convenient staple for beef, veal, and pork roasts and casseroles. It makes a good sauce or gravy, with just a few additional seasonings or some sour cream.

Bacon-Feta Stuffed Chicken

Tina Goss
Duenweg, MO

Makes 4 servings

Prep Time: 10 minutes
Cooking Time: 1½-3 hours
Ideal slow cooker size: 3-qt.

¼ cup crumbled cooked bacon
¼ cup crumbled feta cheese
4 boneless, skinless chicken breast halves
2 14½-oz. cans diced tomatoes
1 Tbsp. dried basil

1. In a small bowl, mix bacon and cheese together lightly.
2. Cut a pocket in the thicker side of each chicken breast. Fill each with ¼ of the bacon and cheese. Pinch shut and secure with toothpicks.
3. Place chicken in slow cooker. Top with tomatoes and sprinkle with basil.
4. Cover and cook on High 1½-3 hours, or until chicken is tender, but not dry or mushy.

Chicken Supreme

Jeanette Oberholtzer
Manheim, PA

Makes 6 servings

Pep Time: 15-20 minutes
Cooking Time: 4-5 hours
Ideal slow cooker size:
4- to 6-qt.

3 slices bacon
6 boneless, skinless chicken breast halves
4-oz. jar sliced mushrooms, drained
10¾-oz. can cream of chicken soup
½ cup shredded Swiss cheese

1. In a large non-stick skillet, cook bacon until crisp. Drain bacon well on paper towels, but reserve drippings. Crumble bacon. Set aside.
2. In bacon drippings, cook 3 chicken breasts over medium heat for 3-5 minutes, or until light brown, turning once. Place chicken in slow cooker. Repeat with remaining 3 breasts.
3. Top with mushrooms.
4. Heat soup in skillet until creamy. Pour over mushrooms and chicken.
5. Cover and cook on Low for 4 hours, or until chicken is tender but not dry.
6. Top chicken with shredded cheese. Sprinkle with bacon.
7. Cover and cook on High 10-15 minutes, or until cheese melts.

Chicken in Mushroom Sauce

Carol Eberly
Harrisonburg, VA
Ruthie Schiefer
Vassar, MI

Makes 4 servings

Prep Time: 10-15 minutes
Cooking Time: 4-5 hours
Ideal slow cooker size:
4- to 5-qt.

4 boneless, skinless
chicken breast halves
10³/4-oz. can cream of
mushroom soup
1 cup (8 ozs.) sour cream
7-oz. can mushroom stems
and pieces, drained,
optional
4 bacon strips, cooked and
crumbled, *or* ¹/4 cup pre-
cooked bacon crumbles

1. Place chicken in slow
cooker.
2. In a mixing bowl, com-
bine soup and sour cream,
and mushroom pieces if you
wish. Pour over chicken.
3. Cover and cook on Low
4-5 hours, or until chicken is
tender, but not dry.
4. Sprinkle with bacon
before serving.
5. Serve over cooked rice
or pasta.

Variations: If you like, add 2
cloves crushed garlic to Step 2.
And lay 2 sprigs of fresh rose-
mary over the chicken and
sauce in Step 2. Add a sprin-

kling of paprika and freshly
snipped parsley to the bacon
topping, just before serving.
— Stanley Kropf
Elkhart, IN

Simply Delicious Chicken Breasts

Donna Treloar
Hartford City, IN

Makes 4 servings

Prep Time: 3 minutes
Cooking Time: 4-6 hours
Ideal slow cooker size: 3-qt.

4 bone-in chicken breast
halves, *or* chicken legs
and thighs
10³/4-oz. can golden
mushroom soup
1 envelope dry onion soup
mix

1. Place chicken in slow
cooker.
2. Pour soup over chicken.
Sprinkle with dry soup mix.
3. Cover and cook on Low
4-6 hours, or until chicken is
tender but not dry.

Quilters' Chicken

Sara Harter Fredette
Goshen, MA

Makes 6 servings

Prep Time: 5 minutes
Cooking Time: 4-8 hours
Ideal slow cooker size: 4-qt.

6 boneless, skinless
chicken breast halves
10³/4-oz. can cream of
mushroom soup
1 envelope dry onion soup
mix
¹/4 -¹/2 cup sour cream
4-oz. can mushrooms,
drained, *optional*

1. Place chicken in slow
cooker.
2. Blend mushroom soup
and onion soup mix together
in a small bowl. Pour over
chicken.
3. Cover and cook on Low
4-8 hours, or until chicken is
tender but not dry.
4. Fifteen minutes before
serving, stir in sour cream
and mushrooms. Cover and
continue cooking. Serve over
rice or noodles.

Creamy Cheddary Chicken

Norma Grieser
Clarksville, MI

Makes 8-10 servings

Prep Time: 10 minutes
Cooking Time: 4-6 hours
Ideal slow cooker size:
  5- to 6-qt.

8-10 chicken breast halves,
  divided
10³/4-oz. can cream of
  chicken soup
10³/4-oz. can cream of
  celery, *or* mushroom,
  soup
1/2 cup cooking wine *or*
  sherry
3/4 cup shredded cheddar
  cheese

1. Place half the chicken in
your slow cooker.
2. In a bowl, mix the
soups and wine together.
Pour half the sauce over the
chicken.
3. Place the other half of
the chicken in the slow
cooker. Pour the remaining
sauce over that layer.
4. Cover and cook on Low
4-6 hours, or until the
chicken is tender.
5. Ten minutes before
serving, sprinkle with cheese.

Variations:
1. Stir your favorite seasonings into Step 2—parsley, thyme,
basil, lemon pepper.
2. Add 1/2 cup toasted
almonds to Step 5.
3. Serve over cooked rice or
mashed potatoes.
— **Carol Armstrong**
Winston, OR

Easy Chicken

Jennifer Kuh
Bay Village, OH

Makes 4 servings

Prep Time: 5-10 minutes
Cooking Time: 4-8 hours
Ideal slow cooker size:
  3- to 4-qt.

4 boneless, skinless
  chicken breast halves,
  fresh *or* frozen
10³/4-oz. can low-fat cream
  of chicken soup
10³/4-oz. can low-fat cream
  of mushroom soup
1/2 cup low-fat sour cream

1. Place chicken in slow
cooker.
2. Mix soups well in a mixing bowl, and then pour over
chicken.
3. Cover and cook on Low
4-8 hours, or until chicken is
tender but not dry.
4. Stir in sour cream 1/2
hour before serving.

Cheesy Chicken

Susan Tjon
Austin, TX
Katrina Eberly
Stevens, PA
Betty Moore
Plano, IL

Makes 6 servings

Prep Time: 10-15 minutes
Cooking Time: 6-8 hours
Ideal slow cooker size:
  3¹/2- to 4-qt.

6 boneless, skinless
  chicken breast halves,
  divided
salt to taste
freshly ground pepper to
  taste
garlic powder to taste, *or*
  2 Tbsp. minced garlic
2 10³/4-oz. cans cream of
  chicken soup
10³/4-oz. can cheddar
  cheese soup

1. Rinse chicken, pat dry,
and then sprinkle with salt,
pepper, and garlic powder or
garlic.
2. Place 3 breasts in bottom of slow cooker.
3. Combine the undiluted
soups in a mixing bowl. Pour
half the soup mixture over
the 3 breasts.
4. Repeat Steps 2 and 3.
5. Cook on Low 6-8 hours,
or until chicken is tender but
not dry.

*Tips: If the sauce looks too
thick 30 minutes before serving,
add a little water.*

Easy Creamy Chicken

Karen Waggoner
Joplin, MO

Makes 8 servings

Prep Time: 5 minutes
Cooking Time: 2-4 hours
Ideal slow cooker size: 4-qt.

8 boneless, skinless
  chicken breast halves
lemon pepper to taste
10³/4-oz. can cream of
  chicken soup
3-oz. pkg. cream cheese,
  softened
8-oz. carton sour cream

1. Place 4 breasts in bottom of slow cooker. Sprinkle with lemon pepper.
2. Mix soup and cream cheese together in a bowl. When blended, fold in sour cream.
3. Pour half the sauce over the breasts in the cooker.
4. Repeat Steps 1 and 3.
5. Cover and cook on High for 2-4 hours, or until chicken is tender but not dry.

Tip: This is good served over cooked rice.

Creamy Italian Chicken

Kathy Esh
New Holland, PA
Mary Ann Bowman
East Earl, PA

Makes 4 servings

Prep Time: 5-10 minutes
Cooking Time: 4 hours
Ideal slow cooker size: 5-qt.

4 boneless, skinless
  chicken breast halves
1 envelope dry Italian
  salad dressing mix
¹/4 cup water
8-oz. pkg. cream cheese,
  softened
10³/4-oz. can cream of
  chicken, *or* celery, soup
4-oz. can mushroom stems
  and pieces, drained,
  optional

1. Place chicken in slow cooker. Combine salad dressing and water. Pour over chicken.
2. Cover and cook on Low 3 hours.
3. In a small bowl, beat cream cheese and soup until blended. Stir in mushrooms if you wish. Pour over chicken.
4. Cover and cook on Low 1 hour, or until chicken is tender but not dry.

Tips:
1. Remove chicken from sauce and serve on a platter. Serve the sauce over cooked noodles.

2. Shred chicken after cooking, and then stir into the sauce. Serve over cooked noodles

Creamy Chicken Curry

Gloria Frey
Lebanon, PA

Makes 4-6 servings

Prep Time: 20 minutes
Cooking Time: 2-4 hours
Ideal slow cooker size:
  3- to 4-qt.

2 10³/4-oz. cans cream of
  mushroom soup
1 soup can water
2 tsp. curry powder
¹/3-¹/2 cup chopped
  almonds, toasted
4 skinless chicken breast
  halves, cooked and
  cubed

1. Combine ingredients in slow cooker.
2. Cover and cook on Low 2-4 hours. Stir occasionally.
3. Serve over cooked rice.

Chicken Delicious

Orpha Herr
Andover, NY

Makes 10 servings

Prep Time: 15-20 minutes
Cooking Time: 4-10 hours
Ideal slow cooker size: 5-qt.

10 boneless, skinless
  chicken breast halves
1 tsp. fresh lemon juice
salt and pepper to taste
2 10¾-oz. cans cream of
  celery soup
⅓ cup sherry *or* wine,
  optional
¼ cup grated Parmesan
  cheese

1. Rinse chicken breasts
and pat dry. Place chicken in
slow cooker in layers. Season
each layer with a sprinkling
of lemon juice, salt, and pepper.
2. In a medium bowl, mix
soups with sherry or wine if
you wish. Pour mixture over
chicken. Sprinkle with
Parmesan cheese.
3. Cover and cook on Low
8-10 hours, or on High 4-5
hours, or until chicken is tender but not dry or mushy.

Savory Chicken Meal #1

Shari Mast
Harrisonburg, VA

Makes 8 servings

Prep Time: 15 minutes
Cooking Time: 4-5 hours
Ideal slow cooker size: 5-qt.

4 boneless, skinless
  chicken breast halves
4 skinless chicken quarters
10¾-oz. can cream of
  chicken soup
1 Tbsp. water
¼ cup chopped sweet red
  peppers
1 Tbsp. chopped fresh
  parsley, *or* 1 tsp. dried
  parsley, *optional*
1 Tbsp. lemon juice
½ tsp. paprika, *optional*

1. Layer chicken in slow
cooker.
2. Combine remaining
ingredients and pour over
chicken. Make sure all pieces
are covered with sauce.
3. Cover. Cook on High 4-5
hours.

Savory Chicken, Meal #2

Shari Mast
Harrisonburg, VA

Makes 3-4 servings

Prep Time: 20 minutes
Cooking Time: 3¼-4¼ hours
Ideal slow cooker size: 3-qt.

leftover chicken and broth
  from Savory Chicken
  Meal #1
2 carrots
1 rib celery
2 medium-sized onions
2 Tbsp. flour *or* cornstarch
¼ cup cold water

1. For a second Savory
Chicken Meal, pick leftover
chicken off bone. Set aside.
2. Return remaining broth
to slow cooker and stir in
thinly sliced carrots and celery, and onions cut up in
chunks. Cook 3-4 hours on
High.
3. In separate bowl, mix
flour or cornstarch with cold
water. When smooth, stir into
hot broth.
4. Stir in cut-up chicken.
Heat 15-20 minutes, or until
broth thickens and chicken is
hot.
5. Serve over rice or pasta.

Creamy Chicken with a Touch of Broccoli

Stacy Petersheim
Mechanicsburg, PA

Makes 4 servings

Prep Time: 10 minutes
Cooking Time: 6-8 hours
Ideal slow cooker size: 2-qt.

4 bone-in, skinless chicken
  breast halves
10³/4-oz. can cream of
  broccoli soup
1 Tbsp. minced garlic
¼ cup finely chopped
  onion
salt and pepper to taste

1. Line your slow cooker with aluminum foil. Place chicken on top of foil.
2. In a mixing bowl, stir together remaining ingredients. Pour over chicken. Seal foil shut.
3. Cover and cook on Low 6-8 hours, or until chicken is tender.

Tip: Serve over cooked rice or noodles.

Elegant Chicken with Gravy

Leesa Lesenski
South Deerfield, MA

Makes 6 serving

Prep Time: 10 minutes
Cooking Time: 3-6 hours
Ideal slow cooker size:
  3- to 4-qt.

6 boneless chicken breast
  halves
10³/4-oz. can cream of
  broccoli, *or* broccoli
  cheese, soup
10³/4-oz. can cream of
  chicken soup
½ cup white wine
4-oz. can sliced
  mushrooms, undrained,
  optional

1. Place chicken breasts in slow cooker.
2. In bowl mix together soups, wine, and mushroom slices. Pour over chicken.
3. Cover. Cook on High 3 hours, or on Low 6 hours, or until chicken is tender but not dry.
4. Serve over rice or noodles.

Creamy Baked Chicken with Stuffing

Vera Martin
East Earl, PA

Makes 8 servings

Prep Time: 10-15 minutes
Cooking Time: 4½ hours
Ideal slow cooker size: 6-qt.

8 boneless chicken breast
  halves, *divided*
10³/4-oz. can cream of
  chicken soup
¼ cup water
1 cup crushed stuffing,
  herb-seasoned
half a stick (4 Tbsp.)
  melted butter
7 slices white American
  cheese

1. Lightly grease slow cooker. Layer half the chicken in bottom of slow cooker.
2. In a small bowl, mix soup and water together. Spoon half of the sauce over the chicken in the cooker.
3. Layer 4 breasts into cooker. Top with remaining sauce.
4. Sprinkle crumbs over top. Drizzle with melted butter.
5. Cover and cook on High for 4 hours, or until chicken is tender.
6. Place cheese slices over crumbs. Cover and cook another 30 minutes.

Chicken and Stuffing

Karen Waggoner
Joplin, MO

Makes 4 servings

Prep Time: 5 minutes
Cooking Time: 2-2½ hours
Ideal slow cooker size: 4-qt.

4 boneless, skinless
  chicken breast halves
6-oz. box stuffing mix for
  chicken
16-oz. pkg. frozen whole-
  kernel corn
half a stick (4 Tbsp.)
  butter, melted
2 cups water

1. Place chicken in bottom
of slow cooker.
2. Mix remaining ingredi-
ents together in a mixing
bowl. Spoon over chicken.
3. Cover and cook on High
2-2½ hours, or until chicken
is tender and the stuffing is
dry.

Scalloped Chicken

Brenda Joy Sonnie
Newton, PA

Makes 4-6 servings

Prep Time: 10 minutes
Cooking Time: 2-3 hours
Ideal slow cooker size: 3-qt.

4 cups cooked chicken
1 box stuffing mix for
  chicken
2 eggs
1 cup water
1½ cups milk
1 cup frozen peas

1. Combine chicken and
dry stuffing mix. Place in
slow cooker.
2. Beat eggs, water, and
milk together in a bowl. Pour
over chicken and stuffing.
3. Cover. Cook on High 2-3
hours.
4. Add frozen peas during
last hour of cooking.

*Variation: For more flavor, use
chicken broth instead of water.*

Apricot Stuffing and Chicken

Elizabeth Colucci
Lancaster, PA

Makes 5 servings

Prep Time: 10 minutes
Cooking Time: 2-3½ hours
Ideal slow cooker size: 5-qt.

1 stick (8 Tbsp.) butter,
  divided
1 box cornbread stuffing
  mix
4 boneless, skinless
  chicken breast halves
6-8-oz. jar apricot
  preserves

1. In a mixing bowl, make
stuffing, using ½ stick (4
Tbsp.) butter and amount of
water called for in instructions on box. Set aside.
2. Cut up chicken into
1" pieces. Place on bottom of
slow cooker. Spoon stuffing
over top.
3. In microwave, or on
stovetop, melt remaining ½
stick (4 Tbsp.) butter with
preserves. Pour over stuffing.
4. Cover and cook on High
for 2 hours, or on Low for
3½ hours, or until chicken is
tender but not dry.

Chicken Cordon Bleu

Beth Peachey
Belleville, PA

Makes 4 servings

Prep Time: 10 minutes
Cooking Time: 6-8 hours
Ideal slow cooker size:
4- to 5-qt.

4 boneless, skinless
  chicken breast halves
1/2 lb. deli-sliced cooked
  ham
1/2 lb. baby Swiss cheese,
  sliced
10³/4-oz. can cream of
  chicken soup
1 box dry stuffing mix,
  prepared according to
  box directions

1. Layer all ingredients in
the order they are listed into
your slow cooker.
2. Cover and cook on Low
6-8 hours, or until chicken is
tender but not dry.

Slow-Cooker Dried Beef and Chicken

Martha Bender
New Paris, IN

Makes 6-8 servings

Prep Time: 15-20 minutes
Cooking Time: 3-9 hours
Ideal slow cooker size:
4- to 5-qt.

6-8 ozs. dried beef
6-8 boneless, skinless
  chicken breasts
10³/4-oz. can cream of
  mushroom soup
1 cup sour cream
1/4 cup flour

1. Arrange dried beef on
the bottom of your slow
cooker.
2. Layer chicken breasts
on top of the dried beef.
3. In a medium-sized mix-
ing bowl, blend together
soup, sour cream, and flour.
Pour over chicken.
4. Cover and cook on Low
7-9 hours, or on High 3-5
hours.
5. To serve, arrange
chicken on platter. Top with
the dried beef. Spoon sauce
over top. Serve with cooked
rice or noodles.

Creamy Chicken and Carrots

Ruth Ann Bender
Cochranville, PA
Audrey L. Kneer
Williamsfield, IL

Makes 2 servings

Prep Time: 5-10 minutes
Cooking Time: 4-5 hours
Ideal slow cooker size:
1¹/2-qt.

2 boneless, skinless
  chicken breast halves,
  about 6 ozs. each
8-oz. pkg. fresh baby
  carrots, cut in half
  lengthwise
10³/4-oz. can cream of
  mushroom soup
4-oz. can mushroom stems
  and pieces, drained

1. Place the chicken in the
slow cooker. Top with
remaining ingredients.
2. Cover and cook on High
4-5 hours or until chicken
pieces are tender.
3. Serve over rice if you
wish.

A Tip —
A slow cooker is great for taking food to a potluck supper,
even if you didn't prepare it in the cooker.
Irma H. Schoen
Windsor, CT

Chicken with Dried Beef and Bacon

Rhonda Freed
Lowville, NY
Darlene G. Martin
Richfield, PA
Sharon Miller
Holmesville, OH
Jena Hammond
Traverse City, MI

Makes 4-6 servings

Prep Time: 15 minutes
Cooking Time: 3-8 hours
Ideal slow cooker size: 4-qt.

4-6 slices bacon
8-12 slices low-sodium
    dried beef, *divided*
4-6 boneless, skinless
    chicken breasts, *divided*
10³/4-oz. can low-fat, low-
    sodium cream of
    mushroom soup
1 cup sour cream

1. Place a paper towel on a paper plate. Top with 4-6 slices of bacon. Cover with another paper towel. Microwave on High for 2 minutes, until bacon is partially cooked. Lift bacon onto fresh paper towel and allow towel to absorb fat.

2. Line slow cooker with half the slices of dried beef.

3. Wrap a slice of bacon around each chicken breast and place the first layer of chicken into the slow cooker. Cover first layer of chicken breasts with the remaining slices of dried beef. Add second layer of chicken.

4. In a mixing bowl, combine soup and sour cream well. Pour over the chicken and dried beef.

5. Cover and cook on Low 7-8 hours, or on High 3-4 hours.

6. Serve over cooked noodles or rice.

Variation: Peel and cube 6 large potatoes. Add half the cubed potatoes after placing the first layer of chicken into the slow cooker (Step 3). Add the other half of the potatoes after the second layer of chicken (Step 3.) Add another can of mushroom soup to Step 4.
— Janie Steele,
    Moore, OK

Mix-It-and-Run Chicken

Shelia Heil
Lancaster, PA

Makes 4 servings

Prep Time: 10 minutes
Cooking Time: 8-10 hours
Ideal slow cooker size:
    4- to 5-qt.

2 15-oz. cans cut green
    beans, undrained
2 10³/4-oz. cans cream of
    mushroom soup
4-6 boneless, skinless
    chicken breast halves
1/2 tsp. salt

1. Drain beans, reserving juice in a medium-sized mixing bowl.

2. Stir soups into bean juice, blending thoroughly. Set aside.

3. Place beans in slow cooker. Sprinkle with salt.

4. Place chicken in cooker. Sprinkle with salt.

5. Top with soup.

6. Cover and cook on Low 8-10 hours, or until chicken is tender, but not dry or mushy.

Chicken Pot Roast

Carol Eberly
Harrisonburg, VA
Sarah Miller
Harrisonburg, VA

Makes 4 servings

Prep Time: 10-15 minutes
Cooking Time: 3-4 hours
Ideal slow cooker size:
4- to 5-qt.

4 boneless, skinless chicken breast halves
salt and pepper to taste
4-6 medium-sized carrots, peeled and sliced
2 cups lima beans, fresh *or* frozen
1 cup water

1. Salt and pepper chicken breasts. Use garlic salt if you wish. Place chicken in slow cooker and start cooking on High.
2. Prepare carrots and place on top of chicken. Add limas on top. Pour water over all.
3. Cover and cook on Low 3-4 hours, or until chicken and vegetables are tender but not dry or mushy.
4. This is good served over rice.

One-Pot Chicken Dinner

Arianne Hochstetler
Goshen, IN

Makes 6 servings

Prep Time: 15 minutes
Cooking Time: 3-6 hours
Ideal slow cooker size:
4- to 5-qt.

12 chicken drumsticks *or* thighs, skin removed
3 medium-sized orange sweet potatoes, cut into 2" pieces
12-oz. jar chicken gravy, *or* 10¾-oz. can cream of chicken soup
2 Tbsp. unbleached flour, *if using chicken gravy*
10-oz. pkg. frozen cut green beans

Optional ingredients:
1 tsp. dried parsley flakes
½ tsp. dried rosemary leaves, crushed
salt and pepper to taste

1. Place chicken in slow cooker. Top with sweet potatoes chunks.
2. In small bowl, combine remaining ingredients, except beans, and mix until smooth. Pour over chicken.
3. Cover and cook on High 1½ hours, or on Low 3½ hours.
4. One and one-half hours before serving, stir green beans into chicken mixture. Cover and cook on Low 1-2

hours, or until chicken, sweet potatoes, and green beans are tender, but not dry or mushy.

Tips:
1. *If you want to include the parsley, rosemary, and/or salt and pepper, add to Step 2.*
2. *Instead of adding the green beans into the slow cooker, stir-fry 1 lb. French-cut green beans with 1 chopped onion. Serve alongside chicken and sweet potatoes.*

Chicken with Vegetables

Janie Steele
Moore, OK

Makes 4 servings

Prep Time: 10-15 minutes
Cooking Time: 6-8 hours
Ideal slow cooker size: 6-qt.

4 bone-in chicken breast halves
1 small head of cabbage, quartered
1-lb. pkg. baby carrots
2 14½-oz. cans Mexican-flavored stewed tomatoes

1. Place all ingredients in slow cooker in order listed.
2. Cover and cook on Low 6-8 hours, or until chicken and vegetables are tender.

Rachel's Chicken Casserole

Maryann Markano
Wilmington, DE

Makes 6 servings

Prep Time: 25-30 minutes
Cooking Time: 4 hours
Ideal slow cooker size: 5-qt.

2 16-oz. cans sauerkraut,
 rinsed and drained,
 divided
1 cup Light Russian salad
 dressing, *divided*
6 boneless, skinless chicken
 breast halves, *divided*
1 Tbsp. prepared mustard,
 divided
6 slices Swiss cheese
fresh parsley for garnish,
 optional

1. Place half the sauer-
kraut in the slow cooker.
Drizzle with 1/3 cup dressing.
2. Top with 3 chicken
breast halves. Spread half the
mustard on top of the
chicken.
3. Top with remaining
sauerkraut and chicken
breasts. Drizzle with another
1/3 cup dressing. (Save the
remaining dressing until serving time.)
4. Cover and cook on Low
for 4 hours, or until the
chicken is tender, but not dry
or mushy.
5. To serve, place a breast
half on each of 6 plates.
Divide the sauerkraut over
the chicken. Top each with a

slice of cheese and a drizzle
of the remaining dressing.
Garnish with parsley if you
wish, just before serving.

Uncle Tim's Chicken and Sauerkraut

Tim Smith
Rutledge, PA

Makes 4 servings

Prep Time: 30 minutes
Cooking Time: 5-8 hours
Ideal slow cooker size: 3¹/2-qt.

4 large boneless, skinless
 chicken breast halves
1-lb. bag sauerkraut
12-oz. can beer
8 medium-sized red
 potatoes, washed and
 quartered
salt and pepper to taste
water

1. Place chicken in slow
cooker.
2. Spoon sauerkraut over
chicken.
3. Pour beer into slow
cooker.
4. Add potatoes. Sprinkle
generously with salt and pepper.
5. Pour water over all until
everything is just covered.
6. Cover and cook on High
for 5 hours, or on Low for 8
hours, or until chicken and
potatoes are tender, but not
dry.

Sunday Chicken Dinner

Beverly Flatt-Getz
Warriors Mark, PA

Makes 4 servings

Prep Time: 15-20 minutes
Cooking Time: 4-8 hours
Ideal slow cooker size:
 4- to 5-qt.

1 large onion, sliced
4-5 potatoes, peeled and
 sliced about 1/4" thick
3-4 lbs. chicken, cut up
10³/4 oz. can cream of
 mushroom soup
1 soup can of milk
garlic powder to taste,
 optional

1. Line bottom of your
slow cooker with onion slices.
2. Spread potatoes over top
of onions. Then add chicken.
3. Mix together soup and
milk. Pour over chicken.
4. If you wish, sprinkle
with garlic powder.
5. Cook on High 4 hours
or on Low 8 hours, or until
potatoes and chicken are tender.

*Tip: Add up to a second can of
milk if you'd like to have more
sauce.*

Lemon Pepper Chicken and Veggies

Nadine Martinitz, Salina KS

Makes 4 servings

Prep Time: 20 minutes
Cooking Time: 4-10 hours
Ideal slow cooker size: 4-qt.

4 carrots, sliced 1/2" thick
4 potatoes, cut in 1"
  chunks
2 cloves garlic, peeled and
  minced, *optional*
4 whole chicken legs and
  thighs, skin removed
2 tsp. lemon pepper
  seasoning
1/4 -1/2 tsp. poultry
  seasoning, *optional*
14 1/2-oz. can chicken broth

1. Layer vegetables and
chicken in slow cooker.
2. Sprinkle with lemon pepper seasoning and poultry seasoning if you wish. Pour broth
over all.
3. Cover and cook on Low
8-10 hours or on High 4-5
hours.

Variations:
*1. Use a 10 3/4-oz. can cream
of chicken or mushroom soup
instead of chicken broth.*
  — **Sarah Herr**
  Goshen, IN

*2. Add 2 cups frozen green
beans to the bottom layer (Step
1) in the cooker.*
  — **Earnest Zimmerman**
  Mechanicsburg, PA

Curried Chicken Dinner

Janessa Hochstedler
East Earl, PA

Makes 6 servings

Prep Time: 20 minutes
Cooking Time: 5-10 hours
Ideal slow cooker size: 3-qt.

1 1/2 lbs. boneless, skinless
  chicken thighs,
  quartered
3 potatoes, peeled and cut
  into chunks, about
  2 cups
1 apple, chopped
2 Tbsp. curry powder
14 1/2-oz. can chicken broth
1 medium-sized onion,
  chopped, *optional*

1. Place all ingredients in
slow cooker. Mix together
gently.
2. Cover and cook on Low
8-10 hours or on High 5
hours, or until chicken is tender, but not dry.
3. Serve over cooked rice.

Chicken Divan

Kristin Tice
Shipshewana, IN

Makes 4 servings

Prep Time: 15 minutes
Cooking Time: 3-4 hours
Ideal slow cooker size: 3-qt.

4 boneless, skinless
  chicken breast halves
4 cups chopped broccoli,
  fresh *or* frozen
2 10 3/4-oz. cans cream of
  chicken soup
1 cup mayonnaise
1/2-1 tsp. curry powder,
  depending upon your
  taste preference

1. Place chicken breasts in
slow cooker.
2. Top with broccoli.
3. In a small mixing bowl,
blend soup, mayonnaise, and
curry powder together. Pour
over top of chicken and broccoli.
4. Cover and cook on High
3-4 hours, or until chicken
and broccoli are tender but
not mushy or dry. Serve with
rice.

Sweet 'N Sour Chicken with Veggies

Jennifer Eberly
Harrisonburg, VA

Makes 6 servings

Prep Time: 10 minutes
Cooking Time: 8-10 hours
Ideal slow cooker size:
3½- to 4-qt.

2 lbs. boneless, skinless chicken thighs (about 12), cut into 1½" pieces
25-28-oz. jar sweet and sour simmer sauce
1-lb. pkg. San-Francisco vegetables (frozen broccoli, carrots, water chestnuts, and red peppers), thawed

1. Combine chicken chunks and cooking sauce in slow cooker.
2. Cover and cook on Low 8-10 hours, or until chicken is tender and no longer pink.
3. Ten minutes before serving, stir in vegetables. Cover and increase heat to High. Cook 10 minutes, or until vegetables are crisp-tender.
4. Serve over hot cooked rice.

Sweet Potato Chicken Casserole

Beverly Flatt-Getz
Warriors Mark, PA

Makes 4-6 servings

Prep Time: 20 minutes
Cooking Time: 3-6 hours
Ideal slow cooker size: 3-qt.

3-4 lbs. chicken, cut up
6 raw sweet potatoes, julienned
20-oz. can pineapple chunks, in juice
14½-oz. can chicken broth
2 Tbsp. cornstarch
2 Tbsp. cold water

1. Place the cut-up chicken into the slow cooker.
2. Top with sweet potatoes.
3. Pour pineapples and juice over the potatoes.
4. Then pour the chicken broth over all ingredients.
5. Cover and cook on Low for 6 hours or on High for 3 hours, or until chicken and potatoes are tender but not dry or mushy.
6. Just before serving, mix cornstarch and cold water together until smooth. Turn cooker to High. Stir cornstarch paste into cooker and cook for a few minutes until sauce thickens.
7. Place chicken and potatoes on serving dish or platter. Top with sauce.

Tip: I sprinkle chives over the chicken when I serve it.

Sweet and Sour Chicken

Kay Kassinger
Port Angeles, WA

Makes 6 servings

Prep Time: 15 minutes
Cooking Time: 8-10 hours
Ideal slow cooker size: 3-qt.

2-3 lbs. boneless, skinless chicken thighs, approximately 12 pieces
14-oz. can pineapple chunks in juice
medium-sized yellow onion, chopped
1¼ cups bottled sweet-and-sour sauce
garlic salt
pepper to taste
¼ cup water, *optional*

1. Spray slow cooker with non-stick cooking spray.
2. Layer chicken in slow cooker. Pour pineapple chunks and juice over chicken. Spread onion over pineapple.
3. Pour sweet-and-sour sauce over all. Sprinkle with garlic salt and pepper. If you'd like plenty of sauce, add water.
4. Cover and cook on Low 8-10 hours, or until chicken is tender, but not dry.

Tip: Wonderful served over jasmine rice.

Sweet and Sour Chicken Breasts

Ruth Fisher
Leicester, NY

Makes 8 servings

Prep Time: 20-65 minutes
Cooking Time: 2 1/2-3 hours
Ideal slow cooker size: 4-qt.

3-4 lbs. boneless, skinless
  chicken breasts
1 3/4 cups ketchup
10 3/4-oz. can tomato soup
1/4 cup brown sugar
8-oz. can pineapple chunks
  with juice
sliced green pepper,
  optional

1. Place chicken breasts in
a large non-stick skillet on
your stove. Add 1/4 cup water.
Cover and cook gently until
tender, about 15 minutes. Or
place in a baking dish, add 1/4
cup water, cover, and bake at
350° until they are tender,
about 40-60 minutes.
2. While chicken is cook-
ing, combine ketchup, soup,
sugar, and pineapples. Mix
well. Stir in green pepper
slices if you wish.
3. Cut cooked chicken into
chunks. Place in slow cooker.
4. Pour sauce over
chicken. Stir slightly.
5. Cover and cook on High
2 hours.

Tips:
*1. This dish is versatile and
can be prepared to match your
schedule. You can do Step 1 the
day before you want to serve
the dish. Just refrigerate the
cooked meat overnight. Or prepare Step 1 2-4 weeks in
advance of serving the chicken
and freeze it until you need it.
On the day you want to
serve Sweet and Sour Chicken,
thaw the chicken if it's been
frozen, and then begin with
Step 2.*

*2. When I make this dish, I
cook rice, and then arrange the
rice in the center of a large
platter. I spoon the chicken
around the rice for an attractive
presentation of the dish.*

Chicken A La Fruit

Teresa Kennedy
Mt. Pleasant, IA

Makes 5-6 servings

Prep Time: 20 minutes
Cooking Time: 6-8 hours
Ideal slow cooker size: 6-qt.

1/2 cup crushed pineapple,
  drained
3 whole peaches, mashed
2 Tbsp. lemon juice
2 Tbsp. soy sauce
1 chicken, cut up

Optional ingredients:
1/2-3/4 tsp. salt
1/4 tsp. pepper

1. Spray slow cooker with
non-stick cooking spray.
2. Mix pineapple, peaches,
lemon juice, and soy sauce in
a large bowl. (Add salt and
pepper if you wish).
3. Dip chicken pieces in
sauce and then place in slow
cooker. Pour remaining sauce
over all.
4. Cover and cook on Low
6-8 hours, or until chicken is
tender but not dry.

Hawaii Chicken

Sandy Clugston
St. Thomas, PA

Makes 4 servings

Prep Time: 10 minutes
Cooking Time: 3-8 hours
Ideal slow cooker size: 3-qt.

4 boneless, skinless
  chicken breast halves
10³/4-oz. can cream of
  mushroom soup
1/2 cup sour cream
10-oz. can pineapple
  tidbits, drained
large red bell pepper, cut
  into strips

Optional ingredients:
1 small red onion, sliced
salt and pepper to taste

1. Spray slow cooker with
non-stick cooking spray. Place
chicken in slow cooker.
2. In bowl, mix soup and
sour cream and pour over
chicken.
3. Place pineapple tidbits
and sliced red pepper over
mixture. Add onion and a
good sprinkling of salt and
pepper, if you wish.
4. Cover and cook on Low
7-8 hours or on High 3-4
hours, or until chicken is tender but not dry.
5. Serve over cooked rice.

Stewed Oriental Chicken

Stanley Kropf
Elkhart, IN

Makes 4-6 servings

Prep Time: 15-20 minutes
Cooking Time: 4 hours
Ideal slow cooker size:
  4- to 5-qt.

1 whole chicken, cut up
3 Tbsp. hot sweet mustard,
  or 2 Tbsp. hot mustard
  and 1 Tbsp. honey
2 Tbsp. soy sauce
1 tsp. ground ginger
1 tsp. cumin

1. Wash chicken and place
in slow cooker. Pat dry.
2. Mix the remaining
ingredients in a bowl. Taste
and adjust seasonings if you
want. Pour over chicken.
3. Cover and cook on High
for at least 4 hours, or until
tender. If it's more convenient, you can cook the meat
an hour or so longer with no
negative effect.

Tips:
1. This is a folk recipe so the
cook should experiment to
taste. I often use a variety of
optional ingredients, depending
on how I'm feeling. These
include teriyaki sauce, oyster
sauce, cardamom, sesame and
olive oil, dry vermouth, and
garlic, in whatever amount and
combination seems right.

2. If you cook the dish
longer than 4 hours, the
chicken tends to fall apart. In
any event, serve it in a bowl
large enough to hold the
chicken and broth.
3. I like to serve this with
cooked plain or saffron rice.

Chicken Oriental

Anne Townsend
Albuquerque, NM

Makes 4 servings

Prep Time: 5 minutes
Cooking Time: 4-8 hours
Ideal slow cooker size: 3-qt.

1 Tbsp. hot chile sesame
  oil
4 large chicken thighs
3 cloves garlic, sliced
1/2 cup brown sugar
3 Tbsp. soy sauce

1. Spread oil around the
bottom of your slow cooker.
2. Rinse chicken well and
remove excess fat. Pat dry.
Place in your slow cooker.
3. Sprinkle garlic slices
over top of the chicken.
Crumble brown sugar over
top. Drizzle with soy sauce.
4. Cover and cook on Low
4-8 hours, or until thighs are
tender, but not dry.
5. Serve over rice, pre-
pared with the juice from the
cooked chicken instead of
water.

Chicken Chow Mein

Clara Yoder Byler
Hartville, OH

Makes 5-6 servings

Prep Time: 30 minutes
Cooking Time: 4-5 hours
Ideal slow cooker size: 4-qt.

1 lb. boneless, skinless chicken breasts, *or* thighs, cubed
2 cups diced celery
1 cup diced onion
2 Tbsp. soy sauce
2 cups water
1/2 tsp. salt, *optional*
1/2 tsp. pepper, *optional*
1 Tbsp. cornstarch
1/4 cup water

1. Place chicken in slow cooker. Add celery, onion, soy sauce, 2 cups water, and salt and pepper, if you wish.
2. Cover and cook on High 4 hours.
3. Just before serving, mix cornstarch with 1/4 cup water in a small bowl. When smooth, add to slow cooker to thicken the sauce a bit. Heat for a few more minutes.
4. I like to serve this over cooked rice, or chow mein noodles, or both.

A Tip —

When buying bakeware and kitchen tools, spend the extra money for good quality.

Thai Chicken

Joanne Good
Wheaton, IL

Makes 6 servings

Prep Time: 5 minutes
Cooking Time: 8-9 hours
Ideal slow cooker size: 4-qt.

6 skinless chicken thighs
3/4 cup salsa, your choice of mild, medium, *or* hot
1/4 cup chunky peanut butter
1 Tbsp. low-sodium soy sauce
2 Tbsp. lime juice

Optional ingredients:
1 tsp. gingerroot, grated
2 Tbsp. cilantro, chopped
1 Tbsp. dry-roasted peanuts, chopped

1. Put chicken in slow cooker.
2. In a bowl, mix remaining ingredients together, except cilantro and chopped peanuts.
3. Cover and cook on Low 8-9 hours, or until chicken is cooked through but not dry.
4. Skim off any fat. Remove chicken to a platter and serve topped with sauce. Sprinkle with peanuts and cilantro, if you wish.
5. Serve over cooked rice.

Variation: Vegetarians can substitute 2 15-oz. cans of white beans, and perhaps some tempeh, for the chicken.

Raspberried Chicken Drumsticks

Pat Bechtel
Dillsburg, PA

Makes 3 servings

Prep Time: 10 minutes
Cooking Time: 5 1/4-6 1/4 hours
Ideal slow cooker size: 3 1/2-qt.

3 Tbsp. soy sauce
1/3 cup red raspberry fruit spread *or* jam
5 chicken drumsticks *or* chicken thighs
2 Tbsp. cornstarch
2 Tbsp. cold water

1. Mix soy sauce and raspberry spread or jam together in a small bowl until well blended.
2. Brush chicken with the sauce and place in slow cooker. Spoon remainder of the sauce over top.
3. Cook on Low 5-6 hours, or until chicken is tender but not dry.
4. Mix together cornstarch and cold water in a small bowl until smooth. Then remove chicken to a serving platter and keep warm. Turn slow cooker to High and stir in cornstarch and water to thicken. When thickened and bubbly, after about 10-15 minutes, spoon sauce over chicken before serving.

Teriyaki Chicken

Elaine Vigoda
Rochester, NY

Makes 6 servings

Prep Time: 15 minutes
Cooking Time: 5-6 hours
Ideal slow cooker size: 5-qt.

1 lb. boneless, skinless
chicken thighs, cut into
chunks
1 lb. boneless, skinless
chicken breasts, cut into
large chunks
10-oz. bottle teriyaki sauce
1/2 lb. snow peas, *optional*
8-oz. can water chestnuts,
drained, *optional*

1. Place chicken in slow
cooker. Cover with sauce. Stir
until sauce is well distributed.
2. Cover and cook on Low
4-5 hours, or until chicken is
tender. Add snow peas and
water chestnuts, if you wish.
3. Cover and cook another
hour on Low.
4. Serve over cooked white
rice or Chinese rice noodles.

Tomato-y Chicken

Joyce Shackelford
Green Bay, WI

Makes 4 servings

Prep Time: 5 minutes
Cooking Time: 3-5 hours
Ideal slow cooker size: 4-qt.

8-oz. can tomato sauce
1 envelope dry spaghetti
sauce mix
1 cup water
4-oz. can mushrooms,
undrained
2-3 lbs. chicken parts

1. Mix tomato sauce, dry
spaghetti mix, water, and
mushrooms together in a
bowl.
2. Place chicken in slow
cooker. Pour sauce over.
3. Cover and cook on High
3 hours, or on Low 4-5 hours,
or until chicken is tender.

Chicken Marengo

Marcia Parker
Lansdale, PA

Makes 4-5 servings

Prep Time: 5-10 minutes
Cooking Time: 6-7 hours
Ideal slow cooker size: 6-qt.

2 1/2-3-lb. frying chicken,
cut-up and skinned
2 envelopes dry spaghetti
sauce mix
1/2 cup dry white wine
2 fresh tomatoes,
quartered
1/4 lb. fresh mushrooms

1. Place chicken pieces in
the bottom of your slow
cooker.
2. In a small bowl, com-
bine the dry spaghetti sauce
mix with the wine. Pour it
over the chicken.
3. Cover and cook on Low
5 1/2-6 1/2 hours.
4. Turn temperature to
High. Then add tomatoes and
mushrooms.
5. Cover and cook on High
30-40 minutes or until the
vegetables are hot.
6. Serve with cooked noo-
dles or your favorite other
pasta.

Chicken Parmigiana

Lois Ostrander
Lebanon, PA

Makes 6 servings

Prep Time: 20 minutes
Cooking Time: 6-8 hours
Ideal slow cooker size: 3½-qt.

1 egg
1 cup dry bread crumbs
6 bone-in chicken breast
  halves, *divided*
10½-oz. jar pizza sauce,
  divided
6 slices mozzarella cheese,
  or ½ cup grated
  Parmesan cheese

1. Beat egg in a shallow, oblong bowl. Place bread crumbs in another shallow, oblong bowl. Dip chicken halves into egg, and then into the crumbs, using a spoon to coat the meat on all sides with crumbs.
2. Saute chicken in a large non-stick skillet sprayed with non-stick cooking spray.
3. Arrange 1 layer of browned chicken in slow cooker. Pour half the pizza sauce over top. Add a second layer of chicken. Pour remaining pizza sauce over top.
4. Cover and cook on Low 5¾-7¾ hours, or until chicken is tender but not dry.
5. Add mozzarella cheese or Parmesan cheese on top. Cover and cook 15 more minutes.

Tips:
1. You can remove the chicken from the slow cooker after Step 4 and place the breasts on a microwave-proof serving platter. Put a slice of mozzarella on each chicken piece and then sprinkle each with Parmesan. Cook in microwave on High for 1 minute to melt cheese.
2. Serve any extra sauce over pasta.

Italian Chicken

Starla Kreider, Mohrsville, PA

Makes 4 servings

Prep Time: 5 minutes
Cooking Time: 2½-8 hours
Ideal slow cooker size: 3-qt.

4 boneless, skinless
  chicken breast halves
28-oz. jar spaghetti sauce,
  your choice of special
  seasonings and
  ingredients
4 ozs. shredded mozzarella
  cheese

1. Place the chicken in your slow cooker.
2. Pour spaghetti sauce over chicken.
3. Cover and cook on High 2½-3½ hours, or on Low 6-8 hours
4. Place chicken on serving platter and sprinkle with cheese.
5. Serve with cooked rice or spaghetti.

That's Amore Chicken Cacciatore

Carol Sherwood
Batavia, NY

Makes 6 servings

Prep Time: 20 minutes
Cooking Time: 7-9 hours
Ideal slow cooker size: 6-qt.

6 boneless, skinless
  chicken breast halves,
  divided
28-oz. jar spaghetti sauce
2 green peppers, chopped
1 onion, minced
2 Tbsp. minced garlic

1. Place a layer of chicken in your slow cooker.
2. Mix remaining ingredients together in a bowl. Spoon half of the sauce over the first layer of chicken.
3. Add remaining breast halves. Top with remaining sauce.
4. Cover and cook on Low 7-9 hours, or until chicken is tender but not dry.
5. Serve with cooked spaghetti or linguine.

Italian Chicken Nuggets

Tina Goss
Duenweg, MO

Makes 4 servings

Prep Time: 5 minutes
Cooking Time: 1 hour
Ideal slow cooker size: 2-qt.

13½-oz. pkg. frozen
  chicken nuggets
⅓ cup grated Parmesan
  cheese
28-oz. jar spaghetti sauce
4 ozs. shredded mozzarella
  cheese
1 tsp. Italian seasoning

1. Put nuggets in bottom
of slow cooker. Sprinkle with
Parmesan cheese.
2. Layer in spaghetti sauce,
mozzarella cheese, and Italian
seasoning.
3. Cover and cook on High
1 hour, or until chicken is
tender but not dry or mushy.

Italian Chicken

Colleen Heatwole
Burton, MI

Makes 4 servings

Prep Time: 5-10 minutes
Cooking Time: 6-8 hours
Ideal slow cooker size:
  3- to 4-qt.

4 boneless, skinless
  chicken breast halves
1 envelope dry Italian
  dressing mix
1 cup chicken broth

1. Place chicken in slow
cooker. Sprinkle with dry
Italian dressing mix.
2. Spoon chicken broth
over top.
3. Cover and cook on High
for 6 hours, or on Low for 8
hours, or until chicken is tender but not dry.

Chicken Stroganoff

Mary C. Wirth
Lancaster, PA

Makes 4 servings

Prep Time: 10-15 minutes
Cooking Time: 5½-6½ hours
Ideal slow cooker size: 3-qt.

4 skinless, boneless
  chicken breast halves,
  cubed
2 Tbsp. butter, melted
1 *or* 2 envelope(s) dry
  Italian dressing mix
8-oz. pkg. light cream
  cheese, softened
10¾-oz. can cream of
  chicken soup

1. Put chicken, melted butter, and dressing mix in slow
cooker. Stir together gently.
2. Cover and cook on Low
5-6 hours.
3. Stir in cream cheese and
soup. Cover and cook on
High 30 minutes, or until
heated through.
4. Serve over cooked rice
or noodles.

A Tip —

Leave the lid on while the slow cooker cooks. The steam
that condenses on the lid helps cook the food from the top.
Every time you take the lid off, the cooker loses steam. After
you put the lid back on, it takes up to 20 minutes to regain
the lost steam and temperature. That means it takes longer
for the food to cook.

Pam Hochstedler
Kalona, IA

Zesty Italian Chicken

Yvonne Kauffman Boettger
Harrisonburg, VA

Makes 4-6 servings

Prep Time: 5 minutes
Cooking Time: 4-8 hours
Ideal slow cooker size: 4-qt.

2-3 lbs. boneless, skinless
  chicken breasts, cut into
  chunks
16-oz. bottle Italian
  dressing
1/4 cup Parmesan cheese

1. Place chicken in bottom
of slow cooker and pour
dressing over chicken. Stir
together gently.
2. Sprinkle cheese on top.
3. Cover and cook on High
for 4 hours, or on Low for 8
hours, or until chicken is tender but not dry.
4. Serve over cooked rice,
along with extra sauce from
the chicken.

Chicken Cacciatore with Green Peppers

Donna Lantgen
Chadron, NE

Makes 6 servings

Prep Time: 10 minutes
Cooking Time: 6 hours
Ideal slow cooker size: 5-qt.

1 green pepper, chopped
1 onion, chopped
1 Tbsp. dry Italian
  seasoning
15 1/2-oz. can diced
  tomatoes
6 boneless, skinless
  chicken breast halves,
  divided

1. In a small bowl, mix
together green pepper, onion,
Italian seasoning, and tomatoes. Place 1/3 in bottom of
slow cooker.
2. Layer 3 chicken breasts
over top. Spoon in 1/3 of
tomato sauce.
3. Layer in 3 remaining
chicken breasts. Top with
remaining tomato mixture.
4. Cover and cook on Low
6 hours, or until chicken is
done, but not dry.

*Variation: Top with grated
mozzarella or Parmesan cheese
when serving.*

Can-You-Believe-It's-So-Simple Salsa Chicken

Leesa DeMartyn
Enola, PA

Makes 4-6 servings

Prep Time: 5 minutes
Cooking Time: 5-8 hours
Ideal slow cooker size: 3-qt.

4-6 boneless, skinless
  chicken breast halves
16-oz. jar chunky-style
  salsa, your choice of
  mild, medium, *or* hot
2 cups shredded cheese,
  your choice of flavor

1. Place chicken in slow
cooker. Pour salsa over
chicken.
2. Cover and cook on Low
5-8 hours, or until chicken is
tender but not dry.
3. Top individual servings
with shredded cheese.
4. Serve this over cooked
rice, or in a whole wheat or
cheddar cheese wrap.

Chicken Cacciatore With Mushrooms

Lucy O'Connell
Goshen, MA

Makes 6-8 servings

Prep Time: 30 minutes
Cooking Time: 8 hours
Ideal slow cooker size: 4-qt.

3-lb. broiler/fryer chicken, cut up
2 medium-sized onions, thinly sliced
1 lb. fresh mushrooms, sliced
48-oz. jar spaghetti sauce
1/2 cup red *or* white wine

Optional ingredients:
3/4 tsp. salt
1/2 tsp. pepper

1. Remove skin from chicken.
2. Place chicken, onions, and mushrooms in slow cooker.
3. In a mixing bowl, combine spaghetti sauce, wine, and salt and pepper if you wish. Pour over chicken.
4. Cover and cook on High for 4 hours, and then on Low for 4 hours.
5. Serve over spaghetti.

Honey Chicken Wings

Bonnie Whaling
Clearfield, PA

Makes 6-8 servings

Prep Time: 20-30 minutes
Cooking Time: 31/2-41/2 hours
Ideal slow cooker size: 4-qt.

3 lbs. chicken wings, tips cut off, *divided*
2 Tbsp. vegetable oil
1 cup honey
1/2 cup soy sauce
2 Tbsp. ketchup

1. Cut each wing into two parts. Place about 1/3 of the wings in a large non-stick skillet and brown in oil. (If the skillet is crowded, the wings will not brown.) Place in slow cooker.
2. Mix remaining ingredients and pour 1/3 of the sauce over the wings in the cooker.
3. Repeat Steps 1 and 2 twice.
4. Cover and cook on High 3-4 hours, or until wings are tender but not dry.

Five-Spice Chicken Wings

Marcia Parker, Lansdale, PA

Makes 6-8 servings

Prep Time: 30 minutes
Cooking Time: 21/2-51/2 hours
Ideal slow cooker size:
  31/2- to 4-qt.

3 lbs. (about 16) chicken wings
1 cup bottled plum sauce (check an Asian grocery, *or* the Asian food aisle in a general grocery store)
2 Tbsp. butter, melted
1 tsp. five-spice powder (check an Asian grocery, *or* the Asian food aisle in a general grocery store)
thinly sliced orange wedges, *optional*
pineapple slices, *optional*

1. In a foil-lined baking pan arrange the wings in a single layer. Bake at 375° for 20 minutes. Drain well.
2. Meanwhile, combine the plum sauce, melted butter, and five-spice powder in your slow cooker. Add wings. Then stir to coat the wings with sauce.
3. Cover and cook on Low 4-5 hours, or on High 2-21/2 hours.
4. Serve immediately, or keep them warm in your slow cooker on Low for up to 2 hours.

5. Garnish with orange wedges and pineapple slices to serve, if you wish.

Variation: For Kentucky Chicken Wings, create a different sauce in Step 2. Use 1/2 cup maple syrup, 1/2 cup whiskey, and 2 Tbsp. melted butter. Then stir in the wings. Continue with Step 3.

Chicken with Broccoli Rice

Maryann Markano
Wilmington, DE

Makes 6 servings

Prep Time: 20 minutes
Cooking Time: 6-8 hours
Ideal slow cooker size: 5-qt.

1 1/4 cups uncooked long-grain rice
pepper to taste
2 lbs. boneless, skinless chicken breasts, cut into strips
1 pkg. Knorr's cream of broccoli dry soup mix
2 1/2 cups chicken broth

1. Spray slow cooker with non-stick cooking spray. Place rice in cooker. Sprinkle with pepper.
2. Top with chicken pieces.
3. In a mixing bowl, combine soup mix and broth. Pour over chicken and rice.

4. Cover and cook on Low 6-8 hours, or until rice and chicken are tender but not dry.

Chicken and Rice in a Bag

Dorothy VanDeest
Memphis, TN

Makes 4-6 servings

Prep Time: 15 minutes
Cooking Time: 8-10 hours
Ideal slow cooker size: 5-qt.

3-lb. fryer, cut into serving pieces, *or* 3 lbs. legs and thighs
1 1/2 cups raw long-grain rice
10 3/4-oz. can condensed cream of chicken soup
1 3/4 cups water
1 envelope dry onion soup mix

1. Rinse chicken pieces and pat dry. Set aside.
2. Combine rice, cream of chicken soup, and water in slow cooker. Stir until well blended.
3. Place chicken pieces in see-through roasting bag. Add onion soup mix. Shake bag to coat chicken thoroughly. Puncture 4 to 6 holes in bottom of bag. Fold top of bag over chicken and lay in slow cooker on top of rice.
4. Cover and cook on Low 8-10 hours, or until chicken is tender and rice is cooked but

not dry. Serve chicken and rice together on a large platter.

Chicken and Rice Casserole

Dale Peterson
Rapid City, SD
Joyce Shackelford
Green Bay, WI

Makes 3-4 servings

Prep Time: 20 minutes
Cooking Time: 4-5 hours
Ideal slow cooker size: 6-qt.

2 10 3/4-oz. cans cream of celery soup, *divided*
2-oz. can sliced mushrooms, undrained
1/2 cup raw long-grain rice
2 whole boneless, skinless chicken breasts, uncooked and cubed
1 Tbsp. dry onion soup mix
1/2 soup can water

1. Spray inside of slow cooker with non-stick cooking spray. Combine 1 can of soup, mushrooms, and rice in greased slow cooker. Stir until well blended.
2. Lay chicken on top. Pour 1 can of soup over all.
3. Sprinkle with onion soup mix. Add 1/2 soup can of water.
4. Cover and cook on Low 4-5 hours, or until both chicken and rice are fully cooked but not dry.

Chicken with Brown *or* Wild Rice

Carol Eveleth
Wellman, IA

Makes 8-10 servings

Prep Time: 10 minutes
Cooking Time: 3-8 hours
Ideal slow cooker size: 6-qt.

1½ cups raw brown, *or* wild, rice
1 envelope dry onion soup mix
10¾-oz. can mushroom soup
10¾-oz. can cream of chicken soup
3½ cups water
8-10 pieces of chicken

1. Spray interior of slow cooker with non-stick cooking spray.
2. Pour rice, soup mix, and soups into slow cooker and mix thoroughly. Pour water on top.
3. Add chicken pieces.
4. Cook on Low 6-8 hours, or on High 3-4 hours, or until chicken and rice are tender but not dry.

Chicken Curry with Rice

Jennifer Yoder Sommers
Harrisonburg, VA

Makes 6 servings

Prep Time: 10 minutes
Cooking Time: 5-10 hours
Ideal slow cooker size:
3- to 4-qt.

1½ lbs. boneless, skinless chicken thighs, quartered
1 onion, chopped
2 cups uncooked, long-grain rice
2 Tbsp. curry powder
14½-oz. can chicken broth

1. Combine all ingredients in your slow cooker.
2. Cover and cook on Low 8-10 hours, or on High 5 hours, or until chicken is tender but not dry.

Variation: Add 1 chopped apple to Step 1. Thirty minutes before the end of the cooking time, stir in 2 cups frozen peas.

A Tip —

When camping, always prepare extra food. You'll likely need six servings to feed four ravenous campers!

Chinese Chicken with Rice

Sharon Anders
Alburtis, PA

Makes 4 servings

Prep Time: 10 minutes
Cooking Time: 3½-6½ hours
Ideal slow cooker size: 3-qt.

⅔ cup soy sauce
½ cup honey
½ tsp. granulated garlic
2 cups hot water
4 boneless, skinless chicken breast halves
1 cup raw, long-grain rice

1. Mix soy sauce, honey, and garlic with hot water in slow cooker.
2. Add chicken breasts, submerging them as much as possible in the sauce.
3. Cover and cook on Low 5-6 hours, or on High 3-4 hours, or until chicken is tender but not dry.
4. Remove chicken to platter and keep warm. Stir uncooked rice into sauce. Cover and cook on High for 30 minutes, or until rice is tender. Add to platter with chicken and serve.

Spicy Chicken with Rice

Dawn Hahn
Lititz, PA

Makes 4 servings

Prep Time: 10 minutes
Cooking Time: 4-6 hours
Ideal slow cooker size:
4- to 5-qt.

1 cup uncooked long-grain rice
1¼ cups chicken broth
1 cup salsa, your choice of mild, medium, *or* hot
4 boneless, skinless chicken breast halves
¾ cup shredded cheddar cheese

1. Spray interior of slow cooker with non-stick cooking spray.
2. Pour rice into bottom of slow cooker.
3. Add chicken broth and salsa. Stir together well.
4. Place chicken breasts on top.
5. Cover and cook for 4-6 hours on Low, or until chicken and rice are tender but not dry.
6. Garnish with cheese just before serving.

Fiesta Chicken

Stacie Skelly
Millersville, PA

Makes 8 servings

Prep Time: 5 minutes
Cooking Time: 6½ hours
Ideal slow cooker size:
4- to 5-qt.

8 boneless, skinless chicken breast halves
16-oz. jar salsa
2 cups instant rice

1. Place chicken in slow cooker. Pour salsa over chicken.
2. Cover and cook on Low 6 hours, or until chicken is tender but not dry.
3. Remove chicken to a serving platter and keep warm.
4. Add rice to hot salsa in slow cooker and cook on High 30 minutes. Serve chicken and rice together on a large platter.

Spicy Chicken Curry

Joan Miller
Wayland, IA

Makes 10 servings

Prep Time: 15-20 minutes
Cooking Time: 3-4½ hours
Ideal slow cooker size:
4- to 5-qt.

10 skinless, bone-in chicken breast halves, *divided*
16-oz. jar salsa, mild, medium, *or* hot
1 medium-sized onion, chopped
2 Tbsp. curry powder
1 cup sour cream

1. Place half the chicken in the slow cooker.
2. Combine salsa, onion, and curry powder in a medium-sized bowl. Pour half the sauce over the meat in the cooker.
3. Repeat Steps 1 and 2.
4. Cover and cook on High for 3 hours. Or cook on High for 1½ hours, and then turn cooker to Low and cook 3 more hours.
5. Remove chicken to serving platter and cover to keep warm.
6. Add sour cream to slow cooker and stir into salsa until well blended. Serve over the chicken.

Cheesy Chicken Chili

Jennifer Kuh
Bay Village, OH

Makes 4 servings

Prep Time: 5-7 minutes
Cooking Time: 6-8 hours
Ideal slow cooker size:
   3- to 4-qt.

4 boneless, skinless
   chicken breast halves
16-oz. jar salsa, your
   choice of spiciness
2 16-oz. cans great
   northern beans, drained
8 ozs. shredded Colby
   Jack, *or* Pepper Jack,
   cheese

1. Place chicken in the bottom of your slow cooker.
2. Cover with salsa.
3. Cover and cook on Low 5½-7½ hours, or until chicken is tender but not dry.
4. Shred or cube chicken in the sauce.
5. Stir in beans and cheese.
6. Cover and cook another 30 minutes on Low.
7. Serve over cooked rice or noodles.

Spanish Chicken

Natalia Showalter
Mt. Solon, VA

Makes 4-6 servings

Prep Time: 15-20 minutes
Cooking Time: 5-6 hours
Ideal slow cooker size:
   3- to 6-qt.

8 chicken thighs, skinned
½-1 cup red wine vinegar,
   according to your taste
   preference
⅔ cups tamari, *or* low-
   sodium soy, sauce
1 tsp. garlic powder
4 6″ cinnamon sticks

1. Brown chicken slightly in non-stick skillet, if you wish, and then transfer to greased slow cooker.
2. Mix wine vinegar, tamari sauce, and garlic powder together in a bowl. Pour over chicken.
3. Break cinnamon sticks into several pieces and distribute among chicken thighs.
4. Cover and cook on Low 5-6 hours, or until chicken is tender but not dry.

Tip: You can skip browning the chicken if you're in a hurry, but browning it gives the finished dish a better flavor.

Chicken Enchiladas

Jennifer Yoder Sommers
Harrisonburg, VA

Makes 4 servings

Prep Time: 20 minutes
Cooking Time: 4 hours
Ideal slow cooker size: 3-qt.

2 10¾-oz. cans cream of
   chicken *or* mushroom
   soup
4½-oz. can diced green
   chilies
2-3 boneless, skinless
   whole chicken breasts,
   cut into pieces
2 cups shredded cheddar
   cheese
5 6″ flour tortillas

1. In a mixing bowl, combine soups, chilies, and chicken.
2. Spray the interior of the cooker with non-stick cooking spray. Put foil handles in place (see Tip on page 114 for instructions).
3. Spoon in ⅕ of the sauce on the bottom. Top with ⅕ of the cheese and then 1 tortilla. Continue layering in that order, and with those amounts, 4 more times, ending with cheese on top.
4. Cover cooker and cook on Low 4 hours.

Green Enchiladas

Jennifer Yoder Sommers
Harrisonburg, VA

Makes 8 servings

Prep Time: 5-7 minutes
Cooking Time: 2-4 hours
Ideal slow cooker size: 3-qt.

2 10-oz. cans green
 enchilada sauce, *divided*
8 large tortillas, *divided*
2 cups cooked chicken,
 divided
1 1/2 cups mozzarella cheese

1. Pour a little enchilada sauce on the bottom of your slow cooker.
2. Layer 1 tortilla, 1/4 cup of chicken, and 1/4 cup of sauce into slow cooker.
3. Repeat layers until all 3 ingredients are used completely.
4. Sprinkle mozzarella cheese over top.
5. Cover and cook on Low 2-4 hours.

Tip: Green enchilada sauce can be found in the Mexican foods section in most grocery stores.

Hot Chicken Salad

Audrey Romonosky
Austin, TX

Makes 8 servings

Prep Time: 10 minutes
Cooking Time: 2 hours
Ideal slow cooker size: 2-qt.

2 Tbsp. onion, minced
1 cup mayonnaise
2 Tbsp. lemon juice
1 1/2 cups shredded cooked
 chicken
1/2 cup slivered almonds *or*
 pecans

1. Mix together all ingredients in slow cooker.
2. Cover and cook on Low 2 hours, or until heated through.
3. Serve hot, or allow to cool and serve on lettuce leaves, along with sliced tomatoes.

Chicken and Noodles

Elena Yoder
Carlsbad, NM

Makes 8 servings

Prep Time: 15 minutes
Cooking Time: 2 hours
Ideal slow cooker size: 4-qt.

1 qt. chicken broth
1 qt. hot water
2 cups cooked chicken, cut
 into small pieces
10-oz. pkg. dry noodles
salt and pepper to taste
10 3/4-oz. can cream of
 mushroom soup

1. Combine all ingredients except soup in slow cooker.
2. Cover and cook on High for 2 hours.
3. Ten minutes before serving, stir in cream of mushroom soup.

Creamy Chicken or Turkey

Clara Yoder Byler
Hartville, OH

Makes 6-8 servings

Prep Time: 30 minutes
Cooking Time: 1½-2 hours
Ideal slow cooker size: 4-qt.

10¾-oz. can cream of
  celery soup
10¾-oz. can chicken
  noodle soup
⅔ cup half-and-half
2 cups cooked chicken *or*
  turkey
10½-oz. can (*or* larger)
  chow mein noodles

1. Put all ingredients in
slow cooker. Mix together
gently until well mixed.
2. Cook on High 1½-2
hours, or until bubbly and
hot.

*Tip: For a light meal, serve this
with raw veggies. For a more
stick-to-the-ribs meal, serve the
creamy meat over rice or
mashed potatoes.*

Chicken Plus Stuffing

Betty B. Dennison
Grove City, PA

Makes 8 servings

Prep Time: 15 minutes
Cooking Time: 2-5 hours
Ideal slow cooker size: 5-qt.

12-serving-size pkg.
  chicken stuffing mix
4 cups cooked chicken
3 10¾-oz. cans cream of
  chicken soup
½ cup milk
2 cups cheddar cheese,
  shredded

1. Prepare stuffing mix as
directed on package and put
in slow cooker.
2. Add chicken, soup, and
milk to slow cooker. Blend all
ingredients together.
3. Sprinkle cheese over the
top.
4. Cover and cook on Low
4-5 hours or on High 2-3
hours.

Chicken Dressing

Mrs. Mahlon Miller
Hutchinson, KS

Makes 3-4 servings

Prep Time: 30 minutes
Cooking Time: 2 hours
Ideal slow cooker size: 1½-qt.

1 cup potatoes, diced and
  boiled
1 cup cooked chicken with
  some broth
3 eggs, beaten
½ cup milk
3 slices bread, cubed

Optional ingredients:
¼ -½ tsp. salt
⅛ -¼ tsp. pepper
1 small onion, chopped
  fine

1. Combine all ingredients
in your slow cooker.
2. Cover and cook on Low
2 hours.

Tender Turkey Breast

Becky Gehman, Bergton, VA

Makes 10 servings

Prep Time: 5 minutes
Cooking Time: 2-6 hours
Ideal slow cooker size: 6-qt.

6-lb. turkey breast,
    boneless *or* bone-in
2-3 Tbsp. water

1. Place the turkey breast in the slow cooker. Add water.
2. Cover and cook on High for 2-4 hours, or on Low for 4-9 hours, or until tender but not dry and mushy.
3. Turn over once during cooking time.
4. If you'd like to brown the turkey, place it in your oven and bake it uncovered at 325° for 15-20 minutes after it's finished cooking in the slow cooker.

Tips:
1. Save the drippings in the bottom of the slow cooker when you remove the meat. Transfer them to a non-stick skillet. Add 1/2 cup water to 1/2 cup drippings. Heat until simmering.

In a small jar, blend 2 Tbsp. flour into 1 cup water. When smooth, stir into simmering broth, continuing to heat and stir until smooth and thickened. Use as gravy over sliced hot turkey.

2. Slice cooked turkey and serve hot. Or allow to cool and then either shred, slice, or cut into chunks for making salads or sandwiches. Freeze any leftovers.

Slow Cooker Turkey Breast

Liz Ann Yoder, Hartville, OH

Makes 8-10 servings

Prep Time: 10 minutes
Cooking Time: 9-10 hours
Ideal slow cooker size:
    6- to 7-qt.

6-lb. turkey breast
2 tsp. oil
salt to taste
pepper to taste
1 medium onion,
    quartered
4 garlic cloves, peeled
1/2 cup water

1. Rinse turkey and pat dry with paper towels.
2. Rub oil over turkey. Sprinkle with salt and pepper. Place, meaty side up, in large slow cooker.
3. Place onion and garlic around sides of cooker.
4. Cover. Cook on Low 9-10 hours, or until meat thermometer stuck in meaty part of breast registers 180°.
5. Remove from slow cooker and let stand 10 minutes before slicing.
6. Serve with mashed potatoes, cranberry salad, and corn or green beans.

Variations:
1. Add carrot chunks and chopped celery to Step 3 to add more flavor to the turkey broth.
2. Reserve broth for soups, or thicken with flour-water paste and serve as gravy over sliced turkey.
3. Freeze broth in pint-sized containers for future use.
4. Debone turkey and freeze in pint-sized containers for future use. Or freeze any leftover turkey after serving the meal described above.

Turkey in the Slow-Cooker

Earnest Zimmerman
Mechanicsburg, PA

Makes 6-8 servings

Prep Time: 5 minutes
Cooking Time: 1-5 hours
Ideal slow cooker size: 6-qt.

3-5-lb. bone-in turkey
  breast
salt and pepper to taste
2 carrots, cut in chunks
1 onion, cut in eighths
2 ribs celery, cut in chunks

1. Rinse turkey breast and pat dry. Season well inside with salt.
2. Place vegetables in bottom of slow cooker. Sprinkle with pepper. Place turkey breast on top of vegetables.
3. Cover and cook on High for 1-3 hours, on Low for 4-5 hours, or until tender but not dry or mushy.

Tips:
1. Strain broth and reserve it. Discard vegetables. The broth makes excellent gravy or base for soups. You can freeze whatever you don't need immediately.
2. Debone the turkey. Slice and serve hot, or chill and use for turkey salad or sandwiches.

Maple-Glazed Turkey Breast with Rice

Jeanette Oberholtzer
Manheim, PA

Makes 4 servings

Prep Time: 10-15 minutes
Cooking Time: 4-6 hours
Ideal slow cooker size:
  3- to 4-qt.

6-oz. pkg. long-grain wild
  rice mix
1½ cups water
2-lb. boneless turkey
  breast, cut into 1½-2"
  chunks
¼ cup maple syrup
1 onion, chopped
¼ tsp. ground cinnamon

Optional ingredient:
½ tsp. salt

1. Combine all ingredients in the slow cooker.
2. Cook on Low 4-6 hours, or until turkey and rice are both tender, but not dry or mushy.

Saucy Turkey Breast

Kelly Bailey
Mechanicsburg, PA
Michele Ruvola
Selden, NY
Ruth Fisher
Leicester, NY

Makes 6-8 servings

Prep Time: 5 minutes
Cooking Time: 1-5 hours
Ideal slow cooker size:
  4- to 6-qt.

3-5-lb. turkey breast, bone-
  in *or* boneless
1 envelope dry onion soup
  mix
salt and pepper to taste
16-oz. can cranberry sauce,
  jellied *or* whole-berry
2 Tbsp. cornstarch
2 Tbsp. cold water

1. Sprinkle salt and pepper and soup mix on the top and bottom of turkey breast. Place turkey in slow cooker.
2. Add cranberry sauce to top of turkey breast.
3. Cover and cook on Low 4-5 hours or on High 1-3 hours or until tender but not dry and mushy. (A meat thermometer should read 180°.)
4. Remove turkey from cooker and allow to rest for 10 minutes. (Keep sauce in cooker.)
5. Meanwhile, cover cooker and turn to High. In a small bowl, mix together cornstarch and cold water

until smooth. When sauce is boiling, stir in cornstarch paste. Continue to simmer until sauce thickens.

6. Slice turkey and serve topped with sauce from cooker.

Sage Turkey Thighs

Carolyn Baer
Conrath, WI

Makes 4 servings

Prep Time: 15 minutes
Cooking Time: 6-8 hours
Ideal slow cooker size: 3-qt.

4 medium-sized carrots, halved
1 medium-sized onion, chopped
1/2 cup water
1 1/2 tsp. dried sage, *divided*
2 skinless turkey thighs *or* **drumsticks, about 2 lbs.**

Optional ingredients:
1 tsp. browning sauce
1/4 tsp. salt
1/8 tsp. pepper
1 Tbsp. cornstarch
1/4 cup water

1. In a slow cooker, combine the carrots, onion, water, and 1 tsp. sage. Top with the turkey. Sprinkle with the remaining sage.

2. Cover and cook on Low 6-8 hours, or until a meat thermometer reads 180°.

3. Remove turkey and keep warm. Remove vegetables from the cooker with a slotted spoon, reserving cooking juices.

4. Keep vegetables warm until ready to serve. Pour cooking juices into a saucepan.

5. Or, place vegetables in a food processor. Cover and process until smooth. Place in a saucepan. Add cooking juices.

6. Bring mixture in saucepan to a boil. Add browning sauce, salt, and pepper, if you wish.

7. In a small bowl, combine cornstarch and water until smooth. Stir into boiling juices. Cook and stir for 2 minutes, or until thickened. Serve over turkey.

8. If you've kept the vegetables warm, add to the serving platter with the turkey.

Tip: Add a little minced garlic to Step 1 if you wish.

Sauerkraut and Turkey

Carol Leaman
Lancaster, PA

Makes 4-6 servings

Prep Time: 5 minutes
Cooking Time: 7-8 hours
Ideal slow cooker size: 5-qt.

1 large boneless turkey breast, whole *or* **half**
32-oz. bag *or* **can of sauerkraut**

1. Place turkey in slow cooker. Top with sauerkraut.

2. Cover and cook on Low 7-8 hours, or until turkey is tender but not dry or mushy.

This is a great recipe to use if you prefer not to eat pork. Believe it or not, most people who eat this dish think they are eating pork!

A Tip —

I like to slow-cook a turkey in advance of needing it. I slice the cooked breast meat into serving pieces and freeze it. And I chop all the rest of the meat and freeze it in 3-cup batches. The chopped turkey is ready for any recipe calling for cooked turkey or chicken, such as turkey or chicken salad, turkey pot pie, and so on.

Sauerkraut and Turkey Sausage

Vera F. Schmucker
Goshen, IN

Makes 8 servings

Prep Time: 5 minutes
Cooking Time: 4-6 hours
Ideal slow cooker size: 3-qt.

1 large can sauerkraut
1/4 -1/2 cup brown sugar, according to your taste preference
8″ link spicy *or* smoked turkey sausage

1. Pour sauerkraut into slow cooker.
2. Sprinkle with brown sugar.
3. Cut turkey sausage into 1/4″ slices and arrange over sauerkraut.
4. Cook on Low 4-6 hours.

Indonesian Turkey

Elaine Sue Good, Tiskilwa, IL

Makes 4 servings

Prep Time: 10 minutes
Cooking Time: 6-8 hours
Ideal slow cooker size:
   2- to 31/2-qt.

3 turkey breast tenderloins (about 11/2-2 lbs.)
6 cloves garlic, pressed and chopped
11/2 Tbsp. grated fresh ginger
1 Tbsp. sesame oil
3 Tbsp. soy sauce, *optional*
1/2 tsp. cayenne pepper, *optional*
1/3 cup peanut butter, your choice of chunky *or* smooth

1. Place the turkey on the bottom of your slow cooker.
2. Sprinkle with garlic, ginger, and sesame oil.
3. Cover and cook on Low 8 hours or until meat thermometer registers 180°.
4. With a slotted spoon, remove turkey pieces from slow cooker. Stir peanut butter into remaining juices. If the sauce is thicker than you like, stir in 1/4-1/3 cup water.
5. Spoon peanut butter sauce over turkey to serve.

Tips:

1. If you like spicier foods, be sure to include the cayenne pepper and add it as part of Step 2. And, if your diet allows, add the soy sauce during Step 2 also.

2. You may substitute 4 whole boneless, skinless chicken breasts or 12 boneless, skinless chicken thighs for the 3 turkey breast tenderloins. I have used both and was pleased with the results.

3. The more meat you have the more evenly it will cook, especially if your slow cooker cooks hot.

A Tip —

Milk products such as cream, milk, and sour cream can curdle and separate when cooked for a long period. Add them during the last 10 minutes if cooking on High, or during the last 20-30 minutes if cooking on Low.

Mrs. J.E. Barthold
Bethlehem, PA
Marilyn Yoder
Archbold, OH

Ground Turkey with Stuffing and Veggies

Brenda Hochstedler
East Earl, PA

Makes 6 servings

Prep Time: 10-15 minutes
Cooking Time: 3-8 hours
Ideal slow cooker size: 3-qt.

1 lb. lean ground turkey
2 cups frozen mixed
  vegetables, your choice
  of combination
1/4 cup Italian dressing
1 tsp. steak sauce, *optional*
16-oz. can wholeberry
  cranberry sauce
6-oz. pkg. stuffing mix for
  turkey

1. Combine ground turkey, vegetables, Italian dressing, and steak sauce, if you wish, in the slow cooker.
2. Pour cranberry sauce over top. Sprinkle with dry stuffing mix.
3. Cover and cook on Low 6-8 hours, or on High 3-4 hours.

Cran-Orange Turkey Roll

Barbara Smith
Bedford, PA
Clarice Williams
Fairbank, IA

Makes 6 servings

Prep Time: 10-20 minutes
Cooking Time: 7-9 hours
Ideal slow cooker size: 4¹/₂-qt.

1/4 cup sugar
2 Tbsp. cornstarch
3/4 cup orange marmalade
1 cup fresh cranberries,
  chopped *or* finely
  ground
2-2¹/₂-lb. frozen turkey roll,
  partially thawed
salt and pepper to taste,
  optional

1. Mix sugar and cornstarch together in a 1- to 2-qt. microwave-safe bowl. Stir in marmalade and cranberries.
2. Cover with waxed paper and cook on High for 1¹/₂ minutes. Stir. Cook on High 1 more minute. If the sauce is slightly thickened, stop microwaving. If the sauce is still thin, stir, cover, and cook another minute on High.
3. Place turkey in slow cooker. Sprinkle with salt and pepper if you wish. Pour sauce over turkey.
4. Cover and cook on Low 7-9 hours, or until turkey reads 180° on a meat thermometer.

Barbecued Turkey for Sandwiches

Joanna Bear
Salisbury, MD

Makes 4-5 servings

Prep Time: 10 minutes
Cooking Time: 1 hour
Ideal slow cooker size:
  1¹/₂- to 2-qt.

1/2 cup ketchup
1/4 cup brown sugar
1 Tbsp. prepared mustard
1 Tbsp. Worcestershire
  sauce
2 cups turkey, cooked and
  cut into bite-sized
  chunks
1 small onion, finely
  chopped, *optional*

1. Mix ketchup, sugar, mustard, and Worcestershire sauce together in the slow cooker. Add turkey and onion, if you wish. Toss to coat well.
2. Cover and cook on High 1 hour, or until heated through.
3. Serve on buns.

71

Hot Turkey Sandwiches

Tracey Hanson Schramel
Windom, MN

Makes 8 servings

Prep Time: 20-30 minutes
Cooking Time: 4-5 hours
Ideal slow cooker size: 3-qt.

6 cups cooked turkey, cut
   into bite-sized chunks
1½ cups mayonnaise *or*
   salad dressing
1 lb. Velveeta cheese,
   cubed
1½ cups celery, chopped

Optional ingredients:
1 small onion, minced
¼ tsp. salt
⅛ tsp. pepper

   1. Combine all ingredients
and place in slow cooker.
   2. Cover and cook on Low
4-5 hours.
   3. Serve in rolls.

Chipped Barbecued Turkey Ham

Velma Sauder
Leola, PA

Makes 8 servings

Prep Time: 10 minutes
Cooking Time: 4 hours
Ideal slow cooker size: 4-qt.

2 lbs. chipped turkey ham
   or regular deli ham
1 small onion, chopped
1 cup ketchup
1 cup water
½ cup brown sugar
2 Tbsp. pickle relish

   1. Combine all ingredients
in slow cooker.
   2. Cover and cook on Low
4 hours. If you're home, stir
occasionally.
   3. Serve in hamburger
buns.

*Tip: Add a slice of your favorite
cheese to the top of each filled
bun, if you wish.*

A Tip —

   If there is too much liquid in your cooker, stick a toothpick under the edge of the lid to tilt it slightly and to allow
the steam to escape.

Carol Sherwood
Batavia, NY

Beef Main Dishes

So Easy Roast Beef

Jean Binns Smith
Bellefonte, PA
Sarah Miller
Harrisonburg, VA
Heidi Hunsberger
Harrisonburg, VA

Makes 6-8 servings

Prep Time: 5 minutes
Cooking Time: 6-8 hours
Ideal slow cooker size: 4-qt.

3-4-lb. beef roast
10³/4-oz. can cream of
　mushroom soup
half or all of 1 envelope
　dry onion soup mix

1. Rinse beef, pat dry, and place in slow cooker.
2. Pour mushroom soup over top. Sprinkle with dry soup mix.
3. Cover and cook on Low 6-8 hours, or until meat is tender but not dry.

Variations:
　1. You can add sliced carrots and halved potatoes after 4 hours of cooking.
　2. For more sauce, mix mushroom soup with a soup-can of water before pouring into cooker.
　— **Lena Hoover**
　　Ephrata, PA
　— **Michelle High**
　　Fredericksburg, PA
　— **Colleen Konetzni**
　　Rio Rancho, NM

3. For more sauce, mix mushroom soup with ¹/2 cup white wine.
　— **Karen Waggoner**
　　Joplin, MO

4. Brown the roast on all sides in 2 Tbsp. olive oil in a non-stick skillet. Place in the slow cooker. In a bowl, mix together mushroom soup, dry soup mix, ¹/2 tsp. salt, ¹/4 tsp. pepper, and ¹/2 cup water. Pour over meat. Proceed with Step 3 above.
　— **Betty Moore**
　　Plano, IL

Zesty Italian Beef

Carol Eveleth, Wellman, IA

Makes 6 servings

Prep Time: 5 minutes
Cooking Time: 4-10 hours
Ideal slow cooker size: 3¹/2-qt.

1 envelope dry onion soup
　mix
¹/2 tsp. garlic powder
1 tsp. dried basil
¹/2 tsp. dried oregano
¹/4 tsp. paprika, *optional*
¹/2 tsp. red pepper, *optional*
2 cups water
2-lb. rump roast

1. Combine soup mix and seasonings with 2 cups water in slow cooker. Add roast.
2. Cook on High 4-6 hours, or on Low 8-10 hours, or until meat is tender but not dry.
3. Allow meat to rest for 10 minutes before slicing. Top slices with cooking juices.

Italian Beef Au Jus

Carol Sherwood
Batavia, NY

Makes 8 servings

Prep Time: 10 minutes
Cooking Time: 8 hours
Ideal slow cooker size: 4-qt.

3-5-lb. boneless beef roast
10-oz. pkg. dry au jus mix
1 pkg. dry Italian salad
   dressing mix
14½-oz. can beef broth
half a soup can water

1. Place beef in slow cooker.
2. Combine remaining ingredients. Pour over roast.
3. Cover. Cook on Low 8 hours.
4. Slice meat and spoon onto hard rolls with straining spoon to make sandwiches.
   Or shred with 2 forks and serve over noodles or rice in broth thickened with flour.

Note: To thicken broth, mix 3 Tbsp. cornstarch into ¼ cup cold water. Stir until smooth.
   Remove ½ cup beef broth from cooker and blend into cornstarch-water. Stir back into broth in cooker, stirring until smooth.
   Cook 10-15 minutes on High until broth becomes of gravy consistency.

Pot-Roasted Beef

Ruth Hofstetter
Versailles, MO

Makes 8 servings

Prep Time: 2 minutes
Cooking Time: 5-10 hours
Ideal slow cooker size: 3-qt.

3-4-lb. bottom round roast
1 envelope dry beef-stew
   seasoning mix
1 cup water

1. Place roast in the slow cooker.
2. In a small bowl, mix together seasoning mix and water. Pour over meat.
3. Cook on Low for 10 hours, or on High for 5 hours.

I-Forgot-to-Thaw-the-Roast Beef!

Thelma Good
Harrisonburg, VA

Makes 10 servings

Prep Time: 20 minutes
Cooking Time: 7-9 hours
Ideal slow cooker size:
   4- to 5-qt.

3-4-lb. frozen beef roast
1½ tsp. salt
pepper to taste
1 large onion
¼ cup flour
¾ cup cold water

1. Place frozen roast in slow cooker. Sprinkle with 1½ tsp. salt and pepper to taste. Slice onion and lay over top.
2. Cover and cook on High 1 hour. Turn heat to Low and roast for 6-8 hours, or until meat is tender but not dry.
3. Spoon 1¼ cups broth from the slow cooker into a saucepan. Bring to a boil.
4. While broth is heating, whisk together flour and cold water in a small bowl until smooth.
5. When the broth boils, stir flour water into the broth, stirring continually until the broth is smooth and thickened.
6. Slice roast and return meat and onions to the slow cooker. Pour gravy over top. Turn on Low until ready to serve.

Tip: This is a stress-free dish to serve to guests.

A Tip —

To get the most flavor from herbs and spices when using them in a slow cooker:
• Use them whole rather than ground or crushed.
• Use fresh herbs whenever you can.

Flavorful Pot Roast

Mary Kay Nolt
Newmanstown, PA

Makes 10-12 servings

Prep Time: 10 minutes
Cooking Time: 7-8 hours
Ideal slow cooker size: 5-qt.

2 2¹/2-lb. boneless beef
  chuck roasts
1 envelope dry ranch salad
  dressing mix
1 envelope dry Italian
  salad dressing mix
1 envelope dry brown
  gravy mix
¹/2 cup water

Optional ingredients:
1 Tbsp. flour
¹/2 cup water

1. Place the chuck roasts in your slow cooker.

2. In a small bowl, combine the salad dressing and gravy mixes. Stir in water. Pour over the meat.

3. Cover and cook on Low 7-8 hours, or until the meat is tender but not dry.

4. If you wish, thicken the cooking juices for gravy. Remove the meat at the end of the cooking time and keep warm on a platter.

5. Turn cooker to High. Bring juices to a boil.

6. Meanwhile, mix 1 Tbsp. flour with ¹/2 cup water in a jar with a tight-fitting lid. Shake until smooth.

7. When juices come to a boil, pour flour-water into cooker in a thin stream, stirring constantly. Continue cooking and stirring until juices thicken.

8. Serve over meat, or in a side dish along with the meat.

Italian Pot Roast

Sandy Osborn
Iowa City, IA

Makes 8 servings

Prep Time: 5-10 minutes
Cooking Time: 5-8 hours
Ideal slow cooker size: 3¹/2-qt.

2¹/2-lb. boneless beef round
  roast
1 medium-sized onion,
  sliced
¹/4 tsp. salt
¹/4 tsp. pepper
2 8-oz. cans no-salt-added
  tomato sauce
1 envelope dry Italian
  salad dressing mix

Optional ingredients:
¹/2 cup flour *or* cornstarch
¹/2 cup water

1. Slice roast in half for even cooking. Then place in your slow cooker.

2. Add onion and remaining ingredients in the order they are listed.

3. Cover and cook on High for 5 hours, or until the roast is tender but not dry. You can also cook it on high 1 hour, then reduce the heat to Low and cook for 7 hours.

4. When the meat is fully cooked, place it on a platter and cover it to keep it warm.

5. To turn cooking juices into gravy, turn the cooker to High to bring juices to a boil.

6. Mix ¹/2 cup flour or cornstarch into ¹/2 cup water. When smooth, pour in a thin stream into boiling juices, stirring continually. Continue to cook until juices thicken.

7. Slice meat. Serve gravy over meat, or place gravy in a separate bowl to serve.

Italian Roast Beef

Dorothy VanDeest
Memphis, TN

Makes 6-8 servings

Prep Time: 15 minutes
Cooking Time: 10-12 hours
Ideal slow cooker size:
4- to 5-qt.

2 onions, *divided*
2 cloves garlic
1 large rib of celery,
    chopped fine, *optional*
3 slices bacon
flour
4-lb. beef rump roast

1. Chop finely 1 onion, the garlic, celery, and bacon. Mix together.
2. Lightly flour roast. Rub on all sides with minced mixture.
3. Slice remaining onion. Place in slow cooker. Place roast on top of onion.
4. Sprinkle any remaining rub—or any that's fallen off the roast—over top the meat.
5. Cover and cook on Low 10-12 hours.

All-Day Pot Roast

Carol Shirk
Leola, PA

Makes 5 servings

Prep Time: 15-20 minutes
Cooking Time: 5-12 hours
Ideal slow cooker size: 4-qt.

1 1/2-lb. boneless eye of beef round roast, round rump roast, *or* chuck roast
4 medium-sized potatoes, quartered
16-oz. pkg. peeled baby carrots
10 3/4-oz. can golden mushroom soup
1/2 tsp. dried tarragon, *or* basil, crushed

1. In a large non-stick skillet, brown meat on all sides.
2. Place potatoes and carrots in slow cooker. Place browned meat on top of vegetables.
3. In a small bowl, mix together soup and tarragon or basil. Pour over meat and vegetables.
4. Cover and cook on Low 10-12 hours, or on High 5-6 hours, until meat and vegetables are tender but not dry.

Whole-Dinner Roast Beef

Betty Moore
Plano, IL
Rhonda Freed
Lowville, NY

Makes 6-8 servings

Prep Time: 10 minutes
Cooking Time: 8-9 hours
Ideal slow cooker size:
3 1/2- to 4-qt.

3-5-lb. beef roast
10 3/4-oz. can cream of mushroom soup
1 envelope dry onion soup mix
4 cups baby carrots
4-5 potatoes, quartered

1. Place the roast in your slow cooker.
2. Cover with mushroom soup. Sprinkle with onion soup mix.
3. Cover and cook on Low 6 hours.
4. Add potatoes and carrots, pushing down into the sauce as much as possible.
5. Cover and cook another 2-3 hours, or until vegetables are tender, but meat is not dry.

Variations:
1. Sprinkle carrots and potatoes with salt and pepper after placing in cooker.
2. Stir a soup can of water into the mushroom soup before adding to cooker in Step 2.

For more flavorful gravy, first brown the meat in a skillet. Scrape all browned bits from the bottom of the skillet and add to the slow cooker along with the meat.
Carolyn Baer
Conrath, WI

3. Add 1 small head of cabbage, quartered, to Step 4.
— **Liz Rugg**
Wayland, IA

4. Add 4 medium-sized onions, cut into chunks, to Step 4.
— **Leona Yoder**
Hartville, OH

Variations:
1. If it fits your schedule better to put all ingredients into the slow cooker at once, place the potatoes and carrots into the cooker first. Then top with the roast. Spoon mushroom soup over all. (For lots of gravy, mix 2 soup-cans water into mushroom soup concentrate before pouring over veggies and meat.)
Sprinkle with the dry soup mix.
Cover and cook on Low 6-8 hours, or until meat and veggies are tender but not dry or mushy.
— **Sherry Kauffman**
Minot, ND
— **Marla Folkerts**
Holland, OH
— **Jean Butzer**
Batavia, NY
— **Janie Steele**
Moore, OK

2. Place veggies in the bottom of the slow cooker. Top with meat. Then instead of adding a can of soup and the dry soup mix, simply mix together until smooth 3/4 cup water, 1 1/2 tsp. salt, 1/4 tsp. pepper, and 2 Tbsp. flour if you'd like a slightly thickened broth. Pour over all.
— **Janice Burkholder**
Richfield, PA
— **Ruth Ann Bender**
Cochranville, PA
— **Betty Hostetler**
Allensville, PA

3. Use 1/2-1 1/2 cups beef broth, or 1 1/2 cups water, instead of the can of mushroom soup.
— **Sarah Herr**
Goshen, IN
— **Karen Ceneviva**
New Haven, CT
— **Frances L. Kruba**
Dundalk, MD
— **Shelia Heil**
Lancaster, PA

Burgundy Roast
Jane Hershberger, Newton, KS

Makes 6-8 servings

Prep Time: 10 minutes
Cooking Time: 5 hours
Ideal slow cooker size: 4-qt.

4-lb. venison, *or* beef, roast
10 3/4-oz. can cream of mushroom soup
1 cup burgundy wine

1 large onion, finely chopped
2 Tbsp. chopped parsley

Optional ingredients:
4 medium-sized potatoes, quartered
4 medium-sized carrots, quartered

1. Place meat in slow cooker.
2. Blend soup and wine together in a mixing bowl. Pour over meat.
3. Top with onion and parsley.
4. Cover and cook on Low 5 hours, or until meat is tender but not dry.

Tips:
1. If you choose to include potatoes and carrots put them in the slow cooker first; then proceed with Step 1 above.
2. Serve the sauce as a gravy over the sliced or cubed meat.

Variation: Replace the wine with 1 soup can of water.
— **Patricia Fleischer**
Carlisle, PA
— **Ethel Mumaw**
Millersburg, OH

Uncle Tim's Pot Roast

Tim Smith
Rutledge, PA

Makes 4 servings

Prep Time: 30 minutes
Cooking Time: 8 hours
Ideal slow cooker size: 5-qt.

4-lb. eye roast of beef
2 Tbsp. crushed garlic
8 medium-sized red
  potatoes, halved *or*
  quartered
1 lb. baby carrots, peeled
water
1 green pepper, cut in half
  and de-seeded

1. Place roast in center of slow cooker. Rub garlic into roast.
2. Add potatoes and carrots. Add water until carrots and potatoes are covered.
3. Cover and cook on Low for 8 hours.
4. One hour before serving, place pepper halves on top of meat (moving vegetables aside as much as possible), cut-side down. Cover and continue cooking.

Variation: Sprinkle roast with salt and pepper in Step 1. And sprinkle potatoes and carrots with salt in Step 2.

Pot Roast with Carrots and Potatoes

Loretta Hanson, Hendricks, MN

Makes 6 servings

Prep Time: 30 minutes
Cooking Time: 4-12 hours
Ideal slow cooker size:
  5- to 6-qt.

3-4 potatoes, pared, and
  thinly sliced
3-4 carrots, pared, and
  thinly sliced
1 onion, chopped, *optional*
salt and pepper to taste
3-lb. brisket, rump roast,
  or pot roast
1 cup beef consommé

1. Place vegetables in bottom of slow cooker.
2. Salt and pepper meat. Place meat in slow cooker.
3. Pour consommé around meat.
4. Cover and cook on Low 10-12 hours, or on High 4-5 hours.

Variatons:
  1. In place of consommé in Step 3, use a 10³/4-oz.-can cream of chicken soup, mixed with 2¹/2 cups strong coffee.
    — Eileen D. Wenger
    Leola, PA

  2. Add 2-3 Tbsp. Worcestershire sauce in Step 3, before adding the consommé.
    — Carol Eveleth
    Wellman, IA

Roast Beef and Mushrooms

Gladys M. High
Ephrata, PA

Makes 4-6 servings

Prep Time: 10 minutes
Cooking Time: 8-10 hours
Ideal slow cooker size: 3-qt.

3-lb. boneless chuck roast
¹/4 lb. fresh mushrooms,
  sliced, *or* 4-oz. can
  mushroom stems and
  pieces, drained
1 cup water
1 envelope dry brown
  gravy mix
1 envelope dry Italian
  dressing mix

1. Place roast in slow cooker.
2. Top with mushrooms.
3. In a small bowl, mix together water, dry gravy mix, and dry Italian dressing mix. Pour over roast and mushrooms.
4. Cover and cook on Low 8-10 hours, or until meat is tender but not dry.

Quick and Easy Mushroom Brisket

Dorothy VanDeest
Memphis, TN
Dede Peterson
Rapid City, SD

Makes 8-10 servings

Prep Time: 5 minutes
Cooking Time: 10-14 hours
Ideal slow cooker size: 4-qt.

4-5-lb. beef brisket
1 envelope dry onion soup
  mix
4-oz. can mushrooms,
  undrained

1. Place brisket in slow cooker with fat side up, cutting to fit the cooker if necessary.
2. In a mixing bowl, combine dry onion soup mix with mushrooms and their liquid. Spread onion soup mixture over top of brisket.
3. Cover and cook on Low 10-14 hours, or until meat is tender but not dry.
4. Remove brisket from slow cooker and allow to rest for 10 minutes. Cut across the grain into thin slices. Serve with meat juices poured over top of sliced meat.

Italian Roast with Potatoes

Ruthie Schiefer
Vassar, MI

Makes 8 servings

Prep Time: 30-35 minutes
Cooking Time: 6-7 hours
Ideal slow cooker size: 5-qt.

6 medium-sized potatoes,
  peeled if you wish, and
  quartered
1 large onion, sliced
3-4-lb. boneless beef roast
26-oz. jar tomato and basil
  pasta sauce, *divided*
1/2 cup water
3 beef bouillon cubes

1. Place potatoes and onion in bottom of slow cooker.
2. Meanwhile, brown roast on top and bottom in nonstick skillet.
3. Place roast on top of vegetables. Pour any drippings from the skillet over the beef.
4. Mix 1 cup pasta sauce and 1/2 cup water together in a small bowl. Stir in bouillon cubes. Spoon mixture over meat.
5. Cover and cook on Low 6-7 hours, or until meat is tender but not dry.
6. Transfer roast and vegetables to serving platter. Cover with foil.
7. Take 1 cup cooking juices from the slow cooker and place in medium-sized

saucepan. Stir in remaining pasta sauce. Heat.
8. Slice or cube beef. Serve with heated sauce.

Roast with Hearty Vegetables

Edna Mae Herschberger
Arthur, IL

Makes 6 servings

Prep Time: 10 minutes
Cooking Time: 8 hours
Ideal slow cooker size: 4-qt.

4-lb. beef roast
2 tsp. salt
6 cups tomato juice
6 carrots, peeled and cut in
  half
6 potatoes, peeled and cut
  in half

1. Place roast in slow cooker. Sprinkle with salt. Pour tomato juice over all.
2. Cover and cook on High 6 hours. Add the potatoes and carrots.
3. Cover and cook on High 2 hours.

Onion Mushroom Pot Roast

Deb Herr
Mountaintop, PA

Makes 6 servings

Prep Time: 10 minutes
Cooking Time: 5-12 hours
Ideal slow cooker size: 6-qt.

3-4-lb. pot roast *or* chuck roast
4-oz. can sliced mushrooms, drained
1 tsp. salt
1/4 tsp. pepper
1/2 cup beef broth
1 envelope dry onion soup mix

Optional ingredients:
1/2 cup flour, *or* cornstarch
1/2 cup water

1. Place pot roast in your slow cooker.
2. Add mushrooms, salt, and pepper.
3. In a small bowl, mix beef broth with the onion soup mix. Spoon over the roast.
4. Cover and cook on High 5-6 hours, or on Low 10-12 hours, or until meat is tender but not dry.

Tip: To make gravy, prepare a smooth paste in a jar or small bowl, mixing 1/2 cup flour or cornstarch with 1/2 cup water.
After the roast is fully cooked, remove the meat and keep it warm on a platter. Turn

cooker to High. When juices begin to boil, pour flour-water paste in a thin stream into the cooker, stirring continually.
Continue cooking and stirring until juices thicken. Serve over sliced roast, or in a bowl along with the meat.

Barbecued Roast Beef

Sherry H. Kauffman
Minot, ND

Makes 8 servings

Prep Time: 15-20 minutes
Cooking Time: 6-7 hours
Ideal slow cooker size: 4-qt.

4-lb. beef roast
1 cup ketchup
1 onion, chopped
3/4 cup water
3 Tbsp. Worcestershire sauce
3/4 cup brown sugar

1. Place roast in slow cooker.
2. In a small bowl, mix together all remaining ingredients except the brown sugar. Pour over roast.
3. Cover and cook on Low 6-7 hours. Approximately 1 hour before serving, sprinkle with 3/4 cup brown sugar.

Barbecued Beef Brisket

Ruthie Schiefer
Vassar, MI

Makes 6-8 servings

Prep Time: 10 minutes
Cooking Time:
6 1/2-8 1/2 hours
Ideal slow cooker size: 5-qt.

2 cups Jack Daniel's Original No. 7 Barbecue Sauce, *divided*
1 medium onion, cut in wedges
3 beef bouillon cubes
3-4 lb. beef roast *or* brisket
3 bay leaves

1. In bottom of slow cooker, combine 1 cup barbecue sauce, onion, and bouillon cubes.
2. Place roast on top of sauce. Top with bay leaves.
3. Cover and cook on Low 6-8 hours or until beef is tender enough to shred easily.
4. Remove meat from slow cooker. Reserve cooking juices in slow cooker. Shred meat with two forks.
5. Return meat to slow cooker. Add remaining barbecue sauce. Mix well.
6. Cover and cook on High until heated through.
7. Serve on sandwich buns.

Sweet 'N Sour Roast

Rosalie D. Miller
Mifflintown, PA

Makes 5 servings

Prep Time: 5 minutes
Cooking Time: 6-8 hours
Ideal slow cooker size: 2-qt.

2-lb. beef roast
1/2 cup pickle juice *or* apple cider vinegar
3 Tbsp. brown sugar
2 tsp. salt
1 Tbsp. Worcestershire Sauce
1 cup water

1. Place roast in your slow cooker.
2. In a small bowl, combine remaining ingredients. Pour over the roast.
3. Cover and cook on Low 6-8 hours, or until meat is tender but not dry.

Variation: Place 5 medium-sized potatoes, cubed, in the bottom of the cooker. Add enough water to just cover the potatoes. Top with 1 qt. frozen green beans. Then add roast and continue with Step 2 above.

Roast Beef with Ginger Ale

Martha Bender
New Paris, IN

Makes 6-8 servings

Prep Time: 15-20 minutes
Cooking Time: 8-10 hours
Ideal slow cooker size: 3 1/2- to 4-qt.

3-lb. beef roast
1/2 cup flour
1 envelope dry onion soup mix
1 envelope dry brown gravy mix
2 cups ginger ale

1. Coat the roast with flour. Reserve any flour that doesn't stick to the roast. Place roast in your slow cooker.
2. Combine the dry soup mix, gravy mix, remaining flour, and ginger ale in a bowl. Mix well.
3. Pour sauce over the roast.
4. Cover and cook on Low 8-10 hours or until the roast is tender.
5. Serve with mashed potatoes or rice.

8-Hour Tangy Beef

Mary Martins
Fairbank, IA

Makes 6-8 servings

Prep Time: 5 minutes
Cooking Time: 8-9 hours
Ideal slow cooker size: 4-qt.

3 1/2-4-lb. beef roast
12-oz. can ginger ale
1 1/2 cups ketchup

1. Put beef in slow cooker.
2. Pour ginger ale and ketchup over roast.
3. Cover. Cook on Low 8-9 hours.
4. Shred with 2 forks and serve on buns. Or break up into chunks and serve over rice, potatoes, or pasta.

Variations:
1. This recipe produces a lot of juice. You can add chopped onions, potatoes, and green beans in Step 2, if you want. Or stir in sliced mushrooms and/or peas 30 minutes before the end of the cooking time.

2. For a tangier finished dish, add chili powder or cumin, along with black pepper, in Step 2.

A Tip —

Browning the meat, onions, and vegetables before putting them in the cooker improves their flavor, but this extra step can be skipped in most recipes. The flavor will still be good.
Dorothy M. Van Deest
Memphis, TN

Zippy Beef Roast

Colleen Heatwole
Burton, MI
Joette Droz
Kalona, IA
F. Elaine Asper
Norton, OH
Ruth Ann Hoover
New Holland, PA

Makes 6-8 servings

Prep Time: 10-15 minutes
Cooking Time: 5-10 hours
Ideal slow cooker size:
4- to 5-qt.

3-4 lb. beef roast
12-oz. can cola
10³/₄-oz. can cream of
mushroom soup
1 envelope dry onion soup
mix

1. Place beef in slow cooker.
2. In a small bowl, blend cola and mushroom soup together. Pour over roast.
3. Sprinkle with dry onion soup mix.
4. Cover and cook on Low for 10 hours, or on High for 5 hours, or until meat is tender but not dry.

Variations:
1. Add a 4-oz. can of mushroom stems and pieces, drained, to Step 2.
— **Ruth Liebelt**
Rapid City, S.D.

2. Brown the roast on both sides in a non-stick skillet before placing in the slow cooker.
— **Shawn Eshleman**
Ephrata, PA

3. Instead of the cola, use 1 cup cooking sherry. Instead of the can of mushroom soup, use 2 10³/₄-oz. cans of golden mushroom soup.
— **Janice Muller**
Derwood, MD

Piquant Chuck Roast

Mary Jane Musser
Manheim, PA

Makes 6 servings

Prep Time: 5 minutes
Cooking Time: 5-10 hours
Ideal slow cooker size:
3- to 4-qt.

3-lb. chuck roast
¹/₂ cup orange juice
3 Tbsp. soy sauce
2 Tbsp. brown sugar
1 tsp. Worcestershire sauce

1. Place meat in slow cooker. In a mixing bowl, combine remaining ingredients and pour over meat.
2. Cover and cook on Low for 8-10 hours, or on High for 5 hours.

Tip: Shred the meat with 2 forks. Mix well with sauce. Serve over cooked rice, noodles, or mashed potatoes.

Tender Texas-Style Steaks

Janice Muller
Derwood, MD

Makes 4-6 servings

Prep Time: 7 minutes
Cooking Time: 6 hours
Ideal slow cooker size: 3-qt.

4-6 steaks or chops
1 cup brown sugar
1 cup ketchup
salt to taste
pepper to taste
few dashes of
Worcestershire sauce

1. Lay steaks in bottom of slow cooker.
2. Combine sugar and ketchup. Pour over steaks. If you need to layer the steaks or chops, make sure each one is covered with sauce.
3. Sprinkle with salt and pepper and a few dashes of Worcestershire sauce.
4. Cover and cook on High for 3 hours, and on Low for 3 hours.

Sweet and Savory Brisket

Donna Neiter
Wausau, WI
Ellen Ranck
Gap, PA

Makes 8-10 servings

Prep Time: 10-12 minutes
Cooking Time: 8-10 hours
Ideal slow cooker size: 5-qt.

3-3¹/₂-lb. fresh beef brisket,
cut in half, *divided*
1 cup ketchup
¹/₄ cup grape jelly
1 envelope dry onion soup
mix
¹/₂ tsp. pepper

1. Place half of the brisket
in a slow cooker.
2. In a bowl, combine
ketchup, jelly, dry soup mix,
and pepper.
3. Spread half the mixture
over half the meat. Top with
the remaining meat and then
the remaining ketchup mixture.
4. Cover and cook on Low
8-10 hours or until meat is
tender but not dry.
5. Allow meat to rest for
10 minutes. Then slice and
serve with cooking juices.

Note: Use fresh *beef brisket,
not corned beef.*

Savory Sweet Roast

Kimberly Burkholder
Millerstown, PA

Makes 6-8 servings

Prep Time: 15 minutes
Cooking Time: 8-9 hours
Ideal slow cooker size:
4- to 5-qt.

3-4-lb. blade roast
10³/₄-oz. can cream of
mushroom soup
¹/₂ cup water
¹/₄ cup sugar
¹/₄ cup vinegar
2 tsp. salt

1. Brown meat on both
sides in a non-stick skillet.
Place in slow cooker.
2. Mix together remaining
ingredients in a bowl and
pour over meat.
3. Cover and cook on Low
8-9 hours, or until meat is
tender but not dry.
4. Remove meat from the
cooker and allow to rest for
10 minutes before slicing or
shredding with 2 forks.

*Tip: Make a good gravy by fol-
lowing the directions with
Peppercorn Roast Beef on pages
84 and 85.*
*Serve gravy alongside or over
top of roast.*

Barbecued Pot Roast

Leann Brown
Ronks, PA

Makes 10 servings

Prep Time: 5 minutes
Cooking Time: 5-6 hours
Ideal slow cooker size:
5- to 6-qt.

5-lb. roast
16-oz. bottle honey
barbecue sauce
1 small onion, chopped
1 clove garlic, minced

Optional ingredients:
black pepper
Montreal seasoning

1. Place roast in slow
cooker.
2. Pour barbecue sauce
over top.
3. Sprinkle onion over
roast, and garlic beside the
roast.
4. If you wish, sprinkle
with pepper and/or seasoning.
5. Cover and cook on Low
5-6 hours.
6. Remove roast from
cooker and allow to rest for
10 minutes. Slice and serve
with cooking juices.

Beef Roast with Tomatoes, Onions, and Peppers

Donna Treloar, Hartford City, IN

Makes 10 servings

Prep Time: 15 minutes
Cooking Time: 8-10 hours
Ideal slow cooker size: 4-qt.

4-5-lb. beef roast
2 14½-oz. cans Mexican-
    style stewed tomatoes
16-oz. jar salsa, your
    choice of mild, medium,
    or hot
2 *or* 3 medium-sized
    onions, cut in chunks
1 *or* 2 green *or* red bell
    peppers, sliced

1. Brown the roast on top and bottom in a non-stick skillet and place in slow cooker.
2. In a bowl, combine stewed tomatoes and salsa. Spoon over meat.
3. Cover and cook on Low 8-10 hours, or until the meat is tender but not dry.
4. Add onions halfway through cooking time in order to keep fairly crisp. Push down into the sauce.
5. One hour before serving, add pepper slices. Push down into the sauce.
6. Remove meat from cooker and allow to rest 10 minutes before slicing. Place slices on serving platter and top with vegetables and sauce.

Tip: *Make Easy Beef Burritos with the leftovers. Shred any leftover beef with 2 forks. Heat on the stovetop with the peppers, onions, and ½ cup sauce. Add 1 Tbsp. chili powder, 2 tsp. cumin, and salt to taste. Heat through. Spoon onto warm flour tortillas. Serve with salsa, sour cream, and/or guacamole.*

Mexican Pot Roast

Susan Segraves, Lansdale, PA

Makes 8 servings

Prep Time: 5 minutes
Cooking Time: 8-10 hours
Ideal slow cooker size: 5-qt.

1½ cups chunky salsa
6-oz. can tomato paste
1 envelope dry taco
    seasoning mix
1 cup water
3-lb. beef chuck roast
½ cup chopped cilantro

1. In a mixing bowl, combine first four ingredients.
2. Place roast in slow cooker and pour salsa mixture over top.
3. Cover and cook on Low 8-10 hours, or until beef is tender but not dry. Remove to a platter.
4. Stir cilantro into sauce before serving with beef.

Peppercorn Roast Beef

Stacie Skelly
Millersville, PA

Makes 6-8 servings

Prep Time: 10-15 minutes
Cooking Time: 8-10 hours
Ideal slow cooker size: 4-qt.

3-4-lb. chuck roast
½ cup soy sauce
1 tsp. garlic powder
1 bay leaf
3-4 peppercorns
2 cups water
1 tsp. thyme, *optional*

Optional ingredients:
½ cup flour
½ cup water

1. Place roast in slow cooker.
2. In a mixing bowl, combine all other ingredients and pour over roast.
3. Cover and cook on Low 8-10 hours.
4. Remove meat to a platter and allow to rest before slicing or shredding.

Tips:
1. Serve sliced with garlic mashed potatoes or macaroni and cheese, or shredded for roast beef sandwiches.
2. To make gravy to go with the meat, turn cooker to High and bring cooking juices to a boil.

In a small bowl, mix together 1/2 cup flour and 1/2 cup water until smooth.

When cooking juices are boiling, pour flour-water paste into hot juices, stirring continually until juices thicken. Then turn off the cooker and serve gravy over the meat.

Green Chili Roast

Anna Kenagy
Carlsbad, NM

Makes 8-10 servings

Prep Time: 15 minutes
Cooking Time: 8 hours
Ideal slow cooker size: 4-qt.

3-4-lb. beef roast
1 tsp. seasoned meat
    tenderizer, *optional*
oil, *optional*
1 tsp. salt
3-4 green chili peppers, *or*
    4-oz. can green chilies,
    undrained
1 Tbsp. Worchestershire
    sauce
1/2 tsp. black pepper

1. Sprinkle roast with meat tenderizer. Brown under broiler or in skillet in oil. Place in slow cooker.
2. Pour in water until roast is half covered.
3. Add remaining ingredients over top.
4. Cover. Cook on Low 8 hours.
5. Serve with mashed potatoes and green beans.

Mexican Brisket

Veronica Sabo
Shelton, CT

Makes 8 servings

Prep Time: 20-30 minutes
Cooking Time: 2-10 hours
Ideal slow cooker size: 5-qt.

1 lb. baking potatoes,
    peeled and cut into
    1" cubes
1 lb. sweet potatoes, peeled
    and cut into 1" cubes
3-3 1/2-lb. beef brisket, fat
    trimmed
1 1/4 cups salsa
2 Tbsp. flour, *or* quick-
    cooking tapioca

1. Place both kinds of potatoes in the slow cooker.
2. Top with the brisket.
3. Put salsa and flour in a small bowl and mix well. Pour evenly over the meat.
4. Cover and cook on Low 6 1/2-10 hours, or on High 2-5 1/2 hours, or until the meat is tender but not dry.
5. To serve, remove the meat from the cooker, keep warm, and allow to rest for 10 minutes. Then slice the meat across the grain. Place slices on a platter and top with the potatoes and sauce.

Beef in Onion Gravy

Donna Neiter
Wausau, WI

Makes 3 servings

Prep Time: 20 minutes
Cooking Time: 6-8 hours
Ideal slow cooker size: 3-qt.

10 3/4-oz. can cream of
    mushroom soup
1 Tbsp. dry onion soup
    mix
2 Tbsp. beef bouillon
    granules
1 Tbsp. quick-cooking
    tapioca
1 lb. beef stew meat, cut
    into 1" cubes

1. Spray the interior of the cooker with cooking spray.
2. In the slow cooker, combine soup, soup mix, bouillon, and tapioca. Let stand 15 minutes.
3. Stir in beef.
4. Cover and cook on Low 6-8 hours, or until meat is tender but not dry.

Tip: Serve over cooked noodles or mashed potatoes.

Variation: Add 2-3 Tbsp. chopped onions, 1/2 cup sliced fresh mushrooms, and/or 1/4 tsp. pepper to the mixture in Step 2.
— **Rosemarie Fitzgerald**
Gibsonia, PA

Easy Stroganoff

Vicki Dinkel
Sharon Springs, KS

Makes 6-8 servings

Prep Time: 5 minutes
Cooking Time: 6¼-8¼ hours
Ideal slow cooker size: 3-qt.

10¾-oz. can cream of
  mushroom soup
14½-oz. can beef broth
1 lb. beef stewing meat *or*
  round steak, cut in
  1" pieces
1 cup sour cream
2 cups cooked noodles

1. Combine soup and
broth in slow cooker. Add
meat.
2. Cover. Cook on High 3-4
hours. Reduce heat to Low
and cook 3-4 hours.
3. Stir in sour cream.
4. Stir in noodles.
5. Cook on High 20 min-
utes.

*Since I'm in school part-time
and work two part-time jobs,
this nearly-complete meal is
great to come home to. It
smells wonderful when you
open the door.*

*A vegetable or salad and
some crispy French bread are
good additions.*

Herby French Dip

Sara Wichert
Hillsboro, KS

Makes 6-8 servings

Prep Time: 5 minutes
Cooking Time: 5-6 hours
Ideal slow cooker size: 4-qt.

3-lb. chuck roast
2 cups water
½ cup soy sauce
1 tsp. garlic powder
1 bay leaf
3-4 whole peppercorns
1 tsp. dried rosemary,
  optional
1 tsp. dried thyme,
  optional
6-8 French rolls

1. Place roast in slow
cooker.
2. Combine remaining
ingredients in a mixing bowl.
Pour over meat.
3. Cover and cook on High
5-6 hours, or until meat is
tender but not dry.
4. Remove meat from
broth and shred with fork.
Stir back into sauce.
5. Remove meat from the
cooker by large forkfuls and
place on French rolls.

Zesty French Dip

Earnest Zimmerman
Mechanicsburg, PA
Tracey Hanson Schramel
Windom, MN

Makes 6-8 servings

Prep Time: 5 minutes
Cooking Time: 8 hours
Ideal slow cooker size:
  4- to 6-qt.

4-lb. beef roast
10½-oz. can beef broth
10½-oz. can condensed
  French onion soup
12-oz. bottle of beer
6-8 French rolls *or*
  baguettes

1. Pat roast dry and place
in slow cooker.
2. In a mixing bowl, com-
bine beef broth, onion soup,
and beer. Pour over meat.
3. Cover and cook on Low
8 hours, or until meat is tender but not dry.
4. Split rolls or baguettes.
Warm in the oven or
microwave until heated
through.
5. Remove meat from
cooker and allow to rest for
10 minutes. Then shred with
two forks, or cut on the diag-
onal into thin slices, and
place in rolls. Serve with dipping sauce on the side.

A slow cooker is perfect for less tender meats such as a
round steak. Because the meat is cooked in liquid for hours,
it turns out tender and juicy.
  Carolyn Baer, Conrath, WI
  Barbara Sparks, Glen Burnie, MD

Beef Roast Sandwiches

Kelly Bailey
Mechanicsburg, PA

Makes 10-12 servings

Prep Time: 15 minutes
Cooking Time: 24 hours
Ideal slow cooker size: 3-qt.

3 lb. beef roast
14³/4-oz. can beef broth
1 envelope dry Italian
  salad dressing mix
10-12 crusty sandwich
  rolls

Optional ingredients:
¹/2 cup mayonnaise
3 Tbsp. prepared mustard

1. Place beef in slow cooker.
2. Combine broth and dressing mix and pour mixture over beef.
3. Cover and cook on Low 12 hours.
4. Remove beef from broth and shred with 2 forks.
5. Return shredded beef to slow cooker and continue to cook on Low for another 12 hours.
6. Serve in crusty rolls, along with mayonnaise mixed with horseradish, if you wish.

Beach Boy's Pot Roast

Jeanette Oberholtzer
Manheim, PA

Makes 6-8 servings

Prep Time: 10 minutes
Cooking Time: 8-12 hours
Ideal slow cooker size:
  3- to 4-qt.

3-4-lb. chuck *or* top round
  roast
8-12 slivers of garlic
32-oz. jar pepperoncini
  peppers, undrained
6-8 large hoagie rolls
12-16 slices of your
  favorite cheese

1. Cut slits into roast with a sharp knife and insert garlic slivers.
2. Place beef in slow cooker. Spoon peppers and all of their juice over top.
3. Cover and cook on Low 8-12 hours, or until meat is tender but not dry.
4. Remove meat from cooker and allow to cool. Then use 2 forks to shred the beef.
5. Spread on hoagie rolls and top with cheese.

Spicy French Dip

Joette Droz
Kalona, IA

Makes 10-12 servings

Prep Time: 10 minutes
Cooking Time: 8-10 hours
Ideal slow cooker size: 4-qt.

3-lb. boneless beef roast,
  cut in thirds
¹/2 cup water
4-oz. can diced jalapeno
  peppers, drained
1 envelope dry Italian
  salad dressing mix
10-12 crusty sandwich
  rolls

1. Place 3 pieces of beef in slow cooker.
2. In a small bowl, combine the water, jalapenos, and dry dressing mix. Pour over beef.
3. Cover and cook on Low 8-10 hours, or until meat is tender but not dry.
4. Remove beef and shred using 2 forks. Place shredded beef back in juices. Stir and serve on rolls.

Slow-Cooked Steak

Radella Vrolijk
Hinton, VA

Makes 6 servings

Prep Time: 10 minutes
Cooking Time: 6½-8½ hours
Ideal slow cooker size:
  3- or 4-qt.

¾ cup flour
1 tsp. pepper
¼ tsp. salt
2 lbs. cubed *or* sirloin
  steak, cut into 6 serving
  pieces
10¾-oz. can cream of
  mushroom soup
1⅓ cups water

1. In a bowl, combine
flour, pepper, and salt.
Dredge steak in flour mixture.
2. Brown in a non-stick
skillet, being careful not to
crowd the skillet. Transfer
browned beef to the slow
cooker.
3. Combine remaining
ingredients in a bowl. Pour
over steak.
4. Cover and cook on Low
6-8 hours.

Variation: Add 1 cup sliced
celery and 1-3 tsp. beef bouillon
granules or brown gravy mix to
Step 3.

Cozy Cabin Casserole

Anna Musser
Manheim, PA

Makes 3-4 servings

Prep Time: 5 minutes
Cooking Time: 6-8 hours
Ideal slow cooker size: 4-qt.

1 lb. lean round steak
1 envelope dry beefy onion
  soup
10¾-oz. can cream of
  mushroom soup
10¾-oz. can cream of
  celery soup
½ cup sour cream

1. Layer first four ingredients in slow cooker.
2. Cover and cook on Low
6-8 hours, or until meat is
tender but not over-cooked.
3. Stir in sour cream 10
minutes before serving.

Creamy Swiss Steak

Margaret Culbert
Lebanon, PA

Makes 6 servings

Prep Time: 20 minutes
Cooking Time: 6-8 hours
Ideal slow cooker size: 5-qt.

2 lbs. round steak, ¾"
  thick, cut into serving-
  size pieces
salt and pepper to taste
1 large onion, sliced thin
10¾-oz. can cream of
  mushroom soup
half a soup-can water

1. Place meat in slow
cooker. Sprinkle with salt and
pepper.
2. Top with onion slices.
3. In small bowl, mix soup
and water together until
smooth. Spoon over top.
4. Cover and cook on Low
6-8 hours, or until meat is
tender but not over-cooked.

Swiss Steak and Gravy

Sherry H. Kauffman
Minot, ND
Virginia Eberly
Loysville, PA
Esther Burkholder
Millerstown, PA
Ruth Retter
Manheim, PA
Wilma Haberkamp
Fairbank, IA
Paula King
Flanagan, IL
Chris Peterson
Green Bay, WI
Phyllis Wykes
Plano, IL
Lois Ostrander
Lebanon, PA
Mary Lynn Miller
Reinholds, PA

Makes 6-8 servings

Prep Time: 5 minutes
Cooking Time: 4-7 hours
Ideal slow cooker size: 5-qt.

2-2¹/₂-lb. round steak, cut
  into serving-size pieces
10³/₄-oz. can cream of
  mushroom soup
half a soup-can milk *or*
  water
half *or* a whole envelope
  dry onion soup mix,
  depending upon your
  taste preference

1. Place steak in slow
cooker.
2. In a bowl, mix soup and
milk together. Pour over
steak.
3. Sprinkle dry onion soup
mix over top.
4. Cover and cook on Low
4-7 hours, or until the meat is
tender but not over-cooked.

Variations:
1. Add a 4-oz. can sliced mush-
rooms, drained, on top of the
steak, in Step 1. Sprinkle the
top of the dish with ¹/₄ tsp.
black pepper at the end of
Step 3.
— **Bonnie Goering**
Bridgewater, VA

2. Cut the steak into 2"x4"
strips. Toss with mushroom
soup mixture. Place in slow
cooker and proceed with
Step 4.
— **Sheila Soldner**
Lititz, PA

3. Use cubed steak instead of
round steak. And use 1 cup
water instead of only half a
soup can.
— **Sara Kinsinger**
Stuarts Draft, VA

Slow-Cooked Round Steak

Kathy Lapp
Halifax, PA

Makes 4-6 servings

Prep Time: 15 minutes
Cooking Time: 4-5 hours
Ideal slow cooker size: 4-qt.

1³/₄-lb. round steak
¹/₄ cup flour
2 onions, sliced thick
1 green pepper, sliced in
  strips
10³/₄-oz. can cream of
  mushroom soup

1. Cut steak into serving-
size pieces. Dredge in flour.
Brown in a non-stick skillet.
2. Place browned steak in
slow cooker. Top with onion
and pepper slices.
3. Pour soup over all, making sure steak pieces are covered.
4. Cover and cook on Low
4-5 hours.

Variations:
1. Add ¹/₂ tsp. salt and ¹/₄
tsp. pepper to flour in Step 1.
2. If you like a lot of gravy,
add a second can of soup to
Step 3.

Steak in a Crock

Judith A. Govotsos
Frederick, MD

Makes 4-5 servings

Prep Time: 10-20 minutes
Cooking Time: 8-12 hours
Ideal slow cooker size:
4- or 5-qt.

1 medium-sized onion,
  sliced and separated
  into rings
4-oz. can of sliced
  mushrooms, liquid
  reserved
2½-lb. round steak, ¾"
  thick, cut into 4-5 pieces
10¾-oz. can cream of
  mushroom soup
2 Tbsp. dry sherry *or*
  water

1. Put onion rings and
mushrooms in bottom of slow
cooker.
2. Brown meat in non-stick
skillet on all sides. Place in
slow cooker over top vegetables.
3. In a bowl, mix reserved
mushroom liquid, soup, and
sherry together. Pour over all.
4. Cover and cook on Low
8-12 hours, or until meat is
tender but not over-cooked.

Round Steak and Vegetables

Judy A. Wantland
Menomonee Falls, WI

Makes 4 servings

Prep Time: 10-15 minutes
Cooking Time: 4-8 hours
Ideal slow cooker size: 4-qt.

1-1½-lb. round steak, cut
  into 1" cubes
10-oz. pkg. frozen peas,
  optional
4 medium carrots, sliced
4 medium potatoes,
  chunked
10¾-oz. can cream of
  mushroom soup
1 envelope dry onion soup
  mix

1. Spray the interior of the
slow cooker. Then mix all
ingredients together in the
cooker.
2. Cover and cook on Low
6-8 hours or on High for 4
hours, or until steak and vegetables are tender.

Slow-Cooker Swiss Steak

Joyce Bowman
Lady Lake, FL

Makes 4 servings

Prep Time: 30 minutes
Cooking Time: 7 hours
Ideal slow cooker size: 3-qt.

1-lb. round steak, ¾"-1"
  thick, cubed
16-oz. can stewed tomatoes
3 carrots, halved
  lengthwise
2 potatoes, quartered
1 medium-sized onion,
  quartered
garlic powder to taste,
  optional

1. Add all ingredients to
your slow cooker in the order
they are listed.
2. Cover and cook on Low
for 7 hours, or until meat and
vegetables are tender, but not
over-cooked or dry.

A Tip —

Meats usually cook
faster than vegetables in
slow cookers.
If you want to know if
your dish is fully cooked,
check the vegetables to
see if they're tender.
If the recipe allows,
place vegetables on the
bottom and along the sides
of your cooker as you're
preparing it.

Tomato-y Swiss Steak

Leona Yoder
Hartville, OH
Heather Horst
Lebanon, PA

Makes 5-6 servings

Prep Time: 5 minutes
Cooking Time: 4-6 hours
Ideal slow cooker size: 4-qt.

2-lb. round steak, 3/4" thick and cut into serving-size pieces
1 tsp. salt
1/8-1/4 tsp. pepper, depending on your taste preference
1 large onion, thinly sliced
14 1/2-oz. can chopped *or* stewed tomatoes

1. Season steak with salt and pepper. Place in slow cooker and top with sliced onion.
2. Spoon tomatoes over top.
3. Cover and cook on Low for 4-6 hours, or until meat is tender but not over-cooked.

Variation: Sprinkle 1 envelope dry onion soup mix over the seasoned meat in Step 1, just before topping with the sliced onion.
— **Esther Porter**
Minneapolis, MN

Basil Swiss Steak

Denise Nickel
Goessel, KS

Makes 6-8 servings

Prep Time: 10 minutes
Cooking Time: 6-8 hours
Ideal slow cooker size: 3-qt.

2-lb. round steak, cut into serving-size pieces
1 onion, sliced
10 3/4-oz. can tomato soup *or* 14 1/2-oz. can stewed tomatoes
1 tsp. salt and pepper
1/2 cup water
1 tsp. dried basil

1. Arrange steak in slow cooker. (Steak need not be browned first.)
2. Lay onion over meat.
3. Mix remaining ingredients together in a bowl. Spoon over the meat and onion.
4. Cover and cook on Low 6-8 hours.

Green-Pepper Swiss Steak

Betty B. Dennison
Grove City, PA

Makes 6-8 servings

Prep Time: 20 minutes
Cooking Time: 6-7 hours
Ideal slow cooker size: 4-qt.

3 lbs. round steak, cut into serving-size pieces
1/2 cup flour
4-oz. can tomato sauce
1 medium-sized onion, sliced
1 green pepper, sliced

1. Dredge meat in flour.
2. In a non-stick skillet, brown meat on both sides, but do not cook.
3. Place browned steak in the slow cooker.
4. Pour tomato sauce over the steak.
5. Arrange onion and pepper over top.
6. Cover and cook on Low 6-7 hours, or until meat is tender, but not over-cooked.

Variation: Add 1 tsp. salt and 1/2 tsp. pepper to flour in Step 1.

Carrots and Swiss Steak
Ruth Zendt
Mifflintown, PA

Makes 5-6 servings

Prep Time: 10 minutes
Cooking Time: 8-10 hours
Ideal slow cooker size:
  4- to 6-qt.

1 lb. baby carrots
1$\frac{1}{2}$-lb. round steak, cut
  into bite-size pieces
1 envelope dry onion soup
  mix
salt and pepper to taste
8-oz. can tomato sauce
$\frac{1}{2}$ cup water

1. Spray the inside of the cooker with non-stick cooking spray. Place carrots in bottom of cooker. Top with steak.
2. In a bowl, combine soup mix, salt and pepper, tomato sauce, and water. Pour over meat.
3. Cover and cook on Low 8-10 hours.

Variation: In a small bowl, mix together 2 Tbsp. cornstarch and 2 Tbsp. cold water until smooth. One-half hour before the end of the cooking time, stir paste into cooker, in order to thicken the sauce.
— Christie Detamore-Hunsberger
Harrisonburg, VA

Italian Round Steak
Chris Peterson
Green Bay, WI
Phyllis Wykes
Plano, IL

Makes 5-6 servings

Prep Time: 5-10 minutes
Cooking Time: 5-8 hours
Ideal slow cooker size: 4-qt.

1$\frac{1}{2}$ lbs. round steak
1 tsp. salt
$\frac{1}{2}$ tsp. oregano
$\frac{1}{4}$ tsp. pepper
medium-sized *or* large
  onion, chopped coarsely
15$\frac{1}{2}$-oz. jar spaghetti
  sauce, your choice of
  flavors

1. Cut steak into 5-6 serving-size pieces.
2. In a bowl, mix together salt, oregano, and pepper. Sprinkle over both sides of pieces of meat. As you finish a piece, place the meat into the slow cooker.
3. Sprinkle with chopped onion.
4. Spoon spaghetti sauce over top, being careful not to disturb the seasoning and onions.
5. Cover and cook on Low 5-8 hours, or until the meat is tender but not over-cooked.

Fajita Steak
Becky Harder, Monument, CO

Makes 6 servings

Prep Time: 10 minutes
Cooking Time: 6-8 hours
Ideal slow cooker size: 4-qt.

15-oz. can tomatoes with
  green chilies
$\frac{1}{4}$ cup salsa, your choice
  of mild, medium, *or* hot
8-oz. can tomato sauce
2 lbs. round steak, cut in
  2"x4"strips
1 envelope dry Fajita spice
  mix
1 cup water, *optional*

1. Combine all ingredients—except water—in your slow cooker.
2. Cover and cook on Low 6-8 hours, or until meat is tender but not over-cooked.
3. Check meat occasionally to make sure it isn't cooking dry. If it begins to look dry, stir in water, up to 1 cup.

Tip: Serve meat with fried onions and green peppers. Offer shredded cheese, avocado chunks, and sour cream as toppings. Let individual eaters wrap any or all of the ingredients in flour tortillas.

Variation: Instead of the salsa, add 1 small onion, chopped, and 1 red bell pepper, cut in 1" pieces to Step 1.
Mix $\frac{1}{4}$ cup flour and $\frac{1}{4}$ cup water in a jar with a tight-fitting lid. Shake until smooth.

Fifteen-20 minutes before the end of the cooking time, pour slowly into stew, stirring while you do so that it blends well. Cover and continue cooking until the stew thickens.
— **Audrey L. Kneer**
Williamsfield, IL

Pepper Steak
Darlene G. Martin
Richfield, PA

Makes 4 servings

Prep Time: 15-20 minutes
Cooking Time: 5-6 hours
Ideal slow cooker size: 3¹/2- to 4-qt.

1-lb. round steak, cut 3/4"-1" thick
14¹/2-oz. can Italian-style stewed tomatoes, undrained
1 tsp. Worcestershire sauce
2 yellow, 2 red, and 2 green bell peppers, sliced in strips
large onion, sliced

1. Cut meat into 4 serving-size pieces. In a large non-stick skillet, brown meat on both sides. Transfer meat to a 3¹/2- or 4-qt. slow cooker.
2. In medium bowl, stir together undrained tomatoes and Worcestershire sauce. Spoon over meat.
3. Arrange vegetables over top.
4. Cover and cook on Low 5-6 hours or until meat and

vegetables are tender but not over-cooked.

New Mexico Steak
Mamie Christopherson
Rio Rancho, NM

Makes 4-6 servings

Prep Time: 10 minutes
Cooking Time: 4 hours
Ideal slow cooker size: 3-qt.

1 large onion, sliced
2-lb. round steak, cut into serving size pieces
salt and pepper to taste
2 7-oz. cans green chili salsa

1. Place onion slices in bottom of slow cooker.
2. Sprinkle steak with salt and pepper. Add steak pieces to cooker.
3. Spoon chili salsa over all, being careful not to wash off the seasonings.
4. Cover and cook on High 1 hour. Turn to Low and cook 3 hours, or until steak is tender but not over-cooked.

Tips:
1. If the chili salsa is too hot, sprinkle a little white sugar over mixture before cooking. Or choose a milder salsa.
2. Add a little liquid (water or beer) if the dish seems too dry toward the end of the cooking time.

Pigs in Blankets
Linda Sluiter
Schererville, IN

Makes 4 servings

Prep Time: 30 minutes
Cooking Time: 6-8 hours
Ideal slow cooker size: 4-qt.

1-2-lb. round steak
1 lb. bacon
1 cup ketchup
1/4 cup brown sugar
1 small onion
1/4-1/2 cup water

1. Cut round steak into long strips. Roll up each meat strip, and then wrap with a slice of bacon. Secure with a toothpick to hold the roll shape.
2. Warm remaining ingredients in saucepan, bringing to a simmer to make a sauce.
3. Place meat rolls in slow cooker. Pour sauce over top.
4. Cover and cook on Low 6-8 hours, or until the meat is tender but not over-cooked.

Beef Roulades

Karen Waggoner
Joplin, MO

Makes 12 servings

Prep Time: 20 minutes
Cooking Time: 2 hours
Ideal slow cooker size: 5-qt.

4 lbs. round steak
4 cups prepared packaged
  herb-seasoned stuffing
  mix
2 10¾-oz. cans cream of
  mushroom soup
1-2 cups water

1. Do it yourself—or ask your butcher—to cut steak into 12 long pieces. Pound each piece until thin and flattened.
2. Place ⅓ cup prepared stuffing on each slice of meat. Roll up and fasten with toothpick. Place in slow cooker.
3. In a bowl, mix soup and water together and then pour over steak.
4. Cover and cook on High 4-6 hours, or until meat is tender but not over-cooked.

Comforting Beef with Potatoes

Dorothy VanDeest
Memphis, TN

Makes 4 servings

Prep Time: 20 minutes
Cooking Time: 2-8 hours
Ideal slow cooker size: 5-qt.

2-3 cups cut-up cooked
  beef roast
2 10-oz. pkgs. frozen hash
  brown potatoes, thawed
1 onion, finely chopped
¼ cup butter, melted
1 cup gravy *or* beef broth

1. Place all ingredients in slow cooker, either in layers or mixed together.
2. Cover and cook on Low 4-8 hours, or on High 2-3 hours, or until thoroughly heated.

Tip: This recipe can easily be doubled.

Buffet Beef

Kate Johnson
Rolfe, IA

Makes 8-10 servings

Prep Time: 10 minutes
Cooking Time: 4-8 hours
Ideal slow cooker size: 4-qt.

12-oz. can beer
1 envelope dry brown
  gravy mix
⅓ cup flour
2½-3-lb. round steak, cut
  into cubes

1. In the slow cooker mix beer and gravy mix together well.
2. In a plastic bag, shake flour and steak cubes together until meat is coated.
3. Empty entire contents of bag into slow cooker. Gently stir to coat meat with liquid.
4. Cover and cook on Low 6-8 hours or on High 4 hours.

Quick and Tasty Beef-in-Gravy

Dede Peterson
Rapid City, SD
Rosalie D. Miller
Mifflintown, PA

Makes 8 servings

Prep Time: 15-20 minutes
Cooking Time: 8-10 hours
Ideal slow cooker size: 6-qt.

3 lbs. stew meat
1 envelope dry onion soup mix
1/2 cup beef broth
10³/4-oz. can cream of mushroom soup
4-oz. can sliced mushrooms, drained

1. Combine all ingredients in slow cooker.
2. Cover and cook on Low 8-10 hours, or until meat is tender but not over-cooked.

Variations:

1. Substitute red wine for the beef broth.
— **Kaye Taylor**
Florissant, MO

2. Brown the beef in 2 Tbsp. olive oil in a non-stick skillet before placing in slow cooker. Do the beef in several batches so as not to crowd the skillet. The meat won't brown well if the skillet is too full.
— **Lauren Eberhard**
Seneca, IL

3. Add 1/4 cup quick-cooking tapioca, if you wish, to Step 1, in order to thicken the sauce.
— **Deb Herr**
Mountaintop, PA

Creamy-Style Beef Tips

Cathy Sellers
Cedar Rapids, IA

Makes 6 servings

Prep Time: 10 minutes
Cooking Time: 6-8 hours
Ideal slow cooker size: 4-qt.

2 lbs. stew meat
2 10³/4-oz. cans cream of mushroom soup
1 soup-can water
half a 12-oz. can evaporated milk
1 tsp. salt

1. Combine all ingredients in slow cooker. Mix well.
2. Cover and cook on Low 6-8 hours, or until the meat is tender but not over-cooked.
3. Serve over rice or noodles.

Creamy Beef and Mushrooms

Joette Droz
Kalona, IA
Betty Moore
Plano, IL
Mary B. Sensenig
New Holland, PA

Makes 6-8 servings

Prep Time: 10 minutes
Cooking Time: 6-8 hours
Ideal slow cooker size: 3-qt.

10³/4-oz. can condensed golden mushroom soup
10³/4-oz. can condensed cream of mushroom soup
10³/4-oz. can condensed French onion soup
1/4 cup seasoned bread crumbs
2 lbs. beef stew meat, cut into 1" cubes

1. In slow cooker, combine soups and breadcrumbs. Mix well.
2. Stir in beef.
3. Cover and cook on Low 6-8 hours, or until meat is tender, but not over-cooked.

Variation: Add 1-1½ cups sliced fresh mushrooms 30 minutes before the end of the cooking time.
— **Sherry Goss Lapp**
Lancaster, PA

Slow-Cooker Beef Stroganoff

Jennifer Eberly
Harrisonburg, VA

Makes 6 servings

Prep Time: 5 minutes
Cooking Time: 6-8 hours
Ideal slow cooker size: 3-qt.

1 lb. lean round steak
　cubes
1 envelope dry beefy onion
　soup mix
10³/4-oz. can cream of
　celery soup
10³/4-oz. can cream of
　mushroom soup
1/2 cup sour cream

1. Place first 4 ingredients
in slow cooker and mix
together thoroughly.
2. Cover and cook on Low
6-8 hours, stirring occasionally if you're around the
kitchen and able to do that.
3. Fifteen minutes before
serving, stir in sour cream.
4. When hot and bubbly,
serve over cooked rice or
noodles.

Variation: Use 2 cans cream
of mushroom soup instead 1
can each of cream of celery and
cream of mushroom soups.
　— Jena Hammond
　　Traverse City, MI

Sweet and Sour Beef Stew

Heather Horst
Lebanon, PA

Makes 6 servings

Prep Time: 10 minutes
Cooking Time: 6-8 hours
Ideal slow cooker size: 3-qt.

1 cup chopped onions
2 lbs. stewing beef
1 Tbsp. Worcestershire
　sauce
1/2 cup vinegar
1/4 cup brown sugar

1. Place onion in bottom of
slow cooker.
2. In a bowl, mix meat and
remaining ingredients
together.
3. Cover and cook on Low
6-8 hours, or until meat and
onions are tender but not
over-cooked.
4. Serve over cooked rice
or pasta.

No-Peeking Beef Tips

Ruth C. Hancock
Earlsboro, OK

Makes 4 servings

Prep Time: 15 minutes
Cooking Time: 4 hours
Ideal slow cooker size: 4-qt.

2 lbs. stew meat
half *or* a whole envelope
　dry onion soup mix
12-oz. can lemon-lime soda
10³/4-oz. can cream of
　mushroom soup *or*
　cream of chicken soup

1. Put meat in slow cooker.
Sprinkle dry onion soup mix
over meat.
2. Mix soda and cream of
mushroom soup together in a
bowl. Spoon over meat, being
careful not to disturb the
onion soup mix.
3. Cover and cook on High
4 hours. Do not stir or
remove lid until the time is
up.
4. Serve over cooked rice
or noodles.

Variations:
1. Add a 4-oz. can of mush-
rooms, undrained, to Step 2.
　— Elaine Rineer
　　Lancaster, PA

2. Add a 4-oz. can of mush-
rooms, undrained, plus 1/2 cup
red wine to Step 2.
　— Leona Yoder
　　Hartville, OH

3. Replace soda with 1 cup sour cream in original recipe. Add either a 4-oz. or an 8-oz. can of mushrooms, undrained, to Step 2.

— **Pauline Morrison**
St. Marys, ON

3. You can prepare this recipe the night before, then refrigerate it overnight. Before you leave in the morning, put the crock in the cooker, and turn it on. Dinner will be ready when you get home.

Beef Stew
Leann Brown
Ronks, PA

Makes 6-8 servings

Prep Time: 10-15 minutes
Cooking Time: 5-6 hours
Ideal slow cooker size:
  5- to 6-qt.

3 lbs. cubed beef
2 12-oz. jars beef gravy
2 cups chopped carrots
1 medium-sized onion, chopped
4 cups chopped potatoes
salt and pepper, optional

1. Place beef in slow cooker. Add remaining ingredients. Stir together well.
2. Cover and cook on Low 5-6 hours, or until meat and veggies are tender but not over-cooked.

Rainy Day Low-Fat Dinner
Ruth Zendt
Mifflintown, PA

Makes 6-8 servings

Prep Time: 10-15 minutes
Cooking Time: 6-10 hours
Ideal slow cooker size: 5-qt.

5-6 medium potatoes, peeled or unpeeled, and cut into 1/2" cubes
1 lb. baby carrots
1 1/2 lbs. lean beef cubes
10 3/4-oz. can fat-free cream of mushroom soup
12-oz. jar fat-free brown gravy

1. Layer potatoes, carrots, and beef in slow cooker in the order listed.
2. In a mixing bowl, blend together the soup and gravy. Pour over cooker contents.
3. Cover and cook on Low 6-10 hours, or until vegetables and meat are tender.

Tips:
1. Add your favorite seasonings to the layers.
2. Vary the vegetable ingredients as you want.

Golfer's Stew
Lucy O'Connell
Goshen, MA

Makes 4-5 servings

Prep Time: 10 minutes
Cooking Time: 7 hours
Ideal slow cooker size: 4-qt.

1 lb. stew beef, cubed
12-oz. jar beef gravy or beef and mushroom gravy
6 medium potatoes, cut in 1/2" chunks
6 carrots, cut in thick slices
3 ribs celery, cut in thick slices, optional
2-3 onions, cut in wedges

1. Place all ingredients in slow cooker. Stir together gently.
2. Cover and cook on High 1 hour and then on Low 6 hours.

Variation: Add 1 tsp. salt and 1/4-1/2 tsp. pepper in Step 1.

Easy Beef Stew

Judi Manos
West Islip, NY

Makes 4-6 servings

Prep Time: 20 minutes
Cooking Time: 7¹/₂-8¹/₂ hours
Ideal slow cooker size: 4-qt.

4 medium-sized red
   potatoes
1¹/₂ lbs. beef stew meat
¹/₃ cup flour
14-oz. can diced tomatoes,
   undrained
2 cups water
3 cups frozen stir-fry bell
   peppers and onions

1. Cut potatoes into quarters. Place on bottom of slow cooker.
2. In a mixing bowl, toss flour with beef to coat. Add to slow cooker.
3. Pour in undrained tomatoes and water.
4. Cover and cook on Low 7-8 hours, or until beef and potatoes are tender but not overcooked.
5. Gently fold stir-fry vegetables into stew. Cover and cook on Low 30-40 minutes, or until vegetables are hot and tender.

Variations:
1. Add 2-3 cups sliced carrots just after the potatoes in Step 1.
2. Add 2 tsp. salt and ³/₄ tsp. pepper to the flour in Step 2, before tossing with the beef.

Roast Beef Stew

Thelma Good
Harrisonburg, VA

Makes 8 servings

Prep Time: 10-15 minutes
Cooking Time: 10-13 hours
Ideal slow cooker size: 6-qt.

2-3-lb. roast, which may be
   frozen!
5-6 potatoes, quartered
4-5 carrots, sliced
2 small onions, sliced
half a head of cabbage,
   sliced

1. In the evening, place roast in slow cooker.
2. Cover and cook on High for 1 hour. Turn to Low and cook overnight, or 6-8 hours, if you're doing this during the daytime.
3. In the morning, place potatoes, carrots, and onions around and over the roast. Fill slow cooker ¹/₂-³/₄ full with water, depending upon how soupy you like your stew.
4. Cover and cook on High 2-3 hours.
5. Lift the lid and put in the cabbage, pushing it down into the broth. Continue cooking on High 1 more hour, or until veggies are done to your liking. The stew should be ready at lunch-time—or dinner-time.

Variations:
1. Sprinkle the roast, top and bottom, with salt and pepper before placing it in the cooker in Step 1. Also, sprinkle the vegetables with salt after you've put them in the cooker in Step 3.
2. Increase the amount of potatoes, carrots, onions, and cabbage to your liking. You may need to increase the cooking time in Steps 4 and 5 to make sure that they get as tender as you like.

Lynn's Easy Stew

Veronica Sabo
Shelton, CT

Makes 5-6 servings

Prep Time: 10 minutes
Cooking Time: 5-8 hours
Ideal slow cooker size:
   4- to 5-qt.

2 lbs. stew beef
4 ribs celery, cut into large
   pieces
3 cups carrots, cut up in
   large pieces
1 large onion, chopped
1 envelope dry onion soup
   mix
water

1. Place all ingredients in slow cooker. Stir together gently, but until well mixed. Add about 2" of water.
2. Cover and cook on High 5-8 hours, or until meat and vegetables are tender.

Succulent Beef Stew

Linda Thomas, Sayner, WI

Makes 6 servings

Prep Time: 30 minutes
Cooking Time: 8 hours
Ideal slow cooker size: 3-qt.

1-1½ lbs. stew meat
1 medium to large onion, chopped
14½-oz. can beef broth
1 broth can of water
½ lb. baby carrots
5 medium white potatoes, peeled *or* unpeeled, cut into ½" chunks

Optional ingredients:
salt and pepper
5 shakes Worcestershire sauce
2 bay leaves

1. In a non-stick skillet, brown stew meat and chopped onion. Sprinkle with salt and pepper if you wish. Transfer mixture to slow cooker.
2. Add broth and water, and Worcestershire sauce and bay leaves if you choose to. Stir together well.
3. Cover and cook on Low 4 hours.
4. Layer in vegetables. Push down into liquid as much as you can. Cover and continue cooking on Low for 4 more hours.
5. If the stew seems to get dry, add ½ cup water.

Mediterranean Beef Stew

Sandy Osborn
Iowa City, IA

Makes 4 servings

Prep Time: 5-10 minutes
Cooking Time: 3-8 hours
Ideal slow cooker size: 3½-qt.

2 medium-sized zucchini, cut into bite-size pieces
¾ pound beef stew meat, cut into ½" pieces
2 14½-oz. cans Italian-style diced tomatoes, undrained
½ tsp. pepper, *optional*
2" stick cinnamon, *or* ¼ tsp. ground cinnamon

1. Place zucchini in the bottom of your slow cooker.
2. Add beef and remaining ingredients in the order they are listed.
3. Cover and cook on High 3-5 hours, or until the meat is tender but not over-cooked. You can also cook the stew on High 1 hour, then on Low for 7 hours, or until meat is tender but not overdone.

Italian Beef

Peggy Forsythe
Bartlett, TN

Makes 6 servings

Prep Time: 20 minutes
Cooking Time: 8 hours
Ideal slow cooker size:
4- to 6-qt.

4-5-lb. beef roast, cut into 1-1½" cubes
2 *or* 3 beef bouillon cubes
1 tsp. garlic salt
2 Tbsp. Italian salad dressing

1. Place roast, bouillon cubes, garlic salt, and dressing in slow cooker. Stir.
2. Add 1-1½" water around the beef, being careful not to disturb the seasoning on the top of the meat.
3. Cover and cook on Low 8 hours, or until tender but not over-cooked.
4. Remove beef from cooker and shred with 2 forks. Return shredded meat to cooker and stir into broth.
5. Serve over rice, or on rolls or garlic bread for a delicious open-face sandwich.

When I want to warm rolls to go with a slow-cooker stew, I wrap them in foil and lay them on top of the stew until they're warm.

Donna Barnitz
Jenks, OK

Beef Ala Mode

Gloria Julien
Gladstone, MI

Makes 6 servings

Prep Time: 5-10 minutes
Cooking Time: 6-8 hours
Ideal slow cooker size: 4-qt.

2-lb. boneless beef roast,
  cut into 6 serving-size
  pieces
1/2 lb. salt pork *or* bacon,
  cut up
3 onions, chopped
pepper to taste
water

1. Place beef and pork in
slow cooker.
2. Sprinkle onions over top
of meat.
3. Add pepper to taste.
4. Pour water in alongside
meat, about 1" deep.
5. Cook on Low 6-8 hours.
6. Serve over mashed potatoes, cooked rice, or pasta.

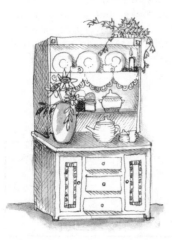

Beef Brisket Barbecue

Sharon Timpe, Jackson, WI

Makes 8 servings

Prep Time: 15 minutes
Cooking Time: 6¹/4-7¹/4 hours
Ideal slow cooker size:
  4- to 5-qt.

2 cups barbecue sauce,
  divided
1 small onion, chopped
3 tsp. beef bouillon
  granules, *or* 2 beef
  bouillon cubes
3-4-lb. boneless beef
  brisket
8 sandwich rolls

1. In the bottom of your
slow cooker combine 1 cup
barbecue sauce, chopped
onion, and bouillon.
2. Place beef brisket on
top.
3. Cover and cook on Low
6-7 hours, or until brisket
shreds easily.
4. Remove brisket from
cooker. Using 2 forks, shred
the meat.
5. Tilt cooker and spoon
off fat from cooking broth.
Discard fat.
6. Pour cooking broth into
a bowl. Again, spoon off any
remaining fat and discard.
7. Measure out 1 cup of
cooking broth. Pour back into
slow cooker, along with
remaining cup of barbecue
sauce. Blend broth and sauce
well.

8. Return shredded meat
to slow cooker. Stir into sauce
thoroughly.
9. Cover and cook on High
for 15 minutes, or until meat
is hot.
10. Serve over sandwich
rolls.

*Tip: You can also serve the
Barbecue on small buns as a
snack or appetizer. Serving from
the slow cooker keeps the meat
hot, and guests can help themselves whenever they want to.*

Easy Roast Beef Barbecue

Rose Hankins, Stevensville, MD

Makes 12-16 servings

Prep Time: 15 minutes
Cooking Time: 12 hours
Ideal slow cooker size:
  4- to 5-qt.

12-oz. bottle barbecue
  sauce
1/2 cup water
1/2 cup ketchup
1/2 cup chopped onions
1/2 cup chopped green
  pepper
3-4-lb. beef roast
12-16 sandwich rolls

1. Combine first 5 ingredients in slow cooker. Smother
roast in sauce.
2. Cover. Cook on Low
12 hours.
3. Shred meat using 2 forks.
Mix thoroughly through sauce.

4. Serve on rolls with cole slaw.

Pulled Beef or Pork

Pat Bechtel, Dillsburg, PA

Makes 16-18 servings

Prep Time: 5-10 minutes
Cooking Time: 8-10 hours
Ideal slow cooker size: 3½-qt.

4-lb. beef *or* pork roast
2 envelopes dry ranch dressing mix
2 envelopes dry Italian dressing mix

1. Cook roast in slow cooker on Low for 8-10 hours, or until tender but not over-cooked. Do not add water or seasonings! By the end of the cooking time there will be broth from cooking— do not discard it!
2. Just before serving remove meat from slow cooker. Using 2 forks, pull meat apart.
3. Add dry dressing mixes to broth and stir thoroughly. Stir pulled meat back into broth in the cooker. Serve immediately in rolls, or over cooked rice or pasta, or over mashed potatoes.

Barbecued Beef Sandwiches

Arianne Hochstetler
Goshen, IN

Makes 24 servings

Prep Time: 15 minutes
Cooking Time: 5½-6½ hours
Ideal slow cooker size: 4-qt.

4-lb. round steak, ¾" thick, cut into 3" cubes
2 cups ketchup
1 cup cola
½ cup chopped onion
2 garlic cloves, minced

1. Spray slow cooker with non-stick cooking spray.
2. Place beef pieces in cooker.
3. Mix remaining ingredients in a large bowl and pour over meat.
4. Cover and cook on High 5-6 hours.
5. About 30 minutes before serving, remove beef from slow cooker and shred with 2 forks. Return beef to slow cooker and mix well with sauce.
6. Cover and cook on High an additional 20 minutes.
7. Spoon about ⅓ cup beef mixture into individual sandwich buns.

Super Beef Barbecue

Linda E. Wilcox
Blythewood, SC

Makes 10-12 servings

Prep Time: 15 minutes
Cooking Time: 9-10 hours
Ideal slow cooker size: 6-qt.

3-4-lb. rump roast
1 clove garlic, minced, *or* ¼ cup finely chopped onion
18-oz. bottle barbecue sauce
1 cup ketchup
16-oz. jar whole dill pickles, undrained

1. Cut roast into quarters and place in slow cooker.
2. In a bowl, stir together garlic, barbecue sauce, and ketchup. When well blended, fold in pickles and their juice. Pour over meat.
3. Cover and cook on Low 8-9 hours, or until meat begins to fall apart.
4. Remove the pickles and discard them.
5. Lift the meat out onto a platter and shred by pulling it apart with 2 forks.
6. Return meat to sauce and heat thoroughly on Low, about 1 hour.
7. Serve in sandwich rolls.

Braised Short Ribs

Leona Yoder
Hartville, OH

Makes 6 servings

Prep Time: 45 mintues
Cooking Time: 4-10 hours
Ideal slow cooker size: 4-qt.

1 tsp. salt
1 cup flour
3 lbs. beef short ribs, cut
  into serving-size pieces
2-3 Tbsp. olive oil
2 medium-sized onions,
  sliced
1 cup water

Optional ingredients:
1¹/₂ Tbsp. flour
¹/₂ cup cold water

1. Combine salt and flour in a shallow bowl. Roll short ribs in the seasoned flour.
2. Brown the ribs in oil on all sides in a large non-stick skillet. Rather than crowd the skillet, which prevents the meat from browning, do the browning in batches. As you finish browning, place pieces of meat in the slow cooker.
3. Add sliced onions and water.
4. Cover and cook on Low 8-10 hours or on High 4-6 hours.

Variations:
1. Add ¹/₂ tsp. pepper to the salt and flour in Step 1.
2. To make gravy, remove fully cooked ribs to a platter and keep warm. Place 1¹/₂

Tbsp. flour in a jar with a tight-fitting lid. Pour in ¹/₂ cup cold water. Shake together until lumps disappear.
Turn cooker to High so that broth begins to simmer. When bubbling, pour in flour-water in a thin stream, whisking as you do it.
Continue whisking until the broth thickens. Serve over, or alongside, ribs.

Tex-Mex Beef Ribs or Roast

Janie Steele
Moore, OK

Makes 6 servings

Prep Time: 5-10 minutes
Cooking Time: 4-10 hours
Ideal slow cooker size: 6-qt.

3-4 lbs. beef short ribs, *or*
  round steak, cut in
  serving-size pieces
1 cup sweet and tangy
  steak sauce
¹/₃ cup picante sauce
1 tsp. chili powder
¹/₂ tsp. dry mustard

1. Place ribs or steak in slow cooker.
2. Combine remaining ingredients in a bowl and pour over meat.
3. Cover and cook on Low 4-10 hours, or until meat is tender but not over-cooked.

Corned Beef and Cabbage

Carrie Darby
Wayland, IA
Leona Yoder
Hartville, OH
Esther Porter
Minneapolis, MN
Betty K. Drescher
Quakertown, PA
Karen Ceneviva
New Haven, CT
Bonita Ensenberger
Albuquerque, NM
Dorothy Lingerfelt,
Stonyford, CA

Makes 6 servings

Prep Time: 30 minutes
Cooking Time: 4-7 hours
Ideal slow cooker size:
  5- or 6-qt.

3-4-lb. corned beef brisket
  (not in a brine), cut into
  6-8 pieces
³/₄-1¹/₄ cups water
5-6 carrots, cut in 2"-3"
  pieces
3 medium-sized onions,
  quartered
salt and pepper
half to a whole head of
  cabbage, cut into wedges

1. Place corned beef in slow cooker. Add water.

2. Place carrots and onions around the meat if possible, pushing the vegetables in so they're at least partly covered by the water. Sprinkle salt and pepper over all.

3. Cover and cook on Low 4-5 hours, or on high 2½-3 hours.

4. Add cabbage to cooker, pushing down into liquid to moisten. Turn to High and cook an additional 1½-2 hours, or until vegetables and meat are tender but not over-cooked.

Tip: You can prepare the cabbage separately in a large soup pot. Place wedges in kettle and add 1 cup broth from cooker. Cook 20 to 30 minutes, covered, or until just-tender. Stir into corned beef and vegetables right before serving.

Variation: Add 3 medium-sized potatoes, peeled or unpeeled, cut into chunks, to Step 2.
— **Sharon Timpe**
Jackson, WI

Apple Corned Beef and Cabbage

Donna Treloar
Hartford City, IN

Makes 6-8 servings

Prep Time: 15 minutes
Cooking Time: 8-10 hours
Ideal slow cooker size: 5-qt.

3-4-lb. corned beef brisket (not in a brine), cut into 6-8 pieces
1 small head of cabbage, cut in thin wedges
3-4 medium-sized potatoes, cut in chunks
2-3 cups baby carrots, *or* sliced full-sized carrots, *optional*
1 qt. pure apple juice
1 cup brown sugar

1. Place corned beef in slow cooker.

2. Place vegetables around and on top of meat.

3. Pour apple juice over everything. Sprinkle with brown sugar.

4. Cover and cook on Low 8-10 hours, or until meat and vegetables are tender but not over-cooked.

Reuben Casserole

Melanie Thrower
McPherson, KS

Makes 4 servings

Prep Time: 10 minutes
Cooking Time: 2-4 hours
Ideal slow cooker size: 2-qt.

2 cups deli-style corned beef, torn into bite-sized pieces, *divided*
15-oz. can sauerkraut, drained, *divided*
½ cup shredded *or* 8 slices Swiss cheese, *divided*
¼ cup Thousand Island salad dressing, *divided*
4 cups dry packaged stuffing mix, *divided*

1. Spray slow cooker with non-stick cooking spray.

2. Layer half of each ingredient in the order listed.

3. Repeat layers.

4. Cover and cook on Low 2-4 hours, until casserole is cooked through and cheese has melted.

Noodle Casserole

Mary B. Sensenig
New Holland, PA

Makes 4 servings

Prep Time: 5 minutes
Cooking Time: 3-3½ hours
Ideal slow cooker size: 4-qt.

8-oz. pkg. dry noodles
10¾-oz. can cream of
  mushroom soup
1 cup milk
¼ lb. dried beef, shredded
1 cup shredded cheese,
  optional

1. Cook noodles as directed on package. Drain and rinse with cold water.
2. In a mixing bowl, blend soup and milk together.
3. Spray the interior of the cooker. Layer ingredients in cooker in this order: cooked noodles, soup-milk mixture, dried beef.
4. Cover and cook on Low for 2½-3 hours. Sprinkle cheese over top, if you wish. Cover and continue cooking another half hour.

Beef Tongue

Lizzie Ann Yoder
Hartville, OH

Makes 6 servings

Prep Time: 15-20 minutes
Cooking Time: 7-8 hours
Ideal slow cooker size:
  4- to 5-qt.

1 beef tongue, fresh *or*
  smoked
2 scant Tbsp. salt
1½ cups water
1 bay leaf
2 lemons, squeezed, *or*
  2 onions quartered
6 peppercorns

1. Place washed tongue in slow cooker.
2. In a bowl, mix all remaining ingredients together. Pour over tongue.
3. Cover and cook on Low 7-8 hours, or until the meat is tender. Cool until you're able to handle the meat, and then remove the outer skin by pulling on it gently.
4. Slice meat and serve hot.
5. Use chilled leftovers in sandwiches.

Roast Venison with Gravy

Becky Gehman
Bergton, VA

Makes 4-6 servings

Prep Time: 5 minutes
Cooking Time: 6-7 hours
Ideal slow cooker size: 3-qt.

2-3-lb. venison roast
1-2 tsp. garlic powder, *or*
  onion powder
10¾-oz. can golden
  mushroom soup
¾ soup can of water

1. Place roast in slow cooker. Sprinkle both sides with seasoning.
2. Cover and cook on Low 4-5 hours, turning the roast twice while cooking.
3. In a bowl, mix together soup and water. Add to meat after it's cooked for 4-5 hours.
4. Cover and cook on Low 2 more hours, turning roast once during this time.

Variations:
  1. Instead of the garlic or onion powder, use 1 envelope dry beefy onion soup mix.
    — Krista Hershberger
    Elverson, PA

  2. Add 1 envelope dry onion soup mix and 2-3 tsp. Worcestershire sauce to the mushroom soup and water.
  Pour over seasoned roast at the beginning of the cooking time.

Cover and cook on Low for 6 hours, or until meat is tender and not over-cooked.
— **Anne Nolt**
Thompsontown, PA

Good and Easy Elk
Evelyn Page
Lance Creek, WY

Makes 3-4 servings

Prep Time: 10-15 minutes
Cooking Time: 4-8 hours
Ideal slow cooker size: 3-qt.

1-2 lbs. elk, cubed
1/2 lb. sliced fresh
  mushrooms
1 cup beef broth
10³/4-oz. can cream of
  mushroom soup
1 envelope dry onion soup
  mix

1. Combine all ingredients in your slow cooker. Mix gently but well.
2. Cover and cook on High 4 hours or on Low 8 hours, or until the meat is tender but not over-cooked.

Tip: You may substitute venison or beef for the elk.

Elk Stroganoff
Evelyn Page
Lance Creek, WY

Makes 3-4 servings

Prep Time: 20 minutes
Cooking Time: 6-8 hours
Ideal slow cooker size: 3-qt.

1 lb. cubed elk
1/2 cup chopped onion
10³/4-oz. can cream of
  celery soup
1/4 tsp. garlic salt
4-oz. can mushroom
  pieces, drained, *optional*
1 cup sour cream

1. Brown meat in a non-stick skillet. Add onions and sauté until wilted.
2. Combine meat and onions, soup, garlic salt, and mushrooms if you wish in slow cooker.
3. Cover and cook on Low 6-8 hours, or until tender.
4. Fifteen minutes before serving, stir in sour cream.

Tips:
1. Serve over cooked rice or noodles.
2. Substitute venison or beef for the elk.

Elk in Mushroom Soup
Evelyn Page
Lance Creek, WY

Makes 4-6 servings

Prep Time: 15 minutes
Cooking Time: 5-8 hours
Ideal slow cooker size: 3-qt.

1-2 lbs. elk steak
10³/4-oz. can cream of
  mushroom soup
soup can of milk

1. Brown steak in a non-stick skillet. Then place in the slow cooker.
2. In a bowl, combine soup and milk. Pour sauce over steak.
3. Cover and cook on Low 5-8 hours, or until meat is tender but not over-cooked.

Tip:
1. I often serve this meat alongside cooked potatoes or rice. Then we pour the soup mixture over the meat and vegetables.
2. You may substitute venison or beef for the elk.

A Tip —

Invest in good quality knives. They make preparation much easier.

Cheesy Hot Dish

Lucille Martin
Barnett, MO

Makes 6 servings

Prep Time: 30-40 minutes
Cooking Time: 2-3 hours
Ideal slow cooker size: 5-qt.

4-5 medium-sized potatoes, cooked and sliced, *divided*
1 lb. ground beef, browned and drained, *divided*
12-oz. pkg. frozen green beans, *divided*
1/2 lb. Velveeta cheese, sliced, *divided*
10¾-oz. can cream of mushroom soup

1. Place half the potatoes in the bottom of a buttered slow cooker.
2. Layer in half the ground beef, followed by a layer of half the green beans. Top with a layer of half the cheese slices.
3. Repeat all the layers.
4. Pour soup over all.
5. Cover and cook on Low for 2 hours if the food is hot when put into the cooker, or on High for 2 hours if the food is cold when put into the cooker.

Creamy Ground Beef

Joleen Albrecht
Gladstone, MI

Makes 5 servings

Prep Time: 10-15 minutes
Cooking Time: 2-4 hours
Ideal slow cooker size: 3-qt.

1 lb. ground beef
garlic powder to taste
salt and pepper to taste
2 10¾-oz. cans cream of mushroom soup
1/2-1 soup-can of water

1. Brown ground beef in non-stick skillet. Drain.
2. Place in slow cooker, along with the seasonings. Taste and add more, if you like.
3. Mix in the soup. Add water until the mixture reaches the consistency of gravy .
4. Cover and cook on Low 2-4 hours.
5. Serve over cooked noodles or rice.

Tip: Serve over baked potatoes. Then sprinkle with grated cheddar cheese.

Tater Tot Casserole

Sharon Wantland
Menomonee Falls, WI

Makes 4 servings

Prep Time: 10 minutes
Cooking Time: 2-3 hours
Ideal slow cooker size: 3-qt.

1 lb. ground beef
1/4 cup chopped onions
10¾-oz. can cream of chicken soup
16-oz. box tater tots

1. Brown ground beef with onions in a non-stick skillet until crumbly. Drain.
2. Place beef and onions in bottom of slow cooker.
3. Top with soup and then with tater tots.
4. Cover and cook on Low 2-3 hours.

Variation: Add a 10¾-oz. can of vegetable soup to Step 3. Mix it together in a bowl with the cream of chicken soup before spooning over the beef and onions. And if you like a lot of sauce, stir half a soup can of water into the two soups.
— Vera Martin
East Earl, PA

Spanish Rice
Sharon Wantland
Menomonee Falls, WI
Sherri Mayer
Menomonee Falls, WI

Makes 4 servings

Prep Time: 20 minutes
Cooking Time: 1 1/2 hours
Ideal slow cooker size: 6-qt.

2 cups minute rice, cooked
1 qt. stewed tomatoes
1/2 cup chopped onions
1/2 cup chopped green pepper
1 envelope dry taco sauce seasoning, mixed with 3/4 cup water, *optional*
3/4 lb. ground beef, browned

1. Combine all ingredients in your slow cooker and mix well.
2. Cover and cook 1 1/2 hours on High, or until heated through.

Variations:
1. Instead of the 2 cups of cooked minute rice, use 1 1/2 cups raw long-grain rice and 2 Tbsp. oil or butter.
Turn the slow cooker to High. Saute the uncooked rice in the oil or butter until golden brown. Then proceed with Step 1 above.
2. Instead of ground beef, use loose sausage. Brown in a non-stick skillet and drain before placing it in your slow cooker. Then proceed with Step 1 above.

— **Linda Overholt**
Abbeville, SC

Meaty Spanish Rice
Susan Wenger
Lebanon, PA

Makes 10 servings

Prep Time: 20 minutes
Cooking Time: 4-8 hours
Ideal slow cooker size: 4- to 5-qt.

2 lbs. ground beef
44-oz. can of stewed *or* diced tomatoes, *or* spaghetti sauce
1 cup water
2 1/2 tsp. chili powder
2 tsp. Worcestershire sauce
1 cup long-grain rice, uncooked

Optional ingredients:
1 medium-sized onion, chopped
1 green pepper, chopped
1 1/2-2 tsp. salt
1/2 tsp. pepper

1. Brown beef in a non-stick skillet. (Include chopped onion and black pepper, if you wish.) Drain. Place mixture in slow cooker.
2. Add remaining ingredients to cooker (including the green pepper and salt, if you wish), stirring well.
3. Cover and cook on Low for 6-8 hours or on High for 4 hours.

Wild Rice Ground Beef Casserole
Esther Gingerich
Parnell, IA

Makes 6 servings

Prep Time: 15 minutes
Cooking Time: 3-6 hours
Ideal slow cooker size: 3-qt.

1 lb. ground beef
1 medium-sized onion, chopped
6.2-oz. pkg. long-grain and wild rice, uncooked
4-oz. can mushrooms, drained
2 10 3/4-oz. cans mushroom soup
1/2 cup water

1. In a non-stick skillet, brown ground beef and onion together. Drain.
2. In the slow cooker, combine ground beef mixture with all remaining ingredients, including the wild rice seasoning.
3. Cover and cook on High 3 hours or on Low 5-6 hours, or until rice is tender but not mushy.

Pizza Rice Casserole

Jennie Martin
Richfield, PA

Makes 6-8 servings

Prep Time: 20 minutes
Cooking Time: 6 hours
Ideal slow cooker size: 5-qt.

1 lb. ground beef
1 medium-sized onion, chopped
3 cups uncooked long-grain rice
1 qt. pizza sauce
3 cups shredded cheese, your choice of flavor
1 cup cottage cheese, *optional*
4 cups water

1. Place ground beef and chopped onion in a non-stick skillet. Brown and then drain.
2. Mix all ingredients in slow cooker.
3. Cover and cook on High for 6 hours, or until the rice is tender.

Granny's Delight

Anna B. Stoltzfus
Honey Brook, PA

Makes 5 servings

Prep Time: 20 minutes
Cooking Time: 1½ hours
Ideal slow cooker size: 6-qt.

1 lb. ground beef
1 small onion, chopped
3 cups dry macaroni
1 cup shredded cheddar cheese
4 cups spaghetti sauce, your favorite packaged *or* homemade
½ cup water

1. Brown beef with chopped onion in a non-stick skillet. Drain.
2. Spray interior of slow cooker with non-stick cooking spray. Place all ingredients into slow cooker and fold together gently.
3. Cover and cook on High for 1½ hours, or until macaroni is tender but not mushy.

Variation: Add ½ tsp. salt, ¼-½ tsp. pepper, according to your taste preference, and 2 cloves minced garlic.
— **Karen Waggoner**
Joplin, MO

Yumazetta

Andrea Cunningham
Arlington, KS

Makes 8 servings

Prep Time: 15 minutes
Cooking Time: 3-5 hours
Ideal slow cooker size: 4- to 6-qt.

1 lb. ground beef
8 ozs. shredded cheese, your choice of flavors
1 onion, diced
10¾-oz. can cream of mushroom soup
12-oz. can diced tomatoes, undrained

1. Brown ground beef in a non-stick skillet. Drain.
2. Combine all ingredients in your slow cooker.
3. Cook on Low 3-5 hours, or until heated through.
4. Serve over cooked pasta.

Here's a real time-saver from our house: Brown large quantities (10 lbs.) of ground beef, seasoned with onion, basil, and oregano to taste. Drain and cool. Freeze in pint freezer containers. The meat is readily available with no prep time or cleanup need when preparing a slow cooker recipe or casserole that calls for browned ground beef.
Dale and Shari Mast, Harrisonburg, VA

Easy Crock Taco Filling

Joanne Good
Wheaton, IL

Makes 4-6 servings

Prep Time: 20 minutes
Cooking Time: 6-8 hours
Ideal slow cooker size: 4-qt.

1 large onion, chopped
1 lb. ground beef
2 15-oz. cans chili beans
15-oz. can Santa Fe corn,
  or Mexican, *or* Fiesta,
  corn
3/4 cup water

Optional ingredients:
1/4 tsp. cayenne pepper
1/2 tsp. garlic powder

1. Brown ground beef and chopped onion in a non-stick skillet. Drain.
2. Mix all ingredients together in the slow cooker, blending well.
3. Cover and cook on Low for 6-8 hours.

Tips:
1. You may want to add more or less than 3/4 cup water to this recipe, depending upon how hot and fast your slow cooker cooks and how tight-fitting its lid is.
2. Serve in warmed, soft corn tortillas or hard taco shells. Or serve as a taco dip with plain corn tortilla chips.
3. Good garnishes for this taco filling include sour cream, guacamole, shredded cheese, diced tomatoes, shredded lettuce, and salsa.

Halloween Hash

Sharon Miller
Holmesville, OH

Makes 4 servings

Prep Time: 20-25 minutes
Cooking Time: 2-4 hours
Ideal slow cooker size: 2-qt.

1 lb. lean ground beef
1/2 cup onion, chopped
16-oz. can whole-kernel
  corn, drained
16-oz. can kidney beans,
  drained
16-oz. can diced tomatoes
1/2 cup shredded cheddar
  cheese, *optional*

1. Brown beef and onion in a non-stick skillet until no longer pink. Drain. Place mixture in your slow cooker.
2. Layer in all remaining ingredients except the cheese.
3. Cover and cook on Low 2-4 hours, or until thoroughly hot.
4. Serve as is, or over a bed of rice or noodles. Sprinkle each serving with cheese, if you wish.

Easy Beef Tortillas

Karen Waggoner
Joplin, MO

Makes 6 servings

Prep Time: 20 minutes
Cooking Time: 1 1/2-3 hours
Ideal slow cooker size: 4-qt.

1 1/2 lbs. ground beef
10 3/4-oz. can cream of
  chicken soup
2 1/2 cups crushed tortilla
  chips, *divided*
16-oz. jar salsa
1 1/2 cups (6 ozs.) shredded
  cheddar cheese

1. Brown ground beef in a non-stick skillet. Drain. Stir in soup.
2. Spray inside of cooker with non-stick cooking spray. Sprinkle 1 1/2 cups tortilla chips in slow cooker. Top with beef mixture, then salsa, and then cheese.
3. Cover and cook on High for 1 1/2 hours, or on Low for 3 hours.
4. Sprinkle with remaining chips just before serving.

Tortilla Casserole

Christie Detamore-
Hunsberger
Harrisonburg, VA

Makes 4 servings

Prep Time: 20 minutes
Cooking Time: 3¼-4¼ hours
Ideal slow cooker size: 3-qt.

4-6 white *or* whole wheat
 tortillas, *divided*
1 lb. ground beef
1 envelope dry taco
 seasoning
16-oz. can fat-free refried
 beans
1½ cups (6 ozs.) lowfat
 cheese of your choice,
 grated, *divided*
3-4 Tbsp. sour cream,
 optional

 1. Spray the inside of the
cooker with non-stick cooking
spray. Tear about ¾ of the
tortillas into pieces and line
the sides and bottom of the
slow cooker.
 2. Brown the ground beef
in a non-stick skillet. Drain.
Return to skillet and mix in
taco seasoning.
 3. Layer refried beans,
browned and seasoned meat,
1 cup cheese, and sour cream
if you wish, over tortilla
pieces.
 4. Place remaining tortilla
pieces on top. Sprinkle with
remaining cheese.
 5. Cover and cook on Low
3-4 hours.

Tamale Casserole

Mamie Christopherson
Rio Rancho, NM

Makes 6-8 servings

Prep Time: 10 minutes
Cooking Time: 5-7 hours
Ideal slow cooker size: 4-qt.

2 lbs. frozen meatballs
28-oz. can chopped
 tomatoes
1 cup yellow cornmeal
14- to 16-oz. can cream-
 style corn
1 cup chopped stuffed
 green olives
½ tsp. chili powder,
 optional

 1. Microwave frozen meatballs for 4 minutes on Power
3, or until thawed. Place in
slow cooker.
 2. Combine remaining
ingredients in a mixing bowl.
Pour over meatballs and mix
well.
 3. Cover and cook on High
1 hour. Turn to Low and cook
4-6 hours. Check after 4
hours of cooking. The casserole is finished when it
reaches a "loaf" consistency.

Stuffed Ground
Beef

Mary B. Sensenig
New Holland, PA

Makes 4 servings

Prep Time: 10 minutes
Cooking Time: 4-6 hours
Ideal slow cooker size: 4-qt.

2 cups ground beef
2 cups cabbage, shredded
salt and pepper to taste
2 cups bread filling
2 cups tomato juice

 1. Brown ground beef in a
non-stick skillet. Drain.
 2. Spray the inside of the
cooker with non-stick cooking
spray. Layer ingredients in
slow cooker in this order:
ground beef, cabbage, salt
and pepper, bread filling.
 3. Pour tomato juice over
top.
 4. Cook on Low 4-6 hours,
or until cabbage is just tender.

German Dinner

Audrey L. Kneer
Williamsfield, IL

Makes 6 servings

Prep Time: 15-20 minutes
Cooking Time: 4-8 hours
Ideal slow cooker size:
   4- to 5-qt.

1 lb. lean ground beef
32-oz. bag sauerkraut,
   drained
1 small green bell pepper,
   chopped fine
2 11½-oz. cans vegetable
   juice
½ cup chopped celery

1. Brown ground beef in non-stick skillet. Drain.
2. Combine all ingredients in slow cooker.
3. Cover and cook on High 1 hour, then on Low 3-7 hours, or until vegetables are done to your liking.

Ground Beef Veggie Casserole

Mary B. Sensenig
New Holland, PA

Makes 6-8 servings

Prep Time: 15-20 minutes
Cooking Time: 4 hours
Ideal slow cooker size:
   4- to 5-qt.

1½ lbs. ground beef
half a medium-sized
   onion, sliced
2 10-oz. pkgs. petite mixed
   vegetables
1 cup tomato juice
8 ozs. cheese, your choice,
   shredded

1. Brown ground beef and onion in a non-stick skillet. Drain.
2. Place browned mixture in slow cooker. Stir in vegetables. Pour tomato juice over top.
3. Cover and cook on Low for 4 hours, or until the veggies are done to your liking.
4. Stir in cheese during the last hour of cooking.

Zucchini Hot Dish

Sharon Wantland
Menomonee Falls, WI

Makes 4 servings

Prep Time: 15-20 minutes
Cooking Time: 2-3 hours
Ideal slow cooker size: 1½-qt.

1 lb. ground beef
1 small onion, chopped,
   optional
salt and pepper to taste
4-5 6"-long zucchini, sliced
10¾-oz. can cream of
   mushroom soup
1-2 cups shredded cheddar
   cheese

1. Brown ground beef with onions, if you wish, along with salt and pepper in a non-stick skillet until crumbly. Drain.
2. Layer zucchini and beef mixture alternately in slow cooker.
3. Top with soup. Sprinkle with cheese.
4. Cover and cook on Low 2-3 hours, or until the zucchini is done to your liking.

Green Bean, Potato, and Ground Beef Meal

Alice Miller, Stuarts Draft, VA

Makes 4-6 servings

Prep Time: 15 minutes
Cooking Time: 4-6 hours
Ideal slow cooker size: 5-qt.

1 lb. ground beef
1/2-1 tsp. salt, according to your taste preference
1/4-1/2 tsp. black pepper, according to your taste preference
1 qt. canned green beans, undrained
4 large potatoes, cut into 1″ chunks
1 cup chopped onions, *optional*

1. In a medium-sized non-stick skillet, brown ground beef until no longer pink. Drain. Add salt and pepper. Set aside.
2. Pour undrained green beans into slow cooker. Top with potatoes, onions if you wish, and then the ground beef.
3. Cover and cook on High 4-6 hours, or until the vegetables are tender.

Variation: In a mixing bowl, combine 2 10³/4-oz. cans cream of mushroom soup and 1/2 cup water until smooth. Pour over the layered ingredients, after completing Step 2.

— **Jena Hammond**
Traverse City, MI

Potato-Beef-and Beans

Vera Martin
East Earl, PA

Makes 6 servings

Prep Time: 15-20 minutes
Cooking Time: 3 hours
Ideal slow cooker size: 4-qt.

1 lb. ground beef *or* turkey, *divided*
1 tsp. onion salt, celery salt, *or both, divided*
15¹/2-oz. can kidney beans, undrained, *divided*
4 potatoes, French-fry cut, *divided*
26-oz. can tomato soup

1. Layer half of all ingredients—except the tomato soup—into the slow cooker in the order listed.
2. Repeat the layers. Pour tomato soup over all.
3. Cover and cook on High 3 hours, or until the potatoes are tender.
4. Stir before serving.

Variation: Mix 1-2 Tbsp. chili powder, depending upon your taste preference, with the tomato soup in Step 2.

Ground Beef Hot Dish

Tracey Hanson Schramel
Windom, MN

Makes 3-4 servings

Prep Time: 15 minutes
Cooking Time: 6-8 hours
Ideal slow cooker size: 3-qt.

1 lb. ground beef
small onion, chopped
4-5 medium-sized potatoes, sliced
1/2 tsp. salt, *optional*
14¹/2-oz. can mixed vegetables, undrained
10³/4-oz. can cream of chicken soup

1. Brown ground beef and onion in a non-stick skillet. Drain.
2. Spray interior of cooker with non-stick cooking spray. Place all ingredients in slow cooker. Stir together gently until well mixed.
3. Cover and cook on Low for 6-8 hours, or until the potatoes are tender.

Variation: Instead of a can of mixed vegetables, use a 10³/4-oz. can undiluted beef vegetable soup. And instead of the salt, add 1 envelope dry onion soup mix.

— **Gloria Julien**
Gladstone, MI

Layered Ground Beef Casserole

Denise Nickel
Goessel, KS

Makes 4-6 servings

Prep Time: 45 minutes
Cooking Time: 6-8 hours
Ideal slow cooker size: 4-qt.

1½ lbs. ground beef
3 large potatoes, cut into 1" chunks
16-oz. pkg. frozen peas
2-3 carrots, sliced
1 medium-sized onion, sliced, *optional*
1 rib celery, diced, *optional*
10¾-oz. can tomato soup
1 soup-can of water

1. Brown ground beef in a non-stick skillet. Drain. Set aside.
2. Spray inside of cooker with non-stick cooking spray. Layer all ingredients in slow cooker in this order: potato chunks, peas, carrot slices, onion slices and celery dice, if you wish, and browned ground beef.
3. Mix tomato soup and water together in a bowl until smooth. Pour over all other ingredients.
4. Cover and cook on Low 6-8 hours, or until vegetables are tender.

Easy Meat Loaf

Karen Waggoner
Joplin, MO

Makes 5-6 servings

Prep Time: 5 minutes
Cooking Time: 2 hours
Ideal slow cooker size:
3- to 4-qt.

2 lbs. ground beef, *or* turkey
6¼-oz. pkg. stuffing mix for beef, plus seasoning
2 eggs, beaten
½ cup ketchup, *divided*

1. Mix beef or turkey, dry stuffing, eggs, and ¼ cup ketchup. Shape into an oval loaf.
2. Place in slow cooker. Pour remaining ketchup over top.
3. Cover and cook on High for 2 hours.

Meat Loaf

Becky Gehman
Bergton, VA

Makes 6-8 servings

Prep Time: 10 minutes
Cooking Time: 2-6 hours
Ideal slow cooker size: 3-qt.

2 lbs. ground beef
½ cup cracker crumbs
1-2 tsp. onion powder
¼ cup ketchup

1. Combine ground beef, cracker crumbs, and onion powder. Form into a loaf. Place in your slow cooker.
2. Spread ketchup over top of meat loaf.
3. Cover and cook on Low for 4-6 hours, or on High for 2 hours.

Tips:
1. You may mix all or half the ketchup into the meat loaf.
2. Remove the cooked meat loaf from the cooker with a slotted spoon, and keep it warm on a platter.
Pour the drippings from the slow cooker into a non-stick skillet. Turn the burner to medium and whisk 2 Tbsp. flour into the drippings until smooth.
Add a beef bouillon cube and stir until the cube is dissolved and the drippings thicken. Serve the gravy with the sliced meat loaf.

Amazing Meat Loaf

Sara Kinsinger
Stuarts Draft, VA
Miriam Nolt
New Holland, PA
Ruth Zendt
Mifflintown, PA
Karen Ceneviva
New Haven, CT

Makes 8 servings

Prep Time: 15 minutes
Cooking Time: 2-8 hours
Ideal slow cooker size: 4-qt.

1/2 **cup ketchup,** *divided*
2 **lbs. ground beef**
2 **eggs**
2/3 **cup dry quick oats**
1 **envelope dry onion soup mix**

1. Reserve 2 Tbsp. ketchup. Combine ground beef, eggs, dry oats, soup mix, and remaining ketchup. Shape into loaf. Place in slow cooker.
2. Top with remaining ketchup.
3. Cover and cook on Low for 6-8 hours or on High for 2-4 hours.

Tip: Chill leftovers, and then slice for sandwiches.

Beef Barbecue

Anna B. Stoltzfus
Honey Brook, PA

Makes 10 servings

Prep Time: 15 minutes
Cooking Time: 2 1/2 hours
Ideal slow cooker size: 4-qt.

2 **lbs. ground beef**
2 **small onions, chopped**
2 **Tbsp. Worcestershire sauce**
1 1/2 **cups ketchup**
4 **Tbsp. brown sugar**
1 **cup water**

1. Brown beef with onions in a large non-stick skillet, breaking up the chunks of meat with a wooden spoon as it cooks. Drain.
2. Place beef and onions into cooker. Add remaining ingredients and mix together thoroughly.
3. Cover and cook on Low for 2 1/2 hours.
4. Pile into sandwich rolls.

Italian Barbecue Sandwiches

Mary B. Sensenig
New Holland, PA

Makes 4 servings

Prep Time: 10 minutes
Cooking Time: 2-6 hours
Ideal slow cooker size: 3-qt.

1 **lb. ground beef**
1 **cup tomato sauce**
half an envelope dry spaghetti sauce mix
salt and pepper to taste
8 **ozs. Velveeta** *or* **American cheese, cubed**

1. In a non-stick skillet, brown ground beef. Drain.
2. Place meat in slow cooker. Stir in sauce and seasonings.
3. Cover and cook on Low 2-6 hours.
4. One hour before serving, stir in cheese.
5. Stir before serving over long rolls.

To remove meat loaf or other meats from your cooker, make foil handles to lift the food out. Use double strips of heavy foil to make 3 strips, each about 20″ x 3″. Crisscross them in the bottom of the pot and bring them up the sides in a spoke design before putting in the food.

John D. Allen
Rye, CO
Esther Lehman
Croghan, NY

Creamy Sloppy Joes

Clara Yoder Byler
Hartville, OH

Makes 8-10 servings

Prep Time: 30 minutes
Cooking Time: 2-3 hours
Ideal slow cooker size: 4-qt.

2 lbs. ground beef
1 onion, finely chopped
1/2 cup ketchup
1 tsp. Worcestershire sauce
10³/4-oz. can cream of
  mushroom soup
1 tsp. salt, *optional*

1. Brown ground beef and onion together in non-stick skillet. Drain.
2. Place in slow cooker. Stir in remaining ingredients.
3. Cook on High for 2-3 hours, or until heated through.
4. Serve in rolls.

Sloppy Joes

Rosalie D. Miller
Mifflintown, PA

Makes 8-10 servings

Prep Time: 10-15 minutes
Cooking Time: 3-8 hours
Ideal slow cooker size:
  3- to 4-qt.

3 lbs. ground beef
1 cup chopped onions
3 16-oz. cans Sloppy Joe
  Sauce
4 Tbsp. brown sugar
4 Tbsp. Worcestershire
  sauce

1. Brown ground beef and chopped onions in non-stick skillet. Drain, but don't lose the onion pieces while you're doing it.
2. Place beef-onion mixture in slow cooker.
3. Stir in remaining ingredients.
4. Cover and cook on Low for 6-8 hours, or on High for 3-4 hours.
5. Spoon mixture into hamburger buns to serve.

Party Meatball Subs

Tamara McCarthy
Pennsburg, PA

Makes 30 servings

Prep Time: 15 minutes
Cooking Time: 8-10 hours
Ideal slow cooker size:
  8- to 10-qt.

10-lb. bag prepared
  meatballs
1 large onion, sliced
10 good-sized fresh
  mushrooms, sliced
2 26-oz. jars spaghetti
  sauce, your choice of
  flavors
2 cloves garlic, minced
1 lb. grated mozzarella
  cheese, *optional*

1. Combine all ingredients except the cheese in your slow cooker. Stir well to coat the meatballs with sauce.
2. Cover and cook on Low 8-10 hours, stirring occasionally throughout cooking time to mix juices.
3. Serve in hoagie rolls and sprinkle mozzarella cheese over top, if you wish.

Tip: This makes a lot of meatball subs! The recipe also works if you reduce the ingredients by half, or even make only quarter of the amounts that are called for.

Tangy Meatballs

Lucy O'Connell
Goshen, MA

Makes 12 main dish servings

Prep Time: 10 minutes
Cooking Time: 6-8 hours
Ideal slow cooker size:
  5- to 6-qt.

3 lbs. Swedish-style
  meatballs (frozen is fine)
16-oz. can whole berry
  cranberry sauce
18-oz. bottle barbecue
  sauce
1/2 cup spicy prepared
  mustard

1. Place meatballs in slow
cooker.
2. Combine remaining
ingredients in a bowl; then
pour over meatballs.
3. Cover and cook on Low
6-8 hours.

*Tip: You can serve this as an
appetizer, or as a main dish
served over rice.*

Sweet and Sour Meatballs

Charlotte Shaffer
East Earl, PA
Michele Ruvola
Selden, NY
Velma Sauder
Leola, PA

Makes 8-10 servings

Prep Time: 15 minutes
Cooking Time: 2 hours
Ideal slow cooker size:
  3- to 4-qt.

2 lbs. precooked meatballs
1 cup grape jelly
2 cups cocktail sauce

1. Place precooked meat-
balls in your slow cooker.
2. In a medium-sized bowl,
mix jelly and cocktail sauce
together with a whisk (it will
be a little lumpy).
3. Pour jelly and cocktail
sauce over meatballs. Stir
well.
4. Cook on High 1-2 hours,
or until the sauce is heated
through.
5. Turn heat to Low until
you're ready to serve.

Fruity Meatballs

Donna Lantgen
Chadron, NE

Makes 8-10 servings

Preparation time: 5-10 minutes
Cooking time: 4-5 hours
Ideal slow cooker size: 4-qt.

2 lbs. frozen meatballs
1 cup brown sugar
16-oz. can crushed
  pineapple with juice

1. Combine ingredients in
slow cooker.
2. Cover and cook on Low
4-5 hours. If you're home
and able, stir every 2 hours.

Tangy Cranberry Meatballs

Char Hagner
Montague, MI

Makes 4 servings

Prep Time: 10 minutes
Cooking Time: 3-4 hours
Ideal slow cooker size: 3-qt.

1 lb. frozen prepared
  meatballs
12-oz. bottle chili sauce
16-oz. can jellied cranberry
  sauce
1/2 cup brown sugar

1. Place meatballs in slow cooker.
2. In a mixing bowl, combine chili sauce, cranberry sauce, and brown sugar, breaking up the cranberry sauce as well as you can. Pour over the meatballs.
3. Cover and cook on Low 3-4 hours.

Variation: Add 1 Tbsp. lemon juice to Step 2.
— Lena Mae Janes
Lane, KS

Tip: You can serve this as an appetizer (with toothpicks) or as a main dish over rice, pasta, or mashed potatoes.

Cranberry Meatballs

Mary Ann Wasick
West Allis, WI

Makes 5-6 servings

Prep Time: 5-10 minutes
Cooking Time: 2-4 hours
Ideal slow cooker size: 4-qt.

1 medium-sized onion,
  finely chopped
2 Tbsp. butter
16-oz. can jellied cranberry
  sauce
16-oz. pkg. prepared frozen
  beef or turkey meatballs
  (approx. 32)
1 tsp. dried orange peel

1. In small saucepan, saute onion in butter.
2. Stir cranberry sauce into saucepan. Heat on low until melted.
3. Combine all ingredients in slow cooker.
4. Cover and cook on Low 2-4 hours.

Sweet Cranberry Meatballs

F. Elaine Asper, Norton, OH

Makes 6 entrée servings,
or 18-20 appetizers

Prep Time: 15 minutes
Cooking Time: 2-6 hours
Ideal slow cooker size: 4-qt.

50 meatballs, about 1 1/2
  lbs.
1 cup brown gravy, from a
  jar, *or* made from a mix
1 cup whole-berry
  cranberry sauce
2 Tbsp. heavy cream
2 tsp. Dijon mustard

1. Put meatballs in slow cooker.
2. Mix remaining ingredients in a bowl. Pour over meatballs.
3. Cover and cook on High 2-3 hours or on Low 5-6 hours.

Easy Meatballs

Carlene Horne, Bedford, NH

Makes 10-12 servings

Prep Time: *7 minutes*
Cooking Time: *4-5 hours*
Ideal slow cooker size: *5-qt.*

2 10¾-oz. cans cream of
    mushroom soup
2 8-oz. pkgs. cream cheese,
    softened
4-oz. can sliced
    mushrooms, undrained
1 cup milk
2-3 lbs. frozen meatballs

1. Combine soup, cream
cheese, mushrooms, and milk
in slow cooker.
2. Add meatballs. Stir.
3. Cover. Cook on Low 4-5
hours.
4. Serve over noodles.

Meatballs With Chili

Colleen Konetzni
Rio Rancho, NM

Makes 8 servings

Prep Time: *10 minutes*
Cooking Time: *8 hours*
Ideal slow cooker size: *5-qt.*

2 lbs. frozen beef
    meatballs
16-oz. jar 505 green chili
    sauce, *or* any other good
    green chili sauce
chili-sauce jar of water

1. Place frozen meatballs
in slow cooker.
2. In a mixing bowl, com-
bine green chili sauce and
water.
3. Pour sauce and water
over meatballs.
4. Cover and cook on Low
8 hours.

*Tip: This is good as a main
dish served with flour tortillas.
Or put out toothpicks and serve
the meatballs as party food.*

A Tip —

   If you wait until you
have all your work done,
you will never have com-
pany. Guests don't usually
care about what's undone
anyway.

My Norwegian Meatballs

Mamie Christopherson
Rio Rancho, NM

Makes 10-12 servings

Prep Time: *5 minutes*
Cooking Time: *45 minutes*
Ideal slow cooker size: *3-qt.*

2-2½-lb. pkg. frozen
    meatballs
2 or 3 10¾-oz. cans cream
    of mushroom soup,
    depending upon how
    saucy you'd like the
    finished dish to be
12-oz. can evaporated milk
1½ cups sour cream
1 cup beef broth
1 tsp. dill weed, *optional*

1. Lay frozen meatballs in
a long, microwave-safe dish
and microwave on High for 4
minutes.
2. Meanwhile, in a large
mixing bowl, combine all
other ingredients.
3. Place meatballs in slow
cooker. Cover with soup mixture.
4. Cover and cook on High
45 minutes (sauce should not
boil).
5. Turn to Low. Keep
warm until serving time.

Tips:
*1. Serve these as an appe-
tizer (with toothpicks), or as a
main dish with mashed potatoes or noodles.*
*2. Substitute other herbs for
the dill weed.*

Meatballs with Cream Sauce

Karen Stoltzfus
Alto, MI

Makes 6-8 servings

Prep Time: 5 minutes
Cooking Time: 3-4 hours
Ideal slow cooker size: 2-qt.

1½ lbs. frozen fully cooked meatballs
8-oz. pkg. cream cheese, softened
10¾-oz. can cream of mushroom soup
½ cup water

1. Place meatballs in slow cooker.
2. In a mixing bowl, combine cream cheese and cream of mushroom soup until well mixed. Add water and stir in thoroughly.
3. Pour sauce over meatballs.
4. Cover. Cook on High for 1 hour; then turn to Low for 2-3 hours. (If meatballs are thawed, cook only on Low 2-3 hours.)

Meatball Sauce

Norma Grieser
Clarksville, MI

Makes 10 servings

Prep Time: 10 minutes
Cooking Time: 3-8 hours
Ideal slow cooker size: 6-qt.

32-oz. bottle of ketchup
16 ozs. ginger ale
3 Tbsp. brown sugar
3 Tbsp. vinegar
3 Tbsp. Worcestershire sauce, *optional*
3 lbs. fully cooked meatballs

1. Combine sauce ingredients in slow cooker. Cover, turn to High, and bring to a simmer.
2. Gently spoon in meatballs, being careful not to splash yourself with the hot sauce.
3. Cover and simmer 3-4 hours on Low if the meatballs are thawed; 6-8 hours if they're frozen when you put them in.

Tip: You can use little smokies instead of meatballs. In fact, this sauce is good on most meats you grill or barbecue. To serve as a sauce for grilled meat, follow Step 1; then brush on grilled meat.

Porcupine Meatballs

Esther J. Yoder
Hartville, OH
Jean Binns Smith
Bellefonte, PA

Makes 8 servings

Prep Time: 30 minutes
Cooking Time: 2-4 hours
Ideal slow cooker size: 4-qt.

1 lb. ground beef
¼ cup uncooked long-grain rice
¼-½ tsp. salt, *optional*
10½-oz. can tomato soup, *divided*
2 Tbsp. shortening, *or* butter
1 cup water

1. In a medium-sized bowl, mix ground beef, rice, salt, and ¼ cup of tomato soup. Shape into 1½" balls.
2. Brown the balls in 2 Tbsp. shortening or butter in a large non-stick skillet, being careful not to crowd them. (If your skillet is small, brown them in two batches.)
3. Place the browned meatballs in your slow cooker.
4. In the bowl, mix together 1 cup of water and the remaining tomato soup. Pour over meatballs.
5. Cover and cook on High 2-4 hours, or until the rice is fully cooked.

Meatball Stew

Beth Peachey
Belleville, PA

Makes 6 servings

Prep Time: 15 minutes
Cooking Time: 6-8 hours
Ideal slow cooker size: 4-qt.

2 lbs. meatballs, frozen *or* homemade
$10^{1/2}$-oz. can tomato soup
1/4 cup water
1 cup carrots, sliced
1 onion, sliced
2 lbs. potatoes, sliced

1. Brown meatballs in a large non-stick skillet, being careful not to crowd the skillet. Brown in two batches rather than pile them up or squeeze them in.

2. When the meatballs are browned, place them and the rest of the ingredients in your slow cooker. Stir together gently.

3. Cover and cook on low 6-8 hours, or until the vegetables are tender.

A Tip —

Write in your cookbook the date when you tried a particular recipe and whether or not you liked it. Develop a rating system for each recipe you try (Excellent, Good, Yummy, Okay). Write notes about what might be a good addition or deletion the next time you make it.

Pork Main Dishes

Honey Barbecue Pork Chops

Tamara McCarthy
Pennsburg, PA

Makes 8 servings

Prep Time: 15 minutes
Cooking Time: 6-8 hours
Ideal slow cooker size: 4-qt.

8 pork chops, *divided*
1 large onion, sliced,
  divided
1 cup barbecue sauce
1/3 cup honey

1. Place one layer of pork chops in your slow cooker.
2. Arrange a proportionate amount of sliced onions over top.
3. Mix barbecue sauce and honey together in a small bowl. Spoon a proportionate amount of sauce over the chops.
4. Repeat the layers.

5. Cover and cook on Low 3-4 hours.
6. If the sauce barely covers the chops, flip them over at this point. If they're well covered, simply allow them to cook another 3-4 hours on Low, or until they're tender but the meat is not dry.

Pork Chops with Tomato Sauce

Margaret H. Moffitt
Bartlett, TN

Makes 4-6 servings

Prep Time: 25 minutes
Cooking Time: 3-7 hours
Ideal slow cooker size: 3-qt.

4 thickly-cut pork chops
1 medium-sized onion,
  sliced *or* **chopped**
1/2 cup ketchup
1/4 cup brown sugar

1/2 tsp. chili powder
1/2 cup water

1. Place pork chops in bottom of slow cooker. Top with onions.
2. In a bowl, mix ketchup, brown sugar, chili powder and water together. Spoon sauce over all. (If the chops need to be stacked in order to fit into your cooker, make sure to top each one with sauce.)
3. Cover and cook on High 3-4 hours, or on Low for up to 6-7 hours, or until meat is tender but not dry.

Tangy Pork Chops

Barbara Gautcher
Harrisonburg, VA

Makes 4-6 servings

Prep Time: 15 minutes
Cooking Time: 4-5 hours
Ideal slow cooker size: 3-qt.

seasoning salt to taste
pepper to taste
4 thickly cut pork loin
   chops, *or* 6 thinner
   chops
1 cup grape jelly
1 bottle prepared chili
   sauce

1. Rub pork chops with seasoning salt and pepper on both sides. Place chops in slow cooker.
2. In a small bowl, combine jelly and chili sauce. Spoon sauce over chops. (If the chops need to be stacked in order to fit into your cooker, make sure to top each one with sauce.)
3. Cover and cook on Low for 4-5 hours, or until meat is tender but not dry.

A Tip —

When sautéing or frying, turn a metal colander or strainer upside down over the skillet. This allows steam to escape and keeps fat from spattering.

Pork Chops with Suit-Yourself Sauce

Clara Newswanger
Gordonville, PA

Makes 4-6 servings

Prep Time: 15 minutes
Cooking Time: 4-5 hours
Ideal slow cooker size: 4-qt.

4-6 pork chops, *divided*
1 tsp. salt
1/4 tsp. pepper
2 Tbsp. olive oil
1/2 cup water
10³/4-oz. can condensed
   cream soup of your
   choice
1 cup barbecue sauce,
   optional

1. Season chops with salt and pepper. Brown on both sides in oil in a hot non-stick skillet. Brown the chops in batches rather than crowding the skillet. As they finish, place a layer of them in the slow cooker.
2. Meanwhile, combine water, soup, and sauce if you wish, in a bowl. Pour a proportionate amount of sauce over the first layer of chops. Add the next layer of chops and pour remaining sauce over top.
3. Cover and cook on Low 4-5 hours, or until chops are tender but not dry.

Creamy Pork Chops

Judi Manos
West Islip, NY

Makes 6 servings

Prep Time: 5-7 minutes
Cooking Time: 4-5 hours
Ideal slow cooker size: 3-qt.

10³/4-oz. can 98% fat-free
   cream of chicken soup
1 onion, chopped
3 Tbsp. ketchup
2 tsp. Worcestershire sauce
6 whole pork chops,
   boneless *or* bone-in,
   divided

1. Mix soup and chopped onions together in a bowl. Stir in ketchup and Worcestershire sauce. Pour half of mixture into slow cooker.
2. Place pork chops in slow cooker. If you have to stack them, spoon a proportionate amount of the remaining sauce over the first layer of meat.
3. Add the rest of the chops. Cover with the remaining sauce.
4. Cover and cook on Low 4-5 hours, or until meat is tender but not dry.

Slow-Cooked Pork Chops

Kimberly Burkholder
Millerstown, PA

Makes 6-8 servings

Prep Time: 15 minutes
Cooking Time: 3-8 hours
Ideal slow cooker size: 3-qt.

1/2 cup flour
1 tsp. salt
1/2 tsp. garlic powder
6-8 lean pork chops, *divided*
10³/4-oz. can chicken and rice soup, *divided*

1. Mix together flour, salt, and garlic powder in a shallow dish. Dredge pork chops in mixture.
2. Heat a non-stick skillet until hot. Then place several chops in skillet and brown on both sides. Do this in batches, rather than crowding the skillet. As you finish browning the chops, place one layer in the slow cooker.
3. Top with a proportionate amount of the soup. Finish browning the meat, add it to the cooker, and top with the remaining soup.
4. Cover and cook on Low 6-8 hours or High 3-4 hours.

Smothered Pork Chops

Marilyn Mowry
Irving, TX

Makes 4 servings

Prep Time: 10 minutes
Cooking Time: 6-8 hours
Ideal slow cooker size: 2-qt.

4 pork chops, center cut
10³/4-oz. can cream of mushroom soup
1 cup milk
2 Tbsp. dry sherry
2 green onions, chopped

1. Place chops in slow cooker.
2. Mix remaining ingredients in a bowl. Pour over chops.
3. Cover and cook on Low 6-8 hours, or until meat is tender but not dry.

Variation: Add salt and pepper to taste to chops before placing in cooker.

Pork Chops Hong Kong

Michelle High
Fredericksburg, PA

Makes 6-8 servings

Prep Time: 65 minutes
Cooking Time: 3-6 hours
Ideal slow cooker size:
  3- to 4-qt.

10-oz. bottle soy sauce
6-8 Tbsp. sugar
6-8 pork chops
10³/4-oz. can cream of mushroom soup

1. Combine soy sauce and sugar. Pour over chops. Marinate 60 minutes.
2. Transfer pork chops to slow cooker. (Discard marinade.)
3. In a bowl, stir soup until creamy. Spoon over chops.
4. Cover and cook on Low for 6 hours or on High for 3 hours.

Spicy Pork Chops

Cynthia Morris
Grottoes, VA

Makes 4 servings

Prep Time: 5 minutes
Cooking Time: 6-8 hours
Ideal slow cooker size: 4-qt.

4 frozen pork chops
1 cup Italian salad
  dressing
1/2 cup brown sugar
1/3 cup prepared spicy
  mustard

1. Place pork chops in slow cooker.
2. Mix remaining 3 ingredients together in a bowl. Pour over chops.
3. Cover and cook on Low 6-8 hours, or until meat is tender but not dry.

Variation: You can substitute chicken breasts for pork chops.

Tip: Check the meat after cooking for 4 hours to make sure the meat is not getting dry or over-cooking.

Pork Chops and Apple Slices

Dorothy VanDeest
Memphis, TN
Dale Peterson
Rapid City, SD

Makes 4 servings

Prep Time: 15 minutes
Cooking Time: 6-8 hours
Ideal slow cooker size:
  3- to 4-qt.

4 pork loin chops, about
  1" thick, well trimmed
2 medium-sized apples,
  peeled, cored, and sliced
1 tsp. butter *or* margarine
1/4 tsp. nutmeg, *optional*
salt and pepper to taste

1. Heat a non-stick skillet until hot. Add chops and brown quickly. Turn and brown on the other side.
2. While chops are browning, place half the sliced apples in the slow cooker. Top with 2 chops. Repeat the layers.
3. Dot with butter and sprinkle with nutmeg. Sprinkle generously with salt and pepper.
4. Cover and cook on Low 6-8 hours, or until meat is tender but not dry.

Variation: Chop one small onion fine. Sprinkle half the onion pieces over the first layer of chops, and the rest of it over the second layer of chops.
  — Kate Johnson
  Rolfe, IA

Barbecued Pork Chops

Sandy Osborn
Iowa City, IA

Makes 8 servings

Prep Time: 10-15 minutes
Cooking Time: 7-8 hours
Ideal slow cooker size: 4-qt.

8 (5 ozs. each) center-cut
  pork chops, 1/2" thick
1/4 tsp. pepper
1/2 cup thick-and-spicy
  honey barbecue sauce
14 1/2-oz. can no-salt-added
  stewed tomatoes
10-oz. package frozen
  vegetable blend

1. Trim fat from the pork chops, and then sprinkle them with pepper.
2. Spray a large non-stick skillet with cooking spray. Set stove burner to medium-high.
3. When the pan is hot, add pork chops in a single layer. Do not crowd the pan or the chops will not brown quickly. Brown on both sides.
4. Spray interior of slow cooker with cooking spray. Place a layer of pork chops in the slow cooker.
5. While the chops are browning, combine barbecue sauce, tomatoes, and frozen vegetable blend in a bowl, stirring well.
6. Pour some of the mixture over the first layer of chops. When you've added the rest of the chops, pour

the rest of the sauce with vegetables over top.

7. Cover and cook on High 1 hour.

8. Reduce heat to Low and cook 6-7 hours, or until meat is tender but not dry.

Slow-Cooked Pork Chops with Green Beans

Vonnie Oyer
Hubbard, OR

Makes 3-4 servings

Prep Time: 10 minutes
Cooking Time: 4-8 hours
Ideal slow cooker size: 3-qt.

3-4 boneless pork chops
salt and pepper to taste
2 cups green beans, frozen
 or fresh
2 slices bacon, cut up
1/2 cup water
1 Tbsp. lemon juice

1. Place pork chops in bottom of slow cooker. Salt and pepper to taste.

2. Top with remaining ingredients in the order listed.

3. Cover and cook on Low 4-8 hours, or until meat and green beans are tender but not dry or over-cooked.

Hassle-Free Pork Chops

Cathy Sellers, Cedar Rapids, IA

Makes 4 servings

Prep Time: 15 minutes
Cooking Time: 3-8 hours
Ideal slow cooker size:
 3- to 4-qt.

4 pork chops
1 small onion, sliced
4 potatoes, peeled and
 sliced
2 10³/4-oz. cans tomato
 soup
1/2 cup milk

1. Heat a non-stick skillet on the stove-top until hot. Add chops and brown on both sides. Do in batches rather than crowd the skillet.

2. Place chops in slow cooker. Brown onions in skillet drippings, and then place over top of chops.

3. Add layer of potatoes to the cooker.

4. In a small bowl, combine soup and milk, mixing well. Pour mixture over potatoes.

5. Cover and cook on Low 6-8 hours, or on High 3-4 hours, or until meat and potatoes are tender but not dry.

Variation: Add salt and pepper to taste to the chops as you place them in the slow cooker. And add salt and pepper to taste to the layer of sliced potatoes after you've placed them in the cooker.

Pork and Sweet Potatoes

Vera F. Schmucker
Goshen, IN

Makes 4 servings

Prep Time: 15 minutes
Cooking Time: 4-4¹/2 hours
Ideal slow cooker size: 4-qt.

4 pork loin chops
salt and pepper to taste
4 sweet potatoes, cut in
 large chunks
2 onions cut in quarters
1/2 cup apple cider

1. Place meat in bottom of slow cooker. Salt and pepper to taste.

2. Arrange sweet potatoes and onions over top of the pork.

3. Pour apple cider over all.

4. Cook on High 30 minutes and then on Low 3¹/2-4 hours, or until meat and vegetables are tender but not dry.

Pork Chops and Yams

Tamara McCarthy
Pennsburg, PA

Makes 4 servings

Prep Time: 15 minutes
Cooking Time: 6-7 hours
Ideal slow cooker size: 4-qt.

4-6 pork chops
16-oz. can yams, drained,
  or 3 medium-sized raw
  yams, peeled and sliced
10³/4-oz. can cream of
  mushroom soup
1/2 cup sour cream
1/4 cup water

1. In a non-stick skillet, brown pork chops over medium heat. Transfer to slow cooker.
2. Place yams over pork chops.
3. In a mixing bowl, combine condensed soup, sour cream, and water. Stir until well blended.
4. Pour sauce over yams and pork chops.
5. Cover and cook on Low 6-7 hours, or until meat and yams are tender but not dry.

Country Pork and Squash

Jean Halloran
Green Bay, WI

Makes 6 servings

Prep Time: 15 minutes
Cooking Time: 6-8 hours
Ideal slow cooker size: 5-qt.

6 boneless country-style
  pork ribs, trimmed of
  fat
2 medium-sized acorn
  squash
3/4 cup brown sugar
2 Tbsp. orange juice
3/4 tsp. Kitchen Bouquet
  browning and seasoning
  sauce

1. Place ribs on bottom of slow cooker.
2. Cut each squash in half. Remove seeds. Cut each half into 3 slices.
3. Place the squash slices over top of the ribs.
4. Combine remaining ingredients in a small bowl. Pour sauce over the ribs and squash.
5. Cover and cook on Low 6-8 hours, or until the meat is tender.
6. Serve 2 rings of squash with each pork rib.

Variation: Add 3/4 tsp. salt to Step 4.

Pork Chops and Rice

Donna Lantgen
Chadron, NE

Makes 4 servings

Prep Time: 5-10 minutes
Cooking Time: 6-8 hours
Ideal slow cooker size: 4-qt.

1¹/2 cups dry long-grain
  rice
2 cups water
4 pork chops
salt and pepper to taste
10³/4-oz. can cream of
  mushroom, *or* celery,
  soup
1 Tbsp. chicken or beef
  bouillon granules, *or*
  1 bouillon cube

1. Spray interior of cooker with non-stick cooking spray. Place rice and water in cooker and mix together well.
2. Place chops over top of rice. Sprinkle with salt and pepper.
3. In a small bowl, stir soup and bouillon together. Spoon over chops.
4. Cover and cook on Low 6-8 hours, or until meat and rice are tender but not dry.

Pork Chops with Sauerkraut

Char Hagner
Montague, MI

Makes 6 servings

Prep Time: 20 minutes
Cooking Time: 6-8 hours
Ideal slow cooker size: 5-qt.

6 pork chops
4 large potatoes, sliced
1 onion, chopped
1 qt. sauerkraut
1/2 cup apple juice

1. Heat a non-stick skillet over medium-high heat. Brown chops on each side. Brown in batches so as not to crowd the skillet.
2. While the chops are browning, place sliced potatoes and onion in the slow cooker.
3. Add browned chops. Top with sauerkraut. Pour apple juice over all.
4. Cover and cook on Low 6-8 hours.

Variations: Salt and pepper chops to taste after browning and before placing in cooker.

Pork Chops 'N Kraut

Heather Horst
Lebanon, PA

Makes 4 servings

Prep Time: 15 minutes
Cooking Time: 3-8 hours
Ideal slow cooker size: 4- to 5-qt.

2 14-oz. cans sauerkraut, rinsed and drained
1 large apple, unpeeled and chopped
4 medium red, *or* white, potatoes, quartered
1 large carrot, shredded
1 tsp. caraway seeds, *optional*
4 pork chops, fat trimmed

1. In slow cooker, mix together sauerkraut, apple, potatoes, carrot, and caraway seeds if you wish.
2. Place chops on top.
3. Cover and cook on Low 6-8 hours, or on High 3-4 hours, or until meat and potatoes are tender but not dry.

Pork Chops with Stuffing

Michelle High
Fredericksburg, PA

Makes 2 servings

Prep Time: 20 minutes
Cooking Time: 4-5 hours
Ideal slow cooker size: 4-qt.

4 slices bread, cubed
1 egg
1/4 cup finely chopped celery
1/4-1/2 tsp. salt
1/8 tsp. pepper
2 thickly cut pork chops
1 cup water

1. In a mixing bowl, combine bread, egg, celery, salt, and pepper.
2. Lay pork chops flat. Cut horizontally part-way through the meat, making a cut that is at least 1" deep. Spread open and fill with stuffing.
3. Pour water into slow cooker. Add chops.
4. Cover and cook on Low 4-5 hours, or until meat is tender but not dry.

Stuffed Pork Chops and Corn

Peggy Forsythe
Bartlett, TN

Makes 5-6 servings

Prep Time: 15 minutes
Cooking Time: 3-6 hours
Ideal slow cooker size:
    4- to 5-qt.

5-6 boneless pork chops
1 box stuffing mix for
    pork, prepared
14-oz. can whole corn,
    optional
10¾-oz. can cream of
    mushroom soup

1. Place pork chops in slow cooker. Spoon prepared stuffing mix over top of chops.
2. Spoon corn over stuffing. Pour soup over all—without adding water.
3. Cover and cook on Low 5-6 hours, or on High 3-4 hours, or until meat is tender but not dry.

A Tip —

   Allow cooked meat to stand for 10-15 minutes before slicing it, so that it can re-gather its juices.

Pork Chops and Stuffing with Curry

Mary Martins
Fairbank, IA

Makes 3-4 servings

Prep Time: 15 minutes
Cooking Time: 6-7 hours
Ideal slow cooker size:
    3- to 4-qt.

1 box stuffing mix
1 cup water
10¾-oz. can cream of
    mushroom soup
1 tsp., or more, curry
    powder, according to
    your taste preference
3-4 pork chops

1. Combine stuffing mix and water. Place half in bottom of slow cooker.
2. Combine soup and curry powder. Pour half over stuffing. Place pork chops on top.
3. Spread remaining stuffing over pork chops. Pour rest of soup on top.
4. Cover. Cook on Low 6-7 hours.
5. Serve with a tossed salad and a cooked vegetable.

Cranberry Pork Roast

Chris Peterson
Green Bay, WI
Joyce Kaut
Rochester, NY

Makes 6-8 servings

Prep Time: 5 minutes
Cooking Time: 6-8 hours
Ideal slow cooker size: 5-qt.

3-4-lb. pork roast
salt and pepper to taste
1 cup finely chopped
    cranberries
¼ cup honey
1 tsp. grated orange peel
½ tsp. ground nutmeg,
    optional
½ tsp. ground cloves,
    optional

1. Sprinkle roast with salt and pepper. Place in slow cooker.
2. Combine remaining ingredients in a bowl. Pour over roast.
3. Cover and cook on Low 6-8 hours, or until meat is tender.

Tip: If you can't find fresh cranberries, substitute with a 16-oz. can of either whole-berry or jellied cranberry sauce.

Cranberry Pork Loin

Annabelle Unternahrer
Shipshewana, IN

Makes 6-8 servings

Prep Time: 10 minutes
Cooking Time: 4-6 hours
Ideal slow cooker size:
*   5- to 6-qt.*

3-lb. boneless pork loin
16-oz. can jellied cranberry
    sauce
1/4 cup sugar
1/2 cup cranberry juice
1 tsp. dry mustard
1/4 tsp. ground cloves,
    optional

1. Place pork loin in slow cooker.
2. Combine remaining ingredients in a bowl. Pour sauce over pork.
3. Cover and cook on Low 4-6 hours, or until meat is tender.

Tip: To thicken the sauce, remove cooked meat to a platter and cover to keep warm. Mix 2 Tbsp. cornstarch with 2 Tbsp. water in a small bowl. Turn cooker to High.
*   Stir cornstarch/water mixture into simmering sauce. Continue stirring until it is thoroughly combined. Then allow sauce to simmer until it thickens, about 10 minutes. Stir occasionally to keep it from getting lumpy.*
*   Serve thickened sauce over or alongside pork slices.*

Fruited Pork

Jeanette Oberholtzer
Manheim, PA

Makes 6 servings

Prep Time: 10 minutes
Cooking Time: 4-6 hours
Ideal slow cooker size:
*   3- to 4-qt.*

2-lb. boneless pork loin
    roast
1/2 tsp. salt
1/4 tsp. pepper
1 1/2 cups mixed dried fruit
1/2 cup apple juice

1. Place pork in slow cooker. Sprinkle with salt and pepper.
2. Top with fruit. Pour apple juice over top.
3. Cover and cook on Low 4-6 hours, or until pork is tender.

Tender Pork Roast

Renee Baum
Chambersburg, PA
Mary Lynn Miller
Reinholds, PA

Makes 8 servings

Prep Time: 10 minutes
Cooking Time: 3-8 hours
Ideal slow cooker size: 5-qt.

3-lb. boneless pork roast,
    cut in half
8-oz. can tomato sauce
3/4 cup soy sauce
1/2 cup sugar
2 tsp. dry mustard

1. Place roast in slow cooker.
2. Combine remaining ingredients in a bowl. Pour over roast.
3. Cover and cook on Low 6-8 hours, or on High 3-4 hours, or until meat is tender but not dry.
4. Remove roast from slow cooker to a serving platter. Discard juices or thicken for gravy.

Tip: To thicken the juices, remove cooked roast to a platter and keep warm. Turn cooker to High.
*   Meanwhile, mix together 2 Tbsp. cornstarch and 2 Tbsp. water in a small bowl. When smooth, stir into bubbling juices. Continue stirring until thoroughly mixed in.*
*   Allow juices to simmer until thickened, about 10 minutes.*
*   Slice pork and serve juices over top or alongside.*

Home-Style Pork

Mary B. Sensenig
New Holland, PA

Makes 8-10 servings

Prep Time: 5 minutes
Cooking Time: 6-8 hours
Ideal slow cooker size: 4-qt.

4 lbs. boneless pork roast,
  cut into pieces
1 medium-sized onion,
  sliced
1 cup water
1/4 cup brown sugar
1/4 cup apple cider vinegar
3 tsp. prepared mustard

1. Place roast pieces in
slow cooker. Top with onion.
2. Pour water around roast
and onions.
3. In a bowl, blend
together last 3 ingredients.
Spoon over meat and onions.
4. Cover and cook on Low
6-8 hours, or until meat is
tender.

Variation: Add 3/4 tsp. salt and
1/4 tsp. pepper to Step 3.

Pork Roast

Kelly Bailey
Mechanicsburg, PA

Makes 8-10 servings

Prep Time: 5 minutes
Cooking Time: 6-12 hours
Ideal slow cooker size:
  4- to 6-qt.

medium-sized to large
  onion, sliced and *divided*
3-4-lb. pork roast
12-oz. can cola
salt and pepper

1. Layer 2/3 of the onions
in bottom of slow cooker,
reserving a few to place on
top of roast.
2. Place roast in cooker.
Pour cola over roast.
3. Season with salt and
pepper and top with remaining onion slices.
4. Cook on Low 6-12 hours
depending on size of roast,
until meat starts to fall apart.

Carolina Pot Roast

Jonathan Gehman
Harrisonburg, VA

Makes 3-4 servings

Prep Time: 20 minutes
Cooking Time: 3 hours
Ideal slow cooker size: 3-qt.

3 medium-large sweet
  potatoes, peeled and cut
  into 1" chunks
1/2 cup brown sugar
1-lb. pork roast
scant 1/4 tsp. cumin
salt to taste
water

1. Place sweet potatoes in
bottom of slow cooker.
Sprinkle brown sugar over
potatoes.
2. Heat non-stick skillet
over medium-high heat. Add
roast and brown on all sides.
Sprinkle meat with cumin
and salt while browning.
Place pork on top of potatoes.
3. Add an inch of water to
the cooker, being careful not
to wash the seasoning off the
meat.
4. Cover and cook on Low
3 hours, or until meat and
potatoes are tender but not
dry or mushy.

As-Basic-As-It-Gets Pork and Sauerkraut

Earnest Zimmerman
Mechanicsburg, PA

Makes 6-8 servings

Prep Time: 5 minutes
Cooking Time: 3-8 hours
Ideal slow cooker size:
   6- to 8-qt.

3-4 lb. pork roast
32-oz. bag, *or* 2 14½-oz.
   cans, sauerkraut, *divided*
salt and/or pepper,
   optional

1. Rinse pork roast; pat dry.
2. Place half the sauerkraut in bottom of slow cooker. Place roast on top.
3. Cover roast with remaining sauerkraut. Season with salt and/or pepper, if you wish.
4. Cover and cook on Low for 6-8 hours or on High 3-4 hours.

Variation: For added flavor, choose a crisp apple, core it, peel it or not, and slice it. Lay over seasoned sauerkraut at the end of Step 3. Crumble 1-2 Tbsp. brown sugar over top.
— **Ethel Mumaw**
Millersburg, OH

No Fuss Sauerkraut

Vera M. Kuhns
Harrisonburg, VA

Makes 12 servings

Prep Time: 7 minutes
Cooking Time: 4-5 hours
Ideal slow cooker size:
   7- to 8-qt.

3-lb. pork roast
3 2-lb. pkgs. sauerkraut
   (drain and discard juice
   from 1 pkg.)
2 apples, peeled and sliced
½ cup brown sugar
1 cup apple juice

1. Place meat in large slow cooker.
2. Place sauerkraut on top of meat.
3. Add apples and brown sugar. Add apple juice.
4. Cover. Cook on High 4-5 hours.
5. Serve with mashed potatoes.

Note: If your slow cooker isn't large enough to hold all the ingredients, cook one package of sauerkraut and half the apples, brown sugar, and apple juice in another cooker. Mix the ingredients of both cookers together before serving.

Savory Pork Roast

Eleya Raim
Oxford, IA

Makes 6 servings

Prep Time: 10 minutes
Cooking Time: 3-6 hours
Ideal slow cooker size:
   4-qt. oval

2-lb. pork roast
1 clove garlic, minced
1 medium-sized onion,
   sliced
1 pint sauerkraut, *or* more
   if you wish
1 tsp. caraway seed

1. If you have time, heat a non-stick skillet over medium-high heat. Place the roast in the hot pan and brown on all sides.
2. Place the roast, browned or not, in the slow cooker.
3. Add remaining ingredients in the order listed.
4. Cover and cook on High 3 hours, or on Low 4-6 hours, or until meat is tender but not dry.

Variation: Salt and pepper the roast before you place it in the cooker.

Pork and Sauerdogs

Leesa DeMartyn
Enola, PA

Makes 12-15 servings

Prep Time: 5 minutes
Cooking Time: 4½-12 hours
Ideal slow cooker size:
  5- to 6-qt.

5-lb. pork roast
32-oz. can sauerkraut,
  undrained
1 pkg. of 8 hot dogs

1. Place pork in slow cooker. Spoon sauerkraut over pork.
2. Cover and cook on Low 9½-11½ hours, or on High 4-5½ hours, or until meat is tender but not dry.
3. Lift roast onto a platter and, using a fork, separate the meat into small pieces.
4. Return pork to cooker and stir into sauerkraut.
5. Cut hot dogs into ½" slices and stir into pork and sauerkraut.
6. Cover and cook for an additional 30 minutes. Serve over a bed of mashed potatoes.

Shredded Pork

Cindy Krestynick
Glen Lyon, PA

Makes 6-8 servings

Prep Time: 10 minutes
Cooking Time: 4-10 hours
Ideal slow cooker size:
  4- to 5-qt.

3-4-lb. pork butt roast
1½ envelopes taco
  seasoning
3-5 cloves garlic, sliced,
  according to your taste
  preference
1 large onion, quartered
4-oz. can whole green
  chilies, drained
1 cup water

1. Place roast in slow cooker.
2. In a bowl, mix all remaining ingredients together. Spoon over meat in cooker.
3. Cover and cook on Low for 8-10 hours, or on High 4-6 hours, or until meat is tender but not dry.
4. Place pork on a platter and shred with 2 forks. Stir shredded meat back into sauce.
5. Serve in tortillas, topped with shredded lettuce, tomato, and sour cream, or over steamed rice.

North Carolina Barbecue

J. B. Miller
Indianapolis, IN

Makes 8-12 servings

Prep Time: 15 minutes
Cooking Time: 5-8 hours
Ideal slow cooker size:
  4- to 5-qt.

3-4-lb. pork loin, roast *or*
  shoulder
1 cup apple cider vinegar
¼ cup, plus 1 Tbsp.,
  prepared mustard
¼ cup, plus 1 Tbsp.,
  Worcestershire sauce
2 tsp. red pepper flakes

1. Trim fat from pork. Place in slow cooker.
2. In a bowl, mix remaining ingredients together. Spoon over meat.
3. Cover and cook on High 5 hours, or Low 8 hours, or until meat is tender but not dry.
4. Slice, or break meat apart, and serve drizzled with the cooking juices. If you use the meat for sandwiches, you'll have enough for 8-12 sandwiches.

Pork Barbecue

Marcia S. Myer
Manheim, PA

Makes 9-12 servings

Prep Time: 10 minutes
Cooking Time: 8-10 hours
Ideal slow cooker size: 4-qt.

3-4-lb. pork roast
16-oz. bottle hickory-
  smoked barbecue sauce
1 medium-large onion,
  chopped
1/8-1/4 tsp. ground cloves

1. Place meat in slow cooker.
2. Cover and cook on Low 6-8 hours, or until very tender.
3. Remove roast to platter. (Drain broth and save for a soup stock, or for making gravy.) Using two forks, shred the meat.
4. Return shredded meat to cooker. Stir in barbecue sauce, chopped onions, and cloves.
5. Cover and cook on Low 2 hours. Serve on sandwich rolls.

Variations:
Drop the ground cloves. Instead, use 1 envelope dry onion soup mix in Step 4.
And add a slice of cheese (your choice) on top of the pork barbecue in each sandwich, if you wish.

— Joan Miller
Wayland, IA

Slow-Cooked Pork Barbecue for a Group

Linda E. Wilcox
Blythewood, SC

Makes 20-24 servings

Prep Time: 15 minutes
Cooking Time: 12-14 hours
Ideal slow cooker size: 6-qt.

6-lb. pork roast
18-oz. bottle favorite
  barbecue sauce
2 Tbsp. brown sugar
2 tsp. dry mustard
2 Tbsp. minced onion

1. Place roast in slow cooker and cook on Low 8-10 hours, or until meat is tender but not dry.
2. Remove roast to platter. (Drain drippings and reserve for a soup stock or for a gravy.) Using 2 forks, shred the pork.
3. Return shredded pork to slow cooker and stir in remaining ingredients.
4. Cook on Low 4 hours. Serve on rolls.

A Tip —

Be sure to read a recipe the whole way through before beginning to cook, so you are certain you have all the ingredients you need.

Simply Pulled Pork Sandwiches

Virginia Blish
Akron, NY

Makes 9-12 servings

Prep Time: 10 minutes
Cooking Time: 5 1/2 hours
Ideal slow cooker size: 5-qt.

3-4-lb. rolled pork loin
  roast
18-oz. bottle barbecue
  sauce of your choice

1. Leave pork roast tied as it came from the store. Rinse with cold water and pat dry with paper towel. Place roast in slow cooker.
2. Pour barbecue sauce over top and sides of roast.
3. Cover and cook on High 5 1/2 hours, or until meat is tender but not dry.
4. Remove roast to a platter. Cut strings and discard. Use 2 forks to pull pork apart until it is shredded.
5. Return pork to slow cooker and mix thoroughly with sauce.
6. Serve on split kaiser rolls.

Pork and Sauerkraut

Sheila Soldner
Lititz, PA

Makes 10-15 servings

Prep Time: 30 minutes
Cooking Time: 10-11 hours
Ideal slow cooker size:
6- to 7-qt.

4-5-lb. lean pork loin roast
1-2-lb. bag sauerkraut,
  divided
half a small head of
  cabbage, thinly sliced,
  divided
1 large onion, thinly sliced,
  divided
1 apple, quartered, cored,
  and sliced, but not
  peeled, *divided*
1 tsp. dill weed, *optional*
1/2 cup brown sugar,
  optional
1 cup water

1. Brown roast for 10 minutes in a heavy non-stick skillet. Place roast in slow
cooker.
2. Cover with a layer of
half the sauerkraut, then a
layer of half the cabbage, a
layer of half the onion, and a
layer of half the apple.
3. Repeat the layers.
4. If you wish to use the
dill weed and brown sugar,
mix them and the water
together in a bowl. Pour over
layers. Or simply pour water
over top.

5. Cover and cook on High
1 hour. Turn to Low and cook
until meat is tender, about 9-
10 hours.

Pork and Potatoes

Dorothy VanDeest
Memphis, TN

Makes 4-6 servings

Prep Time: 10 minutes
Cooking Time: 8-9 hours
Ideal slow cooker size: 5-qt.

3-4 small *or* medium-sized
  sweet potatoes, *or*
  baking potatoes, peeled
  or unpeeled, left whole
3-4-lb. pork loin roast, well
  trimmed
Kitchen Bouquet seasoning
garlic salt
salt and pepper

1. Place potatoes in bottom
of slow cooker.
2. Brush roast well with
Kitchen Bouquet. Sprinkle
with garlic salt, salt, and pepper.
3. Place pork roast on
"rack" of potatoes.
4. Cover and cook on Low
8-9 hours, or until potatoes
and meat are tender but not
dry or mushy.

Veggie Pork Roast

Peggy Forsythe
Bartlett, TN

Makes 8 servings

Prep Time: 10 minutes
Cooking Time: 8-10 hours
Ideal slow cooker size:
4- to 6-qt.

3 medium-sized potatoes,
  quartered
6 carrots, sliced *or* cut into
  3/4" chunks
1 onion, cut into wedges
3-4-lb. pork loin
1-1 1/2 cups mild picante
  sauce

1. Place potatoes, carrots,
and onion in the bottom of
the cooker.
2. Place pork loin on top
of the vegetables.
3. Pour picante sauce over
the meat.
4. Cover and cook on Low
8-10 hours, or until the meat
and vegetables are tender but
not dry or mushy.
5. When finished cooking,
remove the meat and allow to
rest on a platter for 10 minutes. Then slice and surround
with vegetables. Ladle sauce
over top. Serve additional
sauce in a bowl.

Saucy Pork Loin

Carolyn Spohn
Shawnee, KS

Makes 4 servings

Prep Time: 5 minutes
Cooking Time: 3-8 hours
Ideal slow cooker size:
 4- to 6-qt.

4 1" slices boneless pork
 loin
1 clove garlic, minced
scant 1/4 tsp. dry sage
scant 1/4 tsp. rosemary
 leaves
10 3/4-oz. can cream of
 celery soup

1. Place pork in slow
cooker. Sprinkle evenly with
garlic, sage, and rosemary.
 2. Spoon soup over all.
 3. Cover and cook on High
3-4 hours, or on Low 6-8
hours, or until tender but not
dry.
 4. Serve over cooked rice
or bulgur.

Spicy Pork Olé

Mary Kennell
Roanoke, IL

Makes 5 servings

Prep Time: 10-15 minutes
Cooking Time: 3 1/2-4 hours
Ideal slow cooker size: 4-qt.

1 1/2 lbs. pork loin, cut into
 bite-sized pieces
2 Tbsp. taco seasoning
2 cups mild salsa
1/3 cup peach jam
2 Tbsp. cornstarch
1/4 cup water

1. Spray slow cooker with
non-stick cooking spray.
 2. Place pork in slow
cooker. Sprinkle with taco
seasoning and stir to coat.
 3. Add salsa and jam. Stir.
 4. Cook on High 3-3 1/2
hours, or until meat is tender.
Remove meat to serving dish
and keep warm.
 5. In a bowl, blend cornstarch and water. Turn cooker
to High. When sauce sim-
mers, stir in cornstarch-water
mixture. Continue stirring
until fully absorbed. Continue
cooking, stirring occasionally,
until sauce thickens. Serve
over or alongside pork.

Apricot-Glazed Pork Roast

Jean Butzer
Batavia, NY
Virginia Blish,
Akron, NY

Makes 10-12 servings

Prep Time: 10 minutes
Cooking Time: 3-6 hours
Ideal slow cooker size:
 5- to 6-qt.

10 1/2-oz. can condensed
 chicken broth
18-oz. jar apricot preserves
1 large onion, chopped
2 Tbsp. Dijon mustard
3 1/2-4-lb. boneless pork
 loin

1. Mix broth, preserves,
onion, and mustard in a
bowl.
 2. Cut roast to fit, if necessary, and place in cooker.
Pour glaze over meat.
 3. Cover and cook on Low
4-6 hours, or on High 3
hours, or until tender.

*Tip: If you prefer a thickened
sauce, mix 2 Tbsp. cornstarch
and 2 Tbsp. water in a small
bowl. When the pork has finished cooking, remove it to a
platter and cover to keep warm.*
 *Turn cooker to High. Stir
cornstarch/water into simmering
sauce. Stir until it is well mixed.
Continue simmering for 10 minutes, or until sauce thickens.*
 *Serve over or alongside pork
slices.*

Fruity
Slow-Cooked Pork
Margaret Moffitt
Bartlett, TN

Makes 4-6 servings

Prep Time: 15-20 minutes
Cooking Time: 3-6 hours
Ideal slow cooker size: 3-qt.

1½ lbs. pork tenderloin,
  cut in 2″ pieces
20-oz. can pineapple
  chunks, undrained
half a pineapple-can of
  water
½ cup brown sugar
2 large cloves garlic,
  minced
⅓ cup soy sauce, *or*
  teriyaki sauce

1. Combine all ingredients
in slow cooker.
2. Cover and cook on High
3-4 hours, or on Low 5-6
hours, or until meat is tender
but not dry.

Tip: To thicken the sauce,
remove cooked pork pieces and
pineapple chunks with a slotted
spoon to a serving dish. Keep
warm.

Mix together 2 Tbsp. cornstarch and 2 Tbsp. water in a
small bowl until smooth. Turn
cooker to High. When sauce is
simmering, stir in cornstarch-
water mixture until thoroughly
absorbed.

Continue simmering, stirring
occasionally, until juices
thicken, about 10 minutes.

Serve over pork and pineapples, or alongside.

Variation: Add one cup
coarsely chopped green pepper,
30 minutes before the end of
the cooking time.
— **Donna Lantgen**
Chadron, NE

Cranberry Mustard
Pork Tenderloin
Valerie Drobel
Carlisle, PA

Makes 6 servings

Prep Time: 15 minutes
Cooking Time: 6-8 hours
Ideal slow cooker size: 5-qt.

16-oz. can whole cranberry
  sauce
3 Tbsp. lemon juice
4 Tbsp. Dijon mustard
3 Tbsp. brown sugar
2 pork tenderloins, about
  2 lbs. total

1. In a small bowl, com-
bine first four ingredients.
Place about ⅓ of mixture in
bottom of slow cooker.
2. Place tenderloins on top
of sauce. Pour remaining
sauce over tenderloins.
3. Cover and cook on Low
6-8 hours, or until meat is
tender.
4. Allow meat to stand for
10 minutes before slicing.

Tip: To thicken the juices, mix
2 Tbsp. cornstarch with 2 Tbsp.
water in a small bowl. After
removing meat from the cooker,
turn it to High. When juices are
simmering, stir in cornstarch-
water mixture. Continue stirring
until it is absorbed.

Simmer until juices thicken,
about 10 minutes, stirring occasionally.

Serve over or alongside
sliced pork.

Tangy Pork Tenderloin

June S. Groff
Denver, PA

Makes 6 servings

Prep Time: 3-4 hours for
* marinating*
Cooking Time: 6-8 hours
Ideal slow cooker size:
* 4- to 5-qt.*

2 pork tenderloins (a total
  of 2 lbs.)
2/3 cup honey
1/2 cup Dijon mustard
1/2 tsp. chili powder
1/4 tsp. salt

1. Place pork in glass or
ceramic baking dish.
Combine remaining ingredients and spoon over pork.
2. Cover and marinate in
the fridge for at least 3 to 4
hours.
3. Place pork in slow
cooker, cutting to fit if necessary. Spoon marinade over
top.
4. Cover and cook on Low
6-8 hours, or until tender.
5. Remove to a serving
platter and keep warm for 10
minutes before slicing.

Tip: To thicken the sauce, turn
the cooker to High after remov-
ing the pork. Meanwhile, blend
together 2 Tbsp. cornstarch
with 2 Tbsp. water in a small
bowl.
* When the juices are simmer-*
ing, stir in cornstarch-water
mixture until absorbed.

Continue simmering, stirring
occasionally, until juices
thicken, about 10 minutes.
* Serve over or alongside*
sliced pork.

Barbecued Ribs

Sara Harter Fredette
Goshen, MA
Margaret H. Moffitt
Bartlett, TN

Makes 6 servings

Prep Time: 2 minutes
Cooking Time: 5-6 hours
Ideal slow cooker size:
* 4- to 5-qt.*

6 lean pork ribs, *or* chops
salt and pepper to taste
19-oz. bottle hickory, *or*
  sweet and tangy,
  barbecue sauce

1. Place meat in slow
cooker cutting the ribs to fit.
Sprinkle each piece with salt
and pepper.
2. If you need to create
layers of meat, be sure to top
each section of ribs with a
proportionate amount of
sauce.
3. Cover and cook on High
for 1 hour. Then cook on Low
for 4-5 hours, or until meat is
tender, but not dry.
4. When ready to serve,
remove ribs from cooker and
place on serving platter.
Cover to keep warm. Tilt
cooker in order to be able to
spoon off any fat that has

floated to the top of the
sauce. Then spoon sauce over
ribs, and serve any extra in a
separate bowl.

Variations:
* 1. If you have time, broil the*
ribs for about 5-15 minutes per
side, about 6" below the broiler
heat, before placing them in the
cooker. The browning adds
depth of flavor and also cooks
off some of the fat.
   — **Corinna Herr**
     Stevens, PA
   — **Margaret Culbert**
     Lebanon, PA
   — **Dorothy Lingerfelt**
     Stonyford, CA

* 2. Slice one medium-sized*
onion. Then lay the slices into
the bottom of the cooker before
adding the meat.
   — **Corinna Herr**
     Stevens, PA
   — **Karen Ceneviva**
     New Haven, CT
   — **Audrey Romonosky**
     Austin, TX

Seasoned Pork Ribs

Melanie Thrower
McPherson, KS

Makes 2-3 servings

Prep Time: 5-10 minutes
Cooking Time: 4 hours
Ideal slow cooker size:
4- to 5-qt.

3 lbs. pork shoulder ribs,
 cut in serving-size pieces
2 tsp. chipotle seasoning
 spice
1 tsp. coarse black pepper,
 optional
1 Tbsp. prepared
 horseradish
1/4 cup ketchup
1/4 cup apricot jelly

1. Heat a non-stick skillet
over medium-high heat.
2. Season pork with chipotle seasonings and then place
in hot skillet, browning each
piece on top and bottom. Do
in batches so all the pieces
brown well.
3. As you finish browning
ribs, place them in the slow
cooker.
4. Cover and cook on High
for 3 hours.
5. Meanwhile, mix
together pepper if you wish,
horseradish, ketchup, and
apricot jelly in a bowl. Spread
over cooked pork.
6. Cover and cook on High
1 hour, or until the meat is
tender.

Sweet and Saucy Ribs

Jean Butzer
Batavia, NY

Makes 4 servings

Prep Time: 10-15 minutes
Cooking Time: 3-8 hours
Ideal slow cooker size:
3- to 4-qt.

2 lbs. pork baby back ribs
1 tsp. black pepper
2 1/2 cups barbecue sauce
 (not mesquite flavor)
8-oz. jar cherry jam *or*
 preserves
1 Tbsp. Dijon mustard
1/4 tsp. salt

1. Trim excess fat from
ribs. Rub 1 tsp. pepper over
ribs. Cut into 2-rib portions
and place in slow cooker.
2. Combine barbecue
sauce, jam, mustard, and salt
in a small bowl. Pour over
ribs, making sure that each
piece gets a good amount of
sauce.
3. Cover and cook on Low
6-8 hours, or on High 3-4
hours, or until ribs are tender.

*Tip: Try using different flavors
of jam/preserves, such as apricot, plum, or grape.*

Sweet BBQ Ribs

Michele Ruvola
Selden, NY

Makes 6 servings

Prep Time: 10 minutes
Cooking Time: 8-9 hours
Ideal slow cooker size:
3- to 4-qt.

3 1/2 lbs. pork loin back ribs
1/2 tsp. salt
1/4 tsp. pepper
1/2 cup cola
2/3 cup barbecue sauce

1. Cut ribs into 2-3 rib portions and put in slow cooker.
2. Sprinkle each portion
with salt and pepper. Spoon
cola over top, being careful
not to wash off the seasonings.
3. Cover and cook on Low
for 7-8 hours, or until ribs are
tender. Drain liquid.
4. Pour barbecue sauce
into slow cooker. Mix gently
with ribs so the meat is
coated.
5. Cover and cook on Low
for 1 hour, or until ribs are
glazed.

Spare Ribs

Elaine Rineer
Lancaster, PA

Makes 6 servings

Prep Time: *35 minutes*
Cooking Time: *7-8 hours*
**Ideal slow cooker size:*
4- to 5-qt.

3 lbs. country-style
   spareribs
2 Tbsp. olive oil
2 small onions, chopped
1 cup ketchup
2 tsp. Worcestershire sauce
1 cup water

1. Brown spareribs on top and bottom in oil in a large non-stick skillet. As they brown, move them from the non-stick skillet into the slow cooker.
2. Mix together in a saucepan the onions, ketchup, Worcestershire sauce, and water. Simmer for 20 minutes, then pour over ribs.
3. Cover and cook on Low 7-8 hours, or until meat is tender.
4. Place ribs on a serving platter. Spoon sauce over top. Put additional sauce in a bowl and serve along with meat.

Variation: *While the meat is cooking, blend together 1/4 cup flour and 3/4 cup cold water in a jar with a tight-fitting lid. Shake until smooth. After Step 3, place ribs on a serving platter, and*

then cover to keep warm.
   Turn cooker to High. Stir flour-water mixture into simmering sauce in cooker. Stir continuously until sauce is smooth and thickened.
   Serve sauce over or alongside meat.
   —Betty K. Drescher
   Quakertown, PA

Finger-Lickin' Pork Ribs

Marilyn Mowry
Irving, TX

Makes 4 servings

Prep Time: *8-12 hours for marinating*
Cooking Time: *6-8 hours*
**Ideal slow cooker size:*
2- to 3-qt.

4-8 country-style pork ribs
1 cup water
1/2 cup white vinegar
4-oz. bottle liquid smoke
favorite bottled barbecue
   sauce

1. Place ribs in a covered dish. In a bowl, mix together water, vinegar, and liquid smoke. Pour over ribs. Turn ribs over once. Marinate overnight.
2. Next day, drain ribs and discard marinade.
3. Put ribs in slow cooker. Cover with barbecue sauce.
4. Cover cooker and cook on Low 6-8 hours, or until tender.

A-Touch-of-Asia Ribs

Sharon Shank
Bridgewater, VA

Makes 8-10 servings

Prep Time: *5-10 minutes*
Cooking Time: *4-8 hours*
**Ideal slow cooker size:*
5- to 6-qt.

6 lbs. country-style pork
   ribs, cut into serving-size
   pieces
1/4 cup teriyaki sauce
1/4 cup cornstarch
27-oz. jar duck sauce
2 Tbsp. minced garlic,
   optional

1. Place ribs in the bottom of your slow cooker.
2. In a large bowl, stir together teriyaki sauce and cornstarch. Blend in duck sauce and garlic if you wish.
3. Pour the sauce over the ribs, making sure that each layer is well covered.
4. Cover and cook on Low 8 hours, or on High 4-5 hours.

Italian Country-Style Pork Ribs

Kay Kassinger
Port Angeles, WA

Makes 8-10 servings

Prep Time: 20 minutes
Cooking Time: 7-8 hours
Ideal slow cooker size: 5-qt.

3-3½ lbs. country-style pork ribs, cut into serving-size pieces
2 14½-oz. cans Italian-seasoned diced tomatoes
1 cup frozen pearl onions
1½ tsp. Italian seasoning
1 tsp. salt
water as needed

1. Brown ribs on top and bottom in non-stick skillet. Do in batches to assure that each piece browns well.
2. Spray cooker with non-stick cooking spray. Transfer browned meat to slow cooker.
3. Drain tomatoes into hot skillet. Deglaze skillet with tomato juice by stirring up the drippings with a wooden spoon.
4. Layer tomatoes, onions, and seasonings over top of ribs. Pour deglazed pan drippings into slow cooker. Add about 2" of water.
5. Cover and cook on Low 7-8 hours, or until meat is tender but not over-cooked.

Easy Pork Riblets

Ruth C. Hancock
Earlsboro, OK

Makes 3-4 servings

Prep Time: 5-10 minutes
Cooking Time: 8 hours
Ideal slow cooker size:
3- to 4-qt.

2 lbs. pork riblets
8-oz. bottle cocktail sauce
8-oz. jar grape jelly

1. Place ribs in slow cooker.
2. Mix jelly and cocktail sauce together in a bowl. Pour over riblets.
3. Cover and cook on Low 8 hours, or until meat is tender.

Tips —

Thaw meat safely:

1. In the refrigerator on the bottom shelf in a platter or deep dish.
2. In the microwave.
3. As part of the cooking process.
4. In a bowl of cold water, changing the water every 20 minutes.
5. Never at room temperature.

Apple Raisin Ham

Betty B. Dennison
Grove City, PA

Makes 6 servings

Prep Time: 10-15 minutes
Cooking Time: 4-5 hours
Ideal slow cooker size: 4-qt.

1½ lbs. fully cooked ham
21-oz. can apple pie filling
⅓ cup golden raisins
⅓ cup orange juice
¼ tsp. ground cinnamon
2 Tbsp. water

1. Cut ham slices into six equal pieces.
2. In a mixing bowl, combine pie filling, raisins, orange juice, cinnamon, and water.
3. Place 1 slice of ham in your slow cooker. Spread ⅙ of the apple mixture over top.
4. Repeat layers until you have used all the ham and apple mixture.
5. Cover and cook on Low 4-5 hours.

Tips:
1. This is a great way to use leftovers.
2. And you can use any leftovers from this to make wonderful sandwiches.

Country Ham

Esther Burkholder
Millerstown, PA

Makes 12 servings

Prep Time: 10 minutes
Cooking Time: 6 hours
Ideal slow cooker size: 4-qt.

3-lb. boneless, fully cooked
  ham
1/2-3/4 cup brown sugar,
  according to your taste
  preferences
2 Tbsp. prepared mustard
1/4 cup peach preserves

  1. Place ham in slow
cooker.
  2. Combine remaining
ingredients in a small bowl.
Spread over ham.
  3. Cover and cook on Low
6 hours, or until heated
through.

Variation: Use apricot pre-
serves instead of peach.
  — Edwina Stoltzfus
  Narvon, PA

Glazed Ham

Dede Peterson
Rapid City, SD

Makes 4 servings

Prep Time: 20 minutes
Cooking Time: 4-6 hours
Ideal slow cooker size: 6-qt.

4 ham steaks
1/3 cup apricot jam
3/4-1 cup honey, depending
  upon how much
  sweetness you like
1/3 cup soy sauce
1/4 tsp. nutmeg

  1. Place ham in slow
cooker.
  2. In a bowl, mix all other
ingredients together. Pour
over ham.
  3. Cook on Low 4-6 hours,
or until meat is heated
through but not dry.

Glazed Ham in a Bag

Eleanor J. Ferreira
North Chelmsford, MA

Makes 12 servings

Prep Time: 7 minutes
Cooking Time: 6-8 hours
Ideal slow cooker size:
  6- to 7-qt.

5-lb. cooked ham
3 Tbsp. orange juice
1 Tbsp. Dijon mustard

  1. Rinse meat. Place in
cooking bag.
  2. Combine orange juice
and mustard. Spread over
ham.
  3. Seal bag with twist tie.
Poke 4 holes in top of bag.
Place in slow cooker.
  4. Cover. Cook on Low 6-8
hours.
  5. To serve, remove ham
from bag, reserving juices.
Slice ham and spoon juices
over. Serve additional juice
alongside in small bowl.

Cranberry Ham
Janie Steele, Moore, OK

Makes 4 servings

Prep Time: *5-10 minutes*
Cooking Time: *4½ hours*
Ideal slow cooker size: *3-qt.*

1-2-lb. fully cooked ham,
  or 2"-thick slice of fully
  cooked ham
1 cup whole cranberry
  sauce
2 Tbsp. brown sugar

1. Place ham in slow
cooker. Cover with cranberry
sauce. Sprinkle brown sugar
over top.
2. Cook on Low 4½ hours,
or until meat is heated
through but not drying out.

Fruited Ham Slice
Arlene M. Kopp
Lineboro, MD

Makes 4 servings

Prep Time: *10 minutes*
Cooking Time: *3-4 hours*
Ideal slow cooker size: *3-qt.*

1-1½-lb. fully cooked ham
  slice, 1"-thick
8-10 whole cloves
prepared mustard
1-lb. can fruit cocktail,
  drained, with 1 cup
  syrup reserved
½ cup brown sugar, firmly
  packed

1. Stud edges of ham slice
with cloves. Spread top with
mustard. Place ham slice in
slow cooker.
2. In a bowl, mix together
fruit cocktail, 1 cup syrup,
and brown sugar. Spoon over
ham.
3. Cover and cook on Low
3-4 hours, or until ham is
heated through but not drying out.

*Variations: Instead of the fruit
cocktail, use 2 cups of any of
the following: canned pineapple
chunks, sliced peaches, apricot
halves.*

Succulent Ham
June S. Groff
Denver, PA

Makes 6 servings

Prep Time: *10 minutes*
Cooking Time: *4-6 hours*
Ideal slow cooker size: *3-qt.*

1½ lbs. fully cooked
  smoked ham pieces
½ cup brown sugar
¼ cup butter, *or*
  margarine, melted
¼ cup red wine vinegar

1. Place ham in slow
cooker.
2. In a bowl, blend sugar
and melted butter. Stir in
vinegar until sugar dissolves.
Pour over ham.
3. Cover and cook on Low
4-6 hours, or until meat is
heated through but not dried
out.
4. Serve meat sliced, or in
chunks, with juice spooned
over top.

Ham 'n Cola
Dorothy VanDeest
Memphis, TN

Makes 9-12 servings

Prep Time: 15 minutes
Cooking Time: 7-8 hours
Ideal slow cooker size: 4-qt.

1/2 cup brown sugar
1 tsp. dry mustard
1 tsp. prepared horseradish
1/4-1/2 cup cola, *divided*
3-4-lb. precooked ham

1. In a mixing bowl, thoroughly combine brown sugar, mustard, and horseradish. Moisten with just enough cola to make a smooth paste. Reserve remaining cola.
2. Rub entire ham with brown-sugar mixture. Place in slow cooker.
3. Pour remaining cola around the edges of the cooker.
4. Cover and cook on High 1 hour, and then on Low 6-7 hours, or until ham is heated through but is not drying out.

Easy and Elegant Ham
Mary Lynn Miller
Reinholds, PA

Makes 18-20 servings

Prep Time: 10-15 minutes
Cooking Time: 6-7 hours
Ideal slow cooker size:
5- to 6-qt.

2 20-oz. cans sliced
   pineapple, *divided*
6-lb. fully cooked boneless
   ham, halved
6-oz. jar maraschino
   cherries, well drained
12-oz. jar orange
   marmalade

1. Drain pineapple, reserving juice. Set juice aside. Place half the pineapple in an ungreased slow cooker.
2. Top with the ham halves.
3. Spoon cherries, remaining pineapple slices, and reserved pineapple juice over ham. Then spoon marmalade over ham.
4. Cover and cook on Low 6-7 hours, or until heated through.
5. Remove to a warm serving platter. Let stand for 10-15 minutes before slicing.
6. Serve the pineapple and cherries with the sliced ham, either on top of, or alongside, the slices.

Potatoes and Green Beans with Ham
Mary B. Sensenig
New Holland, PA

Makes 4 servings

Prep Time: 5 minutes
Cooking Time: 6-8 hours
Ideal slow cooker size: 3-qt.

1-lb. ham slice, cut in
   chunks
2 cups green beans, frozen
   or fresh
2 cups red-skinned
   potatoes, quartered, but
   not peeled
1/2 cup water
1/2 cup chopped onion
4 slices American cheese

1. Place all ingredients, except cheese, in slow cooker. Gently mix together.
2. Cover and cook on Low 6-8 hours, or until vegetables are tender.
3. One hour before the end of the cooking time, lay cheese slices over top.

Ham and Vegetables

Dorothy VanDeest
Memphis, TN
Betty Hostetler
Allensville, PA

Makes 5-6 servings

Prep Time: 15 minutes
Cooking Time: 3-4 hours
Ideal slow cooker size:
  3- to 4-qt.

2 medium-sized potatoes,
  peeled if you want, and
  cut up
1 lb. green beans,
  Frenched, *or* cut in half
2½ cups water
½ tsp. salt
1 lb. lean cooked ham, in a
  piece *or* cut up, *or* a
  meaty ham hock

1. Place ingredients in
slow cooker in order given.
2. Cover and cook on High
3-4 hours, or until vegetables
are tender.
3. If you're home, check
after the dish has cooked for
2 hours to make sure it isn't
cooking dry. Add ½-1 cup
water if it's looking dry.
4. If you use a ham hock,
remove it, allow it to cool
enough to handle, and
debone it. Stir the chunks of
ham back into the cooker.

Green Beans and Ham

Sara Kinsinger
Stuarts Draft, VA

Makes 12 servings

Prep Time: 5-7 minutes
Cooking Time: 1½-4 hours
Ideal slow cooker size: 4-qt.

2 qts. cooked, *or* canned,
  green beans, undrained
2 cups cooked ham, diced
1 stick (½ cup) butter, cut
  in chunks
1 tsp. hickory smoke
  seasoning

1. Place all ingredients in
slow cooker. Stir together
gently.
2. Cover and cook on High
1½ hours, or on Low 4 hours.

Ham and Cabbage

Tim Smith
Rutledge, PA

Makes 4 servings

Prep Time: 30 minutes
Cooking Time: 6-7 hours
Ideal slow cooker size:
  6- to 7-qt.

2 lbs. ham, uncooked
12 whole cloves
8 medium-sized red
  potatoes
1 medium-sized head
  green cabbage
water

1. Rinse ham, then stick
cloves evenly into ham. Place
in center of slow cooker.
2. Cut potatoes in half.
Add to slow cooker around
the ham.
3. Quarter cabbage and
remove center stem. Add to
cooker, again surrounding the
ham.
4. Fill with water to cover.
5. Cover and cook on High
for 6-7 hours, or until vegetables and meat are tender, but
not dry or mushy.
6. Serve with mustard for
the ham and butter for the
potatoes.

Ham and Dumplings

Donna Lantgen
Chadron, NE

Makes 6 servings

Prep Time: 10 minutes
Cooking Time: 6-7 hours
Ideal slow cooker size: 5-qt.

2¹/2-lb. piece of cooked ham
8 cups water
3 cups all-purpose baking mix
1 cup milk

1. Place ham and water in slow cooker.
2. Cover and cook on High 5-6 hours.
3. In a bowl, mix baking mix and milk together. Drop by spoonfuls into slow cooker.
4. Cover and cook on High 1 more hour.

A Tip —

Grate ends of cheese blocks (cheddar, Swiss, Monterey Jack, etc.) together into a Ziploc bag and keep the grated cheese on hand for sprinkling over salads, casseroles, and toasted cheese bread.

Scalloped Potatoes and Ham

Carol Sherwood
Batavia, NY
Sharon Anders
Alburtis, PA
Mary Stauffer
Ephrata, PA
Esther Hartzler
Carlsbad, NM
Dawn Hahn
Lititz, PA
Diann J. Dunham
State College, PA

Makes 4-6 servings

Prep Time: 20 minutes
Cooking Time: 6-8 hours
Ideal slow cooker size: 5-qt.

2-3 lbs. potatoes, peeled, sliced, and *divided*
12-oz. pkg., *or* 1 lb., cooked ham, cubed and *divided*
1 small onion, chopped and *divided*
2 cups shredded cheddar cheese, *divided*
10³/4-oz. can cream of celery, *or* mushroom, soup

1. Spray the interior of the cooker with non-stick cooking spray.
2. Layer ¹/3 each of the potatoes, ham, onion, and cheese into the cooker.
3. Repeat twice.
4. Spread soup on top.
5. Cover and cook on Low 6-8 hours, or until potatoes are tender.

Variation: For a creamier sauce, combine can of creamed soup with ¹/2 cup water in a bowl before pouring over contents of cooker in Step 4.
—**Jeannine Janzen**
Elbing, KS

Creamy Scalloped Potatoes and Ham

Rhonda Freed
Lowville, NY

Makes 6 servings

Prep Time: 20 minutes
Cooking Time: 4-5 hours
Ideal slow cooker size: 4-qt.

6 cups sliced, raw potatoes
salt and pepper to taste
10³/4-oz. can cream of mushroom, *or* celery, soup
1¹/2 cups milk
1 lb. cooked ham, cubed

1. Place potatoes in slow cooker. Salt and pepper each layer.
2. In a bowl, mix soup, milk, and ham together. Pour over potatoes.
3. Cover and cook on High for 3¹/2 hours. Continue cooking ¹/2-1¹/2 hours more if needed, or until potatoes are tender.

Variation: Substitute 12-oz. can evaporated milk for the 1¹/2 cups milk.
— **Mary Kay Nolt**
Newmanstown, PA

Cheesy Potatoes and Ham

Beth Maurer
Harrisonburg, VA

Makes 4-6 servings

Prep Time: 20 minutes
Cooking Time: 7-9 hours
Ideal slow cooker size: 4-qt.

6 cups sliced, peeled
    potatoes
2½ cups cooked ham,
    cubed
1½ cups shredded cheddar
    cheese
10¾-oz. can cream of
    mushroom soup
½ cup milk

1. In slow cooker, layer
one-third of potatoes, of ham,
and of cheese. Repeat two
more times.
2. Combine soup and milk.
Pour over ingredients in slow
cooker.
3. Cover. Cook on High
1 hour. Reduce to Low for
6-8 hours, or just until potatoes are soft.

Cottage Ham Dinner

Ethel Mumaw
Millersburg, OH

Makes 8 servings

Prep Time: 10-15 minutes
Cooking Time: 8 hours
Ideal slow cooker size: 5-qt.

3-lb. boneless cottage ham
12-oz. can ginger ale
3 unpeeled medium-sized
    potatoes, cut into strips
3 medium-sized onions,
    cut into wedges

1. Place ham in slow
cooker. Pour ginger ale over
top.
2. Add potato strips and
onion wedges around the
ham. Push down into liquid
as much as possible.
3. Cover and cook on Low
for 8 hours, or until vegetables are tender.

Ham Hocks and Kraut

Kathleen Rogge
Alexandria, IN

Makes 3-4 servings

Prep Time: 5 minutes
Cooking Time: 6-8 hours
Ideal slow cooker size: 6-qt.

6 meaty smoked ham
    hocks
15-oz. can sauerkraut
1 large onion, chopped
2 bay leaves
water

1. Place all ingredients in
slow cooker. Fill with enough
water to cover ham hocks.
2. Cover and cook on Low
6-8 hours, or until meat is
tender.
3. Remove hocks and
allow to cool enough to
debone by hand. Stir ham
chunks back into sauerkraut.
4. Remove bay leaves.
Serve with mashed potatoes.

Ham Balls

Edwina F. Stoltzfus
Narvon, PA

Makes 6 servings

Prep Time: 10-15 minutes
Cooking Time: 3½ hours
Ideal slow cooker size:
   3- to 4-qt.

1 cup brown sugar
1 Tbsp. prepared mustard
½ cup water
½ cup vinegar
4-oz. can crushed
   pineapples, undrained
2 lbs. prepared ham loaf,
   divided

1. In a saucepan, bring
brown sugar, mustard, water,
vinegar, and pineapples to a
boil.
2. Meanwhile, shape ham
loaf into balls. Place a layer in
the slow cooker.
3. Spoon a proportionate
amount of boiling sauce over
first layer of meat.
4. Continue with layers
until all meat and sauce are
in the cooker, being sure to
end with sauce.
5. Cook on High 3½
hours.
6. Before serving, tilt
cooker carefully. Spoon off
layer of fat and discard.
7. Place cooked balls on a
serving platter and spoon
sauce over top.

Ham and Cheese Casserole

Kendra Dreps
Liberty, PA

Makes 8-10 servings

Prep Time: 15-30 minutes
Cooking Time: 2-4 hours
Ideal slow cooker size: 3½ qt.

12- *or* 16-oz. pkg. medium
   egg noodles, *divided*
10¾-oz. can condensed
   cream of celery soup
1 pint sour cream
2 cups fully cooked ham,
   cubed, *divided*
2 cups shredded cheese,
   your choice, *divided*

1. Prepare noodles according to package instructions.
Drain.
2. In a small bowl com-
bine soup and sour cream
until smooth. Set aside.
3. In a greased slow
cooker, layer one-third of the
cooked noodles, one-third of
the ham, and one-third of the
cheese.
4. Top with one-fourth of
soup mixture.
5. Repeat steps 3 and 4
twice until all ingredients are
used. The final layer should
be the soup-sour cream mixture.
6. Cook 2-4 hours on Low,
or until heated through.

Ham and Hash Browns

Joette Droz
Kalona, IA
Jonice Crist
Quinter, KS

Makes 4 servings

Prep Time: 10 minutes
Cooking Time: 4-6 hours
Ideal slow cooker size: 4-qt.

26-oz. pkg. frozen hash
   browns
2 cups fully cooked ham,
   cubed
2-oz. jar diced pimentos,
   drained
10¾-oz. can cheddar
   cheese soup
¾ cup milk
¼ tsp. pepper, *optional*

1. In a slow cooker com-
bine potatoes, ham, and
pimentos.
2. Combine soup, milk,
and pepper if you wish in a
bowl until smooth. Mix well
and pour over potato mixture.
Stir.
3. Cover and cook on Low
4-6 hours, or until potatoes
are tender.

Sausage and Apples

Linda Sluiter
Schererville, IN

Makes 4 servings

Prep Time: 10 minutes
Cooking Time: 1-3 hours
Ideal slow cooker size: 8-qt.

1 lb. smoked sausage
2 large apples, cored and sliced
1/4 cup brown sugar
1/2 cup apple juice

1. Cut meat into 2" pieces.
2. Place all ingredients in slow cooker and mix together well.
3. Cover and cook on Low 1-3 hours, or until heated through and until apples are as tender as you like them.

Sausage and Sweet Potatoes

Ruth Hershey
Paradise, PA

Makes 4-6 servings

Prep Time: 15-20 minutes
Cooking Time: 4-10 hours
Ideal slow cooker size: 3-qt.

1 lb. bulk sausage
2 sweet potatoes, peeled and sliced
3 apples, peeled and sliced
2 Tbsp. brown sugar
1 Tbsp. flour
1/4 cup water

1. Brown loose sausage in skillet, breaking up chunks of meat with a wooden spoon. Drain.
2. Layer sausage, sweet potatoes, and apples in slow cooker.
3. Combine remaining ingredients and pour over ingredients in slow cooker.
4. Cover. Cook on Low 8-10 hours, or on High 4 hours.

Sweet and Sour Sausage Dish

Jena Hammond
Traverse City, MI

Makes 8-10 servings

Prep Time: 15 minutes
Cooking Time: 3-6 hours
Ideal slow cooker size: 4-qt.

2 20-oz. cans pineapple chunks, drained
2 large green peppers, sliced into bite-sized strips
3 16-oz. pkgs. smoked sausage, cut into 1" chunks
18-oz. bottle honey barbecue sauce

1. Combine pineapples, peppers, and sausage chunks in slow cooker.
2. Pour barbecue sauce over mixture and stir.
3. Cover and cook on High 3 hours, or on Low 6 hours, or until dish is heated through.

Sausage and Scalloped Potatoes

Melissa Warner, Broad Top, PA
Carolyn Baer, Conrath, WI

Makes 8 servings

Prep Time: 20 minutes
Cooking Time: 4-10 hours
Ideal slow cooker size:
3½- to 4-qt.

2 lbs. potatoes, sliced ¼"
  thick, *divided*
1 lb. fully-cooked smoked
  sausage link, sliced ½"
  thick, *divided*
2 medium-sized onions,
  chopped, *divided*
10¾-oz. can condensed
  cheddar cheese soup,
  divided
10¾-oz. can condensed
  cream of celery soup
10-oz. pkg. frozen peas,
  thawed, *optional*

1. Spray interior of cooker
with non-stick cooking spray.
2. Layer into the cooker
one-third of the potatoes, one-
third of the sausage, one-third
of the onion, and one-third of
the cheddar cheese soup.
3. Repeat layers two more
times.
4. Top with cream of cel-
ery soup.
5. Cover and cook on Low
8-10 hours, or on High 4-5
hours, or until vegetables are
tender.
6. If you wish, stir in peas.
Cover and let stand 5 minutes. (If you forgot to thaw

the peas, stir them in but let
stand 10 minutes.)

Beans with Sausage

Mary B. Sensenig
New Holland, PA

Makes 4-5 servings

Prep Time: 5 minutes
Cooking Time: 4-5 hours
Ideal slow cooker size: 4-qt.

16-oz.-pkg. miniature
  smoked sausage links
1 qt. green beans, with most
  of the juice drained
1 small onion, chopped
½ cup brown sugar
¼ cup ketchup

1. Place sausage in slow
cooker. Top with beans and
then onion.
2. In a bowl, stir together
sugar and ketchup. Spoon
over top.
3. Cover and cook on Low
4-5 hours.

Sausage and Green Beans

Joy Yoder
Harrisonburg, VA

Makes 6 servings

Prep Time: 15 minutes
Cooking Time: 2-5 hours
Ideal slow cooker size:
3- to 4-qt.

1½ lbs. link sausage, cut
  into 2" pieces
1 qt. green beans, frozen
1 apple, diced *or* sliced
  with peel
1 cup water

1. Place sausage in slow
cooker.
2. Add beans, apple, and
water. Mix together well.
3. Cover and cook on High
2 hours, or on Low 4-5 hours,
or until sausage and beans
are both tender.

Creamy Sausage and Potatoes

Janet Oberholtzer
Ephrata, PA

Makes 6 servings

Prep Time: *15 minutes*
Cooking Time: *6-8 hours*
Ideal slow cooker size: *3¹/2-qt.*

3 lbs. small potatoes,
   peeled and quartered
1 lb. smoked sausage, cut
   into ¹/4" slices
8-oz. pkg. cream cheese,
   softened
10³/4-oz. can cream of
   celery soup
1 envelope dry ranch salad
   dressing mix

1. Place potatoes in slow
cooker. Add sausage.
2. In a bowl, beat together
cream cheese, soup, and
salad dressing mix until
smooth. Pour over potatoes
and sausage.
3. Cover and cook on Low
6-8 hours, or until the potatoes are tender, stirring halfway through cooking time if
you're home. Stir again
before serving.

Tips:
*1. Small red potatoes are
great in this dish. If you use
them, don't peel them!*
*2. You may substitute
smoked turkey sausage for the
smoked pork sausage.*

Sausage Comfort Casserole

Kay M. Zurcher, Minot, ND

Makes 6-8 servings

Prep Time: *30 minutes*
Cooking Time: *4-8 hours*
Ideal slow cooker size:
   4- to 5-qt.

2 lbs. beer brats, *or* spicy
   sausage, *divided*
2 14-oz. cans chicken
   broth, *divided*
3 lbs. potatoes, sliced ¹/4"
   thick, *divided*
2 large onions, thinly
   sliced, *divided*
6 ozs. sharp cheddar
   cheese, shredded, *divided*
salt and pepper, *optional,
   divided*

1. Spray slow cooker with
non-stick cooking spray.
2. Brown sausage in a non-
stick skillet until browned on
all sides.
3. Meanwhile, pour 1 cup
chicken broth into slow
cooker. Spread one-third of
the potatoes on the bottom of
the slow cooker. Sprinkle
with salt and pepper if you
wish.
4. Then layer in one-third
of the onions, one-third of the
sausage, and one-third of the
cheese.
5. Repeat the potato, salt
and pepper if you wish,
onion, sausage, and cheese
layers 2 more times.
6. Pour the remaining

chicken broth over top.
7. Cover and cook on Low
8 hours, or on High 4 hours,
or until potatoes and onions
are done to your liking.

*Tip: Do not stir but check
potatoes to make sure they are
finished, but not overcooked.*

Italian Sausage Dinner

Janessa Hochstedler
East Earl, PA

Makes 6 servings

Prep Time: *10 minutes*
Cooking Time: *5-10 hours*
Ideal slow cooker size: *4-qt.*

1¹/2 lbs. Italian sausage, cut
   in ³/4" slices
2 Tbsp. A-1 steak sauce
28-oz. can diced Italian-
   style tomatoes, with
   juice
2 chopped green peppers
¹/2 tsp. red pepper flakes,
   optional
2 cups uncooked minute
   rice

1. Place all ingredients,
except rice, in slow cooker.
2. Cover and cook on Low
7¹/2-9¹/2 hours, or on High 4¹/2
hours.

3. Stir in uncooked rice. Cover and cook an additional 20 minutes on High or Low.

Sausage in Spaghetti Sauce

Mary Ann Bowman
East Earl, PA

Makes 10-12 servings

Prep Time: 15 minutes
Cooking Time: 3-6 hours
Ideal slow cooker size: 5-qt.

4 lbs. sausage of your choice
1 red bell pepper
1 green bell pepper
1 large onion
26-oz. jar spaghetti sauce

1. Heat non-stick skillet over medium-high heat. Brown sausage in non-stick skillet in batches.
As a batch is finished browning on all sides, cut into 1½" chunks. Then place in slow cooker.
2. Slice or chop peppers and onion and put on top of sausage.
3. Add spaghetti sauce over all.
4. Cover and cook on Low 6 hours, or on High 3 hours.

Super Sausage Supper

Anne Townsend
Albuquerque, NM

Makes 3-4 servings

Prep Time: 5 minutes
Cooking Time: 1-6 hours
Ideal slow cooker size: 3-qt.

8-oz. pkg. hot sausage
16-oz. pkg. frozen mixed vegetables
10¾-oz. can cream of broccoli cheese soup

1. Slice sausage and place in slow cooker.
2. Distribute frozen vegetables over the sausage.
3. Spread undiluted soup on top of the vegetables.
4. Cover and cook on High for 1 hour, or on Low 5-6 hours, or until meat is cooked and vegetables are tender.

Tips:
1. This simple meal is quite thick and can be served on dinner plates rather than in soup bowls.
2. It is delicious the next day, as well.

Sausage and Sauerkraut Supper

Bonnie Goering
Bridgewater, VA

Makes 4-5 servings

Prep Time: 10 minutes
Cooking Time: 6-10 hours
Ideal slow cooker size: 4- to 5-qt.

1-lb.-pkg. smoked sausage links, cut into 2" pieces
32-oz. bag refrigerated, *or* canned, sauerkraut, drained
half an onion, chopped
1 apple, cored and chopped
2-3 Tbsp. brown sugar
water

1. Combine all ingredients in slow cooker with water covering half the contents.
2. Cover and cook on Low 6-10 hours, or until vegetables are as tender as you like them.
3. Serve alongside mashed potatoes.

Tip: If you'll be cooking the Supper for more than 8 hours, you may want to use enough water to nearly cover the ingredients in Step 1.

Sausage, Potatoes, and Sauerkraut

Janie Steele
Moore, OK

Makes 6-8 servings

Prep Time: 20 minutes
Cooking Time: 6-8 hours
Ideal slow cooker size:
  4- to 5-qt.

32-oz. can sauerkraut, drained
2 cups peeled, thinly sliced potatoes
1/2 cup chopped onions
1 lb. Polish *or* Italian sausage, *or* any sausage of your choice, cut into 2-3" pieces

1. Place sauerkraut on bottom of slow cooker. Layer in potatoes and onions.
2. Lay sausage pieces over top.
3. Cover and cook on Low 6-8 hours, or until vegetables are tender and sausage is cooked.

Sauerkraut and Kielbasa

Colleen Heatwole
Burton, MI

Makes 4 servings

Prep Time: 10 minutes
Cooking Time: 5-6 hours
Ideal slow cooker size:
  3- to 4-qt.

2 14½-oz. cans sauerkraut
1 lb. Polish kielbasa

1. Drain sauerkraut. Place in slow cooker.
2. Cut kielbasa into 1"-thick slices. Combine with sauerkraut in slow cooker.
3. Cover and cook on Low 5-6 hours.

Sweet and Spicy Kielbasa

Michele Ruvola
Selden, NY

Makes 6-8 servings

Prep Time: 5 minutes
Cooking Time: 2½-3 hours
Ideal slow cooker size: 3-qt.

1 cup brown sugar
1 Tbsp. spicy mustard
2 lbs. smoked fully cooked kielbasa, cut into 1" pieces

1. Combine brown sugar and mustard in slow cooker.
2. Add kielbasa; stir to coat evenly.
3. Cover and cook on Low 2½-3 hours, stirring occasionally.

Harvest Kielbasa

Christ Kaczynski
Schenectady, NY

Makes 6 servings

Prep Time: 20 minutes
Cooking Time: 4-8 hours
Ideal slow cooker size: 4-qt.

2 lbs. smoked kielbasa
3 cups unsweetened
  applesauce
1/2 cup brown sugar
3 medium onions, sliced

1. Slice kielbasa into 1/4"
slices. Brown in skillet.
Drain.
2. Combine applesauce
and brown sugar.
3. Layer kielbasa, onions,
and applesauce mixture in
slow cooker.
4. Cover. Cook on Low 4-8
hours.

The longer it cooks, the bet-
ter the flavor.

A Tip —

If you want to verify
that meat in your cooker is
fully cooked, use a meat
thermometer to check that
the internal temperature
of poultry has reached
180° F. Medium-done beef
and pork should reach an
internal temperature of
160° F. Well-done beef
and pork should reach an
internal temperature of
170° F.

Melt-In-Your-Mouth Sausage

Susan Wenger
Lebanon, PA

Makes 6-8 servings

Prep Time: 15 minutes
Cooking Time: 4-6 hours
Ideal slow cooker size: 4-qt.

2 lbs. fresh sausage, cut in
  3/4" slices
24-oz. jar spaghetti sauce
6-oz. can tomato paste
tomato paste can of water
1 Tbsp. Parmesan cheese

Optional ingredients:
1 tsp. parsley flakes
1 onion, sliced thin
half *or* whole bell pepper,
  sliced
1-2 cups fresh mushrooms,
  sliced

1. Heat non-stick skillet
over medium-high heat.
Brown sausage on all sides.
2. Put browned sausage
and all remaining ingredients
in slow cooker. Stir together
gently but thoroughly.
3. Cover and cook on High
4-6 hours. Serve on steak
rolls, or over mashed potatoes
or corkscrew pasta.

Easy Sausage Sandwiches

Renee Suydam
Lancaster, PA

Makes 8 servings

Prep Time: 10 minutes
Cooking Time: 51/2-8 hours
Ideal slow cooker size: 5-qt.

8 pieces of sausage of your
  choice, sub-roll length
water
26-oz. jar spaghetti sauce,
  your favorite
2-3 cups shredded
  mozzarella cheese
8 sub rolls

1. Place sausage pieces in
slow cooker. Add 1-2" water.
2. Cover and cook on Low
for 5-7 hours. Drain water
3. Stir in spaghetti sauce.
4. Cover and cook 30-60
minutes more until sauce is
heated through.
5. Serve on rolls topped
with mozzarella cheese.

Tip: Serve with sauteed peppers
and onions as condiments for
topping the sandwiches.

Saucy Hot Dogs
Donna Conto, Saylorsburg, PA

Makes 8 servings

Prep Time: *15 minutes*
Cooking Time: *2 hours*
Ideal slow cooker size: *5-qt.*

1 lb. all-beef hot dogs
10-oz. jar grape jelly
1/3 cup prepared mustard
1/4 cup red wine
1/4 tsp. dry mustard

1. Cut hot dogs into 1/2" slices. Place in slow cooker.
2. Mix remaining ingredients together with the hot dogs in the cooker.
3. Cover and cook on Low for 2 hours.
4. Serve in rolls or over cooked pasta.

Tip: *This is also a great buffet dish. Serve it from the warm slow cooker with toothpicks.*

Barbecued Smokies
Radella Vrolijk
Hinton, VA

Makes 10-12 servings

Prep Time: *5 minutes*
Cooking Time: *4-6 hours*
Ideal slow cooker size: *3-qt.*

12-oz. bottle barbecue sauce
8-oz. jar grape jelly
1 1/2 lbs. little smokies, *or* hot dogs, cut into 3/4" slices

1. Mix barbecue sauce and jelly in slow cooker. Add cut-up meat.
2. Cover and cook on Low 4-6 hours.
3. Serve in hot dog buns or over cooked pasta. Or serve on a buffet from the warm cooker with toothpicks.

Barbecued Hot Dogs
Shelia Heil
Lancaster, PA

Makes 10 servings

Prep Time: *15 minutes*
Cooking Time: *2-2 1/2 hours*
Ideal slow cooker size: *2- or 3-qt.*

16-20 hot dogs, cut into 1" chunks
1 jar cocktail sauce
1/2 cup brown sugar
1/2 cup ketchup

1. Place hot dog chunks in slow cooker.
2. Add remaining ingredients to cooker and mix with hot dogs.
3. Cover and cook on Low 2-2 1/2 hours.
4. Serve with mashed potatoes or French fries. Or serve on a buffet from the warm cooker, with toothpicks.

Variation: *Use 1 cup chili sauce instead of cocktail sauce.*
— Sandy Clugston
St. Thomas, PA

Zesty Wieners

Sherril Bieberly
Salina, KS

Makes 10-12 servings

Prep Time: 5 minutes
Cooking Time: 1-2 hours
Ideal slow cooker size:
  2- to 3-qt.

12-oz. bottle chili sauce
12-oz. jar hot pepper jelly
1 1/2 lbs. little smokie
  wieners

1. Combine chili sauce and jelly in slow cooker. Add wieners.
2. Simmer on High until sauce thickens, about 1-2 hours.
3. Serve in buns, or over cooked rice or pasta. Or serve on a buffet from the warm cooker, along with toothpicks to spear the wieners.

Cranberry Franks

Loretta Krahn
Mountain Lake, MN

Makes 15-20 servings

Prep Time: 10 minutes
Cooking Time: 1-2 hours
Ideal slow cooker size: 3-qt.

2 pkgs. cocktail wieners or
  little smoked sausages
16-oz. can jellied cranberry
  sauce
1 cup ketchup
3 Tbsp. brown sugar
1 Tbsp. lemon juice

1. Combine all ingredients in slow cooker.
2. Cover. Cook on High 1-2 hours.

Great picnic, potluck, or buffet food.

Smoked Sausage with Green Beans and New Potatoes

Sheila Soldner
Lititz, PA

Makes 4-6 servings

Prep Time: 15 minutes
Cooking Time: 8-10 hours
Ideal slow cooker size: 4-qt.

2 cups water
1 1/2 lbs. smoked sausage,
  cut into 4" pieces
2 medium-sized onions,
  quartered
1 qt. small new potatoes
2 qts. fresh green beans
salt and pepper to taste

1. Put water in slow cooker. Add sausage and then onions.
2. Layer potatoes on top. Salt and pepper to taste. Place green beans over top. Salt and pepper to taste.
3. Cover and cook on Low 8-10 hours, or until vegetables are tender.

Pot-Luck Wiener Bake

Ruth Ann Penner
Hillsboro, KS

Makes 6 servings

Prep Time: 8 minutes
Cooking Time: 3 hours
Ideal slow cooker size: 3-qt.

4 cups cooked potatoes,
    peeled and diced
$10^3/4$-oz. can cream of
    mushroom soup
1 cup mayonnaise
1 cup sauerkraut, drained
1 lb. wieners, sliced

1. Mix all ingredients in
slow cooker.
2. Cover and cook on Low
3 hours.

A Tip —

You'll get the best
results from your slow
cooker when it's $2/3$-full.
Then it's less likely to
scorch around the edges
(sometimes a problem
with a too-empty cooker),
or not to cook through (if
the cooker's full to the
brim).

And if you're driving
your $2/3$-full cooker to a
pot-luck meal, it won't be
running out into your
trunk as you go around
corners.

Frankfurter Succotash

June S. Groff, Denver, PA

Makes 4-6 servings

Prep Time: 10 minutes
Cooking Time: 4-6 hours
Ideal slow cooker size: 2-qt.

1 lb. hot dogs, cut into $1/2$"
    slices
2 10-oz. pkgs. frozen succo-
    tash, thawed and drained
$10^3/4$-oz. can cheddar
    cheese soup

1. Stir all ingredients
together in slow cooker.
2. Cover and cook on Low
4-6 hours, or until vegetables
are tender.

*Variation: Substitute cooked
ham chunks for the hot dogs.*

Sloppy Jane Sandwiches

Kathleen Rogge
Alexandria, IN

Makes 4-5 servings

Prep Time: 5-10 minutes
Cooking Time: 2-3 hours
Ideal slow cooker size: 2-qt.

1 pkg. hot dogs, cut into
    $3/4$" slices
28-oz. can baked beans
1 tsp. prepared mustard
1 tsp. instant minced
    onion
$1/3$ cup chili sauce

1. In slow cooker, combine
all ingredients.
2. Cover and cook on Low
2-3 hours.
3. Spoon into toasted hot
dog buns.

Tip: This recipe doubles easily.

Pasta & Other Main Dishes

Convenient Slow-Cooker Lasagna

Rachel Yoder
Middlebury, IN

Makes 6-8 servings

Prep Time: 30-45 minutes
Cooking Time: 4 hours
Ideal slow cooker size: 6-qt.

1 lb. ground beef
29-oz. can tomato sauce
8-oz. pkg. lasagna noodles, uncooked
4 cups shredded mozzarella cheese
1½ cups cottage cheese

1. Spray the interior of the cooker with non-stick cooking spray.
2. Brown the ground beef in a large non-stick skillet. Drain off drippings.
3. Stir in tomato sauce. Mix well.
4. Spread one-fourth of the meat sauce on the bottom of the slow cooker.
5. Arrange one-third of the uncooked noodles over the sauce. (I usually break them up so they fit better.)
6. Combine the cheeses in a bowl. Spoon one-third of the cheeses over the noodles.
7. Repeat these layers twice.
8. Top with remaining sauce.
9. Cover and cook on Low 4 hours.

Variations:
1. Add 1 chopped onion to the ground beef in Step 2.
2. Add 1 tsp. salt to the tomato sauce and beef in Step 3.
3. Add ½ cup grated Parmesan cheese to the mozzarella and cottage cheeses in Step 6.
4. Add ½ cup additional shredded mozzarella cheese to the top of the lasagna 5 minutes before serving.

A Tip —

Allow cooked pasta dishes, especially those with cheese, as well as egg dishes, to stand for 10-15 minutes before serving, so that they can absorb their juices and firm up.

Slow-Cooker Lasagna

Mary Jane Musser
Manheim, PA
Janet Oberholtzer
Ephrata, PA
Eleya Raim, Oxford, IA
Orpha Herr, Andover, NY

Makes 6-8 servings

Prep Time: 15 minutes
Cooking Time: 4 hours
Ideal slow cooker size: 4-qt.

12-oz. pkg. lasagna noodles
half a stick (1/4 cup) butter
1 1/2 lbs. ground beef
1 qt. spaghetti sauce
8 ozs. Velveeta cheese,
  cubed, *or* your choice of
  cheeses

1. Cook noodles according to package directions. Drain. Return cooked noodles to saucepan and stir in butter until melted.
2. While the noodles are cooking, brown beef in a non-stick skillet. Drain off drippings.
3. Then layer into the slow cooker one-fourth of the sauce, one-third of the browned beef, one-third of the cooked noodles, and one-third of the cubed cheese.
4. Repeat these layers two more times, ending with one-fourth of the sauce.
5. Cover and cook on Low 3-4 hours, or until heated through and cheese has melted.

Cheesy Cheddar Lasagna

LuAnna J. Hochstedler
East Earl, PA

Makes 4 servings

Prep Time: 15 minutes
Cooking Time: 3-8 hours
Ideal slow cooker size: 3-qt.

1 lb. ground beef
14-oz. jar spaghetti sauce,
  or about 1 1/2 cups if
  you're using homemade
  sauce
1 cup water
12-oz. box macaroni and
  cheese, uncooked,
  divided
8 ozs. cottage cheese
1/2 cup shredded
  mozzarella cheese

1. Brown ground beef in a non-stick skillet. Drain off drippings. In non-stick skillet, mix spaghetti sauce and water into beef.
2. Place half the meat mixture into the slow cooker. Top with half the uncooked macaroni and cheese dinner and sauce packet.
3. Spoon cottage cheese over top.
4. Add the remaining meat.
5. Then add the remaining macaroni and cheese sauce packet.
6. Sprinkle with mozzarella cheese.
7. Cover and cook on Low 6-8 hours or on High 3-4

hours, or until macaroni are tender and cheeses are melted.

Lazy Lasagna

Barb Harvey
Quarryville, PA

Makes 10 servings

Prep Time: 30 minutes
Cooking Time: 3 1/4-4 1/4 hours
Ideal slow cooker size: 4-qt.

1 lb. ground beef
12-oz. pkg. egg noodles
32-oz. jar spaghetti sauce,
  your choice of flavors
8 ozs. mozzarella cheese,
  shredded
16 ozs. cottage cheese

1. Brown ground beef in a non-stick skillet. Drain off drippings.
2. While beef is browning, cook noodles according to package directions. Drain. Return cooked noodles to saucepan.
3. Stir spaghetti sauce into browned and drained ground beef.
4. Stir mozzarella and cottage cheeses into cooked noodles.
5. Layer one-third of the sauce into the bottom of the slow cooker. Top with half the noodles, followed by half the cheeses.
6. Layer in half the remaining sauce, followed by all the remaining noodles and

cheeses. Top with rest of sauce.

7. Cover and cook on Low 3-4 hours.

Variation: Substitute 1 lb. loose sausage for the ground beef.

— Kendra Dreps
Liberty, PA

Quick-'N-Easy Meat-Free Lasagna

Rhonda Freed
Lowville, NY

Makes 6 servings

Prep Time: 10 minutes
Cooking Time: 3-4 hours
Ideal slow cooker size: 4-qt.

28-oz. jar spaghetti sauce, your choice of flavors
6-7 uncooked lasagna noodles
2 cups shredded mozzarella cheese, *divided*
15 ozs. ricotta cheese
1/4 cup grated Parmesan cheese

1. Spread one-fourth of sauce in bottom of slow cooker.

2. Lay 2 noodles, broken into 1" pieces, over sauce.

3. In a bowl, mix together 1 1/2 cups mozzarella cheese, the ricotta, and Parmesan cheeses.

4. Spoon half of cheese mixture onto noodles and spread out to edges.

5. Spoon in one-third of remaining sauce, and then 2 more broken noodles.

6. Spread remaining cheese mixture over top, then one-half the remaining sauce and all the remaining noodles.

7. Finish with remaining sauce.

8. Cover and cook on Low 3-4 hours, or until noodles are tender and cheeses are melted.

9. Add 1/2 cup mozzarella cheese and cook until cheese melts.

A Tip —

Always taste the food you've prepared before serving it, so you can correct the seasonings, if necessary.

Spaghetti and Sauce

Beverly Flatt Getz
Warriors Mark, PA

Makes 8 servings

Prep Time: 15 minutes
Cooking Time: 4-8 hours
Ideal slow cooker size: 4-qt.

1 1/2 lbs. ground beef
1 large onion, chopped
26-oz. jar spaghetti sauce with mushrooms
10 1/2-oz. can tomato soup
14-oz. can stewed, *or* petite diced, tomatoes
soup-can of water

Optional seasonings:
minced garlic, to taste
Italian seasoning, to taste
onion salt, to taste

1. Sauté ground beef and onion in a large non-stick skillet just until meat is browned.

2. Place meat and onion in slow cooker. Stir in spaghetti sauce, tomato soup, cut-up tomatoes, water, and any additional seasonings you would like.

3. Cover and cook on High 4 hours, or on Low 6-8 hours.

4. It's ready to serve over your favorite pasta!

Creamy Spaghetti

Kendra Dreps
Liberty, PA

Makes 10-12 servings

Prep Time: 30 minutes
Cooking Time: 2-4 hours
Ideal slow cooker size:
  4- to 5-qt.

1 lb. dry spaghetti
1 lb. ground beef, *or loose*
  sausage
1 lb. 10-oz. jar spaghetti
  sauce, your favorite
  flavor
1 lb. Velveeta cheese,
  cubed
10³/4-oz. can cream of
  mushroom soup

1. Cook spaghetti according to package directions. Drain. Then place in a large mixing bowl.
2. In a non-stick skillet, brown ground beef or sausage. Drain off drippings. Then add to cooked spaghetti in the large bowl.
3. Stir remaining ingredients into bowl. Mix together well, and then place in slow cooker.
4. Cook on Low 2-4 hours, or until heated through.

Slow-Cooker Pizza

Liz Rugg, Wayland, IA

Makes 8-10 servings

Prep Time: 30 minutes
Cooking Time: 2-3 hours
Ideal slow cooker size: 4-qt.

12-oz. bag Kluski, *or*
  sturdy, noodles
1¹/2 lbs. ground beef
32-oz. jar spaghetti sauce,
  your choice of flavors
16 ozs. mozzarella cheese,
  shredded
8 ozs. pepperoni, thinly
  sliced

1. Cook noodles per directions on package. Drain.
2. While noodles are cooking brown ground beef in a non-stick skillet. Drain off drippings.
3. Meanwhile, grease interior of slow cooker.
4. Pour in one-fourth of spaghetti sauce. Follow with half the noodles, and then half the browned ground beef. Top with one-third of the shredded cheese. Follow with half the pepperoni.
5. Repeat the layers, beginning with one-third of the sauce, followed by a layer of the rest of the noodles, a layer of the remaining ground beef, half the cheese, and the rest of the pepperoni.
6. Top with the remaining spaghetti sauce. Finish with the rest of the cheese.
7. Cover and cook on Low for 2-3 hours, or until heated

through and until the cheese has melted.

Variation: Add sliced mushrooms, chopped or sliced onions, sliced black olives, and diced green peppers to one or more of the layers, if you wish.

Tortellini with Broccoli

Susan Kasting, Jenks, OK

Makes 4 servings

Prep Time: 10 minutes
Cooking Time: 2¹/2-3 hours
Ideal slow cooker size: 4-qt.

¹/2 cup water
26-oz. jar pasta sauce, your
  favorite
1 Tbsp. Italian seasoning
9-oz. pkg. frozen spinach
  and cheese tortellini
16-oz. pkg. frozen broccoli
  florets

1. In a bowl, mix water, pasta sauce, and seasoning together.
2. Pour one-third of sauce into bottom of slow cooker. Top with all the tortellini.
3. Pour one-third of sauce over tortellini. Top with broccoli.
4. Pour remaining sauce over broccoli.
5. Cook on High 2¹/2-3 hours, or until broccoli and pasta are tender but not mushy.

Beef Ravioli Casserole

Elizabeth Colucci
Lancaster, PA

Makes 4-6 servings

Prep Time: 30 minutes
Cooking Time: 2 1/2-3 hours
Ideal slow cooker size: 3-qt.

10-oz. pkg. beef ravioli
16-oz. jar spaghetti sauce,
with peppers, mush-
rooms, and onions,
divided
1/2 cup Italian bread
crumbs
1 cup mozzarella cheese
1/4 cup Parmesan cheese,
optional
1/2 cup cheddar cheese

1. Cook ravioli according
to package directions. Drain.
2. Spoon enough spaghetti
sauce into the slow cooker to
cover the bottom. Place ravioli on top.
3. Cover with remaining
sauce. Top with bread
crumbs. Sprinkle with
cheeses.
4. Stir to mix together
well.
5. Cover and cook on Low
2 1/2-3 hours, or until heated
through, but without over-
cooking the pasta.

Chicken Broccoli Alfredo

Mrs. Mahlon Miller
Hutchinson, KS

Makes 4 servings

Prep Time: 30 minutes
Cooking Time: 1-2 hours
Ideal slow cooker size: 3-qt.

8-oz. pkg. noodles, *or*
spaghetti (half a 16-oz.
pkg.)
1 1/2 cups fresh *or* frozen
broccoli
1 lb. uncooked boneless,
skinless chicken breasts,
cubed
10 3/4-oz. can cream of
mushroom soup
1/2 cup grated mild
cheddar cheese

1. Cook noodles according
to package directions, adding
broccoli during the last 4
minutes of the cooking time.
Drain.
2. Saute the chicken in a
non-stick skillet, or in the
microwave, until no longer
pink in the center.
3. Combine all ingredients
in slow cooker.
4. Cover and cook on Low
1-2 hours, or until heated
through and until cheese is
melted.

Cheesy Chicken and Macaroni

LuAnna J. Hochstedler
East Earl, PA

Makes 4-6 servings

Prep Time: 5-10 minutes
Cooking Time: 3-7 hours
Ideal slow cooker size:
3- to 4-qt.

4 small boneless, skinless
chicken breast halves
7 1/4-oz. pkg. macaroni and
cheese dinner, uncooked
1 cup shredded cheddar
cheese
2 cups water
2 cups frozen vegetable
blend, thawed
1/2 cup water, *optional*

1. Place chicken in slow
cooker.
2. Sprinkle contents of
cheese sauce packet over
chicken.
3. Pour dry macaroni on
top.
4. Sprinkle with cheddar
cheese.
5. Pour water over all, being
careful not to wash off the
cheddar cheese.
6. Cover and cook on High
2 hours, or on Low 4 hours.
7. Stir in thawed vegetables,
mixing them in thoroughly. Add
1/2 cup water if needed to keep
the dish from cooking dry.
8. Cover and cook on High
another hour, or on Low
another 2-3 hours, or until vegetables are tender but pasta is
not mushy or dry.

Creamy Cooker Dinner

Anna Musser
Manheim, PA

Makes 6 servings

Prep Time: 7 minutes
Cooking Time: 2½-3 hours
Ideal slow cooker size: 5-qt.

2 cups shredded cheese,
   your choice
2 cups macaroni,
   uncooked
3 cups milk
2 10¾-oz. cans cream of
   mushroom soup
2 cups cooked ham, *or*
   sliced hot dogs, *or*
   cooked, cubed chicken,
   or cooked ground beef

1. Place all ingredients in slow cooker. Mix together gently, but until well blended.
2. Cover and cook on High 2½-3 hours, or until macaroni is cooked but not overdone.

Macaroni and Cheese

Cynthia Morris, Grottoes, VA
Jennifer A. Crouse
Mt. Crawford, VA
Esther S. Martin, Ephrata, PA
Audrey L. Kneer
Williamsfield, IL
Virginia Eberly, Loysville, PA

Makes 4-5 servings

Prep Time: 5 minutes
Cooking Time: 3 hours
Ideal slow cooker size: 3-qt.

1-3 Tbsp. butter, melted,
   depending upon how
   rich you'd like the dish
   to be
1½ cups uncooked
   macaroni
1 qt. milk
8-12 ozs. grated sharp
   cheddar cheese, *or*
   cubed Velveeta cheese
   (not the low-fat variety)
½-1 tsp. salt, depending
   upon your taste and
   dietary preferences
¼ tsp. pepper

1. Stir all ingredients together in slow cooker.
2. Cover and cook on Low 3 hours.

Variations:
   1. Add 2-3 Tbsp. onion, chopped fine, and 1 tsp. salt to Step 1.
   — **Dale Peterson**
   Rapid City, SD

   2. Instead of macaroni, use ½ lb. uncooked medium noodles.
   — **Vera Martin**
   East Earl, PA
   — **Lucille Martin**
   Barnett, MO

Lotsa Cheese Macaroni and Cheese

Renee Baum
Chambersburg, PA

Makes 10 servings

Prep Time: 15 minutes
Cooking Time: 3 hours
Ideal slow cooker size: 3-qt.

1 lb. dry macaroni
1 lb. Velveeta cheese,
   cubed
8 ozs. extra-sharp cheddar
   cheese, shredded
1 qt. milk
1 stick (½ cup) butter, cut
   into small chunks

1. Follow package instructions for preparing the macaroni, but cook the macaroni only half the amount of time as called for. Drain. Pour macaroni into slow cooker.
2. Add remaining ingredients and stir together well.
3. Cover and cook on High 3 hours, stirring occasionally.

Cheesy Macaronis

Renee Suydam, Lancaster, PA
Patricia Fleischer, Carlisle, PA
Ruth Zendt, Mifflintown, PA

Makes 10-12 servings

Prep Time: 30 minutes
Cooking Time: 3 hours
Ideal slow cooker size: 6-qt.

1 lb. dry macaroni
12-oz. can evaporated milk
3 cups milk
2 lbs. Velveeta cheese,
   cubed, *or* sharp cheese,
   shredded

1. Cook macaroni according to package directions. Drain.
2. Put both milks in slow cooker. Cube cheese and add to milk.
3. Stir in cooked macaroni.
4. Cover and cook on Low 3 hours.

Variations:
1. *¼ cup onion, chopped fine, added to Step 2.*
2. *¼ tsp. chili powder, added to Step 2.*
3. *Chopped fresh parsley, chives, or green and/or red bell pepper, added as a garnish just before serving.*
   — **Bonita Ensenberger**
   Albuquerque, NM

4. *1½ tsp. Worcestershire sauce, added to Step 2.*
   — **Cindy Krestynick**
   Glen Lyon, PA

Two-Cheeses Macaroni

Mary Stauffer
Ephrata, PA
Ruth Ann Bender
Cochranville, PA
Esther Burkholder
Millerstown, PA

Makes 6 servings

Prep Time: 8-10 minutes
Cooking Time: 2½ hours
*Ideal slow cooker size:
   4- to 5-qt.*

1 stick (½ cup) butter, cut
   in pieces
2 cups uncooked macaroni
2 cups grated sharp
   cheese, *divided*
24 ozs. small-curd cottage
   cheese
2½ cups boiling water

1. Place butter in bottom of slow cooker. Add uncooked macaroni, 1½ cups shredded cheese, and cottage cheese. Stir together until well mixed.
2. Pour boiling water over everything. Do not stir.
3. Cover and cook on High for 2 hours.
4. Stir. Sprinkle with remaining ½ cup grated cheese.
5. Allow dish to stand for 10-15 minutes before serving to allow sauce to thicken.

Creamy Spirals

Janet Oberholtzer
Ephrata, PA
Renee Baum
Chambersburg, PA

Makes 10-12 servings

Prep Time: 30 minutes
Cooking Time: 2-2½ hours
*Ideal slow cooker size:
   4- to 5-qt.*

1 lb. uncooked spiral pasta
¾ stick (6 Tbsp.) butter
2 cups half-and-half
10¾-oz. can cheddar
   cheese soup
2-4 cups shredded cheddar
   cheese, depending upon
   how creamy you'd like
   the dish to be

1. Cook pasta according to package directions, being careful not to overcook it. Drain.
2. Return pasta to saucepan. Stir in butter until it melts.
3. Combine half-and-half and soup in slow cooker, blending well.
4. Stir pasta and shredded cheese into mixture in cooker.
5. Cover and cook on Low 2-2½ hours, or until heated through and until cheese melts. (If you're home, stir the dish at the end of the first hour of cooking.)

Lemon Dijon Fish

June S. Groff
Denver, PA

Makes 4 servings

Prep Time: 10 minutes
Cooking Time: 3 hours
Ideal slow cooker size: 2-qt.

1¹/₂ lbs. orange roughy
    fillets
2 Tbsp. Dijon mustard
3 Tbsp. butter, melted
1 tsp. Worcestershire sauce
1 Tbsp. lemon juice

1. Cut fillets to fit in slow
cooker.
2. In a bowl, mix remaining ingredients together. Pour
sauce over fish. (If you have
to stack the fish, spoon a portion of the sauce over the first
layer of fish before adding the
second layer.)
3. Cover and cook on Low
3 hours, or until fish flakes
easily but is not dry or overcooked.

Salmon Souffle

Betty B. Dennison
Grove City, PA
Anne Townsend
Albuquerque, NM

Makes 4 servings

Prep Time: 5 minutes
Cooking Time: 2-3 hours
*Ideal slow cooker size:
2- to 3-qt.*

15-oz. can salmon, drained
    and flaked
2 eggs, beaten well
2 cups seasoned croutons
1 cup grated cheddar
    cheese
2 chicken bouillon cubes
1 cup boiling water
¹/₄ tsp. dry mustard,
    optional

1. Grease the interior of
your cooker with non-stick
cooking spray.
2. Combine salmon, eggs,
croutons, and cheese in the
slow cooker.
3. Dissolve bouillon cubes
in boiling water in a small
bowl. Add mustard, if you
wish, and stir. Pour over
salmon mixture and stir
together lightly.
4. Cover and cook on High
2-3 hours, or until mixture
appears to be set. Allow to
stand 15 minutes before serving.

Tuna Loaf

Tina Goss
Duenweg, MO

Makes 4 servings

Prep Time: 5 minutes
Cooking Time: 1 hour
Ideal slow cooker size: 2-qt.

10³/₄-oz. can cream of
    mushroom soup, *divided*
³/₄ cup milk, *divided*
2 eggs, beaten
2 cups dry stuffing mix
12-oz. can tuna, drained
    and flaked

1. Place ²/₃ of the undiluted soup and ¹/₂ cup of the
milk in a small saucepan.
Blend together; then set
aside.
2. Grease the interior of
the slow cooker with non-stick cooking spray. Mix the
rest of the ingredients
together in the slow cooker.
3. Cover and cook on High
for 1 hour. Allow to stand for
15 minutes before serving.
4. Meanwhile, heat the
reserved soup and milk in the
saucepan. Serve over the
cooked tuna as a sauce.

*Variation: Add ¹/₂ tsp. salt and
¹/₄ tsp. pepper to Step 2.*

Vegetables

Barbecued Beans

Mary Ann Bowman
East Earl, PA

Makes 8-10 servings

Prep Time: 10 minutes
Cooking Time: 3-4 hours
Ideal slow cooker size: 4-qt.

2 16-oz. cans baked beans,
   your choice of variety
2 15-oz. cans kidney *or*
   pinto beans, *or* one of
   each, drained
1/2 cup brown sugar
1 cup ketchup
1 onion, chopped

1. Combine all ingredients
in slow cooker. Mix well.
2. Cover and cook on Low
3-4 hours, or until heated
through.

Barbecued Baked Beans

Anne Nolt
Thompsontown, PA

Makes 6-8 servings

Prep Time: 15 minutes
Cooking Time: 3 hours
Ideal slow cooker size: 3-qt.

6 slices uncooked bacon,
   cut into pieces
2 15-oz. cans pork and
   beans
1 tsp. dry mustard, *or* 1
   Tbsp. prepared mustard
1/2 cup ketchup
3/4 cup brown sugar

1. Brown bacon in a non-
stick skillet until crispy.
Drain.
2. Mix with all remaining
ingredients in the slow
cooker.
3. Cover and cook on High
3 hours. Remove cover during
the last 30 minutes to allow
some of the juice to cook off.

Bonnie's Baked Beans
F. Elaine Asper
Norton, OH

Makes 12-14 servings

Prep Time: 15-20 minutes
Cooking Time: 3-8 hours
Ideal slow cooker size: 4-qt.

1/2 lb. bacon cut into 1/2"
   pieces
2 28-oz. cans pork and
   beans
2 medium-sized onions,
   chopped into 11/2"
   pieces
3/4 cup brown sugar
1 cup ketchup

1. Brown bacon in non-
stick skillet until crispy.
Drain.
2. Place all ingredients into
slow cooker.
3. Cover and cook on High
for 3 hours, or on Low for 7-8
hours.

*Variation: Add 2 green pep-
pers in Step 2, cut into 1"
pieces.*

Mac's Beans
Wilma Haberkamp
Fairbank, IA
Mabel Shirk
Mount Crawford, VA

Makes 6-8 servings

Prep Time: 20 minutes
Cooking Time: 4 hours
*Ideal slow cooker size:
   3- to 4-qt.*

4 slices bacon
3 15-oz. cans kidney beans,
   drained, *or* other beans
   of your choice
1 cup chili sauce
1/2 cup sliced green, *or* red,
   onions
1/3 cup brown sugar

1. In a small non-stick skillet, brown bacon until crisp.
Reserve drippings. Crumble
the bacon.
2. Combine all ingredients
except brown sugar in slow
cooker. Sprinkle brown sugar
over the top.
3. Cover and cook on Low
4 hours.
4. Serve the beans directly
from your slow cooker.

Variations:
*1. Use regular onions
instead of green onions.*
*2. Used canned lima beans
instead of kidney beans.*

Barbecued Beans and Beef
Joan Miller, Wayland, IA

Makes 6 servings

Prep Time: 20-25 minutes
Cooking Time: 9-11 hours
*Ideal slow cooker size:
   31/2- to 4-qt.*

1 medium-sized onion,
   chopped
3 slices bacon, cut into
   squares
11/2 lbs. boneless beef
   chuck roast, *or* ribs
1/2 cup barbecue sauce
3 16-oz. cans baked beans
   (not pork and beans!)

1. Mix onion and bacon
together in slow cooker.
2. Top with beef. Pour barbecue sauce over beef.
3. Cover and cook on Low
8-10 hours, or until beef is
tender but not dried out.
4. Remove beef from slow
cooker and place on cutting
board. Cut beef into 1/2"
pieces.
5. Pour juices from slow
cooker through a strainer into
a small bowl. Reserve the
onion, bacon and only 1/2 cup
of cooking juices.
6. Return cut-up beef,
onions, and bacon and
reserved 1/2 cup juices to slow
cooker. Stir in baked beans.
7. Cover and cook on High
40-50 minutes, or until heated
throughout.

Slow-Cooker Baked Beans

Kimberly Burkholder
Millerstown, PA

Makes 6 servings

Prep Time: 15 minutes
Cooking Time: 6 hours,
 after beans are soaked
Ideal slow cooker size: 4-qt.

2½ cups dry pinto, *or*
 kidney, beans
2½ qts. water
4 cups water
2 cups pizza sauce
3 Tbsp. sorghum molasses
2 tsp. chili powder
2 tsp. salt
2 slices bacon, fried and
 crumbled, *optional*

1. Place dry beans in large soup kettle. Cover with 2½ qts. water. Allow to soak for 8 hours or overnight. Drain.
 Or, for a quicker method, bring beans to a boil after covering with 2½ qts. water. Boil, covered, for 2 minutes. Turn off heat and allow beans to stand for 1 hour, covered. Drain.
2. Place beans and 4 cups fresh water in slow cooker.
3. Add remaining ingredients, stirring together well.
4. Cook on Low 6 hours, or until beans are tender.

Full Meal Deal Beans

Reita Yoder
Carlsbad, NM

Makes 10-12 servings

Prep Time: 25 minutes
Cooking Time: 7-8 hours,
 after beans are soaked
Ideal slow cooker size: 2-qt.

3 cups dry pinto beans,
 sorted and washed
3 qts. water
1 ham bone with lots of
 ham still hanging on!
1 bunch green onions,
 chopped
1 Tbsp. ground cumin,
 optional
5½ cups water
10¾-oz. can Rotel chili
 and tomatoes
salt to taste, *optional*

1. Place dry beans in a large soup kettle and cover with 3 qts. water. Cover and allow to stand overnight or for 8 hours.
 Or for a quicker method, follow the same directions, but instead of standing for 8 hours, bring to a boil and cook for 2 minutes. Keep beans covered, remove from heat, and allow to stand for 1 hour. Drain beans.
2. Place ham bone, green onions, and cumin in the bottom of the slow cooker.
3. Put drained beans on top. Add 5½ cups fresh water and tomatoes.

4. Cover and cook on High 7-8 hours or until beans are soft.
5. Stir in salt if you wish. Let stand 15 minutes before serving.

Makes-A-Meal Baked Beans

Ruth Fisher
Leicester, NY

Makes 6-8 servings

Prep Time: 15 minutes
Cooking Time: 3 hours
Ideal slow cooker size: 3-qt.

1 lb. ground beef
½ cup chopped onions
½ tsp. taco seasoning, *or*
 more
1 *or* 2 15-oz. cans pork and
 beans
¾ cup barbecue sauce

1. Brown ground beef and onions in a non-stick skillet. Drain.
2. Stir all ingredients together in the slow cooker, including the browned ground beef and onions.
3. Cover and cook on Low 3 hours.

Baked Limas

Eleanor Larson
Glen Lyon, PA

Makes 6 servings

Prep Time: 1¹/2-8 hours
Cooking Time: 4-8 hours
Ideal slow cooker size:
*   10- to 12-qt.*

1 lb. dried lima beans
2¹/2 qts. water
¹/4 lb. bacon, cut into
   squares
¹/4 cup molasses
2 Tbsp. brown sugar
1 cup tomato sauce

1. Wash beans. Place in
large soup kettle. Cover with
2¹/2 qts. water. Cover and
soak for 8 hours or overnight.
Drain, reserving soaking
water.
   Or for a quicker method,
bring beans in 2¹/2 qts. water
to a boil. Cover and continue
boiling for 2 minutes.
   Remove from heat, keep
covered, and allow to stand
for 1 hour. Drain, reserving
soaking water.
   2. Meanwhile, brown
bacon in non-stick skillet
until crispy. Drain.
   3. Place soaked beans in
slow cooker. Add remaining
ingredients and stir. Add
enough bean water to cover
beans.
   4. Cover and cook on Low
for 8 hours, or on High for 4
hours, or until beans are tender but not mushy.

Barbecued Black Beans with Sweet Potatoes

Barbara Jean Fabel
Wausau, WI

Makes 4-6 servings

Prep Time: 15 minutes
Cooking Time: 2-4 hours
Ideal slow cooker size: 3-qt.

4 large sweet potatoes,
   peeled and cut into 8
   chunks each
15-oz. can black beans,
   rinsed and drained
1 medium onion, diced
2 ribs celery, sliced
9 ozs. Sweet Baby Ray's
   Barbecue Sauce

1. Place sweet potatoes in
slow cooker.
   2. Combine remaining
ingredients. Pour over sweet
potatoes.
   3. Cover. Cook on High 2-3
hours, or on Low 4 hours.

Creamy Broccoli

Carolyn Fultz
Angola, IN

Makes 4-5 servings

Prep Time: 10 minutes
Cooking Time: 2¹/2-6 hours
Ideal slow cooker size: 3-qt.

2 10-oz. pkgs. frozen
   broccoli spears, thawed
   and cut up
10³/4-oz. can cream of
   celery soup
1¹/4 cups grated sharp
   cheddar cheese, *divided*
¹/4 cup green onion,
   minced
1 cup saltine crackers,
   crushed

1. Spray slow cooker with
non-stick cooking spray.
   2. Combine broccoli, soup,
1 cup cheese, and onion in
slow cooker.
   3. Sprinkle top with crackers and remaining cheese.
   4. Cover and cook on Low
5-6 hours, or on High 2¹/2-3
hours.

A Tip —

Yams and sweet potatoes are not the same. Yams are
much drier. Likewise, there are many varieties of apples,
from very tart to very sweet, from firm texture to soft.
Experiment with different kinds to discover your favorite for
a recipe.

Golden Cauliflower

Rosalie D. Miller
Mifflintown, PA
Dede Peterson
Rapid City, SD

Makes 4-6 servings

Prep Time: 5-10 minutes
Cooking Time: 1 1/2-5 hours
Ideal slow cooker size: 3-qt.

2 10-oz. pkgs. frozen
  cauliflower, thawed
salt and pepper
10 3/4-oz. can condensed
  cheddar cheese soup
4 slices bacon, crisply fried
  and crumbled

1. Place cauliflower in
slow cooker. Season with salt
and pepper.
2. Spoon soup over top.
Sprinkle with bacon.
3. Cover and cook on High
1 1/2 hours, or on Low 4-5
hours, or until cauliflower is
tender.

*Tip: If you forgot to thaw the
cauliflower, cook it 30 minutes
longer.*

Steamed Carrots

Dede Peterson
Rapid City, SD

Makes 4 servings

Prep Time: 15-20 minutes
Cooking Time: 4-6 hours
Ideal slow cooker size: 4-qt.

8 large carrots, sliced
  diagonally
1/4 cup water
2 Tbsp. butter
1 tsp. sugar
1/4 tsp. salt

1. Layer carrots in slow
cooker. Add water and pieces
of butter. Sprinkle with sugar
and salt.
2. Cover and cook on Low
4-6 hours.

*Variation: Stir in 1-2 Tbsp.
brown sugar just before serving.*
— Rhonda Freed
Lowville, NY

Slow-Cooked
Glazed Carrots

Michele Ruvola
Selden, NY

Makes 6-7 servings

Prep Time: 5 minutes
Cooking Time: 6 1/2-8 1/2 hours
Ideal slow cooker size:
  3- to 4-qt.

2-lb. bag baby carrots
1 1/2 cups water
1/4 cup honey
2 Tbsp. butter
1/4 tsp. salt
1/8 tsp. pepper

1. Combine carrots and
water in slow cooker.
2. Cover and cook on Low
6-8 hours, or until carrots are
tender.
3. Drain carrots and return
to slow cooker.
4. Stir in honey, butter,
salt, and pepper. Mix well.
5. Cover and cook on Low
30 minutes, or until glazed.

Golden Carrots

Jan Mast
Lancaster, PA

Makes 6 servings

Prep Time: 5 minutes
Cooking Time: 3-4 hours
Ideal slow cooker size: 2-qt.

2-lb. pkg. baby carrots
1/2 cup golden raisins
1 stick (1/2 cup) butter,
  melted *or* softened
1/3 cup honey
2 Tbsp. lemon juice
1/2 tsp. ground ginger,
  optional

1. Combine all ingredients in slow cooker.
2. Cover and cook on Low 3-4 hours, or until carrots are tender-crisp.

Variation: To use whole carrots, cut into 1"-long chunks.

If the carrots are thick, you may need to cook them 5-6 hours until they become tender-crisp.

Apricot-Glazed Carrots

Marcia S. Myer
Manheim, PA

Makes 8 servings

Prep Time: 5 minutes
Cooking Time: 9 hours, plus
  10-15 minutes
Ideal slow cooker size: 4-qt.

2 lbs. baby carrots
1 onion, chopped
1/2 cup water
1/3 cup honey
1/3 cup apricot preserves
2 Tbsp. chopped fresh
  parsley

1. Place carrots and onions in slow cooker. Add water.
2. Cover and cook on Low 9 hours.
3. Drain liquid from slow cooker.
4. In a small bowl, mix honey and preserves together. Pour over carrots.
5. Cover and cook on High 10-15 minutes
6. Sprinkle with parsley before serving.

Glazed Carrots

Gloria Frey
Lebanon, PA

Makes 4 servings

Prep Time: 10-15 minutes
Cooking Time: 2 1/2-3 1/2 hours
Ideal slow cooker size: 2-qt.

16-oz. pkg. frozen baby
  carrots
1/4 cup apple cider, *or*
  apple juice
1/4 cup apple jelly
1 1/2 tsp. Dijon mustard

1. Put carrots and apple juice in slow cooker.
2. Cover and cook on High 2-3 hours, until carrots are tender.
3. Blend jelly and mustard together in a small bowl.
4. During the last 45 minutes of cooking time, after carrots are tender, stir in blended apple jelly and mustard. Continue to heat until steaming hot.

Candied Carrots
Arlene M. Kopp
Lineboro, MD

Makes 3-4 servings

Prep Time: 10 minutes
Cooking Time: 2¹/₂-3¹/₂ hours
Ideal slow cooker size: 3-qt.

1 lb. carrots, cut into
  1" pieces
¹/₂ tsp. salt
¹/₄ cup water
2 Tbsp. butter
¹/₂ cup light brown sugar,
  firmly packed
2 Tbsp. chopped nuts

1. Place carrots in slow cooker. Sprinkle with salt.
2. Pour water in along the side of the cooker.
3. Cover and cook on High 2-3 hours, or until carrots are just tender. Drain.
4. Stir in butter. Sprinkle with sugar.
5. Cover and cook on High 30 minutes.
6. Sprinkle with nuts about 10 minutes before end of cooking time.

Carrot Casserole
Janessa Hochstedler
East Earl, PA

Makes 4-5 servings

Prep Time: 20 minutes
Cooking Time: 4-5 hours
Ideal slow cooker size: 2-qt.

4 cups sliced carrots
1 medium-sized onion,
  chopped
10³/₄-oz. can cream of
  celery soup
¹/₂ cup Velveeta cheese,
  cubed
¹/₄-¹/₂ tsp. salt

1. Mix all ingredients in slow cooker.
2. Cover and cook on Low 4-5 hours, or until carrots are tender but not mushy.

Zippy Vegetable Medley
Gloria Frey
Lebanon, PA

Makes 4-5 servings

Prep Time: 10-15 minutes
Cooking Time: 2¹/₂ hours
Ideal slow cooker size: 2-qt.

16-oz. pkg. frozen broccoli,
  cauliflower, and carrots
16-oz. pkg. frozen corn
2 10¹/₂-oz. cans fiesta
  nacho cheese soup
¹/₂ cup milk

1. Combine broccoli mixture and corn in slow cooker.
2. Combine soups and milk in a microwave-safe bowl. Microwave for 1 minute on High, or just enough to mix well. When blended, pour over vegetables.
3. Cover and cook on High for 2¹/₂ hours, or until hot and bubbly and vegetables are done to your liking.

Variation: If you'd like a milder dish, replace the one can of fiesta nacho cheese soup with one can of cheddar cheese soup.

— Yvonne Boettger
Harrisonburg, VA

Garden Vegetables

Esther Gingerich
Parnell, IA
Judy A. and Sharon Wantland
Menomonee Falls, WI

Makes 6 servings

Prep Time: 15 minutes
Cooking Time: 2½-4 hours
Ideal slow cooker size: 3-qt.

16-oz. pkg. frozen
   vegetables, thawed
   (combination of
   broccoli, carrots,
   cauliflower, etc.)
10¾-oz. can cream of
   mushroom soup
half a soup can water
⅓ cup sour cream
1-2 cups shredded Swiss,
   or mozzarella, cheese,
   divided
6-oz. can French-fried
   onions, *divided*

1. In slow cooker, combine
thawed vegetables, soup,
water, sour cream, half the
cheese, and half the onions.
2. Cover and cook on Low
2½-4 hours, or until vegetables are as soft as you like
them.
3. Fifteen minutes before
the end of the cooking time,
sprinkle remaining cheese
and onions on top.

Creamy Vegetables

Gloria Frey
Lebanon, PA

Makes 4-5 servings

Prep Time: 5-10 minutes
Cooking Time: 2½-3½ hours
Ideal slow cooker size:
   2- to 3-qt.

16-oz. pkg. frozen broccoli
   and cauliflower
10¾-oz. can cream of
   mushroom soup
8-oz. carton spreadable
   garden vegetable cream
   cheese
1 cup seasoned croutons

1. Place frozen vegetables
in slow cooker.
2. Put soup and cream
cheese in a microwave-safe
bowl. Microwave on High for
1 minute. Stir the soup and
cheese together until smooth.
Microwave for 30-60 seconds
more if necessary to melt the
two ingredients.
3. Pour cheesy soup over
vegetables in slow cooker and
mix well.
4. Cover and cook on Low
2½-3½ hours, or until vegetables are tender.
5. Thirty minutes before
the end of the cooking time,
sprinkle croutons over top.
Continue to cook, uncovered.

Company Corn

Sherril Bieberly
Salina, KS
Jeannine Janzen
Elbing, KS

Makes 8-10 servings

Prep Time: 5-10 minutes
Cooking Time: 5 hours
Ideal slow cooker size:
   3- to 4-qt.

2 20-oz. pkgs. frozen corn
½ tsp. salt
2-4 Tbsp. sugar, according
   to your taste preference
1 stick (½ cup) butter
8-oz. pkg. cream cheese

1. Place frozen corn in
slow cooker. Stir in salt and
sugar.
2. Cut butter and cream
cheese into little pieces and
place on top of corn.
3. Cook on Low for 5
hours, stirring occasionally if
you're at home and able to do
so.

Variations:
   *1. Add 6 slices American
cheese, broken up, to Step 2.*
   — Mary Ann Bowman
   East Earl, PA

   *2. For a cheesier flavor, use
½ lb. Velveeta cheese, cubed, in
place of the cream cheese. And
use ½-1 cup shredded cheddar
cheese instead of the American
cheese (above).*
   — Sheila Soldner
   Lititz, PA

3. Reduce salt to 1/4 tsp. Add 1/4 tsp. pepper and 1/2 tsp. garlic powder.

— **Shawn Eshleman**
Ephrata, PA

4. Drop the salt and sugar, but include everything else.

— **Ruth Hofstetter**
Versailles, MO

Corn Pudding

Clara Newswanger
Gordonville, PA

Makes 4-5 servings

Prep Time: 10-15 minutes
Cooking Time: 4 hours
Ideal slow cooker size: 3-qt.

1/4 -1/2 cup sugar, according to your taste preference
3 Tbsp. cornstarch
2 eggs, beaten slightly
12-oz. can evaporated milk
16-oz. can cream-style corn

1. Combine all ingredients except corn in slow cooker until well blended.
2. Add corn. Mix well.
3. Cook on Low 4 hours. Allow to stand for 15 minutes before serving.

Sweet Dried Corn

Shelia Heil
Lancaster, PA

Makes 14 servings

Prep Time: 5 minutes
Cooking Time: 2-2 1/2 hours
Ideal slow cooker size: 4-qt.

5 15-oz. cans whole-kernel corn, drained
1 stick (1/2 cup) butter, at room temperature
3/4 cup brown sugar

1. Place corn in slow cooker. Add butter and brown sugar. Stir to combine.
2. Cook on High until hot, about 1 1/2 hours. Stir. Continue cooking on Low for another 30-60 minutes, or until corn is very hot.

Dried Corn

Mary B. Sensenig
New Holland, PA

Makes 4 servings

Prep Time: 3-5 minutes
Cooking Time: 4 hours
Ideal slow cooker size: 3-qt.

15-oz. can dried corn
2 Tbsp. sugar
3 Tbsp. butter, softened
1 tsp. salt
1 cup half-and-half
2 Tbsp. water

1. Place all ingredients in slow cooker. Mix together well.
2. Cover and cook on Low 4 hours.

If you're able, check after cooking 3 hours to make sure the corn isn't cooking dry. If it appears to be, stir in an additional 1/4-1/2 cup half-and-half. Cover and continue cooking.

A Tip —

If there is too much liquid in your cooker, stick a toothpick under the edge of the lid to tilt it slightly and to allow the steam to escape.

Carol Sherwood
Batavia, NY

Green Beans Au Gratin

Donna Lantgen
Chadron, NE

Makes 12-14 servings

Prep Time: 10 minutes
Cooking Time: 5-6 hours
Ideal slow cooker size: 4-qt.

2 lbs. frozen green beans,
  or 4 14½-oz. cans,
  drained
1-2 cups cubed Velveeta
  cheese, depending upon
  how much you like
  cheese
½ cup chopped onion
½ cup milk
1 Tbsp. flour

1. Place beans, cheese, and onion in slow cooker. Stir together well.
2. Place milk first, and then flour, in a jar with a tight-fitting lid. Shake together until smooth. Or mix together in a small bowl until smooth. Then stir into other ingredients.
3. Cover and cook on Low 5-6 hours, or until beans are fully cooked and heated through.

Dressed-Up Green Beans

Pat Unternahrer
Wayland, IA

Makes 10-12 servings

Prep Time: 5-10 minutes
Cooking Time: 2½-2¾ hours
Ideal slow cooker size:
  3- to 4-qt.

3 14½-oz. cans green
  beans, drained
2 10¾-oz. cans mushroom
  soup
6-oz. can cheddar, *or*
  original, French-fried
  onions, *divided*

1. Spray interior of slow cooker with non-stick cooking spray.
2. Put drained green beans into cooker.
3. Put 2 cans mushroom soup on top of beans. Stir together gently.
4. Cook on High 2 hours.
5. Add half a can French fried onions. Stir and continue to cook 30-45 minutes.
6. Sprinkle remaining onions on top and serve.

Barbecued Green Beans

Sharon Timpe
Jackson, WI
Ruth E. Martin
Loysville, PA

Makes 10-12 servings

Prep Time: 15 minutes
Cooking Time: 3-4 hours
Ideal slow cooker size: 4-qt.

3 14½-oz. cans cut green
  beans (drain 2 cans
  completely; reserve
  liquid from 1 can)
1 small onion, diced
1 cup ketchup
¾ cup brown sugar
4 strips bacon, cooked
  crisp and crumbled

1. Combine green beans, diced onion, ketchup, and brown sugar in your slow cooker.
2. Add ⅓ cup of reserved bean liquid. Mix gently.
3. Cover and cook on Low 3-4 hours, until beans are tender and heated through. Stir at the end of 2 hours of cooking, if you're home.
4. Pour in a little reserved bean juice if the sauce thickens more than you like.
5. Sprinkle bacon over beans just before serving.

Variation: Use 1½ lbs. fresh green beans instead of canned beans. When using fresh beans, you'll need to increase the cooking time to 5-6 hours on Low,

depending upon how soft or crunchy you like your beans.
— Lois Niebauer
Pedricktown, NJ

Special Green Beans

Sara Kinsinger
Stuarts Draft, VA

Makes 12-14 servings

Prep Time: 30-45 minutes
Cooking Time: 1-2 hours
Ideal slow cooker size: 4-qt.

4 14½-oz. cans green
  beans, drained
10¾-oz. can cream of
  mushroom soup
14½-oz. can chicken broth
1 cup tater tots
3-oz. can French-fried
  onion rings

1. Put green beans in slow cooker.
2. In a bowl, mix soup and broth together. Spread over beans.
3. Spoon tater tots over all. Top with onion rings.
4. Cover and bake on High 1-2 hours, or until heated through and potatoes are cooked.

Creole Green Beans

Jan Mast
Lancaster, PA

Makes 4-6 servings

Prep Time: 10 minutes
Cooking Time: 3-4 hours
Ideal slow cooker size: 2-qt.

2 small onions, chopped
half a stick (¼ cup) butter
4 cups green beans, fresh
  or frozen
½ cup salsa
2-3 Tbsp. brown sugar
½ tsp. garlic salt, *optional*

1. Saute onions in butter in a saucepan.
2. Combine with remaining ingredients in slow cooker.
3. Cover and cook on Low 3-4 hours, or longer, depending upon how soft or crunchy you like your beans.

Greek-Style Green Beans

Diann J. Dunham
State College, PA

Makes 6 servings

Prep Time: 5 minutes
Cooking Time: 2-5 hours
Ideal slow cooker size: 4-qt.

20 ozs. whole *or* cut-up
  frozen beans (not
  French cut)
2 cups tomato sauce
2 tsp. dried onion flakes,
  optional
pinch of dried marjoram
  or oregano
pinch of ground nutmeg
pinch of cinnamon

1. Combine all ingredients in slow cooker, mixing together thoroughly.
2. Cover and cook on Low 2-4 hours if the beans are defrosted, or for 3-5 hours on Low if the beans are frozen, or until the beans are done to your liking.

Green Beans Portuguese-Style

Joyce Kaut, Rochester, NY

Makes 8 servings

Prep Time: 20 minutes
Cooking Time: 3-8 hours
Ideal slow cooker size: 5-qt.

1/4 lb. salt pork, *or* bacon
2 lbs. fresh green beans
2 medium-sized tomatoes
1/2 tsp. each salt and
    pepper
2 cups beef bouillon, *or* 2
    beef bouillon cubes
    dissolved in 2 cups water

1. Dice salt pork or bacon, and spread across the bottom of your slow cooker.
2. Wash the beans, then break into 2"-3" pieces. Layer the beans over the pork or bacon.
3. Peel, seed, and cube tomatoes. Spoon over beans.
4. Sprinkle with salt and pepper. Pour bouillon over all ingredients in slow cooker.
5. Cook on High 3-4 hours, or on Low 6-8 hours, or until beans are done to your liking.

Variations:
1. You may use a 141/2-oz. can of tomatoes instead of fresh ones.
2. You may use canned green beans instead of fresh.
If you use canned tomatoes and/or beans, cook on High for 2-3 hours, or on Low for 4-5 hours.

Super Green Beans

Esther J. Yoder
Hartville, OH

Makes 5 servings

Prep Time: 15 minutes
Cooking Time: 1-2 hours
Ideal slow cooker size: 3-qt.

2 141/2-oz. cans green
    beans, undrained
1 cup cooked cubed ham
1/3 cup finely chopped
    onion
1 Tbsp. melted butter, *or*
    bacon drippings

1. Place undrained beans in cooker. Add remaining ingredients and mix well.
2. Cook on High 1-2 hours, or until steaming hot.

Fresh Green Beans

Lizzie Ann Yoder
Hartville, OH

Makes 6-8 servings

Prep Time: 20 minutes
Cooking Time: 6-24 hours
Ideal slow cooker size:
    4- to 5-qt.

1/4 lb. ham, *or* bacon,
    pieces
2 lbs. fresh green beans,
    washed and cut into
    pieces, *or* Frenched
3-4 cups water
1 scant tsp. salt

1. If using bacon, cut it into squares and brown in non-stick skillet. When crispy, drain and set aside.
2. Place all ingredients in slow cooker. Mix together well.
3. Cover and cook on High 6-10 hours, or on Low 10-24 hours, or until beans are done to your liking.

Cheese-y Potatoes

Barbara Sparks
Glen Burnie, MD

Makes 8-10 servings

Prep Time: 10 minutes
Cooking Time: 5¹/2-8 hours
Ideal slow cooker size: 4-qt.

30-oz. pkg. frozen
    shredded hash brown
    potatoes, partially
    thawed
10³/4-oz. can cheddar
    cheese soup
12-oz. can evaporated milk
2 Tbsp. butter, softened *or*
    melted
¹/2 tsp. salt
pepper to taste, *optional*

1. Spray interior of slow
cooker with non-stick cooking
spray.
    2. Break up partially
thawed potatoes in slow
cooker.
    3. In a bowl stir together
soup, milk, butter, and salt,
and pepper if you wish. Pour
over potatoes. Mix together
gently.
    4. Cover and cook on Low
5¹/2-8 hours, or until potatoes
are tender and fully cooked.

Slow-Cooked Cheese-y Potatoes

Tracey Hanson Schramel
Windom, MN
Sherry H. Kauffman
Minot, ND

Makes 10-12 servings

Prep Time: 8-10 minutes
Cooking Time: 3-9 hours
Ideal slow cooker size: 5-qt.

30-oz. pkg. frozen hash
    browns, shredded *or*
    sliced
2 10³/4-oz. cans cheddar
    cheese soup
12-oz. can evaporated milk
3-oz. can French-fried
    onion rings, *divided*
³/4 tsp. salt
¹/4 tsp. pepper

1. Spray interior of slow
cooker with non-stick cooking
spray.
    2. Combine potatoes, soup,
milk, half the onion rings,
salt, and pepper in the slow
cooker.
    3. Cover and cook on Low
7-9 hours, or on High 3-4
hours, or until potatoes are
heated through.
    4. Sprinkle remaining
onion rings over top before
serving.

Variation: Instead of the
French-fried onion rings, mix
together ¹/4 cup melted butter
and 1¹/2 cups crushed corn-
flakes in a bowl. Sprinkle over
the potatoes during their last 15

minutes of cooking. (No need to
replace the onion rings mixed
into the potatoes in Step 2.)
— **Audrey Romonosky**
Austin, TX

Creamy Easy Potatoes

Loretta Hanson
Hendricks, MN

Makes 6-8 servings

Prep Time: 15 minutes
Cooking Time: 4-6 hours
Ideal slow cooker size: 4-qt.

30-oz. pkg. frozen cubed
    hash browns, thawed
12-oz. can evaporated milk
10³/4-oz. can cream of
    celery soup
10³/4-oz. can cream of
    potato soup
¹/2 cup diced onion,
    optional
1 cup shredded cheddar
    cheese

1. Spray slow cooker with
non-stick cooking spray.
    2. Combine hash browns,
milk, soups, and onion if you
wish in slow cooker.
    3. Sprinkle cheese over
top.
    4. Cover and cook on Low
4-6 hours, stirring occasionally if you're around, until
potatoes are tender and
cooked through.

Easy Cheese-y Potatoes

Carol Sherwood
Batavia, NY

Makes 4 servings

Prep Time: 20 minutes
Cooking Time: 3-8 hours
Ideal slow cooker size: 4-qt.

30-oz. pkg. frozen hash brown potatoes, partially thawed
1-lb. pkg. kielbasa, chopped
1 medium-sized onion, diced
10³/4-oz. can cheddar cheese soup
1 soup can milk

1. Spray interior of slow cooker with non-stick cooking spray.
2. Place first 3 ingredients in slow cooker. Stir together.
3. Mix soup and milk together in a bowl, stirring until well blended. Pour into slow cooker.
4. Fold all ingredients together.
5. Cover and cook on High 3 hours, or on Low 7-8 hours.

Sour Cream Hash Browns

Katrina Eberly
Stevens, PA
Stacy Petersheim
Mechanicsburg, PA
Jeanette Oberholtzer
Manheim, PA

Makes 10-12 servings

Prep Time: 5 minutes
Cooking Time: 3¹/2-4¹/2 hours
Ideal slow cooker size:
4- to 6-qt.

10³/4-oz. can cream of mushroom soup, plain, *or* with roasted garlic
1 cup sour cream, fat-free *or* regular
1¹/2-3 cups shredded cheddar, *or* Monterey Jack, cheese
30-oz. pkg. frozen cubed hash brown potatoes

1. Spray slow cooker with non-stick cooking spray.
2. Combine soup, sour cream, and cheese in a medium bowl. Mix well.
3. Pour half of potatoes into slow cooker.
4. Top with half of the soup mixture.
5. Repeat layers. Spread soup mixture evenly over top.
6. Cook on Low 3¹/2-4¹/2 hours, or until the potatoes are tender and cooked through.

Optional ingredients:
1/4 lb. bacon, cut up, browned until crispy, and drained
1/2 cup sliced green onions
1 garlic clove, minced
salt and pepper to taste

Add any or all of these to the mixture in Step 2.
— **Mary Kennell**
Roanoke, IL

Satisfyingly Creamy Potatoes

Sherry Kauffman
Minot, ND

Makes 8-10 servings

Prep Time: 15 minutes
Cooking Time: 3-4 hours
Ideal slow cooker size: 5-qt.

1 pt. sour cream
10³/4-oz. can cream of chicken soup
2 cups Velveeta cheese, cubed
1/2 cup chopped onions
30-oz. pkg. frozen hash browns

1. Spray interior of slow cooker with non-stick cooking spray.
2. Combine all ingredients in the slow cooker.
3. Cover and cook on Low 3-4 hours, or until potatoes are tender and cooked through.

Creamy Hash Browns

Starla Kreider
Mohrsville, PA

Makes 14 servings

Prep Time: 10 minutes
Cooking Time: 4-5 hours
Ideal slow cooker size: 5-qt.

30-oz. package frozen, diced hash browns
2 cups cubed *or* shredded cheese of your choice
2 cups sour cream
2 10³/4-oz. cans cream of chicken soup
half a stick (¹/4 cup) butter, melted

1. Place hash browns in an ungreased slow cooker.
2. Combine remaining ingredients and pour over the potatoes. Mix well.
3. Cover and cook on Low 4-5 hours, or until potatoes are tender and heated through.

Scalloped Potatoes

Edna Mae Herschberger
Arthur, IL

Makes 6-8 servings

Prep Time: 5 minutes
Cooking Time: 4¹/2-5¹/2 hours
Ideal slow cooker size: 4-qt.

1 pint half-and-half
1 stick (¹/2 cup) butter, softened *or* melted
30-oz. pkg. hash browns
1 tsp. garlic powder
¹/4 tsp. pepper, *optional*
1 lb. Velveeta, cubed

1. Spray interior of slow cooker with non-stick cooking spray.
2. Place all ingredients except Velveeta in slow cooker. Stir together gently but until well mixed.
3. Cover and cook on Low 4-5 hours, or until potatoes are tender and cooked through.
4. Stir in Velveeta. Cook until melted, approximately 30 minutes.

Onion-y Potatoes

Jeannine Janzen
Elbing, KS

Makes 6-8 servings

Prep Time: 5-10 minutes
Cooking Time: 4 hours
Ideal slow cooker size: 4-qt.

30-oz. pkg. frozen hash brown potatoes, thawed
¹/2 cup diced onion, *optional*
5²/3 Tbsp. (¹/3 cup) butter, melted
2 cups French onion dip
16-oz. pkg. American cheese, cut up

1. Spray interior of slow cooker with non-stick cooking spray.
2. Combine all ingredients in slow cooker. Mix well.
3. Cover and cook on Low 4 hours, or until potatoes are tender and cooked through.

A Tip —

It's quite convenient to use a slow cooker to cook potatoes for salads or for fried potatoes or as baked potatoes. Just fill the slow cooker with cleaned potatoes and cook all day until done.

Darla Sathre
Baxter, MN

Bacon Hash Browns

Tierra Woods
Duenweg, MO

Makes 5-6 servings

Prep Time: 15 minutes
Cooking Time: 4 hours
Ideal slow cooker size: 4-qt.

1/4 lb. bacon
6 cups frozen hash brown
  potatoes, partially
  thawed
1 cup mayonnaise
1/2 cup processed cheese
  sauce

1. Cut up bacon. Brown in non-stick skillet until crispy. Drain and set aside.
2. Spray interior of slow cooker with non-stick cooking spray.
3. Measure out 1/4 cup bacon and reserve. Place remainder of bacon, and the rest of the ingredients into the slow cooker. Mix together well.
4. Cover and cook on Low for 4 hours.
5. Sprinkle with reserved bacon just before serving.

Ranch Hash Browns

Jean Butzer
Batavia, NY

Makes 5-6 servings

Prep Time: 5 minutes
Cooking Time: 4-7 hours
Ideal slow cooker size: 6-qt.

30-oz. bag frozen hash
  browns, partially
  thawed
8-oz. pkg. cream cheese,
  softened
1 envelope dry ranch
  dressing mix
10 3/4-oz. can cream of
  potato soup

1. Spray interior of slow cooker with non-stick cooking spray.
2. Place potatoes in slow cooker. Break up with a spoon if frozen together.
3. Mix remaining ingredients in a bowl. Stir gently into potatoes.
4. Cook on Low 4-7 hours, or until potatoes are cooked through. Stir carefully before serving.

Creamy Scalloped Potatoes

Nancy Wagner Graves
Manhattan, KS

Makes 8-10 servings

Prep Time: 5-15 minutes,
* depending upon the kind of*
* potatoes you use*
Cooking Time: 3-4 hours for
* fresh potatoes; 2-5 hours for*
* frozen hash browns*
Ideal slow cooker size:
* 4- to 5-qt.*

2 Tbsp. dried minced
  onion
1 medium clove garlic,
  minced
1 tsp. salt
8-10 medium-sized fresh
  potatoes, sliced, *or* 30-
  oz. bag frozen hash
  browns, *divided*
8-oz. pkg. cream cheese,
  cubed, *divided*
1/2 cup shredded cheddar
  cheese, *optional*

1. Spray interior of slow cooker with non-stick cooking spray.

2. In a small bowl, combine onion, garlic, and salt.

3. Layer about one-fourth of the potatoes into the slow cooker.

4. Sprinkle one-fourth of onion-garlic mixture over potatoes.

5. Spoon about one-third of cream cheese cubes over top.

6. Repeat layers, ending with the seasoning.

7. If using fresh potatoes, cook on High 3-4 hours, or until potatoes are tender.

If using frozen hash browns, cook on High 2 hours, or on Low 4-5 hours, or until potatoes are tender and cooked through.

8. Stir potatoes to spread out the cream cheese. If you wish, you can mash the potatoes at this point.

9. If you like, sprinkle shredded cheese over top of the sliced or mashed potatoes.

10. Cover and cook an additional 10 minutes, or until the cheese is melted.

Plain Old Scalloped Potatoes

Ruth Ann Penner
Hillsboro, KS

Makes 3-4 servings

Prep Time: 10 minutes
Cooking Time: 2 hours
Ideal slow cooker size: 3-qt.

2 cups thinly sliced raw potatoes, *divided*
1 Tbsp. flour
1 tsp. salt
pepper
1 cup milk
1 Tbsp. butter

1. Spray slow cooker with non-stick cooking spray.

2. Put half of thinly sliced potatoes in bottom of slow cooker.

3. In a small bowl, mix together flour, salt, and pepper. Sprinkle half over top of potatoes.

4. Repeat layering.

5. Pour milk over all. Dot with butter.

6. Cover and cook on High for 2 hours.

Tips:
1. Pour milk over all as soon as possible to avoid having potatoes turn dark.
2. A cup of fully cooked ham cubes could be stirred in before serving.
3. Top with shredded cheese, if you wish.

Speedy Potato Dish

Esther J. Yoder
Hartville, OH

Makes 3-4 servings

Prep Time: 15 minutes
Cooking Time: 3-4 hours
Ideal slow cooker size: 4-qt.

5 medium potatoes, peeled and sliced
10³/4-oz. can cream of chicken soup
¹/4 cup chicken broth
¹/4 -¹/2 tsp. pepper

1. Spray interior of slow cooker with non-stick cooking spray.

2. Gently fold ingredients together in slow cooker.

3. Cover and cook on High 3-4 hours, or until potatoes are soft but not mushy or dry.

From-Scratch Scalloped Potatoes

Heather Horst
Lebanon, PA

Makes 12-15 servings

Prep Time: 20 minutes
Cooking Time: 4-5 hours
Ideal slow cooker size:
5- to 6-qt.

6 lbs. potatoes, peeled and thinly sliced, *divided*
2 cups cheddar cheese, shredded
1 cup onion, chopped
2 10³/4-oz. cans cream of mushroom soup
1 cup water
¹/2 tsp. each of salt and pepper
1 tsp. garlic powder, *optional*

1. Place one-third of sliced potatoes in slow cooker.
2. In a medium-sized bowl, mix together shredded cheese, onion, soup, water, and seasonings.
3. Pour one-third of creamy mixture over potatoes.
4. Repeat layers two more times.
5. Cover and cook on High 4-5 hours, or until the potatoes are tender.

Gourmet Scalloped Potatoes

Jean Hindal
Grandin, MO

Makes 10-12 servings

Prep Time: 15 minutes
Cooking Time: 4-8 hours
Ideal slow cooker size: 6-qt.

8 raw potatoes (peeled *or* not), shredded
2 cups sour cream
10³/4-oz. can cream of chicken, *or* mushroom, soup
2 cups shredded cheddar cheese
1 tsp. salt
¹/4 tsp pepper, *optional*
1 tsp. dried onion flakes, *optional*

1. Spray interior of slow cooker with non-stick cooking spray.
2. Combine all ingredients gently in your slow cooker.
3. Cover and cook on High 4 hours, or on Low 6-8 hours, or until potatoes are tender.

From-Scratch Creamy Potatoes

Mary Stauffer
Ephrata, PA

Makes 15 servings

Prep Time: 1 hour preparing;
3 hours chilling
Cooking Time: 5 hours
Ideal slow cooker size: 6-qt.

5¹/2 pounds potatoes
2 10¹/2-oz. cans cheddar cheese soup
3 cups sour cream
1 cup chopped onion
1 tsp. salt
¹/2 tsp. pepper

1. Cook unpeeled whole potatoes in water in a large saucepan until soft. Allow to cool to room temperature. Then refrigerate until fully chilled.
2. Spray cooker interior with non-stick cooking spray.
3. Skin chilled potatoes. Then grate into cooker.
4. Add remaining ingredients to slow cooker and stir together well.
5. Cover and cook on High 5 hours, or until hot and bubbly.

Scalloped Potatoes and Bacon

Jean Butzer
Batavia, NY

Makes 6-8 servings

Prep Time: 10 minutes
Cooking Time: 8-10 hours
Ideal slow cooker size:
  3- to 4-qt.

6 large potatoes, peeled
  and sliced, *divided*
1 small onion, diced
2 cups shredded cheddar
  cheese, *divided*
8 strips bacon, uncooked
  and diced, *divided*
10³/4-oz. can cream of
  mushroom soup

1. Spray the interior of the
slow cooker with non-stick
cooking spray.
2. Place half the sliced
potatoes in bottom of slow
cooker. Top with half the
chopped onion, cheese, and
bacon.
3. Repeat the layers in
order. Top with soup.
4. Cover and cook on Low
8-10 hours, or until the potatoes are tender but not
mushy or dry.

*Tip: You may want to brown
the bacon in a non-stick skillet
until crispy, and then drain it of
its drippings, before placing it
in the cooker. That adds some
time to the process, but it cuts
down on the fat content.*

Sausage and Scalloped Potatoes

Mrs. Mahlon Miller
Hutchinson, KS

Makes 3-4 servings

Prep Time: 15 minutes
Cooking Time: 4 hours
Ideal slow cooker size: 3-qt.

1/2 lb. loose sausage
4 cups raw potatoes, finely
  diced
1/2 cup shredded cheddar
  cheese
1/2 cup sour cream
10³/4-oz. can cream of
  mushroom soup

1. Cook sausage in non-
stick skillet until it loses its
pink color. Drain.
2. Spray the interior of
your slow cooker with non-
stick cooking spray.
3. Combine all ingredients
in your slow cooker.
4. Cover and cook on Low
for 4 hours, or until potatoes
are tender.

Simple Saucy Potatoes

Mary Lynn Miller
Reinholds, PA

Makes 8-10 servings

Prep Time: 15-20 minutes
Cooking Time: 4-5 hours
Ideal slow cooker size: 5-qt.

10 bacon slices
4 15-oz. cans sliced white
  potatoes, drained
2 10³/4-oz. cans cream of
  celery soup
2 cups sour cream
6 green onions, thinly
  sliced

1. Brown bacon in non-
stick skillet. Drain. Crumble
and set aside.
2. Place potatoes in slow
cooker.
3. In a large bowl, com-
bine remaining ingredients,
including the bacon. Pour
over potatoes and mix well.
4. Cover and cook on High
4-5 hours, or until potatoes
are cooked through.

Ranch Potatoes

Jean Butzer
Batavia, NY

Makes 6 servings

Prep Time: 10-15 minutes
Cooking Time: 3¹/2-8 hours
Ideal slow cooker size: 4-qt.

2¹/2 lbs. small red potatoes, quartered
1 cup sour cream
1 envelope dry buttermilk ranch salad dressing mix
10³/4-oz. can cream of mushroom soup

1. Spray the interior of the slow cooker with non-stick cooking spray.
2. Place the potatoes in the slow cooker.
3. Combine the remaining ingredients in a bowl. Spoon over potatoes and stir gently.
4. Cover and cook on Low 7-8 hours, or on High 3¹/2-4 hours, or until potatoes are tender but not dry or mushy.
5. Stir carefully before serving.

Creamy Red Potatoes

Orpha Herr
Andover, NY

Makes 4-6 servings

Prep Time: 25 minutes
Cooking Time: 8 hours
Ideal slow cooker size: 5-qt.

2 lbs. small red potatoes, scrubbed, quartered, unpeeled
8-oz. pkg. cream cheese, softened
10³/4-oz. cream of potato soup
half a soup can milk *or* water
1 envelope dry ranch salad dressing mix

1. Place potatoes in slow cooker.
2. In a small bowl, beat remaining ingredients together until blended. Stir into potatoes.
3. Cover and cook on Low 8 hours, or until potatoes are tender, but not mushy or dry.

Tip: Barbecued pork chops are a great match with this dish.
In a bowl, mix a 10³/4-oz. can of cream of mushroom soup with 1 cup ketchup, 1 Tbsp. Worcestershire sauce, and ¹/2 cup chopped onion.
Place 4 or 5 pork chops in your other slow cooker! Pour sauce over top, making sure all the chops have sauce over them.

Cover and cook on High 4-6 hours, or on Low 6-8 hours, or until the chops are tender but not dry.

Lemon Red Potatoes

Carol Leaman
Lancaster, PA

Makes 6 servings

Prep Time: 15-20 minutes
Cooking Time: 2¹/2-3 hours
Ideal slow cooker size:
3- to 4-qt.

10-12 small to medium-sized red potatoes
¹/4 cup water
¹/4 cup butter, melted
1 Tbsp. lemon juice
3 Tbsp. fresh, *or* dried, parsley
salt and pepper to taste

1. Cut a strip of peel from around the middle of each potato, using a potato peeler.
2. Place potatoes and water in slow cooker.
3. Cover and cook on High 2¹/2-3 hours, or until tender. Do not overcook.
4. Drain water.
5. Combine butter, lemon juice, and parsley. Mix well. Pour over potatoes and toss to coat. Season with salt and pepper.

Rosemary New Potatoes

Carol Shirk
Leola, PA

Makes 4-5 servings

Prep Time: 15 minutes
Cooking Time: 2-6 hours
Ideal slow cooker size:
3- to 4-qt.

1½ lbs. new red potatoes, unpeeled
1 Tbsp. olive oil
1 Tbsp. fresh chopped rosemary, *or* 1 tsp. dried rosemary
1 tsp. garlic and pepper seasoning, *or* 1 large clove garlic, minced, plus ½ tsp. salt, and ¼ tsp. pepper

1. If the potatoes are larger than golf balls, cut them in half or in quarters.
2. In a bowl or plastic bag, toss potatoes with olive oil, coating well.
3. Add rosemary and garlic and pepper seasoning (or the minced garlic, salt, and pepper). Toss again until the potatoes are well coated.
4. Place potatoes in slow cooker. Cook on High 2-3 hours, or on Low 5-6 hours, or until potatoes are tender but not mushy or dry.

Parmesan Potato Wedges

Carol and John Ambrose
McMinnville, OR

Makes 6 servings

Prep Time: 15 minutes
Cooking Time: 4 hours
Ideal slow cooker size: 3-qt.

2 lbs. red potatoes, cut into ½" wedges *or* strips
¼ cup chopped onion
2 Tbsp. butter, cut into pieces
1½ tsp. dried oregano
¼ cup grated Parmesan cheese

1. Layer potatoes, onion, butter, and oregano in slow cooker.
2. Cover and cook on High 4 hours, or until potatoes are tender but not dry or mushy.
3. Spoon into serving dish and sprinkle with cheese.

Garlicky Potatoes

Donna Lantgen, Chadron, NE

Makes 4-5 servings

Prep Time: 30 minutes
Cooking Time: 4½-6 hours
Ideal slow cooker size:
3- to 4-qt.

6 potatoes, peeled and cubed
6 garlic cloves, minced
¼ cup diced onion, *or* one medium-sized onion, chopped
2 Tbsp. olive oil

1. Spray interior of slow cooker with non-stick cooking spray.
2. Combine all ingredients in slow cooker.
3. Cover and cook on Low 4½-6 hours, or until potatoes are tender but not mushy or dry.

Onion Potatoes

Donna Lantgen
Chadron, NE

Makes 6 servings

Prep Time: 20-30 minutes
Cooking Time: 5-6 hours
Ideal slow cooker size: 4-qt.

6 medium-sized potatoes,
   diced
1/3 cup olive oil
1 envelope dry onion soup
   mix

1. Combine potatoes and
olive oil in plastic bag. Shake
well.
2. Add onion soup mix.
Shake well.
3. Pour into slow cooker.
4. Cover and cook on Low
5-6 hours.

The Simplest "Baked" Potatoes

Mary Kathryn Yoder
Harrisonville, MO

Makes 4-12 servings

Prep Time: 20 minutes
Cooking Time: 4-10 hours
Ideal slow cooker size:
   3 1/2- to 5-qt.

4-12 potatoes

1. Prick potatoes. Wrap
each in foil. Place potatoes in
slow cooker. (Do not add
water.)
2. Cover and cook on High
4-5 hours, or on Low 8-10
hours, or until potatoes are
tender when jagged.

Seasoned "Baked" Potatoes

Donna Conto, Saylorsburg, PA

Makes as many servings
as you need!

Prep Time: 5 minutes
Cooking Time: 4-10 hours
Ideal slow cooker size: large
   enough to hold the potatoes!

potatoes
olive, *or* vegetable, oil
Season-All, *or* your choice
   of favorite dry
   seasonings

1. Wash and scrub pota-
toes. Rub each unpeeled
potato with oil.
2. Put about 1 tsp. seasoning per potato in a mixing
bowl or a plastic bag. Add
potatoes one at a time and
coat with seasonings.
3. Place potatoes in slow
cooker as you finish coating
them.
4. Cover and cook on High
for 4 hours, or on Low 8-10
hours, or until potatoes are
tender when jagged.

A Tip —

Slow cookers fit any
season. When it's hot out-
side, they don't heat up
your kitchen. So turn on
your cooker before head-
ing to the pool or the
beach—or the garden.
   Or put your dinner in
the slow cooker, and then
go play or watch your
favorite sport.

Stress-Free "Baked" Potatoes
Leona Yoder
Hartville, OH

Makes 12 servings

Prep Time: 10 minutes
Cooking Time: 4-10 hours
Ideal slow cooker size:
   4- to 5-qt.

12 potatoes
butter, softened

1. Spray slow cooker with non-stick cooking spray.
2. Rub butter over unpeeled whole potatoes. Place in slow cooker.
3. Cover and cook on High 4-5 hours, or on Low 8-10 hours, or until potatoes are tender when jagged.

Tip: Mix 1 Tbsp. pesto into 1/2 cup sour cream for a luscious baked potato topping.

Cornflake Cooker Potatoes
Anne Nolt
Thompsontown, PA

Makes 4-6 servings

Prep Time: 15 minutes
Cooking Time: 4 hours
Ideal slow cooker size: 3-qt.

6-8 potatoes, peeled
2 tsp. salt
2-3 Tbsp. butter
1 cup cornflakes, slightly crushed

1. Place potatoes in slow cooker.
2. Fill cooker with hot water. Sprinkle with salt.
3. Cover and cook on High for 4 hours, or until potatoes are tender.
4. While potatoes are cooking, melt butter. Continue melting until butter browns, but does not burn. (Watch carefully!) Stir in cornflakes. Set aside.
5. Drain potatoes. Spoon buttered cornflakes over potatoes. Or mash potatoes and then top with buttered cornflakes.

Mashed Potatoes
Alice Miller
Stuarts Draft, VA

Makes 4 servings

Prep Time: 15 minutes
Cooking Time: 3-5 hours
Ideal slow cooker size:
   3- to 4-qt.

8 large potatoes, peeled and cut into 1" chunks
water
half a stick (1/4 cup) butter, softened
1 tsp. salt
1 1/2 cups milk, heated until skin forms on top

1. Place potatoes in slow cooker; add water to cover.
2. Cover and cook on High 3-5 hours, or until potatoes are very tender but not watery.
3. Lift potatoes out with a slotted spoon into a bowl. Beat with electric mixer on high speed, scraping sides down.
4. Cut butter in chunks. Add to potatoes. Slowly add milk, being careful not to splash yourself with the hot milk. Add salt. Beat until creamy.

Tip: Put the potatoes in the slow cooker and forget about them while you're occupied otherwise. Come back to the kitchen 3-5 hours later, and you've got soft potatoes, ready to mash!

Refrigerator Mashed Potatoes

Elsie Schlabach
Millersburg, OH

Makes 8-10 servings

Prep Time: 15-20 minutes
Cooking Time: 2-3 hours
Ideal slow cooker size:
 4- to 5-qt.

5 lbs. potatoes (not baking potatoes), peeled and cut into chunks
8-oz. pkg. cream cheese, softened
1-2 cups sour cream
2 Tbsp. butter, softened
1 tsp. salt

1. Cook potatoes in 2-3" water in a large kettle until tender. Drain, reserving 1-2 cups cooking water.
2. Mash until smooth. Add cooking water as needed to keep potatoes from being too stiff.
3. Mash in remaining ingredients and beat until light and fluffy.
4. Cool. Cover and refrigerate.
5. When ready to use, spray interior of slow cooker with non-stick cooking spray.
6. Stir chilled potatoes and then place in slow cooker. Cover and cook on Low 2-3 hours—or until hot throughout.

Variations:
 1. Add 1-2 tsp. garlic salt to Step 3.
  — Colleen Heatwole
  Burton, MI

 2. Add 2 tsp. fresh or dried chives to Step 3.
  — Thelma Good
  Harrisonburg, VA

Tip: This dish is great for a Sunday noon meal, or anytime when you're away from the kitchen but want a comforting potato dish for a meal.

Individual Mashed Potatoes

Mrs. Audrey L. Kneer
Williamsfield, IL

Prep Time: 25 minutes
Cooking Time: up to 3 hours
Ideal slow cooker size:
 1- to 2-qt.

1-2 medium-sized potatoes per person
3 Tbsp. milk per potato
1/2 Tbsp. butter per potato, melted
1/8 tsp. salt per potato

1. Peel and boil potatoes until soft. Mash.
2. While mashing potatoes, heat milk to scalding. Then add hot milk, butter, and salt to mashed potatoes, stirring in well.
3. Put in slow cooker a couple of hours before serving. Set cooker on Low. Stir once in a while. These will be the same as fresh mashed potatoes.

Note: This saves needing to mash potatoes at the last minute.

Seasoned Mashed Potatoes

Elena Yoder
Carlsbad, NM

Makes 12 servings

Prep Time: 30 minutes
Cooking Time: 3-4 hours
Ideal slow cooker size: 4-qt.

potatoes to fill a 4-qt. slow cooker, peeled and cut into chunks
boiling water to cover potatoes
8-oz. pkg. cream cheese, softened
2 cups buttermilk
1 cup dry milk
1 envelope dry ranch dressing mix

1. Place potatoes in slow cooker. Cover with boiling water.
2. Cover and cook on High 3-4 hours, or until very tender.
3. Drain, reserving liquid.
4. Mash potatoes.
5. Beat in cream cheese.
6. Beat in buttermilk, dry milk, and ranch dressing mix.

7. If needed, beat in as much reserved potato water as you want until potatoes reach desired consistency.

Garlic Mashed Potatoes

Katrine Rose, Woodbridge, VA

Makes 6 servings

Prep Time: 20 minutes
Cooking Time: 4-7 hours
Ideal slow cooker size: 4-qt.

2 lbs. baking potatoes, unpeeled and cut into 1/2″ cubes
1/4 cup water
3 Tbsp. butter, sliced
1 tsp. salt
3/4 tsp. garlic powder
1/4 tsp. black pepper
1 cup milk

1. Combine all ingredients, except milk, in slow cooker. Toss to combine.
2. Cover. Cook on Low 7 hours, or on High 4 hours.
3. Add milk to potatoes during last 30 minutes of cooking time.
4. Mash potatoes with potato masher or electric mixer until fairly smooth.
5. Place in slow cooker 2 hours before serving. Cover. Set cooker on Low.
6. Stir before serving.

Note: These potatoes will taste freshly mashed, and they will spare you last-minute work.

Make-Ahead Mashed Potatoes

Tracey Hanson Schramel
Windom, MN

Makes 8-12 servings

Prep Time: 45-60 minutes
Cooking Time: 4-5 hours in slow cooker
Ideal slow cooker size: 2 6-qt. cookers

5 lbs. potatoes, peeled and cubed
8-oz. pkg. cream cheese, softened
1 cup half-and-half
1 stick (1/2 cup) butter, softened
salt and pepper to taste

1. Cook potatoes in water in large saucepan until tender but not mushy. Drain, reserving 1 cup cooking water.
2. In large bowl, beat softened cream cheese and half-and-half together until smooth.
3. Stir in hot potatoes and reserved cooking water and blend well.
4. Stir in butter, salt, and pepper.
5. Place meal-size portions of the mixture in freezer containers. Cool; then freeze.
6. When needed, thaw a container of potatoes. Spray interior of slow cooker. Then place potato mixture in slow cooker.
7. Stir in 1-2 Tbsp. softened butter and 1/2-1 tsp. paprika.

8. Cover and cook on Low 4-5 hours, or until potatoes are heated through, but not dry.

Cheddar Mashed Potatoes

Gloria Good
Harrisonburg, VA

Makes 5-6 servings

Prep Time: 10 minutes
Cooking Time: 3-5 hours
Ideal slow cooker size: 2-qt.

10 3/4-oz. condensed cheddar cheese soup
1/2 cup sour cream
2 Tbsp. chopped green onions
dash of pepper
3 cups leftover, *or* stiff, seasoned mashed potatoes

1. Spray interior of slow cooker with non-stick cooking spray.
2. Mix all ingredients together in slow cooker.
3. Cover and cook on High 3 hours, or on Low 5 hours, or until potatoes are thoroughly hot.

Simply Sweet Potatoes

Leona Yoder
Hartville, OH

Makes 4 servings

Prep Time: 5 minutes
Cooking Time: 6-9 hours
Ideal slow cooker size:
 2- to 3-qt.

---

3 large sweet potatoes
¼ cup water

1. Place unpeeled sweet potatoes into slow cooker.
2. Add ¼ cup water.
3. Cover and cook on High 1 hour. Then turn to Low and cook for 5-8 hours, or until potatoes are tender.

Fruity Sweet Potatoes

Jean Butzer, Batavia, NY
Evelyn Page, Lance Creek, WY

Makes 6 servings

Prep Time: 15 minutes
Cooking Time: 6-8 hours
Ideal slow cooker size:
 3- to 4-qt.

---

2 lbs. (about 6 medium-sized)
 sweet potatoes, *or* **yams**
1½ cups applesauce
⅔ cup brown sugar
3 Tbsp. butter, melted
1 tsp. cinnamon
chopped nuts, *optional*

1. Peel sweet potatoes if you wish. Cut into cubes or slices. Place in slow cooker.
2. In a bowl, mix together applesauce, brown sugar, butter, and cinnamon. Spoon over potatoes.
3. Cover and cook on Low 6-8 hours, or until potatoes are tender.
4. Mash potatoes and sauce together if you wish with a large spoon—or spoon potatoes into serving dish and top with the sauce.
5. Sprinkle with nuts, if you want.

Variation: Instead of raw sweet potatoes, substitute a 40-oz. can of cut-up sweet potatoes, drained. Then cook on Low for only 3-4 hours.
 *— **Shelia Heil***
 Lancaster, PA

Apples n' Yams

Rebecca Plank Leichty
Harrisonburg, VA

Makes 8-10 servings

Prep Time: 25 minutes
Cooking Time: 4-6 hours
Ideal slow cooker size:
 4- to 5-qt.

---

1 Tbsp. lemon juice, *or*
 lemonade
6 apples, peeled and sliced
6 large yams, *or* **sweet**
 potatoes, peeled and
 thinly sliced
¼ cup apple juice
1 Tbsp. butter, melted

1. Toss sliced apples and yams in lemon juice.
2. Combine apple juice and butter. Pour over apples and sweet potatoes. Pour into greased slow cooker.
3. Cover. Cook on High 4 hours or Low 6 hours.

This is a tasty vegetable dish to add to a meal when serving children. The apples smell wonderful when cooking and truly moisten the potatoes when served together. It is a well-rounded and easy way to serve sweet potatoes.

Cinnamon Sweet Potatoes

Deborah Heatwole
Waynesboro, GA

Makes 4-6 servings

Prep Time: 10-15 minutes
Cooking Time: 3 hours
Ideal slow cooker size:
  2- to 3-qt.

1/4 **cup brown sugar**
1/4 **tsp. cinnamon**
3 **medium-sized sweet**
  potatoes, thinly sliced
  and peeled (about 4-6
  cups of slices), *divided*
1/2 **stick (**1/4 **cup) butter,**
  melted
salt to taste

1. Spray slow cooker with non-stick cooking spray.
2. Combine brown sugar and cinnamon in a small bowl.
3. Place one-third of sweet potatoes slices in slow cooker.
4. Drizzle with one-third of butter. Sprinkle with salt and one-third of brown sugar mixture.
5. Repeat layers two more times.
6. Cover and cook on High 3 hours, or until potatoes are tender.

Glazed Sweet Potatoes

Jan Mast
Lancaster, PA

Makes 8-10 servings

Prep Time: 20 minutes
Cooking Time: 3-4 hours
Ideal slow cooker size: 2-qt.

8-10 **medium-sized sweet**
  potatoes
1/2 **tsp. salt**
3/4 **cup brown sugar**
2 **Tbsp. butter**
1 **Tbsp. flour**
1/4 **cup water**

1. Cook sweet potatoes in 2"-3" water in a large saucepan until barely soft. Drain. When cool enough to handle, peel and slice into slow cooker.
2. While potatoes are cooking in the saucepan, combine remaining ingredients in a microwave-safe bowl.
3. Microwave on High for 1 1/2 minutes. Stir. Repeat until glaze thickens slightly.
4. Pour glaze over peeled, cooked sweet potatoes in slow cooker.
5. Cover and cook on High 3-4 hours.

Glazed Maple Sweet Potatoes

Jeannine Janzen
Elbing, KS

Makes 5 servings

Prep Time: 5-10 minutes
Cooking Time: 7-9 hours
Ideal slow cooker size: 4-qt.

5 **medium-sized sweet**
  potatoes, cut in
  1/2"**-thick slices**
1/4 **cup brown sugar,**
  packed
1/4 **cup pure maple syrup**
1/4 **cup apple cider**
2 **Tbsp. butter**

1. Place potatoes in slow cooker.
2. In a small bowl, combine brown sugar, maple syrup, and apple cider. Mix well. Pour over potatoes. Stir until all potato slices are covered.
3. Cover and cook on Low 7-9 hours, or until potatoes are tender.
4. Stir in butter before serving.

Tasty Rice

Starla Kreider, Mohrsville, PA

Makes 6-8 servings

Prep Time: 5-10 minutes
Cooking Time: 2-3 hours
Ideal slow cooker size: 2-qt.

1½ cups raw long-grain rice
3-3½ cups water, *divided*
10¾-oz. can cream of celery soup
2 tsp. chicken bouillon granules
1 onion, chopped
salt and pepper to taste

1. Spray interior of cooker with non-stick cooking spray.
2. Combine rice, 3 cups water, soup, bouillon, onion, and a dash of salt and pepper in the slow cooker.
3. Cover and cook on High 2-3 hours. If after 2 hours, the rice is beginning to dry out, stir in ½ cup water and continue cooking until heated through.

Cooked Rice

Mary Kathryn Yoder
Harrisonville, MO

Makes 8 servings

Prep Time: 5 minutes
Cooking Time: 1½-2½ hours
Ideal slow cooker size: 4-qt.

1 Tbsp. butter
3 cups raw long-grain rice
6 cups water
salt to taste, about 3 tsp.

1. Grease slow cooker with the butter.
2. If you have time, heat the water to boiling in a saucepan on your stovetop, or in a microwave-safe bowl in your microwave. Then pour rice, water (heated or not), and salt into the cooker and stir together.
3. Cover and cook on High 1½-2½ hours. If you're home and able to do so, stir occasionally.

Tips:
   1. To make a smaller amount of rice, try these proportions and cooking time:

1 Tbsp. butter
1 cup raw long-grain, *or* brown, rice
2½ cups water
1 tsp. salt

When I use mushrooms or green peppers in the slow cooker, I usually stir them in during the last hour so they don't get mushy.
Trudy Kutter
Corfu, NY

Follow the directions above, but cook on Low 1 hour and 20 minutes, or until the rice is tender but not dry.
   This makes 4-5 servings.
   — Sarah J. Miller
      Harrisonburg, VA
   — Vera Martin
      East Earl, PA

   2. When the slow cooker is turned off, the rice will keep warm enough for serving for 2-3 hours.
   — Leona Yoder
      Hartville, OH

Wild Rice Casserole

Loretta Hanson
Hendricks, MN

Makes 4 servings

Prep Time: 15 minutes
Cooking Time: 2 hours
Ideal slow cooker size: 4-qt.

6-oz. box long-grain and wild rice
10¾-oz. can cream of mushroom soup
¾ cup water
2 Tbsp. chopped onion, *optional*
2 Tbsp. butter, melted
1 Tbsp. beef bouillon
dash of Worcestershire sauce

1. Place all ingredients in slow cooker, including the seasonings packet from the rice box.

2. Cover and cook on High for 2 hours. Fluff with fork before serving.

Wild Rice Pilaf

Judi Manos
West Islip, NY

Makes 6 servings

Prep Time: 10 minutes
Cooking Time: 3¹/₂-5 hours
Ideal slow cooker size:
3- to 4-qt.

1¹/₂ cups uncooked wild rice
¹/₂ cup finely chopped onion
14-oz. can chicken broth
2 cups water
4-oz. can sliced mushrooms, drained
¹/₂ tsp. dried thyme leaves

1. Spray slow cooker with non-stick cooking spray.
2. Rinse rice and drain well.
3. Combine rice, onion, chicken broth, and water in slow cooker. Mix well.
4. Cover and cook on High 3-4 hours.
5. Add mushrooms and thyme and stir gently.
6. Cover and cook on Low 30-60 minutes longer, or until wild rice pops and is tender.

Variation: Add ³/₄ tsp. salt in Step 3.

Flavorful Fruited Rice

Sandra Haverstraw
Hummelstown, PA

Makes 4 servings

Prep Time: 7 minutes
Cooking Time: 2 hours
Ideal slow cooker size:
2- to 3¹/₂-qt.

¹/₃ cup chopped onion
6-oz. pkg. long-grain and wild rice mix
2 cups chicken broth
¹/₄ cup dried cranberries
¹/₄ cup chopped dried apricots

1. Spray small frying pan with non-stick cooking spray. Add chopped onions and cook on medium heat about 5 minutes, or until onions begin to brown.
2. Place onions and remaining ingredients in the slow cooker, including the seasonings in the rice package. Stir well to dissolve seasonings.
3. Cover and cook on High 2 hours. Fluff with fork to serve.

Variations:
1. Just before serving sprinkle dish with ¹/₂ cup toasted pecans, or other nuts.
2. Use other dried fruits instead of the cranberries, such as raisins or dried cherries.

Cheddar Rice

Natalia Showalter
Mt. Solon, VA

Makes 8-10 servings

Prep Time: 10-15 minutes
Cooking Time: 2-3 hours
Ideal slow cooker size: 3-qt.

2 cups uncooked brown rice
3 Tbsp. butter
¹/₂ cup thinly sliced green onions, *or* shallots
1 tsp. salt
5 cups water
¹/₂ tsp. pepper
2 cups shredded cheddar cheese
1 cup slivered almonds, *optional*

1. Combine rice, butter, green onion, and salt in slow cooker.
2. Bring water to boil and pour over rice mixture.
3. Cover and cook on High 2-3 hours, or until rice is tender and liquid is absorbed.
4. Five minutes before serving stir in pepper and cheese.
5. Garnish with slivered almonds, if you wish.

Red Bean and Brown Rice Stew

Barbara Gautcher
Harrisonburg, VA

Makes 6 servings

Prep Time: 15 minutes, plus 8 hours for soaking beans
Cooking Time: 6 hours
Ideal slow cooker size: 6-qt.

2 cups dried red beans
water
3/4 cup uncooked brown rice
4 cups water
6 carrots, peeled if you wish, and cut into chunks
1 large onion, cut into chunks
1 Tbsp. cumin

1. Place dried beans in slow cooker and cover with water. Allow to soak for 8 hours. Drain. Discard soaking water.
2. Return soaked beans to cooker. Stir in all remaining ingredients.
3. Cover and cook on Low 6 hours, or until all vegetables are tender.

Variation: Add 1 Tbsp. salt to Step 2.

Broccoli Rice Casserole

Liz Rugg
Wayland, IA

Makes 6 servings

Prep Time: 5 minutes
Cooking Time: 3-4 hours
Ideal slow cooker size: 3- to 4-qt.

1 cup uncooked minute rice
1-lb. pkg. frozen chopped broccoli
8-oz. jar processed cheese spread
10 3/4-oz. can cream of mushroom soup

1. Mix all ingredients together in slow cooker.
2. Cover and cook on High 3-4 hours, or until rice and broccoli are tender but not mushy or dry.

Cheese-y Rice

Janice Muller
Derwood, MD

Makes 6 servings

Prep Time: 20 minutes
Cooking Time: 4-6 hours
Ideal slow cooker size: 3 1/2- to 4-qt.

2 cups hot cooked rice
3-oz. can French-fried onions, *divided*
1 cup sour cream
16-oz. jar medium salsa, *divided*
1 cup shredded cheddar, *or taco-blend, cheese, divided*

1. Spray interior of slow cooker with non-stick cooking spray.
2. In a bowl, combine rice and 2/3 cup onions. Spoon half the rice mixture into the slow cooker.
3. Spread sour cream over rice. Layer half the salsa and half the cheese over the sour cream.
4. Top with remaining rice, salsa, and cheese.
5. Cook on Low 4-6 hours, or until cheese is melted and casserole is heated through.

Hometown Spanish Rice

Beverly Flatt-Getz
Warriors Mark, PA

Makes 6-8 servings

Prep Time: 20 minutes
Cooking Time: 2-4 hours
Ideal slow cooker size: 4-qt.

1 large onion, chopped
1 bell pepper, chopped
1 lb. bacon, cooked, and broken into bite-size pieces
2 cups cooked long-grain rice
28-oz. can stewed tomatoes with juice
grated Parmesan cheese, *optional*

1. Sauté onion and pepper in a small non-stick frying pan until tender.
2. Spray interior of slow cooker with non-stick cooking spray.
3. Combine all ingredients in the slow cooker.
4. Cover and cook on Low 4 hours, or on High 2 hours, or until heated through.
5. Sprinkle with Parmesan cheese just before serving, if you wish.

Rice 'N Beans 'N Salsa

Heather Horst
Lebanon, PA

Makes 6-8 servings

Prep Time: 7 minutes
Cooking Time: 4-10 hours
Ideal slow cooker size: 3- to 5-qt.

2 16-oz. cans black, *or* navy, beans, drained
14-oz. can chicken broth
1 cup uncooked long-grain white, *or* brown, rice
1 qt. salsa, mild, medium, *or* hot
1 cup water
1/2 tsp. garlic powder

1. Combine all ingredients in slow cooker. Stir well.
2. Cover and cook on Low 8-10 hours, or on High 4 hours.

New Year's Sauerkraut

Judith A. Govotsos
Frederick, MD

Makes 4-6 servings

Prep Time: 10-15 minutes
Cooking Time: 2-10 hours
Ideal slow cooker size: 3-qt.

3 cups sauerkraut, rinsed and drained
1/2-3/4 cup brown sugar
1 apple, cored and chopped
1 small onion, chopped
water to cover

1. Place sauerkraut in slow cooker. Add sugar, apple, and onions. Stir.
2. Cover with water.
3. Cover with lid and cook on High 2-3 hours, or on Low all day.

Acorn Squash

Janet L. Roggie, Lowville, NY
Mary Stauffer, Ephrata, PA
Leona Yoder, Hartville, OH
June S. Groff, Denver, PA
Trudy Kutter, Corfu, NY

Makes 4-6 servings, depending on the size of the squash

Prep Time: 5 minutes
Cooking Time: 7-8 hours, depending on the size of the squash
Ideal slow cooker size: 4- to 5-qt., depending on the size of the squash

whole acorn squash
water
salt
cinnamon
butter
brown sugar *or* maple
  syrup, *optional*

1. Wash squash. Cut off stem. Place whole squash in slow cooker. Add water to a depth of about 1".
2. Cover and cook on Low 7-8 hours, depending on the size of the squash. Jag with a sharp fork to see if it's tender. Cook longer if it isn't.
   Check every 2 hours during cooking time, if you can, to make sure the squash isn't cooking dry. Add water if it drops below 1" deep.
3. Remove squash from cooker and allow to cool until you can handle it.
4. Cut in half with a long-bladed knife. Scoop seeds out of both halves.

5. Sprinkle flesh with salt and cinnamon. Dot with butter. Drizzle with brown sugar or maple syrup, if you wish. Serve.
   Or scoop out the flesh with a spoon into a mixing bowl. Add remaining ingredients and mash together until well blended and smooth.

Another Method:
   Cut the squash in half before placing in cooker. Scoop out seeds. Wrap each half in foil and place in cooker. Add water to a depth of 1".
   Continue with Step 2 above, but skip Steps 3 and 4.
   — Alice Rush
      Quakertown, PA

Artichokes

Gertrude Dutcher
Hartville, OH

Makes 4-6 servings

Prep Time: 15 minutes
Cooking Time: 6-8 hours
Ideal slow cooker size: 4-qt.

4-6 artichokes
1-1½ tsp. salt
1 cup lemon juice, *divided*
2 cups hot water
1 stick (½ cup) melted butter

1. Wash and trim artichokes. Cut off about 1" from top. If you wish, trim tips of leaves. Stand chokes upright in slow cooker.

2. Sprinkle each choke with ¼ tsp. salt and 2 Tbsp. lemon juice.
3. Pour 2 cups hot water around the base of the artichokes.
4. Cover and cook on Low 6-8 hours.
5. Serve with melted butter and lemon juice for dipping.

Red Cabbage

Kristin Tice
Shipshewana, IN

Makes 8 servings

Prep Time: 30 minutes
Cooking Time: 6 hours
Ideal slow cooker size: 3-qt.

5 cups shredded red
  cabbage
1 cup white sugar
1 cup white vinegar
1 apple, chopped
1 tsp. salt
1 cup water

1. Combine all ingredients in slow cooker.
2. Cover and cook on Low 6 hours.

Tip: This is a great side-dish to serve with pork.

Cheese-y Onions

Janessa Hochstedler
East Earl, PA

Makes 6-8 servings

Prep Time: 10-20 minutes
Cooking Time: 2-4 hours
Ideal slow cooker size: 2-qt.

1¹/2 lbs. small onions
4 slices bacon, cooked and crumbled
10¹/2-oz. can cheddar cheese soup
¹/2 cup milk
¹/4 cup grated Parmesan cheese

1. Peel onions, but leave whole. Place in slow cooker.
2. Mix remaining ingredients together in a bowl.
3. Pour into slow cooker. Gently mix in onions.
4. Cook on High 2 hours, or on Low 4 hours, or until onions are fully tender.

DRIED BEANS

Caramelized Onions

Jeanette Oberholtzer
Manheim, PA

Makes 6-8 servings

Prep Time: 15 minutes
Cooking Time: 10-12 hours
Ideal slow cooker size:
*   4- to 6-qt.*

4-6 large sweet onions
¹/2 cup (1 stick) butter, melted, *or* olive oil

1. Peel onions and slice off the top and the bottom ends.
2. Place onions in slow cooker.
3. Pour butter or olive oil on top of onions. Stir together.
4. Cook on Low 10-12 hours.
5. Use carmelized onions as filling for omelets or sandwiches, as an ingredient in soup, or as a condiment with grilled meat.

A Tip —

When choosing cabbage, select a bright green head that is firm and solid.

Fresh Zucchini and Tomatoes

Pauline Morrison
St. Marys, Ontario

Makes 6-8 servings

Prep Time: 15 minutes
Cooking Time: 2¹/2-3 hours
Ideal slow cooker size: 3¹/2-qt.

1¹/2 lbs. zucchini, peeled if you wish, and cut into ¹/4" slices
19-oz. can stewed tomatoes, broken up and undrained
1¹/2 cloves garlic, minced
¹/2 tsp. salt
1¹/2 Tbsp. butter

1. Place zucchini slices in slow cooker.
2. Add tomatoes, garlic, and salt. Mix well.
3. Dot surface with butter.
4. Cover and cook on High 2¹/2-3 hours, or until zucchini are done to your liking.

Variation: Sprinkle with grated Parmesan cheese when serving, if you wish.

Stewed Tomatoes

Michelle Showalter
Bridgewater, VA

Makes 10-12 servings

Prep Time: 15 minutes
Cooking Time: 3-4 hours
Ideal slow cooker size: 3-qt.

2 qts. canned tomatoes
1/3 cup sugar
1 1/2 tsp. salt
dash of pepper
3 Tbsp. butter
2 cups bread cubes

1. Place tomatoes in slow cooker.
2. Sprinkle with sugar, salt, and pepper.
3. Lightly toast bread cubes in melted butter. Spread over tomatoes.
4. Cover. Cook on High 3-4 hours.

Variation: If you prefer bread that is less moist and soft, add bread cubes 15 minutes before serving and continue cooking without lid.

Mushrooms in Red Wine

Donna Lantgen
Chadron, NE

Makes 4 servings

Prep Time: 10 minutes
Baking Time: 4-6 hours
Ideal slow cooker size: 2-qt.

1 lb. fresh mushrooms, cleaned
4 cloves garlic, chopped
1/4 cup onion, chopped
1 Tbsp. olive oil
1 cup red wine

1. Combine all ingredients in slow cooker. Cook on Low 4-6 hours, or until done to your liking.
2. Serve as a side dish with your favorite meat.

Stuffed Mushrooms

Melanie L. Thrower
McPherson, KS

Makes 4-6 servings

Prep Time: 20-30 minutes
Cooking Time: 2-4 hours
Ideal slow cooker size: 3-qt.

8-10 large mushrooms
1/4 tsp. minced garlic
1 Tbsp. oil
dash of salt
dash of pepper
dash of cayenne pepper, *optional*
1/4 cup grated Monterey Jack cheese

1. Remove stems from mushrooms and dice.
2. Heat oil in skillet. Saute diced stems with garlic until softened. Remove skillet from heat.
3. Stir in seasonings and cheese. Stuff into mushroom shells. Place in slow cooker.
4. Cover. Heat on Low 2-4 hours.

Variations:
1. Add 1 Tbsp. minced onion to Step 2.

2. Use Monterey Jack cheese with jalapenos.

Stuffed Peppers

Virginia Blish
Akron, NY

Makes 4 servings

Prep Time: 15-25 minutes
Cooking Time: 3 hours
Ideal slow cooker size: 5-qt.

4 medium-sized green,
 yellow, *or* red, sweet
 peppers, *or* a mixture of
 colors
1 cup cooked rice
15-oz. can chili beans with
 chili gravy
1 cup (4 ozs.) shredded
 cheese, *divided*
14½-oz. can petite diced
 tomatoes, with onion,
 celery, and green pepper

1. Wash and dry sweet
peppers. Remove tops, mem-
branes, and seeds, but keep
the peppers whole.
2. In a bowl, mix together
rice, beans, and half the
cheese. Spoon mixture into
peppers.
3. Pour tomatoes into slow
cooker. Place filled peppers
on top, keeping them upright.
Do not stack the peppers.
4. Cover and cook on High
3 hours.
5. Carefully lift peppers
out of cooker and place on a
serving platter. Spoon hot
tomatoes over top. Sprinkle
remaining cheese over peppers.

Southwest Hominy

Reita Yoder
Carlsbad, NM

Makes 12-14 servings

Prep Time: 10 minutes
Cooking Time: 1½-3 hours
Ideal slow cooker size:
 3- to 4-qt.

3 29-oz. cans hominy,
 drained
10¾-oz. can cream of
 chicken soup
½ lb. Velveeta, *or* cheddar,
 cheese, grated *or* cubed
1 lb. cubed cooked ham, *or*
 sliced hot dogs
2 2¼-oz. cans green
 chilies, undrained

1. Mix all ingredients
together in slow cooker.
2. Cover and cook on High
for 1½ hours, on Low for 2-3
hours, or until bubbly and
cheese is melted.

Tip: Serve with fresh salsa.

Mexican Hominy

Janie Steele
Moore, OK

Make 6-8 servings

Prep Time: 10 minutes
Cooking Time: 1 hour
Ideal slow cooker size:
 3- to 4-qt.

2 29-oz. cans hominy,
 drained
4-oz. can chopped green
 chilies, mild *or* hot
1 cup sour cream
8-oz. jar Cheez Whiz

1. Combine ingredients in
slow cooker.
2. Cover and heat on Low
for one hour, or until cheese
is melted and dish is thoroughly hot.

A Tip —

Many stove-top and oven recipes can be adapted for a
slow cooker. If you want to experiment, use these conversion
factors:
• Low (in a slow cooker) = 200° in an oven, approximately
• High (in a slow cooker) = 300° in an oven, approximately
• In a slow-cooker, 2 hours on Low = 1 hour, approximately, on High.

Apple Stuffing

Judi Manos
West Islip, NY
Jeanette Oberholtzer
Manheim, PA

Makes 4-5 servings

Prep Time: 20 minutes
Cooking Time: 4-5 hours
Ideal slow cooker size:
4- to 6-qt.

1 stick (1/2 cup) butter,
divided
1 cup chopped walnuts
2 onions, chopped
14-oz. pkg. dry herb-
seasoned stuffing mix
1 1/2 cups applesauce
water, *optional*

1. In non-stick skillet, melt
2 Tbsp. of butter. Saute walnuts over medium heat until
toasted, about 5 minutes, stirring frequently. Remove from
skillet and set aside.

2. Melt remaining butter
in skillet. Add onions and
cook 3-4 minutes, or until
almost tender. Set aside.

3. Spray slow cooker with
non-stick cooking spray. Place
dry stuffing mix in slow
cooker.

4. Add onion-butter mix-
ture and stir. Add applesauce
and stir.

5. Cover and cook on Low
4-5 hours, or until heated
through.

Check after Stuffing has
cooked for 3 1/2 hours. If it's
sticking to the cooker, drying
out, or becoming too brown

on the edges, stir in 1/2-1 cup
water. Continue cooking.

6. Sprinkle with walnuts
before serving.

Pineapple Stuffing

Edwina F. Stoltzfus
Narvon, PA
Krista Hershberger
Elverson, PA

Makes 4-6 servings

Prep Time: 10 minutes
Cooking Time: 3-4 hours
Ideal slow cooker size: 4-qt.

1 stick (1/2 cup) butter,
softened
1/2 cup sugar
3 eggs
20-oz. can crushed
pineapple, drained
6 slices stale bread, cubed

1. In a large mixing bowl,
blend together butter and
sugar.

2. Blend in 1 egg at a time,
mixing until thoroughly combined.

3. Stir in drained pineapple. Fold in bread cubes.

4. Spoon into slow cooker.

5. Cook 3-4 hours on Low,
or until heated through.

6. Allow to stand for 15
minutes before serving.

Corny Cornbread

Pat Unternahrer
Wayland, IA

Makes 8 servings

Prep Time: 5 minutes
Cooking Time:
3 hours and 45 minutes
Ideal slow cooker size: 4-qt.

1 egg
1/2 cup sour cream
1 stick (1/2 cup) butter,
melted
2 14 3/4-oz. cans cream-style
corn
8 1/2-oz. box cornbread mix

1. Spray inside of slow
cooker with non-stick cooking
spray.

2. Mix all ingredients
together in a bowl. Spoon
into greased slow cooker.

3. Cook on High 3 hours
and 45 minutes.

Appetizers, Snacks, & Spreads

Spicy Cheese Dip with Ground Beef

Susan Tjon, Austin, TX

Makes 12-15 servings

Prep Time: 25 minutes
Cooking Time: 2½ hours
Ideal slow cooker size:
  2- to 3-qt.

1 lb. lean ground beef
¼ cup onions, finely
  chopped
half a large onion, finely
  chopped
1½ lbs. Velveeta cheese,
  cubed
15-oz. can Rotel tomatoes
  with green chili peppers

1. Brown ground beef and
¼ cup onions in a large non-
stick skillet. Break beef apart
as needed. Drain.
2. Combine beef with
remaining ingredients in slow
cooker.

3. Cook on Low 2½ hours,
or until cheese is melted.
4. Serve from slow cooker
with scoop-shaped tortilla
chips.

Tip: The smaller the Velveeta
chunks, the faster they will
melt.

Variation: Instead of the
¼ cup onions, use ¾ tsp. garlic
powder.
  — Tierra Woods
  Duenweg, MO

Hot Ground Beef Dip

Jennifer Yoder Sommers
Harrisonburg, VA

Makes 10-12 servings

Prep Time: 10 minutes
Cooking Time: 1 hour
Ideal slow cooker size: 3-qt.

1 lb. ground beef
1 lb. Velveeta cheese,
  cubed
15-oz. can tomato sauce
Worcestershire sauce, to
  taste
green pepper, diced, to
  taste

1. Brown ground beef in
non-stick skillet. Drain.
2. Combine all ingredients
in slow cooker.
3. Cover and cook on High
1 hour.

Variation: Add 2 4¼-oz. cans
diced green chilies to Step 2.
  — Eleya Raim
  Oxford, IA

Tip: Serve hot with tortilla
chips for dipping.

Aunt Cheri's Dip

Cynthia Morris
Grottoes, VA

Makes 20-30 servings

Prep Time: 20-30 minutes
Cooking Time:
45 minutes to 1 hour
Ideal slow cooker size: 6-qt.

1 lb. lean ground beef
2 lbs. Velveeta cheese,
  cubed
2 10¾-oz. cans tomato
  soup
2 10¾-oz. cans cream of
  celery soup
chopped green pepper,
  optional
chopped onion, *optional*

1. Brown ground beef in large non-stick skillet. Drain.
2. Return drained beef to skillet. Turn heat to low. Stir cubed cheese into beef in skillet. Heat gently until cheese melts, stirring occasionally.
3. Place browned beef and melted cheese in slow cooker. Add remaining ingredients and stir well.
4. Cook on High 45-60 minutes, or until heated through.
5. Serve with nacho chips.

Ground Beef Cheese Dip

Carol Eberly
Harrisonburg, VA

Makes about 6 cups dip

Prep Time: 20 minutes
Cooking Time: 2 hours
Ideal slow cooker size: 2-qt.

2-lb. box Velveeta cheese,
  cubed
1 lb. ground beef
1 onion, chopped
10¾-oz. can cream of
  mushroom soup
14½-oz. can diced
  tomatoes with green
  chilies

1. While cutting up cheese, brown beef and onions in skillet. Drain meat mixture and place in slow cooker.
2. Place all remaining ingredients in slow cooker and combine.
3. Cover. Cook on Low 2 hours, or until cheese is melted, stirring occasionally.
4. Serve over baked potatoes or with tortilla chips.

Variation: For more snap, add 4¼-oz. can green chilies in Step 2.

Cheesy Ground Beef Salsa Dip

Mary Jane Musser, Manheim, PA
Colleen Heatwole, Burton, MI

Makes 20 servings

Prep Time: 15 minutes
Cooking Time: 1 hour
Ideal slow cooker size: 3- to 4-qt.

2 lbs. ground beef
2 lbs. Velveeta cheese,
  cubed
16-, *or* 32-oz., jar salsa,
  according to your taste
  preference
tortilla chips

1. Brown beef in non-stick skillet. Drain.
2. Place beef in cooker while hot. Stir in cheese until melted.
3. Add salsa.
4. Turn slow cooker to High for 1 hour. Turn to Low and serve with tortilla chips for dipping.

Variations: Add ¼ cup milk for a creamier consistency.
— **Ruth Ann Bender**
  Cochranville, PA

Add a 4-oz. can of green chilies.
— **Norma Grieser**
  Clarksville, MI

Tip: You can make this ahead of time and refrigerate it, then reheat it in the slow cooker for an hour or two before you're ready to serve it.

Salsa Dip

Barbara Smith
Bedford, PA

Makes 20 servings

Prep Time: 20 minutes
Cooking Time: 4 hours
Ideal slow cooker size:
  3- to 4-qt.

1/2 lb. lean ground beef
1 lb. Velveeta cheese,
  cubed
3-oz. pkg. cream cheese
half an envelope dry taco
  seasoning
14-oz. jar salsa, your
  choice of hotness

1. Brown ground beef in a
non-stick skillet. Drain.
2. Place in slow cooker.
Add remaining ingredients.
Stir well.
3. Cover and cook on Low
4 hours.
4. Stir, and then serve with
taco chips.

A Tip —

To remove onion odor
from your fingers, rub a
metal spoon between your
finger and thumb under
running water.

Mexican Ground Beef-Cheese Dip

Liz Rugg
Wayland, IA

Makes 10 servings

Prep Time: 15 minutes
Cooking Time: 4-5 hours
Ideal slow cooker size: 2-qt.

1 lb. ground beef
15-oz. can enchilada sauce
1 lb. Velveeta cheese,
  cubed

1. Brown ground beef in
non-stick skillet. Drain.
2. Place in slow cooker.
Add sauce and cubed cheese.
Stir well.
3. Cover and cook on Low
4-5 hours.
4. When heated through,
serve with your favorite taco
chips.

Taco Pizza Dip

Arlene Snyder
Millerstown, PA

Makes 8-10 servings

Prep Time: 15 minutes
Cooking Time: 1 1/2-2 hours
Ideal slow cooker size:
  2- to 3-qt.

2 8-oz. pkgs. cream cheese,
  softened
8-12-oz. container French
  onion dip
1 lb. ground beef
half an envelope dry taco
  seasoning mix
1 cup shredded cheddar
  cheese

Optional ingredients:
green pepper, diced
mushrooms, sliced

1. Combine cream cheese
and onion dip. Spread in slow
cooker.
2. Brown ground beef in a
skillet. Drain. Stir taco seasoning into meat.
3. Place seasoned meat on
top of cream cheese mixture.
4. Sprinkle cheddar cheese
on top of meat. Top with peppers and mushrooms, if you
wish.
4. Cover and cook on Low
1 1/2-2 hours. Serve with white
corn chips.

Creamy Taco Dip

Elaine Rineer
Lancaster, PA

Makes 10-12 servings

Prep Time: 15 minutes
Cooking Time: 2-3 hours
Ideal slow cooker size:
  2- to 3- qt.

1½ lbs. ground beef
1 envelope dry taco
  seasoning mix
16-oz. jar of salsa
2 cups sour cream
1 cup cheddar cheese,
  grated

1. Brown ground beef in non-stick skillet. Drain.
2. Return beef to skillet. Add taco seasoning and salsa.
3. Remove from stove and add sour cream and cheese. Pour mixture into slow cooker.
4. Cover and cook on Low 2-3 hours, or until hot.
5. Serve with tortilla chips.

Hearty Broccoli-Beef Dip

Renee Baum
Chambersburg, PA

Makes 24 servings

Prep Time: 15-20 minutes
Cooking Time: 2-3 hours
Ideal slow cooker size: 3-qt.

1 lb. ground beef
1 lb. American cheese,
  cubed
10¾-oz. can cream of
  mushroom soup
10-oz. pkg. frozen chopped
  broccoli, thawed
2 Tbsp. salsa, hot,
  medium, *or* mild

1. Brown ground beef in non-stick skillet. Drain.
2. Combine all ingredients in slow cooker. Mix well.
3. Cover and cook on Low 2-3 hours, or until heated through, stirring after 1 hour.
4. Serve with tortilla chips.

Tip: Serve as a main dish over baked potatoes or cooked rice.
— **Cindy Harney**
Lowville, NY

Hot Chip Dip

Sharon Wantland
Menomonee Falls, WI

Make 8 servings

Prep Time: 15 minutes
Cooking Time: 1½ hours
Ideal slow cooker size: 4-qt.

1 lb. ground beef
1-lb. can chili without
  beans
1 bunch green onions,
  chopped
4¼-oz. can green chilies,
  chopped
1 lb. Velveeta cheese,
  cubed

1. Brown beef in non-stick skillet until crumbly. Drain.
2. Place in slow cooker and add all other ingredients. Mix together well.
3. Cover and cook on High 1½ hours.
4. Turn cooker to Low and serve dip with large tortilla chips.

Chili-Cheese Dip

Dorothy Lingerfelt
Stonyford, CA
Gertrude Dutcher
Hartville, OH
Corinna Herr
Stevens, PA

Makes 10-12 servings

Prep Time: 10 minutes
Cooking Time: 1 hour
Ideal slow cooker size: 4-qt.

1 lb. lean ground beef
1 lb. American cheese,
  cubed
8-10-oz. can tomatoes and
  green chilies
2 tsp. Worcestershire sauce
1/2 tsp. chili powder

1. Brown ground beef in
non-stick skillet. Drain.
2. Place browned beef in
slow cooker. Add all remaining ingredients. Stir well.
3. Cover and cook on High
1 hour, stirring occasionally
until cheese is fully melted.
4. Serve immediately or
turn to Low for serving up to
6 hours later.

Tips:
*1. Serve with tortilla or corn
chips.*
*2. For a thicker dip, stir 2
Tbsp. flour and 3 Tbsp. water
together in a small bowl until
smooth. When dip is hot and
cheese is melted, stir paste into
slow cooker. Continue to stir
until thoroughly blended.*

Nacho Dip

Gladys M. High
Ephrata, PA

Makes 10-12 servings

Prep Time: 15 minutes
Cooking Time: 1 hour
Ideal slow cooker size:
  5- to 6-qt.

1 lb. ground beef
2 lbs. American cheese,
  cubed
16-oz. jar salsa, your
  choice of heat
1 Tbsp. Worcestershire
  sauce

1. Brown ground beef in
non-stick skillet. Drain.
2. Place beef in slow
cooker. Add all other ingredients and blend well.
3. Cover and cook on High
for 1 hour. Stir occasionally
until cheese is fully melted.
4. Serve immediately, or
turn to Low for serving up to
6 hours later.
5. Serve with tortilla or
corn chips.

Easy Pizza Appetizers

Sharon Wantland
Menomonee Falls, WI

Makes 8 servings

Prep Time: 15 minutes
Cooking Time: 1 hour
Ideal slow cooker size: 4-qt.

1 lb. ground beef
1 lb. bulk Italian sausage
1 lb. Velveeta cheese,
  cubed and divided
4 tsp. pizza seasoning
1/2 tsp. Worcestershire
  sauce

1. In a large non-stick skillet, brown beef and sausage
until crumbly. Drain.
2. Add remaining ingredients and place mixture in
slow cooker.
3. Cover and heat on Low
for 1 hour.
4. When thoroughly
warmed, offer a small spoon
or knife for spreading and
serve with party rye bread.

Meaty Queso Dip
Janie Steele
Moore, OK

Makes 15 appetizer servings

Prep Time: 50 minutes
Cooking Time: 30-60 minutes
Ideal slow cooker size:
    3- to 4-qt.

1 lb. ground beef
1 lb. bulk hot Italian
    sausage
1 lb. jalapeno Velveeta
    cheese, cubed
10³/4-oz. can golden
    mushroom soup
tortilla chips

1. Brown ground beef in non-stick skillet. Drain. Place in slow cooker.
2. Brown loose sausage in skillet. Drain. Add to slow cooker.
3. Add all remaining ingredients except tortilla chips to slow cooker. Mix together well.
4. Cook on High for 30-60 minutes, stirring frequently until cheese is melted.
5. Turn to Low. Serve with chips, stirring occasionally to prevent scorching.

Hearty Pizza Dip
Natalia Showalter
Mt. Solon, VA

Makes 18 servings

Prep Time: 30 minutes
Cooking Time: 3 hours
Ideal slow cooker size: 3-qt.

1 lb. bulk smoked sausage
2 8-oz. pkgs. cream cheese,
    cubed
2 cups pizza sauce
2 cups grated mozzarella
    cheese
1 cup grated cheddar
    cheese

1. Brown the sausage in a skillet, breaking it up into small pieces with a spoon as it browns. Drain.
2. Place sausage in slow cooker. Stir in all remaining ingredients.
3. Cover and cook on High for 1 hour. Stir.
4. Cook on Low until heated through, about 2 more hours.

Tip: Serve with corn chips.

Variation: For a stick-to-the-ribs breakfast, stir 2 Tbsp. of the finished dip into 3 eggs while scrambling them. Serve the mixture open-faced on toasted English muffins.
    — **Elaine Patton**
    West Middletown, PA

Hot Beef Dip
Sarah Miller
Harrisonburg, VA

Makes 12-15 servings

Prep Time: 30 minutes
Cooking Time: 2-3 hours
Ideal slow cooker size:
    1- to 2-qt.

2 8-oz. pkgs. cream cheese,
    softened
8 ozs. grated cheddar
    cheese
1 green pepper, chopped
    fine
1 small onion, chopped
    fine
1/4 lb. dried beef, shredded

1. In a medium-sized mixing bowl, combine cream cheese and grated cheese.
2. Fold in peppers, onions, and dried beef. Place stiff mixture in slow cooker.
3. Cover and cook on Low 2-3 hours. Stir occasionally.
4. Serve hot with crackers.

Variations: Use only one pkg. cream cheese. Drop cheddar cheese. Add 1 cup sour cream to Step 1.
    Serve with toasted bread tips for dipping.
    — **Judith A. Govotsos**
    Frederick, MD

Reuben Appetizers

Joleen Albrecht, Gladstone, MI

Makes 10 servings

Prep Time: 15 minutes
Cooking Time: 1-2 hours
Ideal slow cooker size: 2-qt.

1/2 cup mayonnaise
2 cups (10 ozs.) Swiss
  cheese, shredded
1/2 lb. thinly sliced corned
  beef, cut up
14-oz. can sauerkraut,
  drained
1 loaf *or* package party rye
  bread

1. Combine all ingredients,
except bread, in slow cooker.
2. Cover and cook on High
1-2 hours, or until heated
through and cheese is melted.
3. Spread on slices of rye
bread. Serve hot.

*Tip: The consistency is better if
you do not use low-fat cheese or
mayonnaise.*

Variations:
*1. For added flavor, add 2
cups shredded cheddar cheese.
And increase the mayonnaise to
1 cup. These added ingredients
will increase the number of
servings to 14-16.*
  — **Norma Grieser**
  Clarksville, MI

*2. Instead of mayonnaise,
use 1 8-oz. pkg. cream cheese,
softened, and 1/2 cup Thousand
Island salad dressing.*
  — **Jeanette Oberholtzer**
  Manheim, PA

Reuben Spread

Renee Baum,
Chambersburg, PA

Makes 18-20 servings

Prep Time: 15 minutes
Cooking Time: 3 hours
Ideal slow cooker size: 2 1/2-qt.

2 1/2 cups cubed, cooked
  corned beef
16-oz. jar sauerkraut,
  rinsed and drained well
2 cups (8 ozs.) shredded
  Swiss cheese
2 cups (8 ozs.) shredded
  cheddar cheese
1 cup mayonnaise

1. Combine all ingredients
in slow cooker. Mix well.
2. Cover and cook on Low
3 hours, stirring occasionally.
Serve warm.

Sweet 'n Sour
Meatballs

Valerie Drobel, Carlisle, PA
Sharon Hannaby
Frederick, MD

Makes 15-20 servings

Prep Time: 10 minutes
Cooking Time: 2-4 hours
Ideal slow cooker size:
  3- to 4-qt.

12-oz. jar grape jelly
12-oz. jar chili sauce
2 1-lb. bags prepared
  frozen meatballs,
  thawed

1. Combine jelly and sauce
in slow cooker. Stir well.
2. Add meatballs. Stir to
coat.
3. Cover and heat on Low
4 hours, or on High 2 hours.
Keep slow cooker on Low
while serving.

*Variation: Instead of meat-
balls, use 2 1-lb. pkgs. little
smokies.*
  — **Krista Hershberger**
  Elverson, PA

*Tip: If your meatballs are
frozen, add another hour to the
cooking time.*

Tangy Meatballs

Penny Blosser
Beavercreek, OH

Makes 50-60 meatballs

Prep Time: 15 minutes
Cooking Time: 2-4 hours
Ideal slow cooker size: 4-qt.

2 lbs. pre-cooked meatballs
16-oz. bottle barbecue
  sauce
8 ozs. grape jelly

1. Place meatballs in slow cooker.
2. Combine barbecue sauce and jelly in medium-sized mixing bowl.
3. Pour over meatballs and stir well.
4. Cover and cook on High 2 hours, or on Low 4 hours.
5. Turn to Low and serve.

Mini Hot Dogs and Meatballs

Mary Kay Nolt
Newmanstown, PA

Makes 15 servings

Prep Time: 5 minutes
Cooking Time: 2-3 hours
Ideal slow cooker size:
  5- to 6-qt.

36 frozen cooked Italian
  meatballs (1/2-oz. each)
16-oz. pkg. miniature hot
  dogs, *or little smoked*
  sausages
26-oz. jar meatless
  spaghetti sauce
18-oz. bottle barbecue
  sauce
12-oz. bottle chili sauce

1. Combine all ingredients in slow cooker.
2. Cover and cook on High for 2 hours, or on Low for 3 hours, until heated through.

Variation: Add 3 1/2-oz. pkg. sliced pepperoni to Step 1.

Bacon Cheddar Dip

Arlene Snyder
Millerstown, PA

Makes 15 servings

Prep Time: 10-15 minutes
Cooking Time: 1 1/2-2 hours
Ideal slow cooker size: 4-qt.

2 8-oz. pkgs. cream cheese,
  softened
2 cups sour cream
1 lb. bacon, fried and
  crumbled
4 cups shredded cheddar
  cheese, *divided*

1. In a mixing bowl, beat cream cheese and sour cream until smooth.
2. Fold in bacon and 3 cups cheddar cheese.
3. Place mixture in slow cooker and sprinkle with remaining cheese.
4. Cover and cook on Low 1 1/2-2 hours, or until heated through.
5. Serve with white corn chips.

Tip: Save a few bacon crumbs to sprinkle on top.

Variation: For a spicier version, stir some fresh herbs, or some chopped chilies, into Step 2.

A Tip —

Since I work full-time, I often put my dinner into the slow cooker to cook until I get home. My three teenagers and umpire/referee husband can all get a hot nutritious meal no matter what time they get home.

Rhonda Burgoon
Collingswood, NJ

Swiss Cheese Dip

Jennifer Yoder Sommers
Harrisonburg, VA

Makes 12 servings

Prep Time: 5 minutes
Cooking Time: 1-2 hours
Ideal slow cooker size: 1½-qt.

2 cups (8 ozs.) shredded
    Swiss cheese
1 cup mayonnaise
½ cup bacon bits
2 Tbsp. chopped onion
½ cup snack cracker
    crumbs

1. Combine cheese, mayonnaise, bacon bits, and onion in slow cooker.
2. Sprinkle cracker crumbs over top.
3. Cover and cook on Low 1-2 hours.
4. Serve with a variety of snack crackers or cut-up, fresh vegetables.

Pepperoni Pizza Dip

Annabelle Unternahrer
Shipshewana, IN

Makes 10-15 servings

Prep Time: 10 minutes
Cooking Time: 2 hours
Ideal slow cooker size: 3-qt.

2 8-oz. pkgs. cream cheese,
    cubed
14-oz. can pizza sauce
8-oz. pkg. sliced pepperoni,
    chopped
1 small can sliced ripe
    olives, drained
2 cups (8 ozs.) shredded
    mozzarella cheese

1. Place the cream cheese in your slow cooker.
2. In a small bowl, combine the pizza sauce, pepperoni, and olives. Pour over the cream cheese.
3. Sprinkle mozzarella cheese over the top.
4. Cover and cook on Low 2 hours, or until the cheese is melted.
5. Stir and serve with tortilla chips, bagel chips, or little garlic toasts.

Mustard-Lovers' Party Dogs

Barb Harvey
Quarryville, PA

Makes 12 servings

Prep Time: 15 minutes
Cooking Time: 1-2 hours
Ideal slow cooker size: 3-qt.

12 hot dogs cut into bite-
    size pieces
1 cup grape jelly
1 cup prepared mustard

1. Place all ingredients in slow cooker. Stir well.
2. Turn on High until mixture boils. Stir.
3. Turn to Low and bring to the buffet table.

Meaty Buffet Favorites

Judy A. Wantland
Menomonee Falls, WI

Makes 24 servings

Prep Time: 5 minutes
Cooking Time: 2 hours
Ideal slow cooker size:
2- to 3-qt.

1 cup tomato sauce
1 tsp. Worcestershire sauce
1/2 tsp. prepared mustard
2 Tbsp. brown sugar
1 lb. prepared meatballs,
  or 1 lb. mini-wieners

1. Mix first four ingredients in slow cooker.
2. Add meatballs or mini-wieners.
3. Cover and cook on High for 2 hours. Turn to Low and serve as an appetizer from the slow cooker.

Tips:
1. Double the sauce and add both wieners and meatballs.
2. Add 1/4-1/2 cup onion for extra flavor and texture.

Mini-Hot Dogs

Carolyn Fultz
Angola, IN

Makes 20-30 appetizer servings

Prep Time: 5 minutes
Cooking Time: 4-5 hours
Ideal slow cooker size: 4-qt.

2 cups brown sugar
1 Tbsp. Worcestershire
  sauce
14-oz. bottle ketchup
2 *or* 3 lbs. mini-hot dogs

1. In slow cooker, mix together brown sugar, Worcestershire sauce, and ketchup.
2. Stir in hot dogs.
3. Cover and cook on High 1 hour. Turn to Low and cook 3-4 hours.
4. Serve from the cooker while turned to Low.

Sausages in Wine

Mary E. Wheatley
Mashpee, MA

Makes 6 servings
or 24 appetizers

Prep Time: 15 minutes
Cooking Time: 45 minutes-
1 hour
Ideal slow cooker size: 3-qt.

1 cup dry red wine
2 Tbsp. currant jelly
6-8 mild Italian sausages,
  or Polish sausages

1. Place wine and jelly in slow cooker. Heat until jelly is dissolved and sauce begins to simmer. Add sausages.
2. Cover and cook on High 45 minutes to 1 hour, or until sausages are cooked through and lightly glazed.
3. Transfer sausages to a cutting board and slice. Serve with juices spooned over.

A Tip —

Use light brown sugar for a caramel flavor. Use dark brown sugar when you prefer a molasses flavor and color.

Zippy Sausage Cheese Dip

Reita Yoder
Carlsbad, NM

Makes 12 servings

Prep Time: 15 minutes
Cooking Time: 1-2 hours
Ideal slow cooker size: 1-qt.

1 lb. pork sausage, sliced thin, *or* squeezed out of casing and crumbled
2 lbs. Velveeta cheese, cubed
2 10¾-oz. cans Rotel tomatoes with chilies, undrained

1. Brown sausage in large non-stick skillet. Drain.
2. Return browned sausage to skillet and stir in cubed Velveeta cheese.
3. Cook over low heat until cheese melts. Stir occasionally.
4. Place pork and melted cheese in slow cooker. Stir in tomatoes.
5. Cover and cook on Low 1-2 hours until heated through.
6. Serve warm with raw, cut-up veggies or chips.

Tips:
1. If the dip gets too dry, add ¼-½ cup warm water.
2. If the cheese looks curdled, it's okay. Stir the mixture and reduce the heat, or turn off the cooker.

Variation: For a creamier dish, add 2 10¾-oz. cans cream of mushroom soup to Step 4, stirring the soup in with the tomatoes.
— Edna Mae Herschberger
Arthur, IL

Simmered Smoked Sausages

Jonice Crist
Quinter, KS
Mary Lynn Miller
Reinholds, PA
Joette Droz
Kalona, IA
Renee Baum
Chambersburg, PA

Makes 16-20 servings

Prep Time: 15 minutes
Cooking Time: 4 hours
Ideal slow cooker size: 2-qt.

2 16-oz. pkgs. miniature smoked sausage links
1 cup brown sugar, packed
½ cup ketchup
¼ cup prepared horseradish

1. Place sausages in slow cooker.
2. Combine remaining ingredients in a bowl and pour over sausages.
3. Cover and cook on Low for 4 hours.

Slow-Cooked Smokies

Renee Baum, Chambersburg, PA

Makes 12-16 servings

Prep Time: 5 minutes
Cooking Time: 6-7 hours
Ideal slow cooker size: 3- to 4-qt.

2 lbs. miniature smoked sausage links
28-oz. bottle barbecue sauce
1¼ cups water
3 Tbsp. Worcestershire sauce
3 Tbsp. steak sauce
½ tsp. pepper

1. In a slow cooker, combine all ingredients. Mix well.
2. Cover and cook on Low 6-7 hours.

Barbecued Lil' Smokies

Jena Hammond
Traverse City, MI

Makes 48-60 appetizer servings

Prep Time: 5 minutes
Cooking Time: 4 hours
Ideal slow cooker size: 4-qt.

4 16-oz. pkgs. little smokies
18-oz. bottle barbecue
   sauce

1. Mix ingredients together in slow cooker.
2. Cover and cook on Low for 4 hours.

Apple-y Kielbasa

Jeanette Oberholtzer
Manheim, PA

Makes 12 servings

Prep Time: 15 minutes
Cooking Time: 6-8 hours
Ideal slow cooker size: 3-qt.

2 lbs. fully cooked kielbasa
   sausage, cut into 1" pieces
3/4 cup brown sugar
1 cup chunky applesauce
2 cloves garlic, minced

1. Combine all ingredients in slow cooker.
2. Cover and cook on Low 6-8 hours until thoroughly heated.

Easy Barbecue Smokies

Ruth Ann Bender
Cochranville, PA

Makes 12-16 servings

Prep Time: 5 minutes
Cooking Time: 2 hours
Ideal slow cooker size: 3¹/₂-qt.

18-oz. bottle barbecue
   sauce
8 ozs. salsa
2 16-oz. pkgs. little
   smokies

1. Mix barbecue sauce and salsa in slow cooker.
2. Add the little smokies.
3. Heat on High for 2 hours.
4. Stir. Turn to Low to serve.

Crab Spread

Jeanette Oberholtzer
Manheim, PA

Makes 8 servings

Prep Time: 20 minutes
Cooking Time: 4 hours
Ideal slow cooker size: 1- to 3-qt.

1/2 cup mayonnaise
8 ozs. cream cheese,
   softened
2 Tbsp. apple juice
1 onion, minced

1 lb. lump crabmeat,
   picked over to remove
   cartilage and shell bits

1. Mix mayonnaise, cheese, and juice in medium-sized bowl until blended.
2. Stir in onions, mixing well. Gently stir in crabmeat.
3. Place in slow cooker, cover, and cook on Low for 4 hours.
4. Dip will hold for 2 hours. Stir occasionally. Serve with snack crackers, snack bread, or crudites.

Hot Cheese Melt

Tierra Woods
Duenweg, MO

Makes 9-10 servings

Prep Time: 5-10 minutes
Cooking Time: 1¹/₂-2 hours
Ideal slow cooker size:
   3- to 4-qt.

12-oz. can whole, *or*
   chopped, jalapeno
   peppers, drained
15-oz. can Mexican stewed,
   or Rotel, tomatoes,
   undrained
2 lbs. Velveeta cheese,
   cubed
4 slices bacon, cooked
   crisp and crumbled

1. Put chopped jalapenos in bottom of slow cooker. Spoon in tomatoes and then top with chunks of cheese.

2. Cover and cook on Low for 1½ hours, or until cheese is melted.

3. When ready to serve, sprinkle bacon on top.

4. Keep cooker turned to Low and serve Melt with tortilla chips, bread chunks, or fresh, cut-up vegetables.

Pizza Fondue
Bonnie Whaling
Clearfield, PA

Makes 4-6 servings

Prep Time: 15 minutes
Cooking Time: 1 hour
Ideal slow cooker size: 3½-qt.

1 lb. block of cheese, your choice of good melting cheese(s), cut in ½" cubes
2 cups grated mozzarella cheese
19-oz. can Italian-style stewed tomatoes with juice
loaf of Italian bread, slices toasted and then cut into 1" cubes

1. Place cheese cubes, grated mozzarella cheese, and tomatoes in a lightly greased slow cooker.

2. Cover and cook on High 45-60 minutes, or until cheese is melted.

3. Stir occasionally and scrape down sides of slow cooker with rubber spatula to prevent scorching.

4. Reduce heat to Low and serve. (Fondue will keep a smooth consistency for up to 4 hours.)

5. Serve with toasted bread cubes for dipping.

Variation: Add ¼ lb. thinly sliced pepperoni to Step 1.

Mexican Bean and Cheese Dip
Mary Sommerfeld
Lancaster, PA

Makes about 5 cups dip

Prep Time: 5 minutes
Cooking Time: 2-3 hours
Ideal slow cooker size: 2-qt.

15-oz. can refried beans
8-oz. jar taco sauce
1 lb. Velveeta cheese, cubed
1 pkg. dry taco seasoning

1. Combine ingredients in slow cooker.

2. Cover. Cook on Low 2-3 hours, or until cheese is melted.

3. Serve warm from the cooker with tortilla chips.

Note: If you're cautious about salt, choose minimally salted chips.

Mexican Cheese Dip
Dale Peterson
Rapid City, SD

Makes 12 servings

Prep Time: 10 minutes
Cooking Time: 2-3 hours
Ideal slow cooker size: 3-qt.

2 lbs. Velveeta cheese, cubed
2 tsp. taco seasoning
10-oz. can tomatoes and green chilies, undrained

1. Place cubed cheese in slow cooker.

2. Cover and cook on Low 1-1½ hours, or until cheese is melted.

3. Stir in seasoning and tomatoes with green chilies.

4. Cover and cook on Low another 1-1½ hours. Stir occasionally to keep cheese from sticking to the bottom of the cooker.

5. Serve with your favorite sturdy chips.

213

Chili Con Queso

Arlene Leaman Kliewer
Lakewood, CO

Makes 12-16 servings

Prep Time: 15 minutes
Cooking Time: 2 hours
Ideal slow cooker size: 2-qt.

2 Tbsp. oil
1 medium onion, chopped
2 4¼-oz. cans chopped
  green chilies
14½-oz. can Mexican-style
  stewed tomatoes, drained
1 lb. Velveeta cheese, cubed

1. In skillet, sauté onion in oil until transparent. Add chilies and tomatoes. Bring to boil.
2. Add cheese. Pour into slow cooker on Low. Cook for 2 hours.
3. Keep warm in slow cooker, stirring occasionally.
4. Serve with tortilla chips.

Chili Rellanos

Andrea Cunningham
Arlington, KS

Makes 8 servings

Prep Time: 15 minutes
Cooking Time: 6-8 hours
Ideal slow cooker size: 4-qt.

1¼ cups milk
4 eggs, beaten
3 Tbsp. flour

12-oz. can chopped green
  chilies
2 cups grated cheddar
  cheese

1. Combine all ingredients in slow cooker until well blended.
2. Cover and cook on Low for 6-8 hours.
3. Serve with tortilla chips and salsa

Variation: Serve as a burrito filling.

Chili-Cheese Dip

Sharon Timpe
Jackson, WI

Makes 10-12 servings

Prep Time: 5 minutes
Cooking Time: 2-3 hours
Ideal slow cooker size: 2-qt.

1 lb. pasteurized cheese
  spread
15-16-oz. can chili without
  beans
¼ cup chopped onion
4-oz. can chopped green
  chilies

1. Mix all ingredients in slow cooker.
2. Cover and cook on Low 2-3 hours, or until heated through.

Tip: Serve hot from the pot with scoop-shaped corn chips or tortilla chips.

Chili Con Queso Dip

Janie Steele
Moore, OK

Makes 12-15 servings

Prep Time: 5-10 minutes
Cooking Time: 1-2 hours
Ideal slow cooker size: 4-qt.

1 lb. Velveeta cheese,
  cubed
15-oz. can of chili with
  beans
4-oz. can chopped green
  chilies
1 medium onion, chopped

1. Combine all ingredients in slow cooker.
2. Cover and cook on High for 30 minutes, stirring frequently until cheese is melted.
3. Turn to Low, keeping the cooker covered, for 30-60 minutes. Stir occasionally to prevent scorching.
4. Serve with chips.

Mommy Trapp's Chip Dip

Penny Blosser
Beavercreek, OH

Makes 18-24 servings

Prep Time: 15 minutes
Cooking Time: 1 hour
Ideal slow cooker size: 3-qt.

2 pounds Velveeta cheese, cubed
1/4 cup milk
1 cup sharp cheddar cheese, grated
2 2³/4-oz. cans green chilies
1 small jar pimentos

1. Combine all ingredients in slow cooker.
2. Cover and cook on High 1 hour, or until cheese melts. Stir frequently.
3. Turn cooker to Low and serve with chips of your choice.

Tip: Add chopped jalapeno peppers if you want a spicier dip.

Revved-Up Chili Dip

Renee Baum,
Chambersburg, PA
Shirley Sears
Sarasota, FL
Mary Lynn Miller
Reinholds, PA

Makes 15 servings

Prep Time: 5-10 minutes
Cooking Time: 2 hours
Ideal slow cooker size: 2- to 3-qt.

24-oz. jar salsa
15-oz. can chili with beans
2 2¹/4-oz. cans sliced ripe olives, drained
12 ozs. American cheese, cubed

1. In slow cooker, combine salsa, chili, and olives. Stir in cheese.
2. Cover and cook on Low 2 hours, or until cheese is melted, stirring halfway through.
3. Serve with sturdy tortilla chips.

Curried Cheese Dip

Susan Kasting
Jenks, OK

Makes 9-10 servings

Prep Time: 10 minutes
Cooking Time: 45 minutes-1 hour
Ideal slow cooker size: 1- to 2-qt.

2 cups shredded cheddar cheese
8-oz. pkg. cream cheese, softened
1/2 cup milk
1/4 cup chopped scallions
1¹/2 tsp. curry powder

1. Mix ingredients together in slow cooker.
2. Cover and heat on High 45 minutes to 1 hour, or until cheeses are melted and dip is heated through. Stir occasionally.
3. Turn cooker to Low and serve dip with crackers or veggies.

Cider Cheese Fondue—for a buffet table

Ruth Ann Bender
Cochranville, PA

Makes 4 servings

Prep Time: 15 minutes
Warming time: until the
cooker is empty!
Ideal slow cooker size: 1-qt.

3/4 cup apple juice *or* cider
2 cups (8-10 ozs.) shredded
  cheddar cheese
1 cup (4-5 ozs.) shredded
  Swiss cheese
1 Tbsp. cornstarch
1/8 tsp. pepper
1 lb. loaf French bread, cut
  into chunks

1. In a large saucepan,
bring cider to a boil. Reduce
heat to medium low.
2. In a large mixing bowl,
toss together the cheeses with
cornstarch and pepper.
3. Stir mixture into cider.
Cook and stir for 3-4 minutes,
or until cheese is melted.
4. Transfer to a 1-qt. slow
cooker to keep warm. Stir
occasionally
5. Serve with bread cubes
or apple wedges for dipping.

Super-Bowl Dip

Liz Rugg
Wayland, IA

Makes 30 servings

Prep Time: 15 minutes
Cooking Time: 2-3 hours
Ideal slow cooker size:
  3- to 4-qt.

2 lbs. ground beef
1 envelope dry taco
  seasoning mix
24-oz. jar salsa, your
  choice of heat
1 lb. Velveeta cheese,
  cubed
16-oz. can refried beans

1. Brown beef in non-stick
skillet. Drain.
2. Place beef in slow
cooker. Stir in remaining
ingredients.
3. Cover and cook on Low
2-3 hours, or until cheese is
melted.

Tip: Serve with your favorite
tortilla chips.

Refried Bean Dip

Mabel Shirk
Mount Crawford, VA
Wilma Haberkamp
Fairbank, IA

Makes 8-10 servings

Prep Time: 5-10 minutes
Cooking Time: 2-2 1/2 hours
Ideal slow cooker size:
  1- to 2-qt.

20-oz. can refried beans
1 cup shredded cheddar, *or*
  hot pepper, cheese
1/2 cup chopped green
  onions
1/4 tsp. salt
2-4 Tbsp. bottled taco
  sauce (depending on
  your taste preference)

1. In slow cooker, combine
beans with cheese, onions,
salt, and taco sauce.
2. Cover and cook on Low
2 to 2 1/2 hours.
3. Serve hot from the pot
with tortilla chips.

Easy Refried Bean Dip

Katrina Eberly
Stevens, PA

Makes 12 servings

Prep Time: 10 minutes
Cooking Time: 1¹/₂ hours
Ideal slow cooker size: 2-qt.

2 15-oz. cans refried beans
1 envelope taco seasoning mix (use all, *or* ³/4, depending on your taste preference)
¹/2 cup chopped onions
2 cups shredded Monterey Jack, *or* Mexican Blend, cheese
chopped jalapenos, *or* mild chilies, to taste
2-4 drops Tabasco sauce, *optional*

1. Place beans, taco seasoning, onions, and cheese in your slow cooker. Stir well to blend.
2. Stir in jalapenos or chilies and Tabasco sauce.
3. Cook on Low until cheese is melted, about 1¹/2 hours.
4. Add a little water if the dip seems too thick.

Tip: If you have leftovers (unlikely!), wrap the remaining dip in a flour tortilla and top with some sour cream for a light lunch or dinner.
— Joleen Albrecht
Gladstone, MI

Cheesy Bean Dip

Deborah Heatwole
Waynesboro, GA

Makes 18-20 servings

Prep Time: 5-10 minutes
Cooking Time: 1¹/₂-3 hours
Ideal slow cooker size: 2-qt.

16-oz. can refried beans
2 8-oz. pkgs. cream cheese, cubed
2 cups salsa, hot, medium, *or* mild
2 cups shredded cheddar cheese
1 envelope dry taco seasoning mix

1. Mix all ingredients in slow cooker. Stir to combine well.
2. Cover and heat on High for 1¹/2 hours, or on Low for 3 hours, stirring occasionally.
3. Serve with corn chips.

Tip: A potato masher works well for blending the ingredients together.

A Tip —

The Warm setting on a slow cooker holds food at a temperature between 145° and 165° F.

Fiesta Dip

Melissa Warner
Broad Top, PA

Makes 8 servings

Prep Time: 10 minutes
Cooking Time: 30-60 minutes
Ideal slow cooker size: 1-qt.

16-oz. can refried beans
1 cup shredded cheddar cheese
¹/2 cup Mexican salsa
1 green chili pepper, chopped, *optional*

1. Combine all ingredients and place in slow cooker.
2. Cover and heat 30-60 minutes, or until cheese is melted.
3. Serve with tortilla chips or corn chips.

Cheese and Broccoli Dip

Maryann Markano
Wilmington, DE

Makes 24 servings

Prep Time: 20-25 minutes
Cooking Time: 1½-2 hours
Ideal slow cooker size:
  3- to 4-qt.

2 10-oz. pkgs. frozen
  chopped broccoli
1 lb. cubed Mexican
  Velveeta cheese, *or* plain
  Velveeta, *or* a
  combination of the two
2 10¾-oz. cans cream of
  mushroom soup
¼ cup sour cream
1 tsp. garlic powder

1. Cook broccoli until just-tender in a saucepan. Drain.
2. Melt cheese in slow cooker on Low for about 1½-2 hours. (You can jumpstart things by melting the cheese in the microwave—30 seconds on High. Stir. Continue heating on High for 15-second increments, followed by stirring each time, until cheese is melted).
3. In a large mixing bowl, mix together the soup, sour cream, broccoli, and garlic powder. Stir in melted cheese.
4. Spoon into slow cooker. Keep slow cooker on warm while serving with tortilla chips. Stir occasionally.

Hot Broccoli Dip

Brenda Hochstedler
East Earl, PA

Makes 24 servings

Prep Time: 20 minutes
Cooking Time: 1 hour
Ideal slow cooker size: 2-qt.

2 cups fresh *or* frozen
  broccoli, chopped
4 Tbsp. chopped red bell
  pepper
2 8-oz. containers ranch
  dip
½ cup grated Parmesan
  cheese
2 cups shredded cheddar
  cheese

1. Mix together all ingredients in your slow cooker.
2. Cook on Low for 1 hour.
3. Serve with pita chips, veggie chips, or raw, cut-up vegetables.

Hot Mushroom Dip

Carol L. Stroh, Akron, NY

Makes 6-8 servings

Prep Time: 30 minutes
Cooking Time: 3-4 hours
Ideal slow cooker size:
  1½- to 2-qt.

8-oz. pkg. cream cheese
10¾-oz. can cream of
  mushroom soup
4-oz. can mushrooms,
  chopped and drained
⅔ cup chopped shrimp,
  crab, *or* ham
½ cup milk

1. Cut cream cheese into small pieces and place in slow cooker with remaining ingredients. Stir to mix.
2. Heat on Low 3-4 hours, stirring occasionally during first hour.
3. Serve with your choice of dippers—French bread, veggies, or crackers.

Artichokes

Dorothy Lingerfelt
Stonyford, CA

Makes 4 servings

Prep Time: 10 minutes
Cooking Time: 2¹/2-4 hours
Ideal slow cooker size: 4-qt.

4 whole, fresh artichokes
1 tsp. salt
4 Tbsp. lemon juice,
    divided
2 Tbsp. butter, melted

1. Wash and trim off the tough outer leaves and around the bottom of the artichokes.
    Cut off about 1 inch from the tops of each, and trim off the tips of the leaves.
    Spread the top leaves apart and use a long-handled spoon to pull out the fuzzy chokes in their centers.
2. Stand the prepared artichokes upright in the slow cooker. Sprinkle each with ¹/4 tsp. salt.
3. Spoon 2 Tbsp. lemon juice over the artichokes. Pour in enough water to cover the bottom half of the artichokes.
4. Cover and cook on High for 2¹/2-4 hours.
5. Serve with melted butter and remaining lemon juice for dipping.

Artichoke Dip

Colleen Heatwole
Burton, MI

Makes 9-12 servings

Prep Time: 20 minutes
Cooking Time: 1-1¹/2 hours
Ideal slow cooker size: 2-qt.

12-oz. jar marinated
    artichoke hearts
1 cup grated Parmesan
    cheese
²/3 cup sour cream
²/3 cup mayonnaise
2 Tbsp. diced pimento

1. Drain artichoke hearts very well. Chop finely.
2. Place chopped artichokes in slow cooker. Combine with remaining ingredients.
3. Cover and cook on Low 1-1¹/2 hours, stirring occasionally.
4. Serve with tortilla chips.

Apple Dip

Leticia A. Zehr
Lowville, NY

Makes 24 servings

Prep Time: 15 minutes
Cooking Time: 20 minutes
Ideal slow cooker size:
    2- to 3-qt.

2 sticks (1 cup) butter
2 cups brown sugar,
    packed
2 14-oz. cans sweetened,
    condensed milk
1 cup corn syrup
1 cup peanut butter,
    optional
apple slices to dip

1. Combine all ingredients except apple slices in a saucepan until smooth. Heat until scalding, watching to make sure it doesn't stick to the bottom of the pan.
2. Transfer dip to slow cooker.
3. Cover and cook on Low 20 minutes.
4. While the dip is warming, slice the apples and place on a serving plate.
5. Serve the dip from the cooker, while turned on Low to keep it creamy.

219

Butterscotch Dip

Renee Baum
Chambersburg, PA

Makes 10-15 servings

Prep Time: 5-10 minutes
Cooking Time: 45-50 minutes
Ideal slow cooker size: 1-qt.

2 10-11-oz. pkgs.
   butterscotch chips
5-oz. can evaporated milk
2/3 cup chopped pecans
1 Tbsp. rum extract,
   optional
apple and pear wedges

1. Combine butterscotch chips and milk in slow cooker.
2. Cover and cook on Low 45-50 minutes, or until chips are softened. Stir until smooth.
3. Stir in pecans and extract.
4. Serve warm with fruit wedges for dipping.

Slow-Cooker Candy

Eileen M. Landis
Lebanon, PA
Sarah Miller
Harrisonburg, VA
Janet Oberholtzer
Ephrata, PA

Makes 80-100 pieces

Prep Time: 5-10 minutes
Cooking Time: 2 hours
Chilling Time: 45 minutes
Ideal slow cooker size:
   2- to 3-qt.

1 1/2 lbs. almond bark,
   broken
4-oz. Baker's Brand
   German sweet chocolate
   bar, broken
8 ozs. chocolate chips
8 ozs. peanut butter chips
2 lbs. lightly salted, *or*
   unsalted, peanuts

1. Spray inside of cooker with non-stick cooking spray.
2. Layer ingredients into slow cooker in the order given above.
3. Cook on Low 2 hours. Do not stir or lift the lid during the cooking time.
4. After 2 hours, mix well.
5. Drop by teaspoonful onto waxed paper. Refrigerate for approximately 45 minutes before serving or storing.

Peanut Clusters

Jeannine Janzen, Elbing, KS
Marcia Parker, Lansdale, PA

Makes 3 1/2-4 dozen pieces

Prep Time: 20 minutes
Cooking Time: 3 hours
Cooling Time: 30 minutes
Ideal slow cooker size: 4-qt.

2 lbs. white candy coating,
   chopped
12-oz. pkg. semi-sweet
   chocolate chips
4-oz. milk chocolate bar, *or*
   4-oz. pkg. German sweet
   chocolate, chopped
24-oz. jar dry roasted
   peanuts

1. Spray inside of slow cooker with non-stick cooking spray.
2. In slow cooker, combine white candy coating, chocolate chips, and milk chocolate.
3. Cover and cook on Low 3 hours. Stir every 15 minutes.
4. Add peanuts to melted chocolate. Mix well.
5. Drop by tablespoonful onto waxed paper. Cool until set. Serve immediately, or store in a tightly covered container, separating layers with waxed paper. Keep cool and dry.

Tips:
   1. This rich mixture can be lumpy as it melts. Stir often, using a wooden spoon to flatten out the lumps.
   2. This makes great holiday gifts. And the taste improves a day after it's been made.

Haystacks

Cathy Boshart
Lebanon, PA

Makes 3 dozen pieces

Prep Time: 15 minutes
Cooking Time: 15 minutes
Cooling Time: 30 minutes
Ideal slow cooker size: 2-qt.

2 6-oz. pkgs. butterscotch
 chips
3/4 cup chopped almonds
5-oz. can chow mein
 noodles

1. Turn cooker to High.
Place chips in slow cooker.
Stir every few minutes until
they're melted.
2. When the chips are
completely melted, gently stir
in almonds and noodles.
3. When well mixed, drop
by teaspoonful onto waxed
paper.
4. Let stand until
haystacks are set, or speed
things up by placing them in
the fridge until set.
5. Serve, or store in a covered container, placing waxed
paper between layers of
candy. Keep in a cool, dry
place.

Old Fashioned Hot Chocolate Syrup

Jennie Martin
Richfield, PA

Makes 18 servings

Prep Time: 10 minutes
Cooking Time: 4 hours
Ideal slow cooker size: 5-qt.

1 cup dry cocoa powder
2 cups sugar
1 1/2 cups hot water
1/2 tsp. vanilla
3 qts. milk

1. Mix first three ingredients together with a whisk in
a 2-qt. saucepan. Bring to a
boil and boil for 2 minutes.
2. Remove from heat and
stir in vanilla.
3. Add this syrup to
approximately 3 qts. milk.
You can heat the milk in a
5-qt. saucepan, stir the syrup
into it, and then pour the hot
chocolate into your slow
cooker.
Or you can heat the milk
in your slow cooker and add
the syrup to it.
4. Either way, you can
maintain the hot chocolate in
the slow cooker throughout
an evening party.

Slow-Cooker Apple Butter

Sarah Miller
Harrisonburg, VA

Makes 10 cups

Prep Time: 15 minutes
Cooking Time: 12-15 hours
Ideal slow cooker size: 5-qt.

4 qts. unsweetened
 applesauce
3 1/2 cups sugar
1/4 tsp. oil of cinnamon
 (look in the cake/candy
 ingredients aisle of your
 grocery store)
1/4 tsp. oil cloves (look in
 the cake/candy
 ingredients aisle of your
 grocery store)
1/4 cup vinegar
dash *or* two of cinnamon,
 optional

1. Put applesauce in slow
cooker. Cover, and cook on
Low overnight.
2. In the morning, add the
remaining ingredients. Cook
on High, stirring occasionally
until it reaches the thickness
you like. This could take several hours, depending on the
variety of apples.
3. Pour into hot sterilized
jars and process according to
standard canning methods.

Traditional Apple Butter

Wilma Haberkamp, Fairbank, IA
Vera Martin, East Earl, PA

Makes 8 cups

Prep Time: 15 minutes
Cooking Time: 10-13 hours
Ideal slow cooker size: 3-qt.

12-14 medium-sized tart
   cooking apples (about
   16 cups chopped)
2 cups cider
2 cups sugar
1 tsp. ground cinnamon
1/8-1/4 tsp. ground cloves
   (add 1/8 tsp. cloves first;
   taste about halfway
   through the cooking
   time to decide if you
   want to add the other
   1/8 tsp.)

1. Core and chop the
apples. Do not peel them.
Combine apples and cider in
your slow cooker.
2. Cover and cook on Low
9-12 hours, or until apples
turn mushy and then thicken.
3. Puree apples in a food
mill or sieve.
4. Return pureed mixture
to your slow cooker.
5. Add sugar, cinnamon,
and cloves and mix together
well.
6. Cover and cook on Low
1 hour.

*Variations: For a thicker fin-
ished product, drop Step 6 and
do this instead: Cover and cook*

on High 6-8 hours, stirring
about every 2 hours.
   Remove the cover after 3
hours so that the fruit and juice
can cook down and become
thicker and more concentrated.
   Spoon into hot sterilized jars
and process according to standard canning methods.
— **Dorothy VanDeest**
Memphis, TN

Tips:
   *1. This will keep several
weeks in your refrigerator. You
may also can or freeze it.*
   *2. This is good on bread or
toast. Or use it as a topping
over ice cream. Or try it as a
filling for apple turnovers.*
   *3. If you can't find cider, you
can use apple juice instead.*

Lotsa-Apples Apple Butter

Mary Kathryn Yoder
Harrisonville, MO

Makes 5 cups

Prep Time: 30 minutes
Cooking Time: all day
Ideal slow cooker size: 3 1/2-qt.

crock full of chopped apples
2 cups sugar
3 tsp. cinnamon
1/4 tsp. salt

1. Peel, core, and finely
chop apples. You can make
the cooker so heaping full
that the lid doesn't fit at first,
but the apples will cook

down so that the lid will
eventually fit.
2. Drizzle sugar, cinnamon,
and salt over apples.
3. Cover and cook on High
1 hour. Reduce the heat to
Low. Cook all day until mixture becomes thick and dark
in color. Stir occasionally.
4. Place in small jars, cool,
and freeze, leaving room for
expansion.

Apricot Butter

Janet L. Roggie, Lowville, NY

Makes 15 cups

Prep Time: 10 minutes
Cooking Time: 8 hours
Ideal slow cooker size: 5-qt.

4 28-oz. cans apricots,
   drained
3 cups sugar
2 tsp. cinnamon
1/2 tsp. ground cloves
2 Tbsp. lemon juice

1. Puree fruit in food
processor. Pour into slow
cooker.
2. Stir in remaining ingredients.
3. Cover and cook on Low
8 hours.
4. Pour into hot, sterilized
1-cup, or 1-pt., jars and
process according to standard
canning methods.
5. Serve as a spread with
bread, or as a sauce with
pork or chicken dishes.

Beverages

Home-Style Tomato Juice

Wilma Haberkamp
Fairbank, IA

Makes 4 cups

Prep Time: 20 minutes
Cooking Time: 4-6 hours
Ideal slow cooker size: 3-qt.

10-12 large ripe tomatoes
1 tsp. salt
1 tsp. seasoned salt
1/4 tsp. pepper
1 Tbsp. sugar

1. Wash and drain tomatoes. Remove core and blossom ends.
2. Place the whole tomatoes in your slow cooker. (Do not add water.)
3. Cover and cook on Low 4-6 hours, or until tomatoes are very soft.
4. Press them through a sieve or food mill.
5. Add seasonings. Chill.

Tip: If you have more than 10-12 tomatoes, you can use a larger slow cooker and double the recipe.

Spicy Hot Cider

Michelle High
Fredericksburg, PA

Makes 16 servings

Prep Time: 5 minutes
Cooking Time: 3 hours
Ideal slow cooker size: 5-qt.

1 gallon apple cider
4 cinnamon sticks
2 Tbsp. ground allspice
1/4-1/2 cup brown sugar

1. Combine all ingredients in slow cooker.
Begin with 1/4 cup brown sugar. Stir to dissolve. If you'd like the cider to be sweeter, add more, up to 1/2 cup total.
2. Cover and cook on Low 3 hours.
3. Serve warm from the cooker.

Red Hot Apple Cider

Allison Ingels
Maynard, IA

Makes 16 servings

Prep Time: 5 minutes
Cooking Time: 1¹/₂-2 hours
Ideal slow cooker size: 5-qt.

1 gallon apple cider, *or*
  apple juice
1¹/₄ cups red cinnamon
  hearts
16 4″-long cinnamon sticks

1. Combine cider and cinnamon hearts in slow cooker.
2. Cover. Cook on Low 1¹/₂-2 hours.
3. Serve hot with a cinnamon stick in each cup.

Our family enjoys this recipe on cold winter evenings and especially on Christmas Eve. The smell creates a very relaxing atmosphere.

Hot Apple Cider

Jeannine Janzen
Elbing, KS

Makes 4 servings

Prep Time: 5 minutes
Cooking Time: 2-3 hours
Ideal slow cooker size: 3-qt.

1 qt. apple cider
¹/₈ tsp. nutmeg
¹/₂ cup red cinnamon
  hearts

1. Combine all ingredients in slow cooker.
2. Cover and cook on High 2-3 hours, or until very hot.
  If you're at home and available, stir the cider occasionally to help dissolve the red candy.
3. Serve warm from the slow cooker.

Wassail

Dawn Hahn, Lititz, PA

Makes 16 servings

Prep Time: 5 minutes
Cooking Time: 3-5 hours
Ideal slow cooker size: 5-qt.

¹/₂ cup red cinnamon
  hearts
1 gallon apple cider
16 orange slice halves
16 3″- 4″-long cinnamon
  sticks

1. Pour cinnamon hearts into bottom of slow cooker.
2. Add apple cider.
3. Cook on Low 3-5 hours, or until cider is very hot and candy has melted.
  If you're able, stir occasionally to help the candy dissolve.
4. Place one orange slice half and one cinnamon stick in each cup. Pour hot cider over top.

Tip: This is great to serve at a Christmas or Valentine's party.

A Tip —

Slow cookers come in a variety of sizes, from 2- to 8-quarts. The best size for a family of four or five is a 5-6 quart-size.

Dorothy M. Van Deest
Memphis, TN

Citrus Cider

Valerie Drobel, Carlisle, PA

Makes 8-10 servings

Prep Time: 10 minutes
Cooking Time: 2-5 hours
Ideal slow cooker size:
    3- to 5-qt.

2 qts. apple cider
1/2 cup packed brown sugar
2 4"-long cinnamon sticks
1 tsp. whole cloves
1 orange *or* lemon, sliced

1. Pour cider into slow cooker. Stir in brown sugar.
2. Place cinnamon sticks and cloves in cheesecloth and tie with string to form a bag. Float in slow cooker.
3. Add fruit slices on top.
4. Cover and cook on Low 2-5 hours. Remove spice bag. Stir before serving.

Variations:
    1. Add 1/3 tsp. ground ginger to Step 1.
        — **Christie Anne Detamore-Hunsberger** Harrisonburg, VA

    2. Add 1 tsp. whole allspice to the cheesecloth bag in Step 2.
        — **Mary Stauffer** Ephrata, PA

3. Eliminate the brown sugar for a less sweet beverage.
        — **Pauline Morrison** St. Marys, ON

Orange Spiced Cider

Carolyn Baer
Conrath, WI

Makes 8 servings

Prep Time: 5 minutes
Cooking Time: 2-3 hours
Ideal slow cooker size:
    2- to 3-qt.

4 cups unsweetened apple juice
12-oz. can orange juice concentrate, thawed
1/2 cup water
1 Tbsp. red cinnamon hearts
1/2 tsp. ground nutmeg
1 tsp. whole cloves
8 fresh orange slice halves, *optional*
8 3"- 4"-long cinnamon sticks, *optional*

1. Combine first five ingredients in the slow cooker.
2. Place cloves on a piece of cheesecloth. Tie with string to create a bag. Submerge bag in juices in slow cooker.
3. Cover and cook on Low 2-3 hours, or until cider is very hot.
4. Remove bag before serving. Stir cider.
5. If you wish, place a cinnamon stick, topped with an orange slice, in each cup. Pour in hot cider.

Fruit Cider Punch

Becky Frey
Lebanon, PA

Makes 10-12 servings

Prep Time: 5-10 minutes
Cooking Time: 4-10 hours
Ideal slow cooker size: 31/2-qt.

4 cups apple cider
2 cups cranberry juice
1 cup orange juice
12-oz. can apricot nectar
1/4 cup sugar, *optional*
2 4"-long sticks cinnamon

1. Combine all ingredients thoroughly in slow cooker.
2. Cover and cook on Low 4-10 hours.
3. Serve warm from the cooker.

Tip: Taste the punch before adding the sugar to see if you think it's needed.

Cranberry-Apple Cider

Norma Grieser
Clarksville, MI

Makes 20 servings

Prep Time: 10 minutes
Cooking Time: 2-3 hours
Ideal slow cooker size: 8-qt.

1 gallon cider, *or* apple juice
64-oz. can cranberry juice cocktail
1/2 cup brown sugar
1 cup red cinnamon hearts
2 tsp. cinnamon

1. Pour ingredients together in slow cooker. Stir together well.
2. Cover and heat on High for 2-3 hours, or until cider is very hot.
If you're home and able to do so, stir occasionally to help the candy dissolve.
3. Serve warm from the cooker.

Fruity Wassail

Melissa Warner
Broad Top, PA

Makes 10 servings

Prep Time: 5 minutes
Cooking Time: 5-9 hours
Ideal slow cooker size: 3-qt.

2 qts. apple juice, *or* cider
2 cups cranberry juice cocktail
2 4"-long sticks cinnamon
1 tsp. whole allspice
10-oz. can mandarin oranges, with juice

1. Place apple juice, or cider, and cranberry juice in slow cooker.
2. Place cinnamon sticks and whole allspice on a piece of cheesecloth. Tie with a string to make a bag. Place in cooker.
3. Cover and cook on High 1 hour, and then on Low 4-8 hours.
4. Add oranges and their juice 15 minutes before serving.
5. Remove cheesecloth bag before serving.

Spiced Cranberry Cider

Esther Burkholder
Millerstown, PA

Makes 7 servings

Prep Time: 5-10 minutes
Cooking Time: 3-5 hours
Ideal slow cooker size: 3-qt.

1 qt. apple cider
3 cups cranberry juice cocktail
3 Tbsp. brown sugar
2 3"-long cinnamon sticks
3/4 tsp. whole cloves
1/2 lemon, thinly sliced, *optional*

1. Pour apple cider and cranberry juice into slow cooker.
2. Stir in brown sugar.
3. Put spices on a piece of cheesecloth. Tie with a string to create a bag. Place in slow cooker.
4. Stir in lemon slices if you wish.
5. Cover and cook on Low 3-5 hours, or until cider is very hot.
If you're able, stir occasionally to be sure brown sugar is dissolving.
6. Remove spice bag, and lemon slices if you've included them, before serving warm from the cooker.

Variation: Instead of whole cloves, substitute 1 tsp. whole allspice.
— **Jean Butzer**
Batavia, NY

Lime-Cranberry Punch

Sandra Haverstraw
Hummelstown, PA

Makes 10-12 servings

Prep Time: 5 minutes
Cooking Time: 3-4 hours
Ideal slow cooker size: 4-qt.

8 cups cranberry juice
  cocktail
3 cups water
1/2 cup fresh lime juice
2/3 cup sugar
3 4"-long cinnamon sticks,
  broken in half
8 half-slices of an orange,
  optional

1. Place all ingredients except oranges slices in slow cooker. Stir until sugar is dissolved.

2. Cover and simmer on Low 3-4 hours, or until very hot.

3. With a slotted spoon, remove cinnamon sticks and discard before serving.

4. If you wish, float a half-slice of orange on each individual serving of hot punch.

Tip: Refrigerate any leftover punch; then reheat it or enjoy it cold.

Spiced Apricot Cider

Janet Oberholtzer
Ephrata, PA

Makes 4-6 servings

Prep Time: 5 minutes
Cooking Time: 3-4 hours
Ideal slow cooker size: 2-qt.

2 12-oz. cans apricot
  nectar
1/4 cup lemon juice
2 cups water
1/4 cup sugar
3 whole cloves
3 3"- 4"-long cinnamon
  sticks

1. Combine juices, water, and sugar in slow cooker. Mix well.

2. Place whole cloves and cinnamon sticks on a piece of cheesecloth. Tie with a string to create a bag. Submerge in juices in cooker.

3. Cover and cook on Low 3-4 hours, or until cider is very hot.

4. Remove cloves and cinnamon sticks before serving. Serve warm from the cooker.

Delta Tea

Vera F. Schmucker
Goshen, IN

Makes 6 cups

Prep Time: 5 minutes
Cooking Time: 3-4 hours
Ideal slow cooker size:
  2- to 3-qt.

6-oz. can frozen lemonade
5 cups water
1 tsp. vanilla
1 tsp. almond flavoring
3 tsp. dry instant tea

1. Combine all ingredients in slow cooker.

2. Cover and cook on High 3-4 hours, or until very hot.

3. Serve hot from the cooker, or ice it and serve cold.

Johnny Appleseed Tea

Sheila Plock
Boalsburg, PA

Makes 8-9 cups

Prep Time: 15-20 minutes
Cooking Time: 1-2 hours
Ideal slow cooker size: 3-qt.

2 qts. water, *divided*
6 tea bags of your favorite
　flavor
6 ozs. frozen apple juice,
　thawed
1/4 cup, plus 2 Tbsp.,
　firmly packed
　brown sugar

1. Bring 1 qt. water to boil.
Add tea bags. Remove from
heat. Cover and let steep
5 minutes. Pour into slow
cooker.
2. Add remaining ingredi-
ents and mix well.
3. Cover. Heat on Low
until hot. Continue on Low
while serving from slow
cooker.

I serve this wonderful hot
beverage with cookies at our
Open House Tea and Cookies
afternoon, which I host at
Christmas-time for friends and
neighbors.

Spicy Tea

Ruth Retter
Manheim, PA

Makes 9-10 servings

Prep Time: 15 minutes
Cooking Time: 2-3 hours
Ideal slow cooker size: 3 1/2-qt.

6 cups water
6 tea bags, experiment
　with various flavors, *or*
　use your favorite
1/3 cup sugar
2 Tbsp. honey
1 1/2 cups orange juice
1 1/2 cups pineapple juice

1. Place water in a
saucepan and bring to a boil.
Add tea bags to boiling water.
Let stand 5 minutes.
2. Remove tea bags. Pour
tea into slow cooker.
3. Stir in remaining ingredients.
4. Cover and cook on Low
2-3 hours, until very hot.

Variation: Float half an
orange slice on each cup of tea.

Hot Chocolate

Colleen Heatwole
Burton, MI

Makes 10-12 servings

Prep Time: 10 minutes
Cooking Time: 2-3 hours
Ideal slow cooker size: 3-qt.

8 cups water
3 cups dried milk
1/3 cup non-dairy coffee
　creamer
1 cup instant hot chocolate
　mix (the kind you mix
　with milk, not water)
marshmallows

1. Pour water into slow
cooker.
2. Gradually stir in dried
milk until blended.
3. Cover and cook on High
2-3 hours, or until milk is hot.
4. Stir in coffee creamer
and hot chocolate mix.
5. Turn on Low until serving time, up to 3-4 hours.
6. Serve in mugs topped
with marshmallows.

Hot Mint Malt

Clarice Williams
Fairbank, IA

Makes 6 servings

Prep Time: 5 minutes
Cooking Time: 2-3 hours
Ideal slow cooker size:
2- to 3-qt.

6 chocolate-covered cream-
filled mint patties
5 cups milk
1/2 cup chocolate malted
milk powder
1 tsp. vanilla
whipping cream, whipped
stiff

1. In slow cooker, combine mint patties with milk, malted milk powder, and vanilla.
2. Heat on Low 2-3 hours. If you're able, stir occasionally to help melt the patties.
3. When the drink is thoroughly heated, beat with rotary beater until frothy.
4. Pour into cups and top with whipped cream.

Hot Chocolate Malted

Sharon Timpe
Jackson, WI

Makes 8-10 servings

Prep Time: 10 minutes
Cooking Time: 3 hours
Ideal slow cooker size: 3½-qt.

1½ cups hot cocoa mix
1/2 cup chocolate malted
milk powder
6 caramels, unwrapped
1 tsp. vanilla
8 cups water *or* milk
whipped topping, *optional*
25-30 miniature
marshmallows, *optional*

1. Mix all ingredients, except the last 2 optional ones, in a slow cooker.
2. Heat on High 3 hours, stirring occasionally if you're home and able to do so.
3. Taste before serving. Depending upon the hot cocoa mix you've used, you may want to add more water or milk.
(Heat additional liquid in the microwave before adding to the hot chocolate.)
4. Ladle into cups and top each with a dollop of whipped cream or marshmallows, if you wish.

Creamy Hot Chocolate

Deborah Heatwole
Waynesboro, GA

Makes 8 servings

Prep Time: 15 minutes
Cooking Time: 2-4 hours
Ideal slow cooker size: 3-qt.

1/2 cup dry baking cocoa
14-oz. can sweetened
condensed milk
1/8 tsp. salt
7½ cups water
1½ tsp. vanilla
24, *or more*, miniature
marshmallows, *optional*

1. In slow cooker, combine dry cocoa, milk, and salt. Stir until smooth. Add water gradually, stirring until smooth.
2. Cover and cook on High 2 hours, or on Low 4 hours, or until very hot.
3. Just before serving, stir in vanilla.
4. Top each serving with 3 or more marshmallows, if you wish.

Tips:
1. To speed things up, heat the water before adding it to the chocolate mixture.
2. Keep hot chocolate warm on Low up to 4 hours in the slow cooker.
3. Add a mocha flavor by stirring in instant coffee in Step 3.

Italian Hot Chocolate

Cyndie Marrara
Port Matilda, PA

Makes 4-6 small servings

Prep Time: 3-5 minutes
Cooking Time: 1-2 hours
Ideal slow cooker size:
1- to 2-qt.

2 cups brewed strong
  coffee
1/2 cup instant hot
  chocolate mix
1 4"-long cinnamon stick,
  broken into large pieces
1 cup whipping cream
1 Tbsp. powdered sugar

1. Put coffee, hot chocolate mix, and cinnamon sticks into slow cooker. Stir.

2. Cover and cook on High 1-2 hours, or until very hot. Discard cinnamon pieces.

3. Immediately after you've turned on the cooker, place electric mixer beaters and mixer bowl in the fridge to chill (this makes the cream more likely to whip).

4. Just before serving, pour the whipping cream into the chilled electric mixer bowl. Beat cream on high speed until soft peaks form.

5. Fold sugar into whipped cream. Beat again on high speed until stiff peaks form.

6. Ladle hot chocolate coffee into small cups. Top each with a dollop of whipped cream.

Party Mocha

Barbara Sparks
Glen Burnie, MD

Makes 10 servings

Prep Time: 5 minutes
Cooking Time: 3 hours
Ideal slow cooker size:
3- to 4-qt.

1/2 cup instant coffee
  granules
6 envelopes instant cocoa
  mix
2 qts. hot water
2 cups milk
whipped topping, *optional*
10 4"-long cinnamon
  sticks, *optional*
10 peppermint sticks,
  optional

1. Combine all ingredients, except the last 3 optional ones, in the slow cooker. Stir well.

2. Cover and cook on High 3 hours.

3. Stir and turn to Low to keep warm while serving.

4. To serve, pour mocha into cups. Top each with a dollop of whipped topping, or add a cinnamon stick or peppermint stick to each cup, if you wish.

Spiced Coffee

Esther Burkholder
Millerstown, PA

Makes 8 servings

Prep Time: 10 minutes
Cooking Time: 3 hours
Ideal slow cooker size: 3-qt.

8 cups brewed coffee
1/3 cup sugar
1/4 cup chocolate syrup
4 3"-long cinnamon sticks
1 1/2 tsp. whole cloves

1. Pour coffee into slow cooker. Stir in sugar and chocolate syrup.

2. Place cinnamon sticks and whole cloves on a piece of cheesecloth. Tie with string to create a bag. Submerge in slow cooker.

3. Cover and cook on Low 3 hours, or until coffee is very hot. Remove cheesecloth bag.

4. Turn to Low and serve warm from cooker.

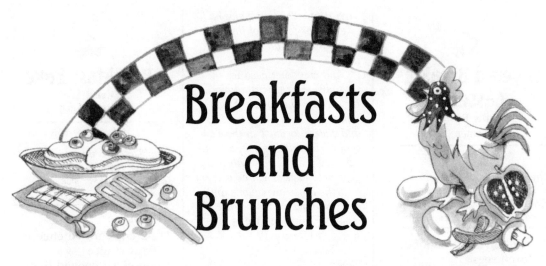

Breakfasts and Brunches

Breakfast Sausage Casserole

Kendra Dreps, Liberty, PA

Makes 8 servings

Prep Time: 15 minutes
Chilling Time: 8 hours
Cooking Time: 4 hours
Ideal slow cooker size: 3-qt.

1 lb. loose sausage
6 eggs
2 cups milk
8 slices bread, cubed
2 cups shredded cheddar
  cheese

1. In a non-stick skillet, brown and drain sausage.
2. Mix together eggs and milk in a large bowl.
3. Stir in bread cubes, cheese, and sausage.
4. Place in greased slow cooker.
5. Refrigerate overnight.
6. Cook on Low 4 hours.

Variation: Use cubed cooked ham instead of sausage.

Easy Egg and Sausage Puff

Sara Kinsinger
Stuarts Draft, VA

Makes 6 servings

Prep Time: 10-15 minutes
Cooking Time: 2-2½ hours
Ideal slow cooker size:
  2- to 4-qt.

1 lb. loose sausage
6 eggs
1 cup all-purpose baking
  mix
1 cup shredded cheddar
  cheese
2 cups milk
¼ tsp. dry mustard,
  optional

1. Brown sausage in non-stick skillet. Break up chunks of meat as it cooks. Drain.
2. Meanwhile, spray interior of slow cooker with non-stick cooking spray.
3. Mix all ingredients in slow cooker.
4. Cover and cook on High 1 hour. Turn to Low and cook 1-1½ hours, or until the dish is fully cooked in the center.

A Tip —

Save the end pieces of loaves of bread in a bag in the freezer. When you have a bag full, run them through a food processor or blender to make bread crumbs. (My children love to do this.) Use the crumbs for breading chicken, in meat loaf, or with melted butter as a topping for macaronis and cheese.

Layered Breakfast Casserole

Cathy Boshart
Lebanon, PA

Makes 8-10 servings

Prep Time: 30 minutes
Cooling Time: 4-8 hours
Cooking Time: 1 hour
Ideal slow cooker size: 6-qt.

6 medium-sized potatoes
2 dozen eggs
1 lb. chopped ham
12 ozs. Velveeta cheese,
  shredded

1. The day before you want to serve the dish, boil the potatoes in their skins until soft.

Chill. When thoroughly chilled, grate.

Spread in bottom of greased slow cooker.

2. Scramble and cook eggs in a non-stick skillet. When just set, spoon cooked eggs over top of potatoes.

3. Layer ham evenly over eggs. Sprinkle with cheese.

4. Bake on Low for 1 hour or until cheese is melted.

Variation: You can make half, or even one-fourth, of this recipe if this quantity is too large.

And you don't need to scramble the eggs before placing them in the cooker. Simply mix the cooked potatoes, ham and cheese together in the slow cooker. Beat the eggs in a separate bowl, along with salt and pepper to taste. Then pour them over the other ingredients and cook on Low for 2-4 hours.

— **Kendra Dreps**
Liberty, PA

Tips:
1. This is a perfect dish to serve on a buffet.
2. Or prepare through the first instruction in Step 3 a day ahead (chill in the fridge overnight), but sprinkle the cheese over top just before cooking.
If you've refrigerated the slow cooker overnight, allow it to reach room temperature before turning it on and reheating the dish.
3. Serve with toasted English muffins and fresh fruit.

Breakfast Bake

Kristi See
Weskan, KS

Makes 10 servings

Prep Time: 15 minutes
Cooking Time: 3-4 hours
Ideal slow cooker size:
  4- to 5-qt.

12 eggs
1¹/2-2 cups grated cheese,
  your choice
1 cup diced cooked ham
1 cup milk
1 tsp. salt
¹/2 tsp. pepper

1. Beat eggs. Pour into slow cooker.

2. Mix in remaining ingredients.

3. Cover and cook on Low 3-4 hours.

Almond Date Oatmeal

Audrey L. Kneer
Williamsfield, IL

Makes 8 servings

Prep Time: minutes
Cooking Time: 4-8 hours,
*   or overnight*
Ideal slow cooker size: 3-qt.

2 cups dry rolled oats
1/2 cup dry grapenuts
    cereal
1/2 cup almonds, chopped
1/4 cup dates, chopped
4 1/2 cups water

1. Combine all ingredients in slow cooker.
2. Cover and cook on Low 4-8 hours, or overnight.
3. Serve with fat-free milk.

Slow Cooker Oatmeal

Martha Bender
New Paris, IN

Makes 7-8 servings

Prep Time: 10-15 minutes
Cooking Time: 8-9 hours
Ideal slow cooker size:
*   4- to 5-qt.*

2 cups dry rolled oats
4 cups water
1 large apple, peeled and
    chopped
1 cup raisins
1 tsp. cinnamon
1-2 Tbsp. orange zest

1. Combine all ingredients in your slow cooker.
2. Cover and cook on Low 8-9 hours.
3. Serve topped with brown sugar, if you wish, and milk.

Breakfast Oatmeal

Donna Conto
Saylorsburg, PA

Makes 6 servings

Prep Time: 5 minutes
Cooking Time: 8 hours
Ideal slow cooker size: 4-qt.

2 cups dry rolled oats
4 cups water
1 tsp. salt
1/2-1 cup chopped dates, *or*
    raisins, *or* cranberries,
    or a mixture of any of
    these fruits

1. Combine all ingredients in slow cooker.
2. Cover and cook on Low overnight, or for 8 hours.

Tip: This is a great dish when you have company for breakfast. No last-minute preparation needed!

Overnight Oatmeal

Jody Moore
Pendleton, IN

Makes 4-5 servings

Prep Time: 5 minutes
Cooking Time: 8 hours
Ideal slow cooker size: 3-qt.

1 cup dry steel-cut oats
4 cups water

1. Combine ingredients in slow cooker.
2. Cover and cook on Low overnight, or for 8 hours.
3. Stir before serving. Serve with brown sugar, ground cinnamon, fruit preserves, jam, jelly, pumpkin pie spice, fresh fruit, maple syrup, or your other favorite toppings.

Tip:
Please note that steel-cut oats are called for. They are different—with more texture, requiring a longer cooking time—than old-fashioned or rolled oatmeal.

Pineapple Baked Oatmeal

Sandra Haverstraw
Hummelstown, PA

Makes 5-6 servings

Prep Time: 5 minutes
Cooking Time: 1½ -2½ hours
Ideal slow cooker size:
2- to 3½-qt.

1 box of 8 instant oatmeal packets (approx. a 12- to 14-oz. box), any flavor
1½ tsp. baking powder
2 eggs, beaten
½ cup milk
8-oz. can crushed pineapple in juice, undrained

1. Spray inside of slow cooker with non-stick cooking spray.
2. Empty packets of oatmeal into a large bowl. Add baking powder and mix.
3. Stir in eggs, milk, and undrained pineapple. Mix well. Pour mixture into slow cooker.
4. Cover and cook on High 1½ hours, or on Low 2½ hours.

Tips:
1. Serve warm as is, or with milk, for breakfast.
2. This is also a good, hearty, not-too-sweet dessert served with ice cream.
3. Individual servings reheat well in the microwave for a quick breakfast.

Breakfast Apples

Joyce Bowman
Lady Lake, FL
Jeanette Oberholtzer
Manheim, PA

Makes 4 servings

Prep Time: 10-15 minutes
Cooking Time: 2-8 hours
Ideal slow cooker size: 3-qt.

4 medium-sized apples, peeled and sliced
¼ cup honey
1 tsp. cinnamon
2 Tbsp. melted butter
2 cups dry granola cereal

1. Place apples in your slow cooker.
2. Combine remaining ingredients. Sprinkle the mixture evenly over top the apples.
3. Cover and cook on Low 6-8 hours, or overnight, or on High 2-3 hours.
4. Serve as a side dish to bacon and bagels, or use as a topping for waffles, French toast, pancakes, or cooked oatmeal.

Polenta or Cornmeal Mush

Dorothy VanDeest
Memphis, TN

Makes 8-10 servings

Prep Time: 10 minutes
Cooking Time: 2-9 hours
Chilling Time: 8 hours,
  or overnight
Ideal slow cooker size: 1½-qt.

4 Tbsp. butter, melted,
  divided
¼ tsp. paprika and/or
  dash of cayenne pepper
6 cups boiling water
2 cups dry cornmeal
2 tsp. salt

1. Use 1 Tbsp. butter to lightly grease the inside of the slow cooker. Sprinkle in paprika/cayenne. Turn to High setting.
2. Add remaining ingredients to slow cooker in the order listed, including 1 Tbsp. butter. Stir well.
3. Cover and cook on High for 2-3 hours, or on Low for 6-9 hours. Stir occasionally.
4. Pour hot cooked polenta/mush into 2 lightly greased loaf pans. Chill overnight.
5. To serve, cut into ¼"-thick slices. Melt 2 Tbsp. butter in large non-stick skillet, then lay in slices and cook until browned. Turn to brown other side.
6. For breakfast, serve with maple syrup, honey, or your choice of sweetener.

Variation: Serve as a main course topped with sausage gravy, or as a side dish topped with a pat of butter.
  — Sara Kinsinger
  Stuarts Draft, VA

Breakfast Hominy

Bonnie Goering
Bridgewater, VA

Makes 5 servings

Prep Time: 5 minutes
Cooking Time: 8 hours
Ideal slow cooker size: 2-qt.

1 cup dry cracked hominy
1 tsp. salt
black pepper, *optional*
3 cups water
2 Tbsp. butter

1. Stir all ingredients together in a greased slow cooker.
2. Cover and cook on Low 8 hours, or overnight.
3. Serve warm for breakfast.

Variation: You can make cheesy hominy by decreasing the salt to ¾ tsp. and adding 1 cup grated cheese (we like American cheese best) to Step 1.

Cheesy Hominy

Deborah Heatwole
Waynesboro, GA

Makes 6-8 servings

Prep Time: 5 minutes
Cooking Time: 2½ hours
Ideal slow cooker size: 2-qt.

1 29-oz., or 2 15½-oz.,
  cans hominy, drained
1 cup diced cheese
  (cheddar *or* Velveeta
  work well)
½ tsp. salt
dash pepper
8 saltine crackers,
  crumbled
½ cup milk
butter, *optional*

1. Spray slow cooker with non-stick cooking spray. Add hominy, cheese, salt, pepper, and saltines. Stir to mix.
2. Pour milk over all. Dot with butter, if you wish.
3. Cover and cook on High 2½ hours.

Tip: Serve for breakfast with sausage and fruit, or for a main meal with a meat and green vegetable.

Blueberry Fancy

Leticia A. Zehr
Lowville, NY

Makes 12 servings

Prep Time: 10-15 minutes
Cooking Time: 3-4 hours
Ideal slow cooker size: 5-qt.

---

1 loaf Italian bread, cubed,
    divided
1 pint blueberries, *divided*
8 ozs. cream cheese, cubed,
    divided
6 eggs
1¹/₂ cups milk

1. Place half the bread
cubes in the slow cooker.
2. Drop half the blueber-
ries over top the bread.
3. Sprinkle half the cream
cheese cubes over the blueberries.
4. Repeat all 3 layers.
5. In a mixing bowl, whisk
together eggs and milk. Pour
over all ingredients.
6. Cover and cook on Low
until the dish is custardy and
set.
7. Serve with maple syrup
or blueberry sauce.

*Variation: Add 1 tsp. vanilla
to Step 5.*

Streusel Cake

Jean Butzer
Batavia, NY

Makes 8-10 servings

Prep Time: 10 minutes
Cooking Time: 3-4 hours
Ideal slow cooker size: 3-qt.

16-oz. pkg. pound cake
    mix, prepared according
    to package directions
¹/₄ cup packed brown sugar
1 Tbsp. flour
¹/₄ cup chopped nuts
1 tsp. cinnamon

1. Liberally grease and
flour a 2-lb. coffee can, or
slow-cooker baking insert,
that fits into your slow
cooker. Pour prepared cake
mix into coffee can or baking
insert.
2. In a small bowl, mix
brown sugar, flour, nuts, and
cinnamon together. Sprinkle
over top of cake mix.
3. Place coffee tin or baking insert in slow cooker.
Cover top of tin or insert with
several layers of paper towels.
4. Cover cooker itself and
cook on High 3-4 hours, or
until toothpick inserted in
center of cake comes out
clean.
5. Remove baking tin from
slow cooker and allow to cool
for 30 minutes before cutting
into wedges to serve.

A Tip —

Keep spatulas, wire
whisks, wooden spoons,
etc. near the stove, within
arms' reach.

Desserts

Cherry Cobbler

Michele Ruvola
Selden, NY

Makes 6-8 servings

Prep Time: 5 minutes
Cooking Time: 2¹/₂-5¹/₂ hours
Ideal slow cooker size: 3-qt.

16-oz. can cherry pie filling
1³/₄ cups dry cake mix of
  your choice
1 egg
3 Tbsp. evaporated milk
¹/₂ tsp. cinnamon

1. Lightly spray the slow
cooker with non-stick cooking
spray.
2. Place pie filling in slow
cooker and cook on High 30
minutes.
3. Meanwhile, mix
together remaining ingredients in bowl until crumbly.
Spoon onto hot pie filling.
4. Cover and cook on Low
2-5 hours, or until a toothpick

inserted into center of topping comes out dry.
5. Serve warm or cooled.

Just Peachy

Betty B. Dennison
Grove City, PA

Makes 4-6 servings

Prep Time: 2-3 minutes
Cooking Time: 4-5 hours
Ideal slow cooker size: 3-qt.

4 cups sliced peaches,
  fresh *or* canned (if using
  canned peaches, reserve
  the juice)
²/₃ cup rolled dry oats
¹/₃ cup all-purpose baking
  mix
¹/₂ cup sugar
¹/₂ cup brown sugar
¹/₂ tsp. cinnamon, *optional*
¹/₂ cup water, *or* reserved
  peach juice

1. Spray inside of slow
cooker with non-stick cooking
spray.
2. Place peaches in slow
cooker.
3. In a bowl, mix together
all dry ingredients. When
blended, stir in water or juice
until well mixed.
4. Spoon batter into cooker
and stir into peaches, just
until blended.
5. Cover and cook on Low
4-5 hours.
6. Serve warm with vanilla
ice cream or frozen yogurt.

Peanut Butter Cake

Velma Sauder
Leola, PA

Makes 6 servings

Prep Time: 5-10 minutes
Cooking Time: 2-3 hours
Ideal slow cooker size: 4-qt.

2 cups yellow cake mix
1/3 cup crunchy peanut butter
1/2 cup water

1. Combine all ingredients in electric mixer bowl. Beat with electric mixer about 2 minutes.
2. Pour batter into greased and floured baking-pan insert, designed to fit inside your slow cooker.
3. Place baking-pan insert into slow cooker. Cover with 8 paper towels.
4. Cover cooker. Cook on High 2-3 hours, or until toothpick inserted into center of cake comes out clean.
   About 30 minutes before the end of the cooking time, remove the cooker's lid, but keep the paper towels in place.
5. When cake is fully cooked, remove insert from slow cooker. Turn insert upside down on a serving plate and remove cake.

Fruity Cake

Janice Muller
Derwood, MD

Makes 10-12 servings

Prep Time: 15 minutes
Cooking Time: 3-5 hours
Ideal slow cooker size:
* 3 1/2- to 4-qt.*

1, *or* 2, 21-oz. can(s) apple, blueberry, *or* peach pie filling
18 1/4-oz. pkg. yellow cake mix
1 stick (1/2 cup) butter, melted
1/3 cup chopped walnuts

1. Spray interior of slow cooker with non-stick cooking spray.
2. Place pie filling in slow cooker.
3. In a mixing bowl, combine dry cake mix and butter. Spoon over filling.
4. Drop walnuts over top.
5. Cover and cook on Low 3-5 hours, or until a toothpick inserted into center of topping comes out clean.

A Tip —

You can use a 2-lb. coffee can, 2 1-lb. coffee cans, 3 16-oz. vegetable cans, a 6-7 cup mold, or a 1 1/2-2-quart baking dish for "baking" cakes in a slow cooker. Leave the cooker lid slightly open to let extra moisture escape.

Eleanor J. Ferreira
North Chelmsford, MA

Pineapple Upside Down Cake

Vera M. Kuhns, Harrisonburg, VA

Makes 10 servings

Prep Time: 20 minutes
Cooking Time: 4-5 hours
Ideal slow cooker size: 4-qt.

1/2 cup butter, *or* margarine, melted
1 cup brown sugar
1 medium-sized can pineapple slices, drained, reserving juice
6-8 maraschino cherries
1 box dry yellow cake mix

1. Combine butter and brown sugar. Spread over bottom of well greased cooker.
2. Add pineapple slices and place cherries in the center of each one.
3. Prepare cake according to package directions, using pineapple juice for part of liquid. Spoon cake batter into cooker over top fruit.
4. Cover cooker with 2 tea-towels and then with its own lid. Cook on High 1 hour, and then on Low 3-4 hours.

5. Allow cake to cool for 10 minutes. Then run knife around edge and invert cake onto large platter.

Easy Autumn Cake

Janice Muller
Derwood, MD

Makes 8 servings

Prep Time: 15 minutes
Cooking Time: 3-5 hours
Ideal slow cooker size: 3 1/2- to 4-qt.

2 16-oz. cans sliced apples, undrained (not pie filling)
18 1/4-oz. pkg. spice cake mix
1 stick (1/2 cup butter), melted
1/2 cup pecans, chopped

1. Spray interior of slow cooker with non-stick cooking spray.
2. Spoon apples and their juice into slow cooker, spreading evenly over the bottom.
3. Sprinkle with dry spice cake mix.
4. Pour melted butter over dry mix. Top with chopped pecans.
5. Cook on Low 3-5 hours, or until a toothpick inserted into topping comes out dry.
6. Serve warm from cooker.

Tomato Soup Spice Cake

Janessa Hochstedler
East Earl, PA

Makes 12 servings

Prep Time: 10 minutes
Cooking Time: 6-7 hours
Ideal slow cooker size: 6-qt.

18 1/4-oz. pkg. spice cake mix
10 3/4-oz. can tomato soup
1/2 cup water
2 eggs

1. Mix cake mix, soup, water, and eggs together in a mixing bowl.
2. Grease and flour a baking-pan insert, designed to fit into your slow cooker.
3. Pour cake batter into the insert.
4. Place insert in slow cooker. Cover insert with 8 paper towels. Cover cooker.
5. Cover and bake on Low 6-7 hours, or until toothpick inserted in center of cake comes out clean.
About 30 minutes before the end of the cooking time, remove the lid of the cooker, but keep the paper towels in place.
6. When cooking is finished, remove paper towels. Remove insert from cooker and allow to stand for 10 minutes. Invert the baking insert upside down on a serving plate and remove the cake.

Pumpkin Pie Dessert

Bonnie Whaling
Clearfield, PA

Makes 4-6 servings

Prep Time: 15-20 minutes
Cooking Time: 3-4 hours
Ideal slow cooker size: 5- to 6-qt.

19-oz. can pumpkin pie filling
12-oz. can evaporated milk
2 eggs, lightly beaten
boiling water
1 cup gingersnap cookie crumbs

1. In a large mixing bowl, stir together pie filling, milk, and eggs until thoroughly mixed.
2. Pour into an ungreased baking insert designed to fit into your slow cooker.
3. Place filled baking insert into slow cooker. Cover the insert with its lid, or with 8 paper towels.
4. Carefully pour boiling water into cooker around the baking insert, to a depth of one inch.
5. Cover cooker. Cook on High for 3-4 hours, or until a tester inserted in center of custard comes out clean.
6. Remove baking insert from slow cooker. Remove its lid. Sprinkle dessert with cookie crumbs. Serve warm from baking insert.

Black Forest Cake

Marla Folkerts
Holland, OH

Makes 8-10 servings

Prep Time: 10 minutes
Cooking Time: 2-2½ hours
Ideal slow cooker size:
* 4- to 5-qt.*

20-oz. can cherry pie filling
  (Lite *or* regular)
18.25-oz. box chocolate
  cake mix, butter-style

1. Preheat slow cooker on
High for 10 minutes.

2. Meanwhile, spray interior of baking insert, designed to fit into your slow cooker, with non-stick cooking spray.

3. In a bowl, stir together pie filling and cake mix until mix is thoroughly moistened. Spoon into insert.

4. Place insert into cooker. Cover insert with 8 paper towels. Cover slow cooker.

5. Cook on High for 1¾ hours. Remove paper towels and cooker lid. Continue cooking for another 30 minutes, or until a toothpick inserted in the center of the cake comes out clean.

6. Remove baking insert from cooker. Serve cake warm directly from the insert.

Brownies with Nuts

Dorothy VanDeest
Memphis, TN

Makes 24 brownies

Prep Time: 10-15 minutes
Cooking Time: 3 hours
Ideal slow cooker size: 5-qt.

half a stick (¼ cup) butter,
  melted
1 cup chopped nuts,
  divided
23-oz. pkg. brownie mix

1. Pour melted butter into a baking insert designed to fit into your slow cooker. Swirl butter around to grease sides of insert.

2. Sprinkle butter with half the nuts.

A Tip —

Always cut brownies with a plastic knife. It prevents clumping and ragged edges.

3. In a bowl, mix brownies according to package directions. Spoon half the batter into the baking insert, trying to cover the nuts evenly.

4. Add remaining half of nuts. Spoon in remaining batter.

5. Place insert in slow cooker. Cover insert with 8 paper towels.

6. Cover cooker. Cook on High 3 hours. Do not check or remove cover until last hour of cooking. Then insert toothpick into center of brownies. If it comes out clean, the brownies are finished. If it doesn't, continue cooking another 15 minutes. Check again. Repeat until pick comes out clean.

7. When finished cooking, uncover cooker and baking insert. Let brownies stand 5 minutes.

8. Invert insert onto serving plate. Cut brownies with a plastic knife (so the crumbs don't drag). Serve warm.

Upside-Down Chocolate Pudding Cake

Sarah Herr, Goshen, IN

Makes 8 servings

Prep Time: 15 minutes
Cooking Time: 2-3 hours
Ideal slow cooker size: 3½-qt.

1 cup dry all-purpose
   baking mix
1 cup sugar, *divided*
3 Tbsp. unsweetened cocoa
   powder, plus ⅓ cup,
   divided
½ cup milk
1 tsp. vanilla
1⅔ cups hot water

1. Spray inside of slow
cooker with non-stick cooking
spray.
2. In a bowl, mix together
baking mix, ½ cup sugar, 3
Tbsp. cocoa powder, milk,
and vanilla. Spoon batter
evenly into slow cooker.
3. In a clean bowl, mix
remaining ½ cup sugar, ⅓
cup cocoa powder, and hot
water together. Pour over batter in slow cooker. Do not
stir.
4. Cover and cook on High
2-3 hours, or until toothpick
inserted in center of cake-y
part comes out clean.

*Tip: The batter will rise to the
top and turn into cake.
Underneath will be a rich
chocolate pudding.*

Chocolate Soufflé

Rachel Yoder
Middlebury, IN

Makes 10-12 servings

Prep Time: 5 minutes
Cooking Time: 6 hours
Ideal slow cooker size: 6-qt.

18¼-oz. pkg. chocolate
   cake mix
½ cup vegetable oil
2 cups sour cream
4 eggs, beaten
3-oz. box instant chocolate
   pudding mix
1 cup chocolate chips,
   optional

1. Combine all ingredients
in a large mixing bowl.
2. Spray interior of slow
cooker with non-stick cooking
spray. Pour soufflé mixture
into cooker.
3. Cover and cook on Low
for 6 hours. (Do not lift the
lid until the end of the cooking time!)
4. Insert toothpick into
center of cake to see if it
comes out clean. If it does,
the soufflé is finished. If it
doesn't, continue cooking
another 15 minutes. Check
again. Repeat until it's finished cooking.
5. Serve warm from the
cooker with ice cream or
frozen yogurt.

Chocolate Peanut Butter Cake

Esther Hartzler
Carlsbad, NM

Makes 8-10 servings

Prep Time: 7 minutes
Cooking Time: 2-2½ hours
Ideal slow cooker size:
   5- to 6-qt.

2 cups dry milk chocolate
   cake mix
½ cup water
6 Tbsp. peanut butter
2 eggs
½ cup chopped nuts

1. Combine all ingredients
in electric mixer bowl. Beat
for 2 minutes.
2. Spray interior of a baking insert, designed to fit into
your slow cooker. Flour interior of greased insert. Pour
batter into insert. Place insert
in slow cooker.
3. Cover insert with 8
paper towels.
4. Cover cooker. Cook on
High 2-2½ hours, or until
toothpick inserted into center
of cake comes out clean.
5. Allow cake to cool.
Then invert onto a serving
plate, cut, and serve.

Chocolate Fondue
Diann J. Dunham
State College, PA

Makes 2¹/2-3 cups

Prep Time: 5 minutes
Cooking Time: 2¹/2 hours
Ideal slow cooker size: 2-qt.

1 stick (¹/2 cup) butter,
   melted
1¹/2 cups sugar
¹/4 cup whipping cream
3 Tbsp. creme de cocoa,
   rum, *or* orange-flavored
   liqueur (or 1 tsp. orange,
   rum, *or* vanilla
   flavoring)
6 1-oz. squares
   unsweetened chocolate

1. Combine butter and sugar in the slow cooker until well mixed.
2. Stir in whipping cream until well blended. Stir in liqueur or flavoring until well blended.
3. Stir in squares of chocolate.
4. Cover and cook on High 30 minutes.
5. Stir well, turn cooker to Low, and cook 2 hours.
6. Serve warm from the cooker with angel food or pound cake, cut into bite-sized pieces, marshmallows, apple slices, banana chunks, and strawberries, whole or halved.

Tip: As long as an inch or more of the fondue remains in the cooker, you can keep the cooker turned on Low for up to 6 hours. Stir occasionally.

Dessert Fondue
Sara Kinsinger
Stuarts Draft, VA
Bonita Ensenberger
Albuquerque, NM

Makes about 3 cups

Prep Time: 10-15 minutes
Cooking Time: 2 hours
Ideal slow cooker size: 4-qt.

1 Tbsp. butter
16 1-oz. candy bars, half
   milk chocolate; half
   semi-sweet chocolate,
   broken
30 large marshmallows
¹/3 cup milk
1 cup whipping cream

1. Grease slow cooker with butter. Turn to High for 10 minutes.
2. Meanwhile, mix broken candy bars, marshmallows, and milk together in a bowl.
3. Put candy/milk mixture into slow cooker.
4. Cover and cook on Low for 30 minutes. Stir. Cover and cook another 30 minutes. Stir.
5. Gradually stir in whipping cream. Cover and cook on Low another hour.
6. Serve the fondue warm from the cooker with pieces of pound cake, angel-food cake, bananas, and pretzels for dipping.

Best Bread Pudding
Betty B. Dennison
Grove City, PA

Makes 8-10 servings

Prep Time: 10 minutes
Cooking Time: 2-3 hours
Ideal slow cooker size: 5-qt.

³/4 cup brown sugar
6 slices raisin-and-
   cinnamon-swirl bread,
   buttered and cubed
4 eggs
1 qt. milk
1¹/2 tsp. vanilla
¹/2 tsp. lemon extract,
   optional

1. Spray interior of slow cooker with non-stick cooking spray.
2. Spread brown sugar in bottom of cooker. Add cubed bread. (Do not stir sugar and bread together.)
3. In a mixing bowl, beat eggs well. Beat in milk and vanilla, and lemon extract if you wish. Pour over bread.
4. Cover and cook on High 2-3 hours, or until pudding is no longer soupy. Do not stir. Brown sugar will form a sauce on the bottom.
5. When the pudding is finished, spoon it into a serving dish, drizzling the sauce over top of the bread.

Baked Custard

Barbara Smith
Bedford, PA

Makes 5-6 servings

Prep Time: 10-15 minutes
Cooking Time: 2-3 hours
Ideal slow cooker size:
4- to 5-qt.

2 cups whole milk
3 eggs, slightly beaten
1/3 cup, plus 1/2 tsp., sugar,
divided
1 tsp. vanilla
1/4 tsp. cinnamon

1. Heat milk in a small uncovered saucepan until a skin forms on top. Remove from heat and let cool slightly.
2. Meanwhile, in a large mixing bowl combine eggs, 1/3 cup sugar, and vanilla.
3. Slowly stir cooled milk into egg-sugar mixture.
4. Pour into a greased 1-qt. baking dish which will fit into your slow cooker, or into a baking insert designed for your slow cooker.
5. Mix cinnamon and 1/2 tsp. reserved sugar in a small bowl. Sprinkle over custard mixture.
6. Cover baking dish or insert with foil. Set container on a metal rack or trivet in slow cooker. Pour hot water around dish to a depth of 1 inch.
7. Cover cooker. Cook on High 2-3 hours, or until custard is set. (When blade of a knife inserted in center of custard comes out clean, custard is set.)
8. Serve warm from baking dish or insert.

Variations: Instead of the cinnamon, use 1/4 tsp. nutmeg, or 1-2 Tbsp. grated coconut.
— **Jean Butzer**
Batavia, NY

Tapioca

Ruth Ann Hoover
New Holland, PA
Sharon Anders
Alburtis, PA
Pat Unternahrer
Wayland, IA

Makes 10-12 servings

Prep Time: 5-10 minutes
Cooking Time: 3 hours and
20 minutes
Chilling Time: 4-5 hours
Ideal slow cooker size: 3-qt.

2 qts. whole milk
1 1/4 cups sugar
1 cup dry small pearl
tapioca
4 eggs
1 tsp. vanilla
whipped topping, *optional*

1. Combine milk and sugar in slow cooker, stirring until sugar is dissolved as well as possible. Stir in tapioca.
2. Cover and cook on High 3 hours.
3. In a small mixing bowl, beat eggs slightly. Beat in vanilla and about 1 cup hot milk from slow cooker. When well mixed, stir into slow cooker.
4. Cover and cook on High 20 more minutes.
5. Chill. Serve with whipped topping if you wish.

Variations:
1. For a less stiff pudding, use only 3 eggs and/or only 3/4 cup small pearl tapioca.
— **Susan Kasting**
Jenks, OK
— **Karen Stoltzfus**
Alto, MI

2. For an airier pudding, beat chilled pudding with a rotary beater until fluffy. Fold in an 8-oz. container of whipped topping.
— **Evelyn Page**
Lance Creek, WY

3. Top chilled pudding with a crushed or broken chocolate candy bar. Or serve the tapioca warm without any topping.
— **Karen Stoltzfus**
Alto, MI

4. Top chilled pudding with cut-up fruit or berries of your choice (peaches, strawberries, or blueberries are especially good).
— **Virginia Eberly**
Loysville, PA

Pineapple Tapioca

Janessa K. Hochstedler
East Earl, PA

Makes 4-6 servings

Prep Time: 15 minutes
Cooking Time: 3 hours
Chilling time: 2-3 hours
Ideal slow cooker size: 3-qt.

2½ cups water
2½ cups pineapple juice
½ cup dry small pearl
   tapioca
¾-1 cup sugar
15-oz. can crushed
   pineapple, undrained

1. Mix first four ingredients together in slow cooker.
2. Cover and cook on High 3 hours.
3. Stir in crushed pineapple. Chill for several hours.

Slow-Cooker Rice Pudding

Nadine Martinitz
Salina KS

Makes 6 servings

Prep Time: 5-20 minutes,
depending upon whether or
not you need to cook the rice
Cooking Time: 2-4 hours
Ideal slow cooker size: 2-qt.

2½ cups cooked rice
12-oz. can evaporated milk
½ cup sugar
2 eggs, beaten
1 tsp. vanilla
½ cup raisins, *optional*

1. Spray interior of slow cooker.
2. Mix all ingredients together in slow cooker.
3. Cover and cook on High 2 hours, or on Low 4 hours.
4. Stir after first hour. If the rice seems to be nearly done, check again after another 30 minutes, and adjust cooking time accordingly.
5. Serve warm or cold.

Rice Pudding from Scratch

Rhonda Freed
Lowville, NY

Makes 8-10 servings

Prep Time: 25 minutes
Cooking Time: 3¼-3¾
Ideal slow cooker size: 4-qt.

8 cups milk
1 cup raw long-grain rice
1 cup sugar
2 Tbsp. butter
2 tsp. vanilla

1. In a large microwave-safe bowl, mix milk, rice, sugar, and butter together. Cover.
2. Microwave on High for 5 minutes, and then stir. Cover, microwave 4 minutes, and then stir. Repeat for three, two, and one minutes of cooking time, stirring between each cooking time.
3. Pour into slow cooker. Stir in vanilla.
4. Cover and cook on High 1½ hours. Stir occasionally if you're home and able to do so.
5. Cook on High an additional 1½-2 hours with the cover off, or until the rice is cooked through and creamy but not dry or mushy.

Tip: Rice pudding thickens as it cools. If you like a thinner pudding, reduce the cooking time.

Old-Fashioned Rice Pudding

Ruth Zendt
Mifflintown, PA
Arianne Hochstetler
Goshen, IN

Makes 10-12 servings

Prep Time: 5 minutes
Cooking Time: 4-7 hours
Ideal slow cooker size:
3- to 4-qt.

2 qts. skim, *or* 2%, milk
1 cup raw long-grain rice
1 cup sugar
pinch of salt
1/4 cup butter, melted,
    optional
1/2-3/4 cup raisins, *optional*

1. Spray interior of slow cooker with non-stick cooking spray.
2. Place all ingredients in slow cooker. Stir thoroughly.
3. Cook on High 4-5 hours, or on Low 6-7 hours, stirring occasionally if you're home and able to do so.

The cooking time varies depending upon how thick and stiff you'd like the finished rice to be. The pudding will thicken slightly as it cools.

Tip: To serve, sprinkle with cinnamon, sugar, or pour a little milk over each serving.

Baked Stuffed Apples

Miriam Nolt
New Holland, PA
Ruth Hofstetter
Versailles, MO
Sara Kinsinger
Stuarts Draft, VA
Betty Drescher
Quakertown, PA
Dorothy Lingerfelt
Stonyford, CA
Kaye Taylor
Florissant, MO
Dale Peterson
Rapid City, SD
Karen Ceneviva
New Haven, CT

Makes 6-8 servings

Prep Time: 15-30 minutes
Cooking Time: 2 1/2-5 hours
Ideal slow cooker size: 5-qt.

2 Tbsp. raisins
1/4 cup sugar
6-8 medium-sized baking
    apples, cored but left
    whole and unpeeled
1 tsp. ground cinnamon
2 Tbsp. butter
1/2 cup water

1. Mix raisins and sugar together in a small bowl.
2. Stand apples on bottom of slow cooker. Spoon raisin-sugar mixture into centers of apples, dividing evenly among apples.
3. Sprinkle stuffed apples with cinnamon. Dot with butter.

4. Add 1/2 cup water along the edge of the cooker.
5. Cover and cook on Low 3-5 hours, or on High 2 1/2-3 1/2 hours, or until apples are tender but not collapsing.
6. Serve warm as is, or with ice cream or frozen yogurt.

Variations:

1. Instead of raisins, use chopped walnuts or pecans.
— **Connie Casteel**
Mt. Pleasant, IA

2. Instead of keeping the apples whole, core them and cut them in half. Lay them cut-side up and fill the core area. Lay apples in slow cooker with cut- and stuffed-sides up, stacking them if necessary.
— **Carol Eberly**
Harrisonburg, VA

3. Instead of granulated sugar, use 1/4 cup brown sugar. And instead of cinnamon use apple pie spices, or a mixture of ground allspice, cloves, and cinnamon to equal 1 tsp.
— **Linda E. Wilcox**
Blythewood, SC
— **Arlene M. Kopp**
Lineboro, MD

4. Instead of sugar, use 1/4 cup Splenda.
— **Leona Yoder**
Hartville, OH

Baked Apples

Donna Lantgen
Rapid City, SD

Makes 4 servings

Prep Time: 15 minutes
Cooking Time: 4-5 hours
Ideal slow cooker size:
* 3- to 4-qt.*

4 baking apples, left
  whole, cored and
  unpeeled
1 tsp. cinnamon
1/4 cup brown sugar
4 Tbsp. butter

1. Place apples in slow
cooker, making sure each is
standing on the bottom of the
slow cooker.
2. Combine cinnamon and
brown sugar. Stuff into apples.
3. Top each apple with
1 Tbsp. butter.
4. Cover. Cook on Low 4-5
hours.
5. Delicious as a side dish
served warm, or as a topping
for waffles, pancakes, or ice
cream.

Sugarless Applesauce

Lauren M. Eberhard
Seneca, IL

Makes 12 servings

Prep Time: 20 minutes
Cooking Time: 3-5 hours
Ideal slow cooker size: 3-qt.

8 cups apples, peeled and
  thinly sliced
1-2 tsp. cinnamon
half-whole 12-oz. can diet
  7-Up, *or* any sugar-free
  white soda

1. Toss apples with cinnamon in slow cooker.
2. Pour enough soda over
apples to cover one-third of
them.
3. Cover and cook on Low
3-4 hours, or until apples are
tender enough to mash into
sauce.
4. Remove cover and turn
cooker to High. Cook until
sauce reaches the thickness
you prefer. Stir occasionally,
breaking up the chunks.
5. Remove from cooker
and allow to reach temperature. Chill and then serve.

Homestyle Applesauce

Paula King, Flanagan, IL
Lizzie Ann Yoder
Hartville, OH
Dorothy Lingerfelt
Stonyford, CA
Ellen Ranck, Gap, PA
Janet L. Roggie
Lowville, NY
Mary E. Wheatley
Mashpee, MA
Sharon Miller, Holmesville, OH
Donna Treloar
Hartford City, IN

Makes 6-8 servings

Prep Time: 15-20 minutes
Cooking Time: 4^1/2-6^1/2 hours
Ideal slow cooker size:
* 3- to 4-qt.*

8-10 medium-sized cooking
  apples, peeled, cored,
  and diced
1/2 cup water
scant 1/2-3/4 cup sugar,
  according to the kind of
  apples you use
1/2-1 tsp. cinnamon,
  optional

1. In slow cooker, combine
apples and water.
2. Cover and cook on Low
4-6 hours, or until apples are
very soft. Add sugar, and cinnamon if you wish (or reserve
the cinnamon and sprinkle
over finished sauce), and
cook on Low another 30 minutes.
3. Sprinkle with cinnamon
at serving time if you wish

(unless you've already added it in Step 2).

Tip: This applesauce will be slightly chunky. If you prefer a smoother sauce, puree or sieve the apples after they've been cooked.

Applesauce
Jean Butzer
Batavia, NY
Trudy Cutter
Corfu, NY

Makes 8 servings

Prep Time: 15 minutes
Cooking Time: 1½-2 hours
Ideal slow cooker size: 4- to 5-qt.

8 medium-sized tart apples, peeled, cored, and cut into quarters
2/3 cup sugar
3/4 cup apple juice, *or* water, *or* cranberry juice
2 Tbsp. butter, melted
1 tsp. ground cinnamon
2 tsp. lemon juice, *optional*

1. Mix all ingredients, except the lemon juice, in the slow cooker.
2. Cover and cook on High 1½-2 hours.
3. Stir well to break up larger pieces of apples.
4. Do a taste test. If the sauce is sweeter than you like, stir in up to 2 tsp. lemon juice.
5. Serve warm or chilled. The sauce is especially good

served with pork roast or chops. It's also good as a breakfast fruit or over toast.

Variation: Adjust the amount of cinnamon to suit your personal or family tastes. You may also use ½ tsp. nutmeg in place of the cinnamon.

Chunky Cranberry Applesauce
Christie Anne Detamore-Hunsberger
Harrisonburg, VA

Makes 6 servings

Prep Time: 15 minutes
Cooking Time: 3-4 hours
Ideal slow cooker size: 3-qt.

6 MacIntosh, *or* Winesap, *or* favorite baking apple, peeled *or* unpeeled, cut into 1" cubes
½ cup apple juice
½ cup fresh *or* frozen cranberries
¼ cup sugar
¼ tsp. ground cinnamon, *optional*

1. Combine all ingredients in slow cooker.
2. Cover and cook on Low 3-4 hours, or until apples are as soft as you like them.
3. Serve warm, or refrigerate and serve chilled. Serve the sauce as a side dish during the main course. Or have it for dessert, topping pound cake or ice cream.

Caramel Apples
Lucy O'Connell
Goshen, MA

Makes 4 servings

Prep Time: 10 minutes
Cooking Time: 2-3 hours
Ideal slow cooker size: 3-qt.

4 large tart apples, cored
14-oz. jar caramel sauce
½ cup apple juice
1 tsp. apple pie spice

1. Remove peel from top inch of whole apples.
2. Place apples in slow cooker, making sure that each one is sitting flat on the bottom of the cooker. Fill the center of each apple with one-fourth of the caramel sauce.
3. Pour apple juice into the bottom of the cooker.
4. Sprinkle apples with apple pie spice.
5. Cover and cook on High 2-3 hours.

Tips:
1. Cooking time will vary according to the size of the apples.
2. Serve with vanilla ice cream or whipped cream if you wish.

247

Caramel Apples on Sticks

Becky Harder
Monument, CO
Jeanette Oberholtzer
Manheim, PA

Makes 8-10 servings

Prep Time: 30 minutes
Cooking Time: 1-1¹/₂ hours
Ideal slow cooker size: 2-qt.

2 14-oz. bags of caramels
¹/₄ cup water
8-10 medium apples
sticks
waxed paper
granulated sugar

1. Combine caramels and water in slow cooker.
2. Cover. Cook on High for 1-1¹/₂ hours, stirring every 5 minutes.
3. Wash and dry apples. Insert a stick into stem end of each apple. Turn cooker to Low. Dip apple into hot caramel, turning to coat entire surface.
4. Holding apple above cooker, scrape off excess accumulation of caramel from bottom of apple.
5. Dip bottom of caramel-coated apple in granulated sugar to keep it from sticking. Place apple on greased waxed paper to cool.

This is a good recipe for Fall/Harvest/Halloween parties. Children won't forget the hands-on experience of dipping their own apples. Room mothers can make the caramel mix ahead of time and bring it into the classroom. This recipe is also a fun intergenerational activity for church groups or family reunions.

In the late 1950s and early 1960s, my sister and I were rewarded with a store-bought caramel apple, only after our Saturday night baths and our Sunday school lessons had been completed. I remember that the waxed paper wrapped around each apple had colorful clowns printed on it, and they sold for less than 50¢ each.

—Becky Harder

Apple Dish
Vera Martin
East Earl, PA

Makes about 7 cups

Prep Time: 15-20 minutes
Cooking Time: 2-2¹/₂ hours
Ideal slow cooker size:
3- to 4-qt.

³/₄ **cup sugar**
3 **Tbsp. flour**
1¹/₂ **tsp. cinnamon,**
optional
5 **large baking apples, pared, cored, and diced into ³/₄" pieces**
half a stick (¹/₄ cup) butter, melted
3 **Tbsp. water**

1. Spray interior of slow cooker with non-stick cooking spray.
2. In a large bowl, mix sugar and flour together, along with cinnamon if you wish. Set aside.
3. Mix apples, butter, and water together in slow cooker. Gently stir in flour mixture until apples are well coated.
4. Cover and cook on High 1¹/₂ hours, and then on Low 30-60 minutes, or until apples are done to your liking.
5. Serve with milk poured over top.

Variation: Add ¹/₂ cup dry quick or rolled oats to Step 2, if you wish.

— **Deb Herr**
Mountaintop, PA

Apple Dessert

Barbara Sparks
Glen Burnie, MD

Makes 5 servings

Prep Time: 15 minutes
Cooking Time: 1¹/2-3 hours
Ideal slow cooker size: 2-qt.

---

3 large baking apples
1 Tbsp. lemon juice
1 Tbsp. butter, melted
1¹/2 Tbsp. brown sugar
1/2 tsp. cinnamon

1. Core, peel if you wish, and then cut apples in eighths. Place in slow cooker.
2. Drizzle butter and lemon juice over apples.
3. Sprinkle sugar and cinnamon on top.
4. Cover and cook on Low 3 hours, or on High 1¹/2 hours.
5. Serve as a main-course side dish, as a dessert (warm or cold) topped with whipped cream or drizzled with evaporated milk, or as a topping for vanilla ice cream.

Jellied Apples

Patricia Howard
Green Valley, AZ

Makes 10 servings

Prep Time: 20 minutes
Cooking Time: 4-6 hours
Chilling time: 5-6 hours
Ideal slow cooker size: 4-qt.

---

10 tart apples, peeled, cored, and sliced
1/2-1 cup sugar, depending upon how much sweetness you like
2 cups hot water
3/4 cup red hots candy
juice of 1 lemon
1/2 cup cold water
1 envelope unflavored gelatin

1. Place prepared apples in slow cooker.
2. Combine sugar, hot water, and red hots candy in a saucepan. Heat over medium heat, stirring until sugar and candy dissolve. Continue cooking, uncovered, until mixture becomes syrupy and somewhat thickened.
3. Pour syrup over apples.
4. Cover cooker. Cook on Low 4-6 hours, or until apples are tender.
5. Turn off cooker. Using a slotted spoon, remove apples, reserving the syrup in the cooker. Place apple slices in a deep serving dish.
6. Place cold water in a small bowl. Stir in gelatin until dissolved.
7. Add lemon juice, along with dissolved gelatin and water, to hot syrup in slow cooker. Stir well.
8. Let mixture cool. Then pour over apples.
9. Place in refrigerator until set, about 3-4 hours.

Tip: Start this recipe the day, or the night, before you want to serve it.

Apple Appeal

Anne Townsend
Albuquerque, NM

Makes 6 servings

Prep Time: 10 minutes
Cooking Time: 4-5 hours
Ideal slow cooker size: 3-qt.

6 baking apples, peeled,
  cored, and quartered
1/4 tsp. nutmeg
2 Tbsp. sugar
3/4 tsp. Asian five-spice
  powder
1/4 cup apple juice

1. Place prepared apples in
slow cooker.

2. In a small mixing bowl,
combine all remaining ingredients.

3. Pour into slow cooker,
stirring gently to coat apples.

4. Cover and cook on Low
4-5 hours, or until apples are
as tender as you want them.

5. Serve the apples sliced
or mashed and warm, cold,
or at room-temperature.

6. These versatile apples
may be served as a side-dish
with ham, scalloped potatoes,
green beans almandine, cornbread, pecan tarts, and as a
topping for toast!

A Tip —

Keep nuts in the freezer
so you'll have them when
you need them.

Apples and Pineapple Dessert

Joan S. Eye
Harrisonburg, VA

Makes 5-6 servings

Prep Time: 25-30 minutes
Cooking Time: 7-8 hours
Ideal slow cooker size:
  4- to 5-qt.

5-6 baking apples, peeled
  and cored
2-4 Tbsp. dark brown
  sugar, according to your
  taste preference*
1-2 tsp. cinnamon,
  according to your taste
  preference*
1/2 cup canned crushed
  pineapple, drained but
  with liquid reserved
1/4 cup chopped walnuts

1. Slice the peeled apples
into the slow cooker.

2. In a separate bowl, mix
together sugar, cinnamon,
and pineapple, starting first
with the lesser amounts of
sugar and cinnamon. *Taste,
and then add more if you prefer, according to the full
amounts suggested.

3. Spoon sugar-juice mix-
ture over apple slices. Stir
together well.

4. Sprinkle with walnuts.

5. Cover and cook on Low
7-8 hours, or until the apples
are done to your liking.

Pineapple Pudding

Lois Niebauer
Pedricktown, NJ

Makes 4-5 servings

Prep Time: 10 minutes
Cooking Time: 4 hours
Ideal slow cooker size: 1 1/2-qt.

20-oz. can crushed
  pineapple, undrained
1/4 cup water
2 eggs, beaten
2 Tbsp. cornstarch
1/2-3/4 cup sugar, depending
  upon your preference
  for sweetness

1. Spray interior of slow
cooker with non-stick cooking
spray.

2. Mix all ingredients
together in the slow cooker.

3. Cover and cook on High
for 1/2 hour, and then on Low
for 3 1/2 hours.

4. Serve warm with a
scoop of vanilla ice cream or
frozen yogurt, or a dollop of
whipped cream on each serving, if you wish.

Whole Cranberry Sauce

Sherril Bieberly
Salina, KS

Makes 5-6 servings

Prep Time: 5 minutes
Cooking Time: 5-6 hours
Chilling Time: 6-8 hours,
*   or overnight*
Ideal slow cooker size: 2-qt.

12-oz. pkg. cranberries
2 cups sugar
1/2 cup brandy, *or* white
    grape juice, *or* apple
    juice
1/4–1/2 cup walnuts,
    optional

1. Place first 3 ingredients in slow cooker. Cook on Low for 5-6 hours, stirring occasionally if you're home and able to do so.
2. Remove cooked cranberries to refrigerator dish and refrigerate overnight. Serve cold.
3. If you wish, chop the nuts. Spread out in a single layer in a dry non-stick skillet over medium heat. Stir occasionally, heating nuts until toasted. Allow to cool, and then stir into cranberry sauce before serving.

Tip: You can prepare this several days ahead of serving it, and then refrigerate it until you're ready for it.

Southwest Cranberries

Bernita Boyts
Shawnee Mission, KS

Makes 8 servings

Prep Time: 5 minutes
Cooking Time: 2-3 hours
Ideal slow cooker size:
*   1 1/2- to 2-qt.*

16-oz. can whole berry
    cranberry sauce
10 1/2-oz. jar jalapeno jelly
2 Tbsp. chopped fresh
    cilantro

1. Combine ingredients in slow cooker.
2. Cover. Cook on Low 2-3 hours.
3. Cool. Serve at room temperature.
4. Serve these spicy cranberries as a side dish or as a marinade for poultry or pork.

Warm Fruit Compote

Renee Baum
Chambersburg, PA

Makes 14-18 servings

Prep Time: 15 minutes
Cooking Time: 2-2 1/2 hours
Ideal slow cooker size: 5-qt.

2 29-oz. cans sliced
    peaches, drained
2 29-oz. cans pear halves,
    sliced and drained
20-oz. can pineapple
    chunks, drained
15 1/4-oz. can apricot halves,
    sliced and drained
21-oz. can cherry pie filling

1. In slow cooker, combine peaches, pears, pineapples, and apricots. Top with pie filling.
2. Cover and cook on High 2-2 1/2 hours, or until hot throughout.
3. Serve hot as a side dish with the main course. Or chill and serve, also as a side dish, or as dessert. It's also good as a topping for angel food cake, vanilla ice cream, and frozen yogurt.

Rhubarb-Pineapple Compote

Dorothy VanDeest
Memphis, TN

Makes 4-6 servings

Prep Time: 15-20 minutes
Cooking Time: 2-6 hours
Ideal slow cooker size: 3¹/₂-qt.

1 lb. fresh rhubarb
2 cups fresh pineapple
  chunks
¹/₂ cup orange soda
1 Tbsp. sugar
nutmeg, *optional*

1. Wash rhubarb, and then cut into 1" pieces. Place in slow cooker.
2. Stir in pineapple.
3. Add soda, and then sprinkle with sugar. Stir into fruit.
4. Cover and cook on High 2 hours, or on Low 4-6 hours, or until rhubarb is tender.
5. Serve warm or chilled. If you wish, sprinkle with nutmeg before serving.

Tip: This is a good go-along with a platter of roasted pork or beef. Or serve as a topping for vanilla ice cream or frozen yogurt.

Variation: Stir in 1 Tbsp. minute tapioca 15 minutes before the end of the cooking time to thicken the compote slightly.
— **Betty Drescher**
Quakertown, PA

Quickie
Go-Alongs
(using your stove or oven)

Breads

Apple Nut Ring
Naomi Cunningham
Arlington, KS

Makes 10 servings

Prep Time: 10 minutes
Baking Time: 25-30 minutes

2 7.5-oz. pkgs. refrigerated
  buttermilk biscuits
1/4 cup butter, *or*
  margarine, melted
2/3 cup sugar
2 Tbsp. ground cinnamon
3-4 medium-sized apples
1/3 cup nuts, chopped

1. Separate biscuits.
2. In a saucepan, melt the butter or margarine.
3. Combine sugar and cinnamon in a small bowl.
4. Dip biscuits in butter, and then roll in sugar mixture. Arrange biscuits, so that they overlap, around the edge and into the center of a greased 9 x 13 baking pan.
5. Peel, core, and slice the apples. Cut slices in half crosswise. Place an apple slice between each biscuit and around the outer edge of the baking dish.
6. Mix the nuts with any remaining sugar mixture. Sprinkle over top of biscuits and apples.
7. Bake at 400° for 25-30 minutes, or until biscuits are a deep golden brown.

Low-Fat Chocolate Muffins
Teresa Martin
Gordonville, PA

Makes 12 servings

Prep Time: 15-20 minutes
Baking Time: 15-20 minutes

1¹/₂ cups flour
³/₄ cup sugar
¹/₄ cup baking cocoa
2 tsp. baking powder
1 tsp. baking soda
¹/₂ tsp. salt
²/₃ cup fat-free vanilla yogurt
²/₃ cup skim milk
¹/₂ tsp. vanilla
confectioners sugar, *optional*

1. In a large mixing bowl, combine flour, sugar, baking cocoa, baking powder, baking soda, and salt.
2. In a separate bowl, stir together yogurt, milk, and vanilla until well mixed.
3. Stir wet ingredients into dry ingredients, just until moistened.
4. Fill greased muffin tins ²/₃ full.
5. Bake at 400° for 15-20 minutes, or until toothpick inserted in centers of muffins comes out clean.
6. Cool for 5 minutes before removing from pan to wire rack.
7. Dust with confectioners sugar, if you wish.

Tip: These muffins freeze well.

Pillow Pizza
Sharon Miller
Holmesville, OH

Makes 8 servings

Prep Time: 20 minutes
Baking Time: 20 minutes

2 tubes refrigerated biscuits (10 biscuits per tube)
1¹/₂ lbs. ground beef
16-oz. can pizza sauce
optional ingredients:
    chopped onions
    chopped peppers
    canned mushrooms
    pepperoni
1 lb. mozzarella cheese, shredded

1. Cut each biscuit into quarters and place in the bottom of a greased 9 x 13 baking dish.
2. In a skillet, brown beef. Drain off drippings. Add sauce to beef in skillet and stir together.
3. Pour over biscuit quarters.
4. Top with any optional ingredients as you would a pizza. Sprinkle cheese over top.
5. Bake at 400° for 20 minutes.

Ham and Cheese Sticky Buns
Rosanne Weiler
Myerstown, PA

Makes 12 servings

Prep Time: 10 minutes
Baking Time: 20 minutes

24 party-size potato rolls
1 lb. sliced Swiss cheese
¹/₂ lb. sliced ham
2 sticks (1 cup) butter
¹/₃ cup brown sugar
2 Tbsp. Worcestershire sauce
2 Tbsp. prepared mustard
2 Tbsp. poppy seeds

1. Slice rolls in half and place bottoms in 9 x 13 baking pan.
2. Layer on cheese and ham, and top with roll tops.
3. Melt butter in a saucepan and add sugar, Worcestershire sauce, mustard, and poppy seeds. Bring to boil and let boil 2 minutes.
4. Immediately pour over rolls and bake at 350° for 20 minutes.

Tip: These can be made ahead and heated when ready to serve.

When I serve these as an appetizer, everyone comes back for seconds!

Vegetables

Green Beans Supreme

Deb Martin
Pennsylvania

Makes 4-6 servings

Prep Time: 15 minutes
Cooking Time: 15 minutes

4 slices of bacon
1/4 cup onion, chopped
1 can cream of celery, *or* mushroom, soup
1/3 cup milk
1 lb. fresh green beans, *or* two 9-oz. pkgs., frozen green beans

1. Cook bacon until crisp in a large saucepan. Remove bacon and crumble. Set aside.
2. Sauté onion in 2 Tbsp. bacon drippings until tender.
3. Blend in soup, milk, and green beans. Heat, stirring occasionally, until beans are cooked as tender as you like.
4. Top with bacon and serve.

Broccoli Casserole

Ruth H. White
Pennsylvania

Makes 4-6 servings

Prep Time: 30 minutes
Baking Time: 15-20 minutes

2 bunches of broccoli
1/4-1/2 lb. cheese of your choice, grated
1 stick (1/2 cup) butter
about 36 snack crackers

1. Cook broccoli until just tender.
2. Melt cheese with butter in a saucepan.
3. Crush crackers.
4. In a greased 2-qt. casserole dish, alternate layers of broccoli, cheese sauce, and crackers.
5. Bake uncovered at 325° for 15-20 minutes.

Crustless Spinach Pie

Helene Kusnitz
West Hempstead, NY

Makes 6-8 servings

Prep Time: 10 minutes
Baking Time: 30 minutes

10-oz. pkg. frozen, chopped spinach
half a stick (1/4 cup) butter or margarine, melted
3 Tbsp. flour
3 eggs, lightly beaten
1/2 tsp. salt
1/8 tsp. pepper
8-oz. carton cottage cheese
1/2 cup grated mozzarella cheese

1. Thaw and drain spinach.
2. Combine all ingredients and mix well. Spoon into a greased pie plate or quiche dish.
3. Bake at 350° for 30 minutes.

Crispy Cauliflower
Pat Taylor
Paw Paw, WV

Makes 4 servings

Prep Time: 30 minutes
Cooking/Baking Time:
25 minutes

1 fresh head of cauliflower
water
1 stick (1/2 cup) butter
1 cup dry bread crumbs
1 tsp. Italian seasoning
1 cup shredded cheddar
cheese

1. Separate cauliflower
into florets. Place in
microwavable dish. Sprinkle
with 1 Tbsp. water. Cover
and cook on High for 3-4
minutes.

2. Drain florets and allow
to cool until you can handle
them.

3. Place melted butter in a
shallow dish. Mix the bread
crumbs and seasoning
together in another shallow
dish.

4. Dip each floret into
melted butter, and then into
the seasoned bread crumbs,
rolling to cover well.

5. Place in greased 9 x 13
baking dish. Bake, uncovered,
at 375° for 20 minutes. Turn
off oven. Sprinkle with shredded cheese and return to
oven to melt.

Stewed Tomatoes
Esther J. Mast
Lancaster, PA

Makes 4-5 servings

Prep Time: 5 minutes
Cooking Time: 10 minutes

2 Tbsp. chopped onions
2 Tbsp. freshly chopped
celery leaves
2 Tbsp. butter
2 cups canned diced
tomatoes, undrained
2 Tbsp. cornstarch
4 Tbsp. sugar
1/2 tsp. salt
1/8 tsp. cinnamon

1. In a large skillet or
saucepan, sauté onions and
celery leaves in butter until
soft but not brown.

2. Add tomatoes and stir in
well.

3. In a small bowl, com-
bine cornstarch, sugar, salt,
and cinnamon. Pour just
enough tomato mixture into
dry mixture to moisten.
Immediately stir into remaining tomato mixture. Continue
cooking and stirring until
thickened.

Tip: *If the mixture gets too
thick, add water until the tomatoes reach the consistency you
want.*

Variations:
*1. Stir 1 1/2 tsp. prepared
mustard into Step 2.*
*2. Butter and toast 3 slices
of bread. Then cut them into
cubes and place them on top of
the tomatoes at the end of Step
3. Slide under broiler to brown.*
— **Dorothy Hartley**
Carmichaels, PA

*3. Stir 1 Tbsp. fresh basil,
chopped, or 3/4 tsp. dried basil,
into Step 2.*
*4. If you add #2 Variation
(just above), sprinkle the buttered toast with a dusting of
dried oregano before cutting the
toast into cubes.*
— **Colleen Heatwole**
Burton, MI

*I got this recipe from the
school cafeteria where I worked
when our sons were in junior
high school. It became a family
favorite—served as a side dish
to macaroni and cheese.*
— **Esther J. Mast**
Lancaster, PA

A Tip —

A teaspoon or two of
brown sugar in tomato
dishes enhances the flavor
and helps to smooth out
the acid.

Yam Fries

Kathy Keener Shantz
Lancaster, PA

Makes 6 servings

Prep Time: 10 minutes
Baking Time: 20 minutes

2 Tbsp. olive oil
1 tsp. salt
1 tsp. pepper
1 tsp. curry
1/2 tsp. hot sauce
4 medium-sized yams,
    sliced like French fries

1. In a large mixing bowl, combine oil, salt, pepper, curry, and hot sauce.
2. Stir in sliced yams.
3. When thoroughly coated, spread on lightly greased baking sheet.
4. Bake at 375° for 20 minutes, or until tender.

Parmesan Baked Potatoes

Edith Groff
Pennsylvania

Makes 8 servings

Prep Time: 10 minutes
Baking Time: 40-45 minutes

6 Tbsp. butter, melted
3 Tbsp. Parmesan cheese,
    grated
8 medium red potatoes,
    unpeeled and halved
    lengthwise

1. Pour butter into a 9 x 13 baking pan.
2. Sprinkle cheese over butter.
3. Place potatoes cut-side down on top of cheese.
4. Bake uncovered at 400° for 40-45 minutes, or until tender.

Baked Potato Wedges

Sally A. Price
Reston, VA

Makes 4 servings

Prep Time: 15 minutes
Baking Time: 35-40 minutes

4 large baking potatoes
1 stick (1/2 cup) butter, *or*
    margarine, melted
1/4 cup ketchup
1 tsp. prepared mustard
1/2 tsp. paprika
1/4 tsp. salt
1/4 tsp. pepper

1. Wash potatoes and pat dry. Quarter each potato. Cut each quarter crosswise into 1/4"-thick slices, cutting to, but not through, bottom of potato to resemble a fan.
2. Place each potato wedge, skin-side down, on large baking sheet. Set aside.
3. Combine all remaining ingredients and mix well. Brush tops and sides of potatoes with mixture.
4. Bake, uncovered, at 425° for 35-40 minutes.

Salads

Dried Cherry Salad

Stacy Schmucker Stoltzfus
Enola, PA

Makes 12 servings

Prep Time: 20 minutes
Cooking Time: 10 minutes

half a head of romaine
    lettuce, torn
half a head of red leaf
    lettuce, torn
half a large red onion,
    sliced
1 cup dried cherries
1 cup feta cheese
1/3 cup sugar
1 cup pecan halves

Raspberry Dressing:
4 Tbsp. raspberry vinegar
1/2 tsp. Tabasco sauce
1/2 tsp. salt
4 Tbsp. sugar
pepper to taste
1 Tbsp. chopped parsley
1/2 cup vegetable oil

1. Place lettuces in a large salad bowl. Sprinkle with onion slices, dried cherries, and feta cheese.

2. In a skillet, over medium heat, combine 1/3 cup sugar and pecans. Stir constantly until sugar melts and pecans are coated. Immediately pour pecans onto waxed paper to cool.

3. Sprinkle cooled nuts over salad.

4. To make dressing, combine vinegar, Tabasco sauce, salt, 4 Tbsp. sugar, pepper, and parsley in a small mixing bowl. While whisking, slowly pour in oil until emulsified. Just before serving, pour over salad.

Bibb Lettuce with Pecans and Oranges

Betty K. Drescher
Quakertown, PA

Makes 8 servings

Prep Time: 10-15 minutes

4 heads Bibb lettuce
3/4 cup pecan halves,
    toasted
2 oranges, peeled and
    sliced

Dressing:
1/3 cup vinegar
1/2 cup sugar
1 cup vegetable oil
1/2 tsp. salt
half a small onion,
    chopped
1 tsp. dry mustard
2 Tbsp. water

1. Place lettuce, pecans, and oranges in a salad bowl.

2. Combine dressing ingredients in blender. (You can make this ahead of time and refrigerate it.)

3. Toss dressing with salad ingredients just before serving.

Spinach-Strawberry Salad

Pat Bechtel
Dillsburg, PA
Sarah M. Balmer
Manheim, PA

Makes 6-8 servings

Prep Time: 20 minutes

12 ozs. fresh spinach
1 qt. fresh strawberries,
  sliced
2 Tbsp. sesame seeds
1 Tbsp. poppy seeds

Dressing:
1/2 cup vegetable oil
1/2 cup sugar
1 1/2 tsp. grated onion
1/4 tsp. Worcestershire
  sauce
1/4 tsp. paprika
1/4 cup cider vinegar

1. Layer spinach, strawberries, sesame seeds, and poppy seeds in a large salad bowl.
2. Combine the dressing ingredients in a blender. Blend for 2 minutes.
3. Just before serving pour the dressing over the spinach and toss lightly to coat the spinach and berries.

This is one of our favorite salads. I make the dressing and store it in the refrigerator. Then I make the amount of salad I want and just add as much dressing as it needs.

Variations:
1. For the dressing, use 1/4 cup honey, heated until thin, instead of the 1/2 cup sugar.
— **Ellie Oberholtzer**
Smoketown, PA

2. To the salad itself, add 1 cup shredded Monterey Jack cheese and 1/2 cup chopped walnuts.
— **Tina Snyder**
Manheim, PA

Mozzarella / Tomato / Basil Salad

Makes 6 servings

Prep Time: 8 minutes

1 pint buffalo mozzarella
  cheese balls, or 1/4-1/2 lb.
  buffalo mozzarella
  cheese, sliced
2 large tomatoes, sliced
  and quartered
1/2 cup black olives, sliced
1/2 cup basil leaves, torn
1 Tbsp. olive oil
1 Tbsp. red wine vinegar
1/4 tsp. salt
1/8 tsp. pepper

1. If the mozzarella balls are in liquid, rinse and drain them. Place in a mixing bowl.
2. Add tomatoes, black olives, and basil leaves. Mix together gently.
3. Mix olive oil, vinegar, salt, and pepper together. Pour over salad ingredients and and mix gently.

Variations:
1. Add 1 sweet Vidalia onion, sliced, to Step 2.
2. Serve the dressed salad on a bed of arugula leaves.
— **Bonita Ensenberger**
Albuquerque, NM

Crunchy Pea Salad

Dottie Schmidt
Kansas City, MO

Makes 4 servings

Prep Time: 20 minutes
Chilling Time: 30 minutes

10-oz. pkg. frozen peas
1 cup diced celery
1 cup chopped fresh
  cauliflower florets
1/4 cup diced green onions
1 cup chopped cashews
1/4 cup crisp-cooked and
  crumbled bacon
1/4 cup sour cream
1/2 cup Ranch salad
  dressing
1/4 tsp. Dijon mustard
1 small clove garlic, minced

1. Thaw peas. Drain.
2. In a large mixing bowl,
combine peas, celery, cauliflower, onion, cashews, and
bacon with sour cream.
3. In a small bowl, mix
together Ranch dressing,
mustard, and minced garlic.
4. Begin by pouring only
half the dressing over the
salad mixture. Toss gently.
Add more if needed. (The
dressing amount is generous.)
5. Chill before serving.

Easy Fruit Salad

Shirley Sears
Tiskilwa, IL

Makes 12 servings

Prep Time: 20-25 minutes
Chilling Time: 3-4 hours

20-oz. can pineapple
  chunks, drained and
  halved
11-oz. can mandarin
  oranges, drained
15-oz. can apricot halves,
  drained and quartered
15-oz. can peach slices,
  drained and quartered
2 cups fresh green grapes,
  halved
3 bananas, sliced
20-oz. can peach pie filling
1/2 cup pecan halves,
  optional

1. In a large mixing bowl,
stir all drained, canned fruit
together.
2. Add grapes and sliced
bananas.
3. Mix in peach pie filling.
4. Refrigerate several
hours before serving.
5. Garnish with pecan
halves just before serving, if
you wish.

Tips:
1. Drain the fruit well.
*2. If you need a larger salad,
just use larger cans or more
cans of fruit. You could add
marshmallows or apples, too, if
you want.*

*This is quick to make. I
keep these canned ingredients
on hand all the time for last-
minute preparation. I only need
to purchase fresh grapes and
bananas. My mom introduced
me to this recipe in 1968, and
I've given it to others many
times.*

Desserts

Grilled Peach Melba

Stacy Schmucker Stoltzfus
Enola, PA

Makes 4 servings

Prep Time: 10 minutes
Grilling Time: 5-10 minutes

4 large, unpeeled peaches
  or nectarines
2 tsp. sugar
2 cups red raspberries,
  fresh *or* frozen
sugar, *optional*
vanilla ice cream

1. Halve and pit peaches or nectarines.
2. Press fresh or thawed raspberries through sieve. Save juice and discard seeds. Sweeten to taste with sugar, if needed.
3. Grill unpeeled peaches cut-side down for approximately 2 minutes. Turn

peaches over. With cut-side up, fill each cavity with 1/2 tsp. sugar, and continue grilling until grill marks appear on skins.
4. Serve immediately with a scoop of vanilla ice cream and drizzle with the raspberry sauce.

Cherry Berry Cobbler

Carol DiNuzzo, Latham, NY

Makes 6 servings

Prep Time: 20 minutes
Baking Time: 45 minutes

21-oz. can cherry pie filling
10-oz. pkg. frozen red
  raspberries, thawed and
  drained
1 tsp. lemon juice
1/2 cup flour
1/4 cup sugar
1/8 tsp. salt
half a stick (1/4 cup) butter

1. In a saucepan, combine pie filling, raspberries, and lemon juice. Bring to a boil over medium heat.
2. Turn into a greased 1-qt. casserole.
3. In a bowl, mix together flour, sugar, and salt. Cut in butter until crumbly. Sprinkle over fruit.
4. Bake at 350° for 45 minutes, or until browned and bubbly.
5. Serve warm (not hot) alone, or over ice cream.

Butter Rum Bananas

Shari Jensen
Fountain, CO

Makes 4 servings

Prep Time: 5 minutes
Cooking Time: 10 minutes

2 Tbsp. butter
1/2 cup sugar
2 Tbsp. water
2 Tbsp. light rum
1/2 Tbsp. lemon juice
grated rind of half a lemon
1/2 tsp. vanilla, *or* rum,
  flavoring
4 small bananas, peeled
  and halved
whipping cream, *or* ice
  cream

1. Melt butter in a large skillet. Add sugar and water. Stir well. Cook until reduced to heavy syrup, stirring occasionally so the mixture doesn't stick to the bottom of the pan.
2. Add rum, lemon juice, rind, and your choice of flavoring. Cook 2 minutes, or until golden in color.
3. Remove from stove and add banana pieces. Plunge them into the syrup, covering them as well as possible.
4. Serve warm, not hot, topped with a dollop of whipped cream or alongside scoops of ice cream.

Ultimate Apple Crisp

Judi Manos, West Islip, NY

Makes 6-8 servings

Prep Time: 15 minutes
Cooking/Baking Time:
*   25 minutes*

6-8 apples (use baking
   apples if you can find
   them)
1 cup brown sugar
1 cup dry oats, quick *or*
   rolled (both work, but
   rolled have more
   texture)
1 cup flour
1 Tbsp. cinnamon
1½ sticks (¾ cup) butter,
   melted
half a stick (¼ cup) butter,
   cut in pieces

1. Core, peel if you want,
and slice apples. Place in
microwave and oven-safe
baking dish (a Pyrex-type pie
plate works well).
2. In a separate bowl, mix
together brown sugar, oats,
flour, and cinnamon. Add
melted butter and mix with a
fork until thoroughly mixed.
3. Place mixture on top of
the apples. Microwave on
High, uncovered, for 10 minutes. Let stand for 2 minutes.
4. Cut up the half stick of
butter, and place on top of
the heated apple mixture.
5. Place in oven and bake
at 350° for 15 minutes.

Tapioca Pudding

Miriam Christophel
Goshen, IN

Makes 5 servings

Prep Time: 10 minutes
Cooking Time: 5 minutes
Cooling Time:
*   20 minutes-2 hours*

3 Tbsp. dry instant tapioca
⅓ cup sugar
⅛ tsp. salt
1 egg, beaten
3 cups milk
¾ tsp. vanilla

1. In a 2-quart saucepan,
combine all ingredients
except vanilla. Let stand 5
minutes.
2. Bring ingredients to a
boil, stirring constantly. Boil
for 1 minute.
3. Remove from heat. Stir
in vanilla.
4. Stir once after cooling
for 20 minutes.
5. Serve warm or cold.

*This is good just as it is, or
with a sliced banana and some
whipped cream stirred in. It is
our kids' favorite dessert. I like
it because it isn't as sweet as
some puddings are.*

Sunny Spice Cake

Karla Baer, North Lime, OH

Makes 15-20 servings

Prep Time: 10 minutes
Baking Time: 35 minutes
Cooling Time: 30-60 minutes

18¼-oz. pkg. dry spice
   cake mix
3⅝-oz. pkg. butterscotch
   instant pudding
2 cups milk
2 eggs
peach halves, drained
frozen whipped topping,
   thawed

1. In a mixing bowl, blend
together cake mix, pudding
mix, milk, and eggs.
2. Pour into a greased 9 x
13 baking pan. Bake at 350°
for 35 minutes.
3. Cool.
4. When ready to serve,
cut into serving-sized pieces.
Place a peach half on each
serving of cake. Top each
with a dollop of whipped topping.

Assumptions about Ingredients in
Fix-It and Forget-It 5-Ingredient Cookbook

flour = unbleached *or* white, and all-purpose

oatmeal or oats = dry, quick *or* rolled (old-fashioned), unless specified

pepper = black, finely ground

rice = regular, long-grain (not minute or instant unless specified)

salt = table salt

shortening = solid, not liquid

sugar = granulated sugar (not brown and not confectioners)

Three Hints

1. If you'd like to cook more at home—without being in a frenzy—go off by yourself with your cookbook some evening and make a week of menus. Then make a grocery list from that. Shop from your grocery list.

2. Thaw frozen food in a bowl in the fridge (not on the counter-top). If you forget to stick the food in the fridge, put it in a microwave-safe bowl and defrost it in the microwave just before you're ready to use it.

3. Let roasted meat, as well as pasta dishes with cheese, rest for 10-20 minutes before slicing or dishing. That will allow the juices to re-distribute themselves throughout the cooked food. You'll have juicier meat, and a better presentation of your pasta dish.

Equivalent Measurements

dash = little less than 1/8 tsp.

3 teaspoons = 1 Tablespoon

2 Tablespoons = 1 oz.

4 Tablespoons = 1/4 cup

5 Tablespoons plus 1 tsp. = 1/3 cup

8 Tablespoons = 1/2 cup

12 Tablespoons = 3/4 cup

16 Tablespoons = 1 cup

1 cup = 8 ozs. liquid

2 cups = 1 pint

4 cups = 1 quart

4 quarts = 1 gallon

1 stick butter = 1/4 lb.

1 stick butter = 1/2 cup

1 stick butter = 8 Tbsp.

Beans, 1 lb. dried = 2-2 1/2 cups (depending upon the size of the beans)

Bell peppers, 1 large = 1 cup chopped

Cheese, hard (for example, cheddar, Swiss, Monterey Jack, mozzarella), 1 lb. grated = 4 cups

Cheese, cottage, 1 lb. = 2 cups

Chocolate chips, 6-oz. pkg. = 1 scant cup

Crackers (butter, saltines, snack), 20 single crackers = 1 cup crumbs

Herbs, 1 Tbsp. fresh = 1 tsp. dried

Lemon, 1 medium-sized = 2-3 Tbsp. juice

Lemon, 1 medium-sized = 2-3 tsp. grated rind

Mustard, 1 Tbsp. prepared = 1 tsp. dry or ground mustard

Oatmeal, 1 lb. dry = about 5 cups dry

Onion, 1 medium-sized = 1/2 cup chopped

Pasta

Macaronis, penne, and other small or tubular shapes, 1 lb. dry = 4 cups uncooked

Noodles, 1 lb. dry = 6 cups uncooked

Spaghetti, linguine, fettucine, 1 lb. dry = 4 cups uncooked

Potatoes, white, 1 lb. = 3 medium-sized potatoes = 2 cups mashed

Potatoes, sweet, 1 lb. = 3 medium-sized potatoes = 2 cups mashed

Rice, 1 lb. dry = 2 cups uncooked

Sugar, confectioners, 1 lb. = 3 1/2 cups sifted

Whipping cream, 1 cup unwhipped = 2 cups whipped

Whipped topping, 8-oz. container = 3 cups

Yeast, dry, 1 envelope (1/4 oz.) = 1 Tbsp.

Substitute Ingredients—
for when you're in a pinch

For one cup **buttermilk**—use 1 cup plain yogurt; or pour 1 1/3 Tbsp. lemon juice or vinegar into a 1-cup measure. Fill the cup with milk. Stir and let stand for 5 minutes. Stir again before using.

For 1 oz. **unsweetened baking chocolate**—stir together 3 Tbsp. unsweetened cocoa powder and 1 Tbsp. butter, softened.

For 1 Tbsp. **cornstarch**—use 2 Tbsp. all-purpose flour; or 4 tsp. minute tapioca.

For 1 **garlic clove**—use 1/4 tsp. garlic salt (reduce salt in recipe by 1/8 tsp.); or 1/8 tsp. garlic powder.

For 1 Tbsp. **fresh herbs**—use 1 tsp. dried herbs.

For 1/2 lb. **fresh mushrooms**—use 1 6-oz. can mushrooms, drained.

For 1 Tbsp. **prepared mustard**—use 1 tsp. dry or ground mustard.

For 1 medium-sized **fresh onion**—use 2 Tbsp. minced dried onion; or 2 tsp. onion salt (reduce salt in recipe by 1 tsp.); or 1 tsp. onion powder. Note: These substitutions will work for meat balls and meat loaf, but not for sautéing.

For 1 cup **sour milk**—use 1 cup plain yogurt; or pour 1 Tbsp. lemon juice or vinegar into a 1-cup measure. Fill with milk. Stir and then let stand for 5 minutes. Stir again before using.

For 2 Tbsp. **tapioca**—use 3 Tbsp. all-purpose flour.

For 1 cup **canned tomatoes**—use 1 1/3 cups diced fresh tomatoes, cooked gently for 10 minutes.

For 1 Tbsp. **tomato paste**—use 1 Tbsp. ketchup.

For 1 Tbsp. **vinegar**—use 1 Tbsp. lemon juice.

For 1 cup **heavy cream**—add 1/3 cup melted butter to 3/4 cup milk. Note: This will work for baking and cooking, but not for whipping.

For 1 cup **whipping cream**—chill thoroughly 2/3 cup evaporated milk, plus the bowl and beaters, then whip; or use 2 cups bought whipped topping.

For 1/2 cup **wine**—pour 2 Tbsp. wine vinegar into a 1/2 -cup measure. Fill with broth (chicken, beef, or vegetable). Stir and then let stand for 5 minutes. Stir again before using.

Kitchen Tools and Equipment You May Have Overlooked

1 Make sure you have a little electric vegetable chopper, the size that will handle 1 cup of ingredients at a time.

2 Don't try to cook without a good paring knife that's sharp (and holds its edge) and fits in your hand.

3 Almost as important—a good chef's knife (we always called it a "butcher" knife) with a wide, sharp blade that's about 8 inches long, good for making strong cuts through meats.

4 You really ought to have a good serrated knife with a long blade, perfect for slicing bread.

5 Invest in at least one broad, flexible, heat-resistant spatula. And also a narrow one.

6 You ought to have a minimum of 2 wooden spoons, each with a 10-12 inch-long handle. They're perfect for stirring without scratching.

7 Get a washable cutting board. You'll still need it, even though you have an electric vegetable chopper (#1 above).

8 A medium-sized whisk takes care of persistent lumps in batters, gravies, and sauces when there aren't supposed to be any.

9 Get yourself a salad spinner.

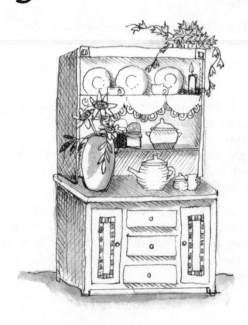

Index

About the Author

Phyllis Pellman Good is a *New York Times* bestselling author whose books have sold more than 9.2 million copies.

Good has authored the national #1 bestselling cookbook *Fix-It and Forget-It Cookbook: Feasting with Your Slow Cooker* (with Dawn J. Ranck), which appeared on *The New York Times* bestseller list, as well as the bestseller lists of *USA Today*, *Publishers Weekly*, and *Book Sense*. And she is the author of *Fix-It and Forget-It Lightly: Healthy, Low-Fat Recipes for Your Slow Cooker*, which has also appeared on *The New York Times* bestseller list. In addition, Good authored *Fix-It and Forget-It Recipes for Entertaining: Slow Cooker Favorites for All the Year Round* (with Ranck) and *Fix-It and Forget-It Diabetic Cookbook* (with the American Diabetes Association), also in the series.

Good has also authored *Fix-It and Enjoy-It Cookbook: All-Purpose, Welcome-Home Recipes*, for stove-top and oven use. (*Fix-It and Enjoy-It Cookbook* is the first in a "cousin" series to the *Fix-It and Forget-It* books.)

Good's other cookbooks include *Favorite Recipes with Herbs, The Best of Amish Cooking,* and *The Central Market Cookbook.*

Phyllis Pellman Good is Senior Editor at Good Books. (Good Books has published hundreds of other titles by more than 125 different authors.) She received her B.A. and M.A. in English from New York University. She and her husband, Merle, live in Lancaster, Pennsylvania. They are the parents of two young-adult daughters.

For a complete listing of books by Phyllis Pellman Good, as well as excerpts and reviews, visit www.Fix-ItandForget-It.com, or www.GoodBooks.com.